Democracy Online

Democracy Online

The Prospects for Political Renewal Through the Internet

Editor
Peter M. Shane

ROUTLEDGE
NEW YORK AND LONDON

Published in 2004 by
Routledge
270 Madison Avenue
New York, NY 10016
www.routledge-ny.com

Published in Great Britain by
Routledge
2 Park Square
Milton Park, Abingdon,
Oxon Ox14 4RN U.K.
www.routledge.co.uk

Routledge is an imprint of the Taylor and Francis Group.
Printed in the United Stated of America on acid-free paper.

10 9 8 7 6 5 4 3 2 1

Library of Congress Cataloging-in-Publication Data

Democracy online : the prospects for political renewal through the Internet / Peter M.
Shane, editor.
    p. cm.
  Includes bibliographical references and index.
  ISBN 0-415-94864-9 (hb : alk. paper) — ISBN 0-415-94865-7 (pb : alk. paper) 1. Inter-
net—Political aspects—United States. 2. Internet in public administration—United States.
3. Political participation—United States—Computer network resources. I. Shane, Peter M.
  JK468.A8D456 2004
  352.3'8'02854678—dc22

                                                                      2004001294

Contents

Acknowledgments

The preparation of a volume of this ambition entails innumerable debts. Versions of these papers were first presented at a Carnegie Mellon University conference entitled "Prospects for Electronic Democracy," held in September 2002. Financial support for the conference was provided by the William and Flora Hewlett Foundation and by the H. J. Heinz III School for Public Policy and Management, my professional home from 2000 to 2003. I am especially grateful for the personal interest and support of Paul Brest, president of the Hewlett Foundation, and Terry Amsler, our Hewlett program officer.

At Carnegie Mellon, this effort would not have been possible without the collaboration of InSITeS, the Institute for the Study of Information Technology and Society. For their encouragement and support in building InSITeS, I will always be indebted to Provost Mark Kamlet and to three deans of the Heinz School, Linda Babcock, Jeffrey Hunker, and Mark Wessel. Staff members Dorothy Bassett, Kim Falk-MacArthur, and Ari Luber all provided critical help along the way.

The conference was actually part of a larger Hewlett-funded research enterprise entitled "Community Connections." That project, which existed in only nebulous shape in the confines of my imagination in 2000, was refined into something concrete and feasible through many conversations with Carnegie Mellon colleagues. Key among them was Peter Muhlberger, who not only contributed to this volume but also helped select the roster of presenters. I am grateful to Peter not only because his interests dovetail with mine but also because his combined expertise in democratic theory, experimental design, quantitative social science, and computer programming was critical to moving our project from vision to reality.

Parts of various of the essays in this volume have appeared in other works and are reprinted with permission:

Portions of "Technologies for Democracy," by A. Michael Froomkin, appeared in the January 2003 issue of *Harvard Law Review* as "Habermas@discourse.net: Towards a Critical Theory of Cyberspace."

Portions of "Unchat: Democratic Solution for a Wired World," by Beth Simone Noveck, have appeared in the *Boston University Journal of Science and Technology Law* 9, 1 (2003).

Portions of "Getting Past Electronic Democracy," by Dan Hunter, appeared in the spring 2003 issue of *Loyola of Los Angeles Law Review* as "ICANN and the Concept of Democratic Deficit."

Portions of the chapter, *Internet-based political Discourse: A Case Study of Electronic Democracy in Hoogeveen*, by Nicholas W. Jankowski and Renee van Os, appeared in the Dutch language anthology *Jaarboek ICT & Samenleving 2004, as* "Digitale Democratie binnen de gemeente Hoogeveen" [Digital Democracy in the city of Hoogeveen], edited by J. de Haan & O. Klumper, (Boom, Amsterdam, The Netherlands).

Finally, I would like to thank the authors themselves for their insights and camaraderie, and the team at Routledge for their support and patience. It has been a privilege to collaborate on what all hope will be a significant step in advancing the global conversation about the prospects for democratic renewal through new technologies.

Introduction: The Prospects
for Electronic Democracy

PETER M. SHANE

The phenomenon of "electronic democracy," variously labeled, has come to have two distinct meanings. The first is the design and deployment of digital information and communications technologies (ICTs) to enhance democratic political practice. The second is a new stage of democracy, a stage during which the proliferation of digital ICTs will have deepened democracy's vitality and legitimacy, whether on a local, national, or even global basis.

In this volume, an international group of scholars drawn from communications studies, information science, law, philosophy, political psychology, political science, and sociology considers the prospects for electronic democracy in both senses:

- In terms of enhanced democratic practice, what is the world likely to see in terms of the evolution of new online forms of democratic initiative? What are the opportunities and challenges most likely to arise? What new institutional forms are possible? How will the future of ICT-enabled democratic practice be shaped by the social, psychological, and political contexts in which new technologies are deployed?
- In terms of deepening democracy's vitality and legitimacy, what can and should the world hope for? What should be the ambitions of "electronic democrats" if genuine revitalization is to occur, and how likely is the realization of these ambitions?

It should to come as no surprise if even so talented a group of commentators fails to answer these questions definitively. What the papers do provide is an important set of insights on these critical questions and a display of the extraordinarily interdisciplinary research agenda that is necessary if we are to grasp the complexity of the e-democratic ambition and its implications.

It is by now well understood that technological potential is hardly the sole or even primary predictor of the likely impacts of electronic networks on democracy. First of all, ICTs are as inherently adaptable to programs of control as they are to programs of empowerment. The networks that facilitate information sharing and discourse also, and to an unprecedented degree, facilitate filtering, surveillance, and the evasion of democratically adopted norms. The capacities of new ICTs could thus be deployed as much to suppress democracy as to enhance it. Moreover, the evolution of any technology depends on its interaction with human agency in specific economic, social, political, and cultural circumstances. What ICTs can accomplish for any particular political system will have very much to do with what members of particular communities, individually and collectively, determine to do with such technologies in particular contexts. Economic and cultural forces, public policy, democratic design, and grassroots initiative will all have a role in framing the future of electronic democracy.

Building on these starting points, this volume is intended to help carry forward an emerging school of what might be called "cyberrealist" thought about the prospects for electronic democracy. The authors do not treat as self-evident either what we should hope for, in principle, in terms of democratic revitalization or the potential for facilitating the realization of those hopes through technology. They embrace neither the hyperoptimistic technological determinism of the early 1990s nor the doomsday anxieties of the pessimistic backlash. Instead, drawing on insights from their diverse disciplines, this distinguished group of academic researchers and electronic democracy practitioners offers a framework for thinking about what ICT-enabled democratic revitalization would require of new technologies in principle and what those technologies are likely to offer in practice. What emerges is both an important statement of our current state of knowledge and, just as important, a platform for further inquiry.

The book is organized around four large questions:

- Do new technologies truly have the potential to support democratic practices and new democratic institutions?
- What would electronic democracy have to accomplish in order to revitalize democracy?
- What do existing practices teach us about the challenges and opportunities for implementing electronic democracy initiatives?
- How will the resources available to individual citizens—whether economic, social, political, cognitive, educational, or motivational—as well as the larger economic, social, and political landscape within which electronic democracy projects take shape affect the potential of such projects?

Part I: The Potential for Democratic Technologies and New Political Practices

In "Technologies for Democracy," A. Michael Froomkin opens the volume by providing a brief overview of the most influential vision of democratic discourse among current electronic democracy theorists, namely, the work of Jürgen Habermas. After reviewing the requirements of Habermas's "practical discourse," Froomkin shows the plausibility of deploying existing technologies to improve democratic conversation along the lines Habermas would recommend. Froomkin's survey discusses new forms of software and practice, as well as the hardware needed to support them. His review encompasses weblogging or "blogging," collaborative document creation, community-based (and community-creating) discussion forums with collaborative filtering, and open government and community filtering initiatives.

In "Unchat: Democratic Solution for a Wired World," Beth Simone Noveck complements Froomkin's bird's-eye view of the technological possibilities with a ground-level analysis of the design choices facing the creators of Unchat, a software program intended to sustain an online environment for democratic deliberation. Noveck's implicit message is that to the extent technology is to be used to support democratic practice, democratic intention must infuse every aspect of design choice.

The two papers that follow illustrate the prospects for deploying digital technologies in the form of new or drastically reformed democratic institutions. Starting with arguably the most familiar and venerated institution of democratic practice in the United States, Nancy Marder observes in "Cyberjuries: A Model of Deliberative Democracy?" that the World Wide Web has already enabled the creation of a new mechanism for dispute resolution. Cyberjuries are available for civil matters, whether or not strictly legal in nature, and give disputing parties a verdict that they may use on an advisory or binding basis, as they choose. Marder argues that the early versions of cyberjury design, by borrowing more fully the most important deliberative features of ordinary juries, can provide a model of online deliberation that offers a quick, inexpensive, and accessible form of dispute resolution in many contexts.

Moving to an entirely different scale, philosopher James Bohman argues, in "Expanding Dialogue: The Internet, Public Sphere, and Transnational Democracy," that under particular conditions, the Internet could sustain new institutions that, in turn, would support a new transnational public sphere of democratic deliberation. Noting the immense challenges of such an undertaking, Bohman nonetheless sees possibilities emerging for such a public sphere in the activities of the European Union. His position implies that innovative forms of public discussion can evolve solutions to problems of cosmopolitan identity and solidarity that, according to some observers, belie the prospects for democratic transnational governance.

Part II: Electronic Democracy and Democratic Revitalization

What makes the democratic possibilities illustrated in Part I so enticing is the fact that they arise precisely at a time of deep and widespread anxiety around the world about the performance of democratic governments even in highly functional postindustrial societies. Part II, therefore, considers what should be the ambitions of electronic democracy's champions if electronic democracy is to facilitate a period of genuine revitalization.

Viewing the matter in a domestic context, Peter Shane argues in "The Electronic Federalist: The Internet and the Eclectic Institutionalization of Democratic Legitimacy" that electronic democrats should take two lessons from America's founding generation, which also had to deal with a deep crisis of legitimacy and discontent with prevailing governance. The first is that political ideals and normative commitments have to be translated into working political institutions if they are to have genuine force in shaping people's attitudes toward governance. The second is that democratic vitality requires robustness in political institutions that simultaneously implement multiple models of democratic legitimation. He thus argues it would be mistaken to pursue a democratic reform agenda focusing exclusively on either the premises of representative democracy or deliberative democracy; genuine revitalization requires both.

Israeli legal scholar Oren Perez makes a distinct but thematically related argument in a transnational context. In "Global Governance and Electronic Democracy: E-Politics as a Multidimensional Experience," Perez argues the Internet's suitability for contributing to the development of new and inclusive global decision-making structures. Like Shane, Perez believes that the pursuit of enhanced legitimacy necessarily entails issues of institutional design. He is critical, however, of contemporary institutional theorizing that, in his view, pays insufficient attention to the multidimensionality of democratic practice. The Internet's promise for supporting transnational democratic practice, in Perez's view, lies precisely in its capacity to facilitate multidimensional decision frameworks that take account of the range of individual and social pluralism characterizing global society. Developing his argument based on World Bank environmental assessment processes, Perez urges that electronic democrats avoid conceptualizing their goal as a single new and more legitimate unitary governing structure. Instead, he says, we should favor "a polycentric and experimental approach."

Recommendations at this level of ambition may seem to some would-be reformers to make the perfect enemy of the good. Yet papers by political scientists Lori Weber and Sean Murray and by communications scholar Tamara Witschge indicate that empirical studies strongly support the proposition that deployment of online political initiatives without well-conceived democratic design will do little to further democratic aims. In "Interactivity, Equality, and the Prospects for Electronic Democracy: A Review," Weber and Murray review a selection of the emerging empirical research on electronic democracy. Observing that the shortfalls of U.S. democracy are very much linked to prevailing social inequalities, they argue, based on empirical studies, that electronic democracy efforts cannot overcome such inequalities unless they take full advantage of the Internet's interactive capabilities. Democracy-enhancing initiatives limited to information provision cannot, in their judgment, overcome the antidemocratic impacts of offline social inequality.

Tamara Witschge presses this argument further. In "Online Deliberation: Possibilities of the Internet for Deliberative Democracy," she points out that the features of political conversation that make it salient for democratic legitimacy, namely, the presence of difference and disagreement, are precisely the features that make people avoid deliberative politics offline. So far, empirical studies show that the Internet does not spontaneously spawn deliberative forums in which political discussion is less difficult and demanding, thereby increasing heterogeneity and equality within political discussions. Designers of online democratic initiatives must attend consciously to the political psychology of Internet users if there is to be any genuine electronic enhancement of deliberative democracy.

In "Hacktivism and the Future of Democratic Discourse," Alexandra Samuel argues that the future of electronic democracy will involve more than even a diligent mapping of best offline institutional practices into cyberspace. However ambitious the ideals of deliberative democrats, cyberspace has already spawned novel forms of online political action, or "hacktivism," that challenge the adequacy of deliberative democratic thinking about free speech norms and the relationship between identity and accountability. For this reason, purely proceduralist accounts of democratic legitimacy may never fully capture the nature of democratic life as it is likely to emerge online. Hacktivism challenges electronic democracy theorists to be more creative in imagining the richness of an ICT-enabled democratic world.

A challenging alternative perspective on these arguments is provided by Dan Hunter. In "ICANN and Electronic Democratic Deficit," he argues that democracy in and of itself does not offer a coherent general theory of political action. In his view, the most celebrated actual attempt to instantiate online transnational democracy—namely, elections for the board of directors for the Internet Corporation for Assigned Names and Numbers (ICANN)—failed miserably according to democratic criteria. Rather than demonstrating a shortfall in the capacity of the Internet to sustain ideal democracy, however, Hunter stresses that the ICANN experience really taught a different lesson. It exposed democracy as a poor substitute for a number of other conceptions of our political commitments that run deeper. Rather than worry about how offline expectations of democracy are found wanting in cyberspace or even about the nature of online democratic life, Hunter would direct attention to the development of alternative guiding theories of how best to meet what he takes to be our more fundamental political commitments. His argument offers a provocative counterpoint to the other authors in this volume. Rather than insist that electronic democrats need to think ambitiously if ICTs are truly to help revitalize democracy, he would, by implication, deemphasize democracy per se as the goal of online political initiatives.

Part III: The Lessons of Electronic Democracy Practice

Having considered both the alluring range of technological possibilities for electronic democracy and the daunting level of ambition most of the contributors recommend for its deployment, the volume next examines a variety of real-life electronic democracy initiatives. Four case studies illuminate the challenges and opportunities that lie ahead.

In "Digital Deliberation: Engaging the Public Through Online Policy Dialogues," Thomas C. Beierle reports on what might be considered an online metadialogue, that is, a dialogue about dialogue. For two weeks during the summer of 2001, the United States Environmental Protection Agency (EPA) conducted a "National Dialogue on Public Involvement in EPA Decisions," covering issues that ranged from the information and assistance the public needs to be effectively involved in EPA decision making to the particulars of participation in rule making, permitting, and Superfund activities. A total of 1,166 people participated, mainly from the United States, but also from Brazil, South Africa, and elsewhere. Beierle found that the dialogue, unlike typical public comment processes, public hearings, and advisory committee sessions, succeeded in creating an essentially unique opportunity to engage a large group of individuals in dialogue-based interaction. Beierle carefully chronicles ways in which the dialogue both achieved and fell short of various attributes associated with ideal democratic deliberation. He concludes that a long-term effort to test and refine online dialogues requires conscious refinements in format, software, behavioral norms, institutional strategy, and access.

In "Participation, Deliberative Democracy, and the Internet: Lessons from a National Forum on Commercial Vehicle Safety," J. Woody Stanley, Christopher Weare, and Juliet Musso report on an effort by the Federal Motor Carrier Safety Administration to employ an Internet-based forum for a public discussion focused on substantive policy. Between August 2000 and June 2001, the FMCSA supplemented its traditional docket for public comment with an online forum involving private citizens, interest group representatives, and agency managers in a conversation about the role of the federal government in improving commercial vehicle safety. Comparing comments in the public docket to the messages in the Internet forum yields evidence that computer-mediated communication encourages public discussion and broadens the level of participation by individuals and groups previously uninvolved in the policy-making process. At the same time, the initiative did not achieve its full promise in terms of promoting deliberative discourse. The authors argue that "[t]he potential of the Internet to improve the processes of government is likely to be realized only under conditions where a network or community exists to support its use, institutional barriers to political communication are overcome or minimized, and the legitimacy of a forum is further affirmed by the actions of agency managers." Of particular interest is their observation that agency officials failed to integrate the forum fully with existing deliberative and decision-making processes and activities in a way that would communicate to discussants the impact of their participation.

In a different national context, Nicholas W. Jankowski and Renée van Os's "Internet-Based Political Discourse: A Case Study of Electronic Democracy in the City of Hoogeveen" illustrates the likelihood of limited impact for electronic democracy initiatives undertaken without a firm basis in empirically tested process models of online deliberation. Their analysis focuses on online political discussions organized through the Hoogeveen Digital City site, one of the Netherlands' more advanced community networks. Jankowski and van Os found that the discussions had few ramifications in terms of policy discussion among Hoogeveen city officials. To the degree such officials were attentive to the initiative at all, organizational concerns seemed to have priority over political substance in the online discussions, whether the ostensible focus of such discussions was information provision, deliberation, or actual decision making.

Finally, "The League of Women Voters' DemocracyNet (DNet): An Exercise in Online Civic Engagement" offers a case study in online political activity of a different sort. Rather than providing a deliberative forum, the DNet program seeks to support democratic engagement by providing voters with thorough, nonpartisan online information concerning both candidates and ballot measures in thousands of communities across the country. Authors Jackie Mildner and Nancy Tate pose the question whether such a project should truly count as an initiative in "online civic engagement." What they found is that although DNet, as organized in 2000, could claim only limited impacts on the communities it serves, if assessed in terms of effects on candidates and voters, it had a more profound impact in galvanizing civic engagement by the volunteers who were mobilized to assemble content for the DNet Web site. The insight points to an intriguing potential direction for champions of electronic democracy—deploying technological initiatives as a way not only of luring uninvolved citizens online but also of engaging more citizens in the offline processes of creating the informational foundations for community deliberation.

Part IV: Social, Psychological and Political Contexts for Electronic Democracy

The case studies of Part III point to important issues of design and institutional integration in relation to the effectiveness of electronic democracy initiatives. Such initiatives, however, do not and will not occur in a vacuum. Even projects that are well designed in terms of process models and democratic theory can be deployed only in specific social, economic, and political contexts. And, of course, they involve human beings, whose behaviors will necessarily reflect their personal resources of motivation, cognitive capacity, education, and skill. How this array of factors is likely to shape the prospects for electronic democracy is illuminated by real-world research, using experiments, surveys, and case studies as complementary methodologies.

In "Virtual Distance and America's Changing Sense of Community," Paul G. Harwood and Wayne V. McIntosh look at what computer-mediated communication can do for individuals' sense of community connectedness—also a major concern for electronic democrats. To examine the potential contribution of computer-mediated experience to individuals' sense of community, they use the Social Capital Benchmark Survey (2000), comprising a national sample of 3,003 respondents, to help determine "whether individuals' computer-mediated community experiences reinforce or stand juxtaposed to their offline sense of belonging." Their research suggests that people who experience impediments in enjoying a sense of community offline are often able to develop a sense of community online. Intriguingly, members of minority racial groups in the sample—who may experience some measure of social isolation in their real-world contexts of work and school—show "a strong proclivity to seek out a comfortable electronic social niche." Such findings are highly suggestive of at least a potential capacity for electronic democracy initiatives to attract to online deliberative communities those citizens who feel relatively unconnected to their communities in real space.

Whether citizens who go online in search of community will want to talk politics is, of course, another question. The importance of individual attitudes and resources to the success of online democratic initiatives is thus stressed in Peter Muhlberger's study, "Access, Skill, and Motivation in Online Political Discussion: Testing Cyberrealism." Muhlberger finds, based on a representative survey of adult Pittsburghers, that people currently talk politics relatively little and that they talk politics online even less. According to his analysis, the best strategies for increasing online political discussion would be oriented toward proliferating home Web access, encouraging Web use more generally, and encouraging people's willingness to share their views with people who disagree with them and in public settings. There is also evidence to suggest that improving discussion quality will lure more participation, especially from educated Web users.

In addition to motivation, another resource obviously relevant to the potential impact of online democratic initiatives is public policy knowledge. In "Virtual Deliberation: Knowledge from Online Interaction Versus Ordinary Discussion," Jason Barabas finds, however, that relatively unstructured online discussions are likely to do no better than ordinary conversation—which does not do very well—in improving the distribution among discussants of accurate information on public policy issues. To evaluate the effects of policy discussion and online activity on knowledge, he analyzed data from two nationally representative surveys conducted in 1998 concerning social security reform. The results were comparable; neither approximated the beneficial information effects associated with organized deliberative forums.

The final contribution, by Grant Kippen and Gordon Jenkins, turns our attention from the relationship between the potential successes of electronic democracy and the individual resources and capacities that individuals bring to online experience to the ways in which our contemporary social, political, and institutional contexts have to be taken into account. Focusing specifically on political parties and writing in a Canadian context, Kippen and Jenkins find that parties have been conspicuously slow to adopt new technologies for building stronger relationships with their constituents. As analyzed in "The Challenges of E-Democracy for Political Parties," the lag is all the more notable when viewed against the background of e-business and e-government, where practices have much more rapidly been transformed by customer- and citizen-centric models. Two factors predominate in the explanation for this lag. First, political parties have yet to be persuaded that the quality of electronic democracy initiatives can or will be linked to their core mission, winning at the polls. Second, political parties lack the financial resources available to businesses and administrative agencies to develop advanced technology. The implication is strong that the appeal of electronic democracy in principle may be insufficient to elicit from powerful contemporary political actors the resources necessary to launch and sustain online initiatives.

* * *

The following eighteen papers go far in illuminating the technological potential for electronic democracy and identifying factors likely to determine how successful electronic democracy initiatives will be. They also demonstrate that the kinds of research most likely to be productive in guiding electronic democracy initiatives challenge the conventions of university research in key ways. First, the research that the field both needs and warrants is transnational, multi-institutional, and multidisciplinary. The seven disciplines represented in this volume—communications studies, information science, law, philosophy, political psychology, political science, and sociology—do not come close to exhausting the relevant fields. Few universities are likely to have across-the-board strengths in all the significant areas, making interinstitutional cooperation an imperative.

Moreover, if we are not to mistake culturally specific behaviors for more generalizable findings about human-computer interaction, cross-cultural study is a must.

Second, the research community must help to build a lot of what it seeks to test. Research into the likely impacts of incandescent lighting would not have been enormously helpful if confined to experimental study and speculation based on the use of even really good candles. To some extent, we cannot really know the promise or limitations of new ICTs until people can actually experience them. Electronic democracy researchers might even advance their insights by their personal and collaborative use of the very technologies that hold democratic promise.

It is clearly the view of most of the writers in this volume that both broadly utopian and categorically despondent predictions of our ICT-enabled democratic future are premature. The prevailing mood is cautionary. The most consistent implicit strain of optimism is one that might be expected of research scholars—the recognition that human ingenuity is providing us with tools that can be used in extraordinary new ways to connect, educate, and empower humanity and that we can maximize their potential by thinking rigorously about our deepest values, human psychology, and the impact of social, economic, and cultural forces on political possibility. This volume aspires to be an important step in that direction.

PART 1

The Potential for Democratic Technologies and New Political Practices

CHAPTER 1

Technologies for Democracy

A. MICHAEL FROOMKIN

That democracy can function properly only with an informed and engaged citizenry is at once a cornerstone of serious legal and moral philosophy, a high school civics verity, and a cliché. While some suggest that the main contribution of the Internet to civic life is to increase social fragmentation (Sunstein 2001), new technology may enhance the quantity and especially the quality of mass participation in a representative democracy, perhaps even make it possible to find a path toward the enhanced democracy suggested by Jürgen Habermas. Although it is far too early to know for sure, this essay seeks to lay a foundation for the latter claim: that Internet tools may enrich political debate, permit the growth of new social networks, and (we can hope) help realize what Benjamin Barber calls the "Jeffersonian Scenario" (Barber 1989–99: 582), in which we improve the quality and deliberativeness of both geographic communities and communities of practice (Agre 2002).

1. A Very Short Summary of Habermas's Vision of a Path Toward Improved Democratic Discourse

This is not the place to attempt to recount the convolutions of Habermas's work. Instead, I will summarize Habermas's frankly speculative account of the process by which current, and in his view highly imperfect, democratic discourse might come to be improved. (This is, of course, only a small aspect of his very large project.)

An informed and engaged citizenry enriches the political process in at least two ways. It stimulates what we hope are better decisions by

3

contributing to the policy stew and by holding politician-cooks to account. More fundamentally, participation legitimates the process by which we reach decisions. Habermas has argued that only a decision-making process that is meaningfully open to all is capable of making decisions that we should regard as morally legitimate. He also argues that a system that routinely fails to make decisions pursuant to a process that meets his demanding criteria for moral decision making will, in time, suffer from a crisis of legitimacy, leading either to reform or to some form of repression.

In the most optimistic and forward-looking portion of his grand project to reformulate the ethical underpinnings of lawmaking, Habermas suggests that the forces needed to push public decision-making in the directions advocated by his philosophy are likely to come from a reenergized, activist, engaged citizenry, working together to create new small-scale communicative associative institutions that over time merge into larger ones, or at least join forces.

Habermas's own discussion of a concrete political agenda includes recommendations for increased decentralization in order to allow pluralistic decision making. Decentralization also serves to counteract the "generation of mass loyalty" sought (and increasingly, he believes, achieved) by mass institutions such as political parties and states (Baynes 1992: 179–80). Habermas seems to be suggesting that, under these conditions, the best practical discourse cannot be achieved directly within society as a whole; subgroups must break off to form smaller discourse communities, either to practice good discourse or to create the conditions under which someday a coming together of many parts may produce a suitably discursive whole (Habermas 1992: 422).

It seems that one solution—or is it a hope?—is for the members of each subgroup to build good discourse habits within a distinctive community where the commonalities of experience and taste make good discourse and perhaps agreement easier (Habermas 1992: 455; 1996: 366–67, 373–84). Once inculcated in the practices of proper discourse, the participants in these small communities can venture out and engage in dialogue with others from different backgrounds who have also undergone similar (re)formative experiences (Habermas 1996: 165–67).

Ultimately, Habermas "locates rational collective will formation outside formal organizations of every sort" (McCarthy 1992: 63). As Habermas puts it, "Discourses do not govern. They generate a communicative power that cannot take the place of administration[] but can only influence it. This influence is limited to the procurement and withdrawal of legitimation" (Habermas 1992: 452). Over time, Habermas has changed his account of the means by which "spontaneously formed publics" affect public decisions. Where in earlier writings he categorized civil society as part of the public sphere, in *Between Facts and Norms*, Habermas relocates civil society in the "lifeworld," that is, the sphere centered around private life. Although important (Baxter 2002: 580–81), this change need not concern us here, as both versions accept and build on the empirical reality that discourses in civil society do sometimes—but only sometimes—have an influence on formalized public policy decision making in government and elsewhere.

The ideal discourse would encompass all those affected by the outcome (Luhmann 1996: 944). Indeed, Habermas's critics have argued that the demanding discourse required to actualize discourse ethics is nothing more than an unrealizable, imaginative construct. To the extent that Habermas may have relied upon an "ideal speech situation" in his earlier work, this criticism had more than a little justice (Power 1996). But in his more recent work, particularly in *Between Facts and Norms* and *The Theory of Communicative Action*, Habermas has provided an account of discourse ethics that depends upon an ideal that is realizable, although it does call for a far more demanding type of discourse than one commonly encounters in the political arena (Habermas 1984, 1987, 1996).

Habermas does not naively claim that people can resolve all problems simply by sitting around and talking about them from the heart. Instead, he recognizes that, in reality, much social interaction is "strategic," meaning that people bring their personal agendas to many discourses and seek to exercise their power and influence to achieve what they consider to be personally advantageous results, rather than selflessly seeking the true and the just. Strategic communication consists of using force, such as economic threats or promises, rather than attempting to persuade others of the rational merits of one's cause (Habermas 1982: 236).

Guarding against strategic communication in oneself and others is particularly difficult: it requires that participants in discourse understand that their true interests will be better served by a more honest policy. Habermas does not make this assertion on the basis of a utilitarian calculation of enlightened self-interest. Instead, he grounds the claim in reason and the commitments that he argues a rational party must make when actually trying to communicate with another person rather than simply attempting to manipulate him or her.

In reality, people are capable only of "practical discourse," which, at its best, produces provisionally legitimate laws or rules that apply only to the group or polity that produced them. Habermas's discourse principle generates minimum parameters for this practical discourse: participants must "take part, freely and equally, in a cooperative search for truth, where nothing coerces anyone except the force of the better argument. . . . Practical discourse can also be viewed as a communicative process simultaneously exhorting all participants to ideal role taking" (Habermas 1982: 198). Outcomes tainted by threats, force, coercion, trickery, or impairment of participants are not legitimate.

To achieve Habermasian practical discourse, participants must come as close as possible to an ideal in which "(1) all voices in any way relevant get a hearing, (2) the best arguments available to us given our present state of knowledge are brought to bear, and (3) only the unforced force of the better argument determines the 'yes' and 'no' responses of the participants" (Habermas 1996b: 163; see also Alexy 1989). Rather than seeing even these requirements as unrealistic or utopian, Habermas argues that the commitments required for practical discourse arise from a good-faith commitment to honest debate. Once parties undertake to debate nonstrategically, they embark on a course that requires all affected parties to deliberate together in a reasoned conversation that aims at reasoned agreement. This requirement, Habermas claims, emanates from the requirements of reason and the cognitive requirements of language (Habermas 1987: 148; Baynes 1992: 113). Specifically, Habermas argues that the decision to communicate carries four implicit assertions that anyone who honestly seeks to communicate presupposes: (1) that the utterance is comprehensible, (2) that the utterance is true, (3) that the speaker is truthful, and (4) that the utterance is the right one for the situation (Habermas 1979: 41, 59–60). These shared fundamental values—without which, Habermas claims, any real discourse is impossible—suffice to provide a foundation for an ethic of social interaction.

Practical discourse, Habermas writes, is "a procedure for testing the validity of norms that are being proposed and hypothetically considered for adoption" (Habermas 1990: 103). Although the discourse principle does not require that communications between parties be ideal in order to generate legitimate rules, it nevertheless demands that parties at least engage in a practical discourse that is the best it can be. While rules can be legitimate absent procedures necessary for practical discourse if they are the same ones that participants would have adopted under the proper procedures, we cannot be sure when we have met that condition or that proper procedures have been used (Habermas 1996: 107). The parties have to understand the limited, contingent nature of any agreement they may reach in order to remain open to further possible improvements (Habermas 1990: 43, 103).

Since discourse lies at the heart of Habermas's vision of the collective formation of legitimate rules, his theory inevitably requires a fairly strong understanding of the community in which the discourse will take place. If nothing else, members of the community must be able to communicate with one another. Habermas rejects the idea that a common language is required. What is required is the practical ability to understand statements sufficiently to evaluate the reasons for their acceptance. They must also agree on fundamental concepts so that meaningful communication is possible. Indeed, participants need to be sufficiently familiar with one another's worldviews, or at least be able to reconstruct them mentally when needed:

> In order to understand an utterance in the paradigm case of a
> speech act oriented to reaching understanding, the interpreter has
> to be familiar with the conditions of [an utterance's] validity; he
> has to know under what conditions the validity claim linked with it
> is acceptable, that is, would have to be acknowledged by a hearer.
> But where could the interpreter obtain this knowledge if not from
> the context . . . ? He can understand the meaning of communicative
> acts only because they are embedded in contexts of action oriented
> to reaching understanding. (Habermas 1984: 115)

Thus, a completely formless society, or an anarchy in which people not only live separate lives but hold divergent aesthetics so alien to one another that they defy mutual comprehension, is a society that is not capable of engaging in the practices that allow it to generate legitimate rules.

It does not follow, however, that even a society in which participants are capable of understanding one another will be able to govern itself through some Rousseauistic process of collective will formation combined with direct democracy (Habermas 1996: 100–4). Understanding does not suffice to compel agreement on matters of substance; only fundamental procedural parameters for the testing of proposed norms can be derived from reasoned agreement and understanding. Indeed, Habermas argues that total "pluralism and pure procedural justice are ultimately incompatible" (Habermas 1996: 480–90).

Given the "multiplicity of individual life projects and collective forms of life," Habermas asserts that only the procedures of discourse required to achieve rational agreement can command universal assent (Habermas 1993: 150). Habermas responds to the criticism that some people may have no interest in participating in or achieving universal assent, and might instead prefer to agree to disagree, or choose to disagree entirely, by stating that this objection misunderstands his point. It would be perfectly consistent with discourse ethics, for example, for a group to agree that it will decide disputed questions by majority vote, given the need to make decisions in real time, so long as the "decision [is] reached under discursive conditions that lend their results the presumption of rationality: the content of a decision reached in accordance with due procedure must be such as can count as the rationally motivated but fallible result of a discussion provisionally brought to a close under the pressure of time" (Habermas 1993: 159; see also 1992: 449–50). In other words, procedurally sound discourses allow us to claim that the discourses' outputs are legitimate, and hence to enforce the rules even against resisting nonparticipants. As for persons who just wish to disagree, presumably they are invited to participate in the discourse, but if they persistently refuse the invitation, the discourse must proceed as best it can without them, just as it does without those persons who consider themselves so superior that they do not think the participants are worthy partners for debate (Rosenfeld 1996). If rules that coerce result from a practical discourse in which the coerced were welcome to participate, then the results, Habermas argues, nevertheless satisfy the discourse principle.

It is too early to predict, but not too early to hope (Agre 1998), that the Internet supplies at least a partial answer to the powerful challenge raised against the possibility of ever applying discourse theory to broad ranges of public life:

> For Habermas, not only lawmaking but also governance in its ongoing, administrative aspect must draw its energy and authority from the citizenry's generation of communicative power. This bold vision would seem to call for a vast increase in the amount of "communicative power" presently flowing through this or any other contemporary democracy. As Habermas points out, communicative power is generated only "from below," from mobilized citizenries. Thus, "his vision seems to demand a substantial renovation of our existing public spheres, and the creation of many new spaces and institutional forms for citizenly engagement in the processes of lawmaking and governance." (Forbath 1996: 1445 quoting Jürgen Habermas.)

If this is a fair description of what the widespread actualization of discourse ethics would require, it seems a tall order, especially in an era of "bowling alone" (Putnam 2000). The "creation of many new spaces and institutional forms for citizenly engagement in the processes of lawmaking and governance" may seem beyond our capabilities, and perhaps it is. But perhaps there is a technological solution. Technology may not compel outcomes, but it certainly can make difficult things easier (Schwartz and Phoenix 2001). The Internet radically empowers the individual. The Internet also creates new tools that make possible the construction of new communities of shared interest. In Habermasian terms, the Internet draws power back into the public sphere, away from other systems. It also makes it possible, as never before, to create as many "new spaces and new institutional forms" as one desires. Could it be that emerging technologies will enable new types of Internet-based discourses that generate the "communicative power" Habermas argues is needed to educate and mobilize citizens to demand that their governments make decisions that are better and more legitimate?

The Habermasian new spaces begin with individuals in "pluralistic, differentiated civil societies" who gradually unite in communities of shared interests and understanding. Using democratized access to a new form of mass media—the Internet—these individuals first engage in self-expression, then engage each other in debate. In so doing, they begin to form new communities of discourse. Whether these new communities of discourse can grow into forces capable of influencing the public sphere is only speculation—but it suddenly seems more plausible than it used to.

2. Technologies for Democracy

The Internet can be seen as a giant electronic talkfest, a medium that is discourse-mad. Thanks to the significant hardware and software that make it possible, for most users the Internet is the exchange of information, and a good part of that information is debate and argument—discourse itself, albeit not always the calmest, and most certainly not often adhering to the strictures derived from Habermas's discourse principle.

As the Internet user base increases, the network is harnessed to serve an increasingly wide range of purposes. Meanwhile, discourse-enabling tools are being developed at a rapid pace, and some combination of these may suffice someday to overcome the daunting problems of scale that stand in the way of an engaged, networked citizenry. This part briefly sketches four families of software initiatives and one family of hardware initiative, each illustrating a different way in which Internet tools enable substantially improved discourses.

Blogs represent one of the latest examples of the Internet's democratization of publishing. They illustrate how ease of publishing can stimulate debate: bloggers often read and react to one another's work, creating a new commons of public, if not necessarily always deeply deliberated, debate. Wiki webs illustrate collaborative document creation tools. The process of creating these documents is a form of discourse, and the finished or continually evolving products are contributors to discourse. Slashdot is a leading example of a community-based (and community-creating) discussion forum with collaborative filtering. Finally, open government and community filtering initiatives provide examples of proposed and actual instances of governments using Internet resources to improve communication and in some cases influence or even control decision making based on community input.

First, however, comes the hardware that makes the other things possible.

2.1 Hardware for Democracy

Internet software does not exist in a vacuum. It requires hardware to run on and connectivity to run over. Although computers are falling in price, they are not free, and neither is Internet connectivity. The cost of connectivity has led many commentators to bemoan the "digital divide" between and within countries (Bridges.org 2002). Any Internet-based discourse threatens to exclude those who cannot afford access; any decision that affects people whose material circumstances make them unable to participate in it is deeply suspect and lacks legitimacy.[1] In wealthier countries, such as the United States and some Western European countries, publicly provided free Internet access (as is found in many U.S. public libraries) combined with the rise of cafés that sell Internet access by the hour means that many people without a computer have at least some access to the Internet. Still, the legitimacy of any rule formation that affects these people requires that this access be sufficient to allow them to participate meaningfully.

Because content and software tend to be visible worldwide, they are the most noticeable signs of the Internet's growth. Less visible, in part because they are more local, are an impressive number of community-based projects to provide a hardware infrastructure for Internet access. Some are freenets—free Internet service providers—while others are ambitious projects to provide free wireless Internet connections to neighborhoods and even cities (Flickenger 2002).[2] Using tools such as empty Pringles cans for antennas (Flickenger 2002), community networks are extending the range of wireless access and providing free high-speed access to their neighbors. Even with free bandwidth, one still needs a device that can access the Internet, but as personal digital assistants become increasingly Internet-aware, people have more, cheaper options for Internet access.

2.2 Weblogs and Blogs

The Internet was democratizing publishing even before the Web was invented. Today, new user-friendly tools make it possible to create elegant Web pages without any knowledge of HTML, formatting languages, or unfamiliar scripting tools. Specialized hosting also removes technical barriers to entry and provides centralized locations where readers can find blogs, and bloggers can find each other.[3] This development not only expands the number of speakers; by making updating so easy, it also changes the nature of online conversations.

While Web pages are naturally a one-to-many medium, political bloggers often read and link to each other's sites, invite feedback from readers, and comment on what other bloggers are saying. A medium that is architecturally one-to-many is thus effectively a hybrid, a peer-to-peer conversation with many eavesdroppers. Although the stream-of-consciousness form of some blogs may not necessarily lend itself to reflection, some blogs are at least self-conscious about the nature of the "blogisphere," if not yet engaged in thorough Habermasian self-reflection.

The blogisphere is young, but it shows some signs of potentially evolving into a miniature public sphere of its own, one of shared interests rather than shared geography. Conceivably, the rise of a blog culture, even one composed primarily of nonpolitical, wholly personal diaries, may enrich the public sphere. The impulse to read some blogs may not be that different from the impulse that brings viewers to soap operas, but the experience of regularly encountering another person's diary, of following along in a stranger's life, might have value. Blogging encourages citizens to embark on the intellectual exercise of viewing life from the perspective of others, to try to walk in each other's shoes, to respect each other enough to engage in honest discourse, and to recognize in each other sufficient basic rights so as to create the autonomy needed to make the discourse possible. That encouragement is only part of what is needed for discourse ethics to flourish, but it is a start.

2.3 Wiki Webs and Other Collaborative Drafting Tools

Collaborative drafting systems allow many people to work together on a shared document or set of documents. The collaborators need not be online at the same time; the system allows for asynchronous communications across a network. Wiki Wiki (which means "quick" in Hawaiian) is an example of collaborative drafting software.

Wiki users create general categories and then classify their contributions. Singular category names refer to specific objects of discussion, while plural ones refer to broader discussions or topics. Today the original Wiki contains more than twenty thousand titles or pages, organized into sixteen categories. The main categories fall into three broad areas: technology (primarily computer-related), more general intellectual pursuits, and Wiki. Within the general intellectual category, topics include book discussions, language skills, entertainment, stories, and film reviews. Wiki Wiki describes itself as a "composition system; it's a discussion medium; it's a repository; it's a mail system; it's a tool for collaboration. . . . [I]t's a fun way of communicating."[4] Indeed, the original Wiki gave rise to a large, highly unorganized, collaborative community that has produced a very large set of texts.

Wiki webs are accessed by Web browsers in the ordinary way. First, any visitor can update or delete any existing content on any page of a Wiki site—which illustrates a potentially serious security problem in a basic Wiki Wiki installation. Second, any visitor can create new pages or add content to the Wiki. Unlike ordinary Web pages, Wiki sites display all the internal links that lead to a given page, in addition to all the links that start from it. There is also a special category that tracks recent changes to the Wiki.

Unlike some Wiki clones, the original Wiki web is wide open. Although users may identify themselves, either by an IP address or a username, and create home pages in the system, they are not required to do so. Any user of a Wiki can add or change content anywhere in the system. Given the extreme openness of the original Wiki and its resulting vulnerability to electronic vandalism, its persistence as a viable collaborative tool suggests that the authors may have found a way for the community to police itself. Of course, part of the explanation for Wiki flourishing might be the basic clunkiness of the content-editing process; vandals just might not have the patience it takes to change many pages. Wiki's users think that another reason their content survives is that the time it takes to create content plus the relative ease with which it can be replaced actually welcomes and encourages deliberation and discourages name-calling and tantrums, since these are what get deleted quickly.

Similarly, the Openlaw project at the Berkman Center for Internet and Society at Harvard Law School uses the Annotation Engine, "a set of Perl scripts and a database that allows readers anywhere to add comments to Web pages anywhere else" (Berkman Center 2004a). The center describes Openlaw as

> [a]n experiment in crafting legal argument in an open forum . . .
> [to] develop arguments, draft pleadings, and edit briefs in public,
> online. Non-lawyers and lawyers alike are invited to join the process by adding thoughts to the "brainstorm" outlines, drafting and
> commenting on drafts in progress, and suggesting reference
> sources. . . . Building on the model of open source software, [Openlaw is] working from the hypothesis that an open development
> process best harnesses the distributed resources of the Internet
> community. By using the Internet, [Openlaw] hope[s] to enable the
> public interest to speak as loudly as the interests of corporations.
> Openlaw is therefore a large project built through the coordinated
> effort of many small (and not so small) contributions. (Berkman
> Center 2004b).

2.4 Slash and Other Collaborative Filtering Tools

Although far from being the best practical discourse in a box, Slash, the software behind the popular Web site Slashdot.org (Chromatic, Aker, and Krieger 2002), is a leading example of how software can facilitate discourse without relying on the strategic behavior of actually deleting unhelpful participation. Slashdot is a community discussion tool that allows largely unfettered and almost unlimited discussion, yet nonetheless permits participants to organize and manage their reading—for example, by limiting themselves to contributions that other members of the community have deemed as worth reading. The Slashdot site itself is proudly devoted to "news for nerds" and "stuff that matters," with these terms referring to a wealth of technical talk amid discussions of social issues such as the Columbine massacre or governmental censorship policies (Katz 1999a, 1999b; Slashdot 2004). Reflecting the reprogrammers' commitment to fostering community-based discourse, the software is open-source and freely available. Indeed, a wide variety of online communities use it to organize their conversations.

Anyone visiting the Slashdot Web site can suggest a topic of discussion, but in principle the "article" appears on the front page of the site only if one of the several "editors," the people running the software, approve it.

Editors can also initiate their own articles. Once an article is posted for discussion, anyone can append comments to it. Posted remarks may be signed, pseudonymous, or anonymous. What makes Slashdot effective is that the user community is then recruited to assist in rating the comments.

Every comment posted to Slashdot carries a rating designed to reflect the community's decision as to whether the comment contributes to the discussion. Anonymous comments enter the system rated at zero points. Comments signed with a new, and thus untrusted, user's name or pseudonym enter the system rated at one point. Veterans who have a demonstrated track record of making useful contributions find that their comments enter the system with two points.

Once a user enters a comment into the system, other users are recruited to decide whether the comment's rating should be raised or lowered. The Slash software selects a random and constantly changing group of users who have visited the site a sufficient number of times to serve as temporary moderators and gives each user five "moderation points" to apply to the comments of others. (In my experience, moderation opportunities come every other month or so, or faster if one of my comments is rated up to the maximum level.) Moderators can use each of their moderation points to raise or lower the status of someone else's comment by a point but cannot moderate posts on a topic about which they have chosen to comment; if a user later joins in the discussion on a topic he chose to moderate, his moderation points vanish.

Meanwhile, every visitor to the Slashdot web site can set her user preferences so that the site displays only those comments that have acquired a minimum number of points. No comment is deleted for low status, so there is no actual censorship, only collaborative filtering. Furthermore, the system builds in feedback. A poster gains one point of "karma" every time a moderator gives one of her comments a point. Conversely, having her comment downgraded by a point reduces a poster's karma by one. High karma, acquired by a history of posting comments appreciated by moderators, allows one to post a comment with a higher initial status of two points instead of one. Thus, for example, I can read the Slashdot site with my viewing threshold set at two, knowing that what I read either will come from people who the community has found tend to make valuable contributions or will be comments to which someone else gave a point. While I may sometimes miss a small part of the gold, I also ensure that I wade through relatively little of what I and like-minded readers consider dross.

"Metamoderation" reduces the incidence of abuse by moderators. Habitual users of the site are offered a daily set of ten randomly chosen moderation decisions made by others and are asked if each is correct or abusive. Users whose moderation decisions are consistently marked as abusive by metamoderators will find that their karma shrinks, as do their odds of being asked to moderate in the future.

While Slashdot is a very useful tool for enabling an interesting and useful community discussion, there are important ways in which it is not, and standing alone cannot be, the sort of best practical discourse that produces decisions entitled to our respect. Slashdot is not really a decision-making tool at all; it is a discussion tool. The openness of the discussion means that anyone can join or leave at will and that individuals can assume multiple identities within the system. Although it is possible that a consensus might be reached, most discussions do not last long enough to achieve a consensus, if only because the site is news-oriented and new material rapidly sends the old to the archive. In the absence of consensus, there is no obvious way to make a decision; on the current site, voting is not possible because one does not know who the electorate should be or how many of the posters are multiple identities of the same person.

Because the editors choose which topics make the Slashdot front page, they have an agenda-setting role that permits them to skew the discourse. However, one could easily imagine practices that would blunt the impact of the editors, such as a rotating editorial board chosen from high-karma users. In fact, some Slashdot-like systems avoid the danger of editorial domination by placing control of the front page in the hands of the community. At Kuro5hin.org, for example, every article submitted for publication goes into a special "moderation queue," where members each get one vote to determine the fate of the article. Or, because the software is free, although the computer needed to run it is not, one could envision a set of complementary or competing fora.

In addition, recent versions of the Slashdot software include a "journaling" feature that allows every user of the software to set up a private Web page that functions much like a blog—except that, if the author chooses, she can invite other members of the community to comment on her journal entries. If Alice has a journal, Bob has the option of setting his reading preferences so that he will be notified every time Alice posts something. Bob can also choose to view a column on the front page of his customized Slashcode home page that lists the most recently modified journals. This feature substantially democratizes the community's ability to raise topics independently of a site's editors, thereby enhancing the variety of discourse, albeit at the risk of slight fragmentation.

It would be foolhardy to predict that some hypothetical version of Slashdot will someday include tools that encourage communities to self-generate morally valid community decisions. But it is not too soon to speculate that a multiplicity of Slashdot-like sites could become the nuclei of pluralistic "public spheres" in which the participants self-organize, educate each other, and then bring that shared understanding to bear in more traditional social processes for decision making, such as elections. For several years, those fortunate enough to have access to a computer and an Internet service provider have had access to an uncensored feed of first-person experience from many countries and alternative commentary sometimes quite different from what the mass media provide. Now, perhaps, this same fortunate—and rapidly growing—population with access to new communications technology will have access to tools that make community building and quality discourse easier. That is still a long way from generalizing the best practical discourse, but it seems a step in the right direction, one in which we might be more willing to move if we were persuaded that the endpoint is achievable.

2.5 From Open Government to Community Deliberation Tools

Unlike weblogs, a tool that citizens can use to speak to each other, "open government" initiatives allow information to flow between government and citizen, although in its simplest form the flow is one-way. Having official government information available online does not constitute discourse, but it does improve it: "in the deliberative process, information plays a central role along with achieving equality of access to it. Equality of access to information and an unrestricted means of access are fundamental to a more ambitious practice of discourse" (Gimmler 2001: 31). Easy access to information empowers citizens, enhances debates, and in time may change outcomes.

Once governments provide official information online, it is only a small step to creating facilities for citizens to send e-mail or other feedback. For example, Britain's UK Online provides one-stop access to government consultation documents and invites readers to discuss draft bills and to comment on other parliamentary processes (Bertelsmann Foundation 2002: 11).[5] England and Scotland allow citizens to propose legislation via the Internet, but the nature of the parliamentary system—in which the government exercises tight control over the legislative agenda—makes it highly unlikely their proposals will become law. So long, however, as e-government initiatives involve little more than moving traditional practices such as notice and comment rule making online, the most they can offer is to change the volume and quality, but not the nature, of citizen participation in government.[6] These are worthy goals, but they are a long way from a true Habermasian discourse. In an interesting twist that deserves emulation, one U.S. bureaucrat has set up a personal and unofficial policy page in which he discusses his ideas for regulatory reform and invites reader comment (Galbi undated).

Perhaps in the future, "e-government shall be a balanced combination of electronic services and forms of electronic participation" (Bertelsmann Foundation 2002: 4). As yet, however, "not much progress has… been made in connection with the development of instruments, processes and principles… for the direct integration of the popular will into political decision-making processes" (ibid.: 10). The Habermasian goal is not direct democracy as such; simply transposing plebiscites to the Internet is unlikely to increase the level of deliberation given the number of decisions that need to be made. Rather, we need different structures that enhance democracy, supplement debate, and encourage citizen involvement in what ultimately will be more like, and feel more like, self-governance.

It remains uncertain to what extent one can export the community-creation virtues of a Wiki or a Slash to wider spheres, just as it is unclear to what extent one can use Internet tools to enhance awareness, debate, and deliberation within existing, usually geographically based, institutions. Three things, however, are clear: First, there is room for improvement, both in the quality of most governance structures and in the apparent legitimacy they enjoy. Second, Internet technologies that enable and structure discourse offer hope for improvement, as long as it is understood that the most we can hope for from them is that they will enable and enhance but not determine or discourage (Agre 2003). Third, a high level of discourse and valid rule creation is attainable, and thus worth striving for, as demonstrated by the work of the Internet Engineering Task Force (IETF), an international, participatory, open, and deliberative standards body that does most of its work online.

Today's early experiments in the design of online discourse-reinforcing institutions may be no more than portents of future designs for improved governance (Bertelsmann Foundation 2002: 14), but you have to start somewhere. One government has begun experimenting with online systems in which neighborhoods are asked to prioritize public works projects—which pothole gets fixed first, for example. Another experiment would allow citizens to put items on bureaucrats' agendas. Every citizen would be given a small annual quota of opportunities to add an item to a government agency's agenda. The agency receiving a citizen's request for action would not be required to do what the citizen suggested, but if the agency did not take action, it would have to publish a reasoned opinion on its Web site explaining its decision. Software products such as Benjamin R. Barber and Beth Simone Noveck's Unchat offer novel ways to structure small-group real-time online discussions by building in means for participants to choose (and unchoose) discussion leaders and moderators, to generally set their own ground rules, and to have private side conversations about procedure that need not disrupt the discussion of substance (Noveck 2004). To encourage decision making, the software includes a module for straw polls of the group. To encourage good decisions, Unchat provides for easy integrated linking to outside sources of information. Unchat's biggest limitation, however, is that it is designed for a relatively small group of people and does not seem likely to scale well.

More ambitious projects are on the drawing board. A team of Carnegie Mellon University researchers, led by Peter Shane, Robert Cavalier, and Peter Muhlberger, has created software configurable to support an online version of James Fishkin's Deliberative Polling. Deliberative Polling is a technique of structured conversation, "designed to measure what public opinion on major issues would be like if citizens had the time and resources to become better informed."[7] Delibera, the Carnegie Mellon software, combines text, video, and audio elements to try to realize the advantages of face-to-face deliberation online.

At the Massachusetts Institute of Technology School of Architecture and Planning, students led by Dean William J. Mitchell and Professor Daniel Greenwood are developing an "open governance environment" that they hope will enhance the deliberativeness and effectiveness of New England open town meetings.[8] The aim is to meld the most useful features of community filtering—collaborative filtering of contributed ideas and proposals—with a more structured and formal process by which the ideas that receive the most support in the first phase are subjected to structured, sometimes time-limited debate culminating in a decisional moment, usually a vote (governance filtering).[9] In the initial phase, members of the town meeting are encouraged to brainstorm and to comment on each other's suggestions. When a proposal reaches a certain critical mass of support, or when a proposal originates from the appropriate government official, people are appointed to make the case for and against it, and everyone is invited to comment on the proposal and to respond to other comments within a few weeks' time. The process culminates either with an agenda for the physical town meeting, one backed up by considerably more discussion than would be possible in a single evening, or perhaps with an online vote of the town's residents.

A town-meeting-size group is small compared even to a small country, and very small compared to a big one. Slash systems work well with over half a million participants, but it is unclear how far they can scale. Regardless of their scalability, they do not structure decisions, just a series of conversations. Unchat, Delibera, and the open governance environment may help structure decisions, but they offer no obvious method for dealing with large groups. Even inviting citizens to help set bureaucratic agendas may not work in anything larger than a medium-size city. As one attempts to find discourse tools for bigger groups, one must find cyberfederalist ways to subdivide them yet keep them in contact, find different tools, or be prepared to argue that habits inculcated in small group settings spill over into larger discourses. My personal experience with the Internet, in which I seem to find myself among varied groups, inclines me toward a vision of many smaller groups with overlapping membership, each attempting to achieve a best practical discourse within its limited realm. It might be that a multitude of subspheres of interlocking, cross-pollinating discourses would provide an environment in which an informed citizenry could revitalize the public sphere as a whole and engage in the creation of better, and perhaps even more legitimate, rules at even a national level (Keane 2000: 77–78). At best, however, we are in the very early days of that experiment.

3. Conclusion

I have not sought to argue that the Internet will somehow magically transform participants in public discourse into philosopher-kings, or that the Internet necessarily pushes us in the direction of the revitalization of the public sphere that Habermas's theory calls for. It is important to avoid falling prey to what Benjamin Barber has called the "Pangloss Scenario" (Barber 1998–99: 576). The Internet as a whole is not some freestanding public sphere of its own filled with transformed denizens who will magically drop the attitudes, practices, and objectives that shape our familiar institutions of government. Indeed, given their linguistic and other diversities, there seems no reason to claim that Internet users as a whole somehow form a public sphere of their own.

One should, however, be equally wary of excessive pessimism. The "Jeffersonian Scenario" may be attainable and is certainly worth striving for, even if it means we move from bowling alone to bowling together virtually.

The Internet supports a variety of new tools that show a potential for enabling not just discourse but *good* discourse. While it is far too soon to claim that the widespread diffusion and use of these tools, or their successors, might actualize the best practical discourse in an ever-wider section of our lives, it is not too soon to hope, and perhaps to install some software.

Notes

1. A more fundamental problem is that in the absence of widely deployed seamless voice recognition and reading software, Internet-based discourse also requires literacy.

2. For sample lists, see "Freenets & Community Networks," available at http://www.lights.com/freenet/ (accessed August 28, 2002); "Community Computer Networks, Free-Nets and City-Regional Guides," available at http://victoria.tc.ca/Resources/freenets.html (accessed April 2002); PersonalTelco, "Wireless Communities," available at http://www.personaltelco.net/index.cgi/WirelessCommunities (accessed March 2004).

3. See, e.g., Blogger.com, at http://www.blogger.com; Weblogs.com, at http://www.weblogs.com.

4. "Front Page," available at http://c2.com/cgi/wiki (accessed October 14, 2002).

5. See http://www.ukonline.gov.uk/ (accessed September 5, 2002).

6. For a transnational survey of efforts to expand traditional notice and comment rulemaking to include Internet provision of information and electronic comments, see Pauline Poland, "Online Consultation in GOL Countries: Initiatives to Foster E-Democracy" (2001), available at http://governments-online.org/documents/e-consultation.pdf.

7. "What is a Deliberative Poll?" available at http://www.pbs.org/newshour/btp/dop_background.html (accessed December 12, 2003).

8. The home page of the MIT E-Commerce Architecture Project Graduate Seminar Series, 4.285 Designing Online Self-Governance: Digital & Physical Place, Process and Presence, is at http://www.contractsxml.org/ecap2002/spring/. *See also* Jim Youll, ECitizen project page, at http://agentzero.com/~jim/ecitizen/tool-selection.html (accessed March 2004).

9. See MIT E-Commerce Architecture Project Graduate Seminar Series, "Collaborative Filters for Community and Governance: Can We All Now Finally Talk at Once?" available at http://www.contractsxml.org/ecap2002/spring/Filters.htm.

References

Agre, Philip E. 1998. "Information Technology in the Political Process." Available at http://polaris.gseis.ucla.edu/pagre/political.html.

Agre, Philip E. 2002. "Real-Time Politics: The Internet and the Political Process," *The Information Society* 18, 5: 311–31.

Alexy, Robert. 1989. *A Theory of Legal Argumentation.* Trans. Ruth Adler and Neil MacCormack. New York: Oxford University Press. Originally published 1978.

Barber, Benjamin. 1998–99. "Three Scenarios for the Future of Technology and Strong Democracy." *Political Science Quarterly* 113, 4: 573–89.

Baxter, Hugh. 2002. "System and Lifeworld in Habermas's Theory of Law," *Cardozo Law Review* 23, 2: 473–615.

Baynes, Kenneth. 1992. *The Normative Grounds of Social Criticism.* Albany: State University of New York Press.

Berkman Center for Internet and Society 2004a. "Annotation Engine." Available at http://cyber.law.harvard.edu/projects/annotate.html.

Berkman Center for Internet and Society 2004b. "Openlaw." Available at http://cyber.law.harvard.edu/openlaw.

Bertelsmann Foundation. 2002. "E-Government—Connecting Efficient Administration and Responsive Democracy." Available at http://www.begix.de/en/studie/studie.pdf.

Bridges.org. 2002. "What Is the Digital Divide?" Available at http://www.bridges.org/digitaldivide/index.html.

Chromatic, Brian Aker, and Dave Krieger. 2002. *Running Weblogs with Slash.* Sebastopol, CA: O'Reilly.

Flickenger, Rob. 2002. *Building Wireless Community Networks.* Sebastopol, CA: O'Reilly.

Forbath, William E. 1996. "Short-Circuit: A Critique of Habermas's Understanding of Law, Politics, and Economic Life." *Cardozo Law Review* 17, TK: TK–TK.

Galbi, Douglas. (undated). *Think!-New Ideas, Institutions, and Examples in Telecommunications Policy.* Available at http://www.galbithink.org/.

Gimmler, Antje. 2001. "Deliberative democracy, the public sphere and the internet" *Philosophy & Social Criticism* 27, 4: 21–39.

Habermas, Jürgen. 1979. "What is Universal Pragmatics?" In *Communication and the Evolution of Society.* Trans. Thomas McCarthy. Boston: Beacon Press. Originally published 1976.

Habermas, Jürgen. 1982. "A Reply to My Critics." In John B. Thompson and David Held, eds., *Habermas: Critical Debates.* Cambridge, MA: MIT Press.

Habermas, Jürgen. 1984. *The Theory of Communicative Action,* vol. 1: *Lifeworld and System: A Critique of Functionalist Reason.* Trans. Thomas McCarthy. Boston: Beacon Press. Originally published 1981.

Habermas, Jürgen. 1987. *The Theory of Communicative Action,* vol. 2: *Reason and the Rationalization of Society.* Trans. Thomas McCarthy. Boston: Beacon Press. Originally published 1981.

Habermas, Jürgen. 1990. "Discourse Ethics: Notes on a program of Philosophical Justification." In *Moral Consciousness and Communicative Action.* Trans. Christian Lenhardt & Shierry Weber Nicholsen. Cambridge, MA: MIT Press. Originally published 1983.

Habermas, Jürgen. 1992. "Further Reflections on the Public Sphere." Trans. Thomas Burger. In Craig Calhoun, ed., *Habermas and the Public Sphere.* Cambridge, MA: MIT Press.

Habermas, Jürgen. 1993. *Justification and Application: Remarks on Discourse Ethics.* Trans. Ciaran Cronin. Cambridge, MA: MIT Press. Orginally published 1990 and 1991.

Habermas, Jürgen. 1996. *Between Facts and Norms: Contributions to a Discourse Theory of Law and Democracy.* Trans. William Rehg. Cambridge, MA: MIT Press.

Katz, Jon. 1999b. Halloween Horrors Story (1999). Available at http://slashdot.org/features/99/11/03/1117256.shtml.

Katz, Jon. 1999a. Voices from the Hellmouth. Available at http://slashdot.org/features/99/04/25/1438249.shtml.

Keane, John. 2000. "Structural Transformations of the Public Sphere." In Kenneth L. Hacker and Jan van Dijk, eds., *Digital Democracy.* Thousand Oaks, CA: Sage.

Luhmann, Niklas. 1996. "*Quod Omnes Tangit*: Remarks on Jürgen Habermas's Legal Theory," *Cardozo Law Review* 17, 4–5: 883–900.

McCarthy, Thomas. 1992. "Practical Discourse: On the Relation of Morality to Politics." In Craig Calhoun, ed., *Habermas and the public Sphere*. Cambridge, MA: MIT Press.

Noveck, Beth. 2004. "Unchat: Democratic Solution for a Wired World." In Peter M. Shane, ed., *Democracy Online: The Prospects for Democratic Renewal Through the Internet*. New York: Routledge.

Poland, Pauline. 2001. "Online Consultation in GOL Countries: Initiatives to Foster E-Democracy." Available at http://governments-online.org/documents/e-consultation.pdf.

Power, Michael K. 1996. "Habermas and the Counterfactual Imagination." *Cardozo Law Review* 17, 4–5: 1005–26.

Putnam, Robert. 2000. *Bowling Alone: The Collapse and Revival of American Community*. New York: Simon and Schuster.

Rosenfeld, Michel. "Can Rights, Democracy, and Justice Be Reconciled Through Discourse Theory? Reflections on Habermas's Proceduralist Paradigm of Law." *Cardozo Law Review* 17, 4–5: 791–824.

Schwartz, Randal L., and Tom Phoenix. 2001. *Learning Perl*. 3rd ed. Sebastopol, CA: O'Reilly.

Slashdot 2004. Censorship [category index]. Available at http://slashdot.org/search.pl?topic=153.

Sunstein, Cass. 2001. *Republic.com*. Princeton: Princeton University Press.

CHAPTER 2

Unchat: Democratic Solution for a Wired World

BETH SIMONE NOVECK

It is a half-truth to say that democracy depends upon free speech. Rather, the participative practices of democratic life require open, equal, reasoned deliberation. Deliberation is more than just talk; it involves weighing approaches to problem solving in such a way that the viewpoints of all members of the community can be heard. Deliberation is a special form of speech structured according to democratic principles and designed to transform private prejudice into considered public opinion and to produce more legitimate solutions.

New technology could be an asset to democracy, not because it creates more outlets for speech but because software can impose the structure that transforms communication into deliberation. Democratic rules of conversation can be "coded" into the software itself to ensure, for example, that each participant speaks once before anyone else speaks again.

The future of electronic democracy requires the construction of technical architectures conducive to the goals of deliberative democracy, not just commerce. Deliberative processes must be *designed* for cyberspace. This requires first developing the tools to facilitate deliberation and then developing methods for implementing them in political and social institutions.

This chapter describes one of the first such deliberative design experiments. An interdisciplinary team of technologists and democratic theorists (including the author) developed Unchat, Web-based software for deliberative practice in cyberspace.[1] The following essay relates this design

21

research and addresses the prospective uses of software to promote deliberative democracy.

1. Of Yurts, Yaks, and Telephone Booths: Designing for Deliberation

When Mongolia wanted to expand its telecommunications infrastructure, one of the impediments encountered was how to construct a telephone booth big enough to fit two Mongols in full sheepskin winter wear yet small enough to prevent them from corralling yaks (Taylor **2001**). Design matters; value choices translate into design choices. Web sites are constructed to make transacting straightforward; the "shopping cart" must never be more than one mouse click away. In the same way that we construct e-commerce technologies, we can build sites tailor-made for political, social, and cultural uses, but we do not yet do so adequately. Such technology would enable the group collaboration processes that underlie deliberation. This means that if we are to structure the space and procedure for deliberation in cyberspace, we need to be explicit about what the procedures of deliberation ideally comprise.

1.1 Accessibility

To be deliberative, the conversation must be accessible to *all* members of the community (sometimes known as the demos). Therefore, the space in which it occurs—whether physical or virtual—has to be available to as wide a range of participants as possible. A baseball stadium or town hall may be an important locus of public congregation, but unless it is easily reached by public transportation as well as by car, large segments of the public will be excluded.

Space has to be aesthetically as well as technically usable. If the acoustics in the church basement are bad, admitting people for free is not enough to ensure participation. Similarly, electronic spaces for deliberation have to be "technology-neutral" so that access is not limited only to those running one particular operating system.

1.2 No Censorship

To be deliberative, the conversation must be free from censorship. Therefore, the space needs to safeguard freedom of thought and expression. Censorship goes beyond physical threat. It includes any distortion or restraint of speech that would hinder the independence of the discussion or cause participants to self-censor. Such incursions are just as likely to come from the market as from the government.

1.3 Autonomy

Participants in a deliberative dialogue are not consumers but autonomous citizens. The process must treat them not as passive recipients of information but as active participants in a public process. Therefore, participants cannot be used for data profiling in the course of deliberating. To do so would not only chill free expression but also transform citizens from autonomous decision makers into statistical probabilities whose actions are to be predicted. Autonomy also demands that participants have a controlling role in the deliberative process. In colonial New England, citizens ran their own town meetings; by virtue of running the conversation, they became better and more active participants in it (Barber 1984).

1.4 Accountability

A deliberative dialogue can take place only where members of a community engage with one another in accountable and reasoned public discourse. They cannot be anonymous. Though the right to anonymous speech must be protected online and off, productive group collaboration and decision making in political, cultural, educational, and business life also require accountable, interpersonal engagement.

1.5 Transparency

Participants in the debate must be "visible" to each other and to those setting the agenda (to the extent they are not the participants themselves). Transparency means that the structure and rules of the space must be public so that citizens know who owns the space, whether monitoring is taking place, and the bias of any information contributed to the discussion. It is relevant that America Online moderates its chat rooms, deleting messages that are critical of its corporate policy.

1.6 Equality

Deliberative democracy requires equality among members. To be equal, participants need not be stripped of their uniqueness, but individual attributes should not translate into a greater or smaller chance to be heard. Creating a public sphere is not about rending boundaries but about rendering social and power relationships visible. In the constructed space, all participants must be equal players with like opportunities for access and voice. The architecture cannot privilege one group over another.

1.7 Pluralism

In order to allow everything worth saying to be heard, it is necessary to ensure that viewpoints representing a broad spectrum be clearly expressed. As Owen Fiss eloquently argued: "[The state] may have to allocate public resources—hand out megaphones—to those whose voices would not otherwise be heard in the public square. It may even have to silence the voices of some in order to hear the voices of the others" by regulating the rules of the space (Fiss 1996: 4).

1.8 Inclusiveness

Countless philosophers have envisioned the small group as the ideal democratic unit (Gastil 1983). In a deliberative and public forum, participants must be able to "see" each other, their identities and interests laid bare. Yet at the same time, a deliberative forum must be inclusive and open to all members of the relevant community. Without capturing a wide array of voices and viewpoints, it is impossible to obtain a genuine sense of public opinion. Therefore, deliberation groups must be both small and inclusive. Both goals can be accomplished by linking small groups.

1.9 Staying Informed

Successful deliberation demands discipline. Participants need to take the time to inform themselves in order to base their judgments upon reasonable information. A deliberative dialogue cannot be divorced from information, and participants must have access to a wide variety of viewpoints in order to make effective and educated decisions (Fishkin 1991).

1.10 Publicness

The dialogue must be open, accessible, and explicitly dedicated to the interests of the group, rather than those of any individual or particular interest group. By thinking explicitly as citizens and members of a community, participants articulate rationales to serve not only themselves but also what they perceive to be the interests of a wider community.

1.11 Facilitation

One final prerequisite to deliberation is structural—namely, effective facilitation. The only way to manage the competing voices of participants is to moderate them. Facilitation may be as simple as having someone call on people as they raise their hands or as complex as the elaborate procedures used in a courtroom proceeding.

2. From Theory to Practice: Software as Deliberative Structure

Unchat is an implementation of this deliberative theory in technology. The goal of the project was to create software for synchronous small group deliberation and see how it could be used to realize these deliberative qualities. The focus was less on bringing people to the table electronically than on what occurred when they got there. We were curious as to whether deliberation online might be possible. So we embarked on a two-year research experiment to build and deploy a tool to enable deliberation in different domains.

2.1 How It Works

In the Yale Law School International Cyberlaw discussion group, a dozen law students met online once a week for two hours with academics, policy makers, and technologists from around the world. By convening on the Internet, these American law students could converse with representatives of the European Commission and the Council of Europe to gain a deeper understanding of media and intellectual property regulation in the European legal tradition. They exchanged keyboarded messages in real time, which, though slower than speaking, conditioned the group to the reasoned exchange of ideas. Participants uploaded informational resources, such as statutes and cases, to shared electronic libraries. The array of shared information enabled them to compare American and European traditions through discussion with native experts.

With twenty highly vocal people in the room at once, moderation was enabled. Participant postings would go through a moderator, who would preview and organize the comments. The moderator could reject or hold any interventions that were not on topic. But to prevent the moderator from abusing this power, we rotated the moderation from one participant to another so that everyone had an opportunity to wield the electronic gavel (self-moderation). By taking responsibility for running the conversation, members learned to participate better and more effectively.

In another project, twenty-five fourteen-year-old high school students convened from their respective suburban, urban, and inner-city schools to discuss harmful Internet content.[2] Having read in the Unchat library beforehand, they intelligently debated what should be included in an Internet acceptable-use policy. Exceeding their age in terms of sophistication and civility, they discussed balancing free-speech rights and educational openness against the interests of the school community in creating a safe environment for educating young students.

When they got excited about the topic, the young people could "shout" a message, bypassing the moderator altogether. One of the first things we did was to decide how many interruptions each participant would be entitled to (Figure 2.1).

After a participant uses up his or her shouts, the software shuts off the ability of that person to interrupt. The shout option not only takes advantage of the flexibility of the software to enable impassioned outcries but also encourages participants to reflect on the impact their disruptions have on the dynamic of the larger group.

Like the shout, a whisper does not go to the moderator for posting to the larger group. Rather, it is a private message between two participants. In a third project, Spiritual Friendship in the Digital Age, Episcopal priest

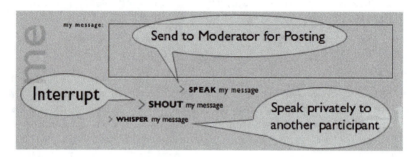

Figure. 2.1 Copyright © Bodies Electric LLC.

and facilitator Reverend Steve Kelsey required participants to "huddle" with a partner by whispering one-on-one for five minutes to create a more intimate climate prior to the group discussion.

Principles of deliberative democracy suffuse the concept and functionality of Unchat. The knowledge of how to structure successful participation offline informs the design of this online deliberation tool, which is intended to capture the ideas of deliberative structure outlined earlier.

2.2 The Design Process: Translating Values into Code

2.2.1 Accessibility. To be accessible, the software tool we wanted to build needed to be available to participants regardless of technological ability or choice of technology. Therefore, Unchat works on Windows, Mac, and Linux operating systems using both major browsers, Internet Explorer and Netscape. The universality of access was a central criterion for design.

Initially, Unchat ran on an Oracle database with a WebLogic "middleware" platform. These are powerful yet expensive technologies. This would have been akin to building the town hall from Carrera marble and then having to charge speakers for every use to recoup the expense. So we moved the application to an entirely free back end.

2.2.2 No Censorship. Unchat runs via the browser, communicating with a server via an open port. Some networks do not permit this kind of communications traffic. We wanted our technology to create a reason for openness and keeping ports open. The trade-off is not unlike the risks of a large crowd gathering to protest. Free speech is a necessary activity of democracy that must be protected despite its costs for security and safety.

2.2.3 Autonomy. We wanted to build software that would give users the choice of how to structure their own communication. In real life, conversation can take place in a café, a town hall, or a classroom. Cyberspace is flexible enough that users ought to be able to convene in different sorts of spaces according to the rules they set for themselves. With Unchat, a group can not only set the rules of the space but also change them as needed.

2.2.4 Accountability and Transparency. Chat rooms are anonymous. Participants choose handles by which to hide their identities and role-play in the virtual space. Yet when communication functions as a means for public decision making and not as entertainment, participants must be identifiable and accountable (Gutmann and Thompson 1996). Being known by name encourages responsible participation because it connects public action with personal reputation.

Though anonymity is at times a liberating feature of cyberspace, social relations are iterative, not itinerant. People cannot easily change the social, business, or political community they inhabit. Accordingly, they must learn to participate in these communities on an ongoing basis, which means that hateful and hurtful words or actions carry a cost. Accountability creates an incentive for productive and respectful participation.

Because Unchat is a tool intended to serve real communities, participants log in with a first name and a last name. Logging in immediately signals to the participant the seriousness of the exercise, thereby linking real-life consequences directly to virtual conversation.[3]

2.2.5 Relevancy and Responsiveness. Communications technologies can be broken down into synchronous and asynchronous technologies (Mitchell 1997). Asynchronous communication in the form of bulletin boards or weblogs has become the ubiquitous standard mode of Web-based communication. But we wanted to mimic in cyberspace the effect of getting people together in the same place at the same time to confront new ideas. Hence, it had to be a synchronous application.

2.2.6 Equality: Democratic Architecture and Graphic Design. The look and feel of the technology had to be inviting and inclusive. An overly designed space with an excessively modernist or classical design would preclude people from imagining how to use the space. Adopting a typeface and look that were too futuristic would alienate those ill at ease with the technology. The initial design emphasized a feeling of lightness, openness, and airiness.

The challenge to present an open look and feel was greatest in the design and building of the discussion application, otherwise known as the applet. How could we create a sense of place and purpose with very little space? So many public-purpose buildings are intentionally monumental, imbuing the visitor with a sense of awe. Yet in this tiny space—minimized by the need to design for the smallest standard monitor size—room was needed to display a group dialogue with all its participants and also leave room to type contributions to the discussion, create ballots, and share information.

Unchat eschews the chat convention of listing participant names in favor of a visual metaphor of the table.[4] Participants appear in text by their first and last names in a semicircle around a table. This circumvents the need for graphically intensive video-based technologies to create a sense of group in a space. The name of the moderator appears at the top of the screen. The name of the participant appears in the middle of the screen. These are visual aids to help situate the participant in the space and at the table. When someone "speaks," his or her name flashes and changes its color to blue.

2.2.7 Facilitation

2.2.7.1 Selection of a moderator A good facilitator makes all the difference between a productive meeting and a divisive one because he or she sets the tone and controls the agenda. To empower participants to engage in productive deliberation, this experiment had to build in a mechanism by which participants could elect moderators democratically and also revolt against them. Unchat permits the participants to set a moderator, vote for a moderator, or rotate the moderation function from person to person. If citizens meet to discuss an issue, an expert facilitator might moderate the first session. The next time the group convenes, participants might take charge of their own dialogue and start electing moderators from among their ranks. Each moderator might serve a fifteen-minute term—long enough to allow adequate time for that moderator to get acclimated, but short enough to give several people a turn.

2.2.7.2 Moderator macros One of the primary impediments to using technology to enhance democratic life is the hurdle that technology imposes on those who are not used to it. The problem stems from the opacity of the technology. The user must acclimatize to the technology rather than the other way around. We realized that for democratic deliberation to be possible, the tool had to be simple and easy to use. To this end, the moderator functionality includes four macro buttons: Post, Bounce, Hold, and Delete. These buttons allow the moderator to perform a series of standard tasks with one click. When a participant sends a message to the moderator, the moderator can broadcast it to the group (post). If the message is rude or otherwise irrelevant, the moderator can send it back to the sender with an explanation (bounce). A comment that is not yet relevant can be held, and deletion is an option of last resort. In this way, for example, the moderator can queue all the questions to a guest speaker, ordering them and eliminating redundant messages. The macro buttons make it possible to manage the communication at a distance.

Each macro button comes with preprogrammed comments or "tags" that explain the reasoning behind the moderator's action. For example, if a moderator wants to bounce a message, he or she must append a reason, such as "Please stick to the subject." This structures the conversation without a psychological cost to the participants. They experience no public shame from receiving a private message from the moderator. The tag system is designed to make the moderator's job easier while opening a channel of communication between the moderator and the participant.

The moderator macro tags can be changed at the start of every conversation. Though the software comes with preprogrammed defaults, participants can set up a discussion with French or Spanish tags or with responses designed to appeal to children, for example.

2.2.7.3 Autopass With one click, the moderator can allow messages to be broadcast directly to the group without awaiting moderator action. Autopass allows the new moderator to learn the ropes and assess the group dynamic while messages continue to post automatically at a reasonable interval. It also permits the moderator to leave the room for a time without halting the discussion. Autopass is an important tool to teach and learn the skills and timing of moderation.

2.2.8 Pluralistic and Inclusive: Devolving Power Downward via Role-Based Permissions.

If a single administrator controls who can participate, the inclusiveness of the discussion may be threatened. Often the individual responsible for a cyberdialogue must have technical ability, thereby further limiting the potential for democratic participation. Unchat clearly needed to give participants control over their own conversation—the ability to choose participants and set the agenda. People needed to have options to self-organize just as in real life they call meetings, convene groups, and organize spontaneous water-cooler colloquies. Whereas in real life any two people can have a conversation and set the agenda for it, in larger group settings it is usually one person who has permission to book the conference room at the office or an assembly room at school. We wanted to offer a tool for managed discussion without imposing a gatekeeper.

Unchat has a sitewide administrator, responsible for initial installation, setup, and role assignment (Table 2.1). At the next level it has topic creators, who have the power to create new discussion themes, known as topics, and designate the users who may participate in them. Topic creators have the power to create Unchat sessions under that topic as well as to assign the role of chat creator. Chat creators can create new Unchat sessions and accompanying rules. These roles are hierarchical. The sitewide administrator has all the permissions of a topic creator and a chat creator. A topic creator, in turn, has the power and permissions of a chat creator. A participant with access to a topic has access to all the Unchat sessions in that topic, but a participant who only has access to an Unchat session does not have access to other sessions within the topic. Multiple people can occupy each role. In other words, every member of the group can control it and be able to set up conversations, change the libraries, and amend the

TABLE 2.1

Roles	Site Administrator	Topic Administrator	Unchat Administrator
Set-up	Set-up site		
Management	Set-up **topics**	Set-up **topics**	
-create & edit	Set-up **Unchats**	Set-up **Unchats**	Set-up **Unchats**
-create & customize library			
-create & customize quiz			
User Management	Manage **site** users		
-add, edit and delete participants	Manage **topics** users	Manage **topics** users	
	Manage **Unchats** users	Manage **Unchats** users	Manage **Unchats** users

rules, or only a handful, such as a teacher, may be empowered. The settings can always be changed.

The same tool allows the regulator to set up a citizen consultation with invited stakeholders and then to turn over the tool to citizens to conduct their own networking. This permission matrix has been designed for a combination of control and freedom to maximize the ability to devolve power downward without degenerating into unstructured chaos.

2.2.9 Deliberative Communication: Speak, Shout, and Whisper. In the same way that Unchat allows different people to possess keys to the public meeting space through the assignment of access roles and permissions, it also allows participants democratically to choose the style of deliberation just as in real life they could choose to debate in a café or a boardroom. With Unchat, we wanted participants to select their own rules of moderation and modes of speaking.

Ordinary conversation has quiet interruptions and loud interjections, private sidebars and caucusing. The ability to vary the conversational cadence is often essential to the effectiveness of the dialogue. In a controlled and well-ordered conversation, the occasional impassioned outburst signals the importance of an issue to the speaker. Unchat mimics this by allowing the participant to choose among speaking, shouting, and whispering a message. When a participant types a message and hits return, the software will, by default, send that message to the moderator, who decides whether or not to post it. Understanding that sometimes people need to interrupt to make an impassioned point, the participant can shout and bypass the moderator, broadcasting the message directly. In order to prevent the moderator from taking any blame for the interruption, a shouted message is labeled.

A whisper is the equivalent of leaning over in your chair at a meeting and remarking quietly to the person next to you. Suddenly in cyberspace anyone in the room is next to you. I can whisper to someone in Singapore without interrupting the flow. Whispering can be essential for a few people to discuss and agree on a position before broadcasting their view.

In real life, if someone interrupts repeatedly, he or she will be asked to refrain or leave the room. This conversational etiquette is missing in the typical cyberspace chat room, where interruption is the dominant mode of expression. To address this, we made Unchat's shout and whisper features configurable. A participant can interrupt by typing a message and selecting shout, but the shout button will stop working after the participant has used up a preset number of interruptions. For a more anarchic, free-for-all dialogue, the number can be set very high. To control interruptions, the number of shouts can be set low. The explicit imposition of this rule leads participants to reflect on the rules of communication and adjust their behavior accordingly. It follows logically that a participant will be judicious in what he or she says by interruption if it is understood that each person can shout only five times. Highlighting the rules and making the structures visible causes people to begin to conform their behavior to the constraints.

2.2.10 Staying Informed and Publicness: Archiving. A deliberative discussion requires the structure created by facilitation, but it also requires the development of institutional memory to allow one conversation to build and grow to the next. A Web conference, unlike a conference call, allows for easy transcription of a conversation. This ability to record the conversation also makes the discussion more inclusive by allowing those who cannot participate to keep abreast of the dialogue.

With Unchat, every conversation is logged in real time. Someone entering late can see what was said at the beginning of the conversation. This is far less disruptive than entering a real-life meeting late and having to ask someone what took place. The latecomer can catch up on what was said and immediately participate in the conversation, whereas in a real-life conversation latecomers may be hesitant to jump in.

Unchat has two kinds of logs: a transcript of the conversation and a history of all the actions and statements made, including the moderator's various actions, such as bouncing, holding, and deleting. The history is intended to make the moderator more accountable for his or her actions. However, it is more than a control against moderator abuses; it is also a mechanism to study the effectiveness of different rule structures and their impact on the group. The next version of the software should include text fields for summarizing transcripts and a function for automatically e-mailing transcripts to participants. Additional functions might include search tools for finding particular postings, such as threading, and collaborative filtering technology to reorganize and sort comments by substance instead of chronology.

2.2.11 Staying Informed: Integrated Libraries. By integrating content into the discussion tool, Unchat connects information to the conversation. The original Unchat design called for three levels of library: a universal library, a topic library, and a personal library, each one with a standard document-organizing taxonomy. But the taxonomy, designed to make using the library easier, proved to be unworkable. Needed resources got buried amid too many categories. There also turned out to be little need for a universal library independent of the topic of discussion.

Instead, the redesign of the library structure incorporated a flexible content management engine to make it possible to create custom libraries associated with a particular topic, Unchat session, or participant. A topic library can be the repository for a class syllabus and all the materials required for a semester's civic or educational discussion. For each individual weekly session, that week's organizer creates an Unchat session library by downloading relevant materials from the topic library and any independent materials of the organizer's choice. The organizer can also assign each participant to perform a certain task, such as writing an essay or performing research on the Web, and then upload those results to each participant's personal "My Library." In this way, participants can do hands-on learning without corrupting the library structure. Any number of people, from a single individual to everyone, can have the right to edit the libraries.

2.2.12 The Deliberative Speed Bump: Navigation. A distribution of working papers or documents often precedes meetings in real life. Participants may also be required to attend an introductory lecture or a training session before being allowed to participate in a more advanced working group. Unchat is similarly designed to encourage this reflection and preparation prior to discussion.

Pundits laud the speed of the Internet—how it makes everything that much faster (Gleick 1999). However, we were interested in taking advantage of the Internet's flexibility to slow people down. The navigation of Unchat is expressly designed to promote the goals of deliberation. A participant wanting to jump into a conversation must first pass through the library. Depending upon the configuration, a user may also encounter a topical quiz, designed to frame the issues for debate and prompt reflection. While no person can be forced to read, designing the system such that participants interact with the content makes deliberation easier. This navigation exploits the Web's informational resources and ties them more closely to the human interaction that takes place inside an Unchat forum.

2.2.13 The Virtual Speed Bump: Point-Counterpoint. After the library, participants may be asked to take a quiz. The quiz is not a test but a point-counterpoint interaction with the participant to frame the issues for conversation. When the quiz taker answers a question, the system responds to that answer. For instance, if this user answers with a typically left-wing point of view, the system might suggest a right-wing argument and further reading. Quiz functionality could eventually be used in a variety of ways, including testing participant knowledge before and/or after a discussion, as a sorting mechanism for organizing discussion groups according to viewpoint (i.e., to mix or segregate people of different viewpoints based on their answers to quiz questions), to poll opinions before as well as after a discussion, to measure feedback to a discussion, and to organize deliberative focus groups. This reduces the cost of constructing pluralistic groups and ensuring diversity of opinion.

3. Conclusion

This first fully functional real-time cyberdeliberation tool, which allows a group to set up a discussion according to democratic principles and to self-moderate its conversation, enables new forms of dialogue and collaboration never before possible. The technical architecture of the software is flexible and allows experimentation with different conversational rules. It can also lead to the development of new tools. In addition to whispers and shouts, for example, there could be new categories of speech—guffaws to signal heckling, or yawns to express boredom. Unchat and its progeny might incorporate the choice of whether to speak accountably or anonymously and whether or not to have comments logged on the transcript or appear off the record. Providing such options might foster greater openness in controversial contexts. Moderator term limits might be imposed. The timer on the built-in voting tool could be set to increments of days or weeks, rather than minutes, to encourage thoughtful and deliberative discussion prior to decision making. Additional graphical tools might be incorporated to represent the opinions in the room visually and make the culture of the conversation more transparent. These new rules will affect the way participants interact with one another. In order to develop best practices for doing deliberation online, the next step is to test which rules work best to accomplish which goals.

Eventually, with a toolkit of available deliberative software, we can begin to institutionalize cyberdemocracy to enable citizen consultation and self-governance across domains. Armed with the right tools and the knowledge of how to use them, we can experiment with new ways to improve democratic participation and with better methods of online participation, from citizen juries to deliberative polls to consensus councils. For fifty years after World War II, we have understood that television and other media are important vehicles for teaching the values of democracy. The technology may be changing, but its impact for democracy has not.

Notes

1. See Bodies Electric LLC's official Web site of Unchat, http://www.unchat.com. The Unchat software was created by an interdisciplinary design team led by the author and Benjamin R. Barber, Kekst Professor of Civil Society at the University of Maryland, with technical support from Thaumaturgix, Inc., a software development company in New York, http://www.tgix.com, and additional advising from Jack M. Balkin, Knight Professor of Constitutional Law and the First Amendment, Yale Law School, and members of the Information Society Project at Yale Law School. After searching in vain for tools that could be adapted to "do deliberation" online, the team embarked on this original design project, which is ongoing.

2. For more on the Internet Ethics in Schools project, see New York Law School, "Internet Use in Schools," available at http://www.nyls.edu/democracy.php?ID=26 (accessed January 10, 2003).

3. Though a seemingly modest requirement, this request to have real names stymied the first programmer, who was convinced that the database would not read a space between the first name and last name and could only accept "firstnamelastname" or "firstname_lastname." It took a second consultation and more technical research to uncover that the immutable "truth" of cyberspace, where individuals exist only as nicknames, could be changed to meet the demands of democracy.

4. Conversational groups very quickly develop a "culture" whereby people start to respond to each other by name and identify comments that they are responding to by cutting and pasting from that comment or referencing it in some way.

References

Barber, Benjamin R. 1984. *Strong Democracy: Participatory Politics for a New Age.* Berkeley: University of California Press.
Fishkin, James S. 1991. *Democracy and Deliberation: New Directions for Democratic Reform.* New Haven: Yale University Press.
Fiss, Owen M. 1996. *The Irony of Free Speech.* Cambridge, MA: Harvard University Press.
Gastil, John. 1983. *Democracy in Small Groups: Participation, Decision Making and Communication.* Philadelphia: New Society.
Gleick, James. 1999. *Faster: The Acceleration of Just About Everything.* New York: Pantheon.
Gutmann, Amy, and Dennis Thompson. 1996. *Democracy and Disagreement.* Cambridge, MA: Belknap.
Taylor, Veronica. 2001. Interview with Author. Dec. 4, 2001.

CHAPTER 3

Cyberjuries: A Model
of Deliberative Democracy?

NANCY S. MARDER

The traditional jury plays a vital role in our justice system and in our democracy. It provides both a mechanism for resolving disputes and—even more important, as Alexis de Tocqueville noted almost 170 years ago—a means for citizens in a democracy to participate in their own self-governance.[1] Deliberation is at the heart of both of these functions.

With the technology of the Web, a new form of jury, the cyberjury, has emerged. The cyberjury is still in a rudimentary stage, but it has great potential. Like the traditional jury, the cyberjury could resolve certain types of disputes and teach citizens lessons in self-governance. Although the roles of cyberjuries should be understood in the context of the roles of traditional juries, cyberjuries need not do everything that traditional juries now do. Rather, we should borrow features of traditional juries, such as deliberation, that will improve cyberjuries' decision making and inspire greater confidence in their verdicts, but we should not adopt features that will undercut the advantages that the new technology affords: the capacity to reach many people and to provide them with a fast, inexpensive method of dispute resolution.

In my view, cyberjuries are best understood in the context of traditional juries. Accordingly, the first part of this essay focuses on traditional juries and the ways in which they are democratic institutions that rely on deliberation to reach accurate decisions, to speak on behalf of the community, and to teach self-governance. The remainder of this essay focuses on cyberjuries. After I describe cyberjuries, I ask whether they too can function as democratic institutions. Although cyberjuries should not mimic traditional juries, there are improvements that should be made in their design. At the very least, cyberjuries, to be the embodiment of deliberative democracy in cyberspace, need to include deliberation as part of the decision-making process.

1. The Jury as the Embodiment of Deliberative Democracy

The American jury, in both civil and criminal cases, is an institution that embodies the deliberative democratic ideal. The jury is a truly democratic institution in that it draws ordinary citizens from all walks of life and charges them with the task of working together as equals to render judgment. The jury is a truly deliberative institution in that after seeing the evidence and hearing the testimony and arguments, the jurors meet behind closed doors to exchange ideas until they reach a verdict. Alexis de Tocqueville described the American jury as providing a "free school," educating citizens about the responsibilities of a democracy.[2] Today the jury continues to serve as a free school, giving citizens one of the few opportunities, in addition to voting in elections, that they have to participate in their own governance.

1.1 The Jury as a Democratic Institution

One way in which the jury constitutes a truly democratic institution is that it consists of ordinary citizens. Jurors typically do not have any training in the law. Although a juror must meet some statutory criteria, such as being a citizen and at least eighteen years old, jury service does not require any prior knowledge of or experience with the law.[3] Legal professionals, such as lawyers and judges, though not precluded from jury duty, do not receive any special treatment because of their familiarity with the law.

Jurors are summoned to serve temporarily. They do not start out as professionals in the law, and they are not permitted to develop into professional jurors. They are summoned, they serve, and then they return to their private lives. They are valued for the common sense perspective they bring to the case and are said to embody the voice of the community.[4] By hearing only one case, they avoid becoming hardened, as might befall a professional. Indeed, as the U.S. Supreme Court recognized in *Duncan v. Louisiana*,[5] one of the advantages that jurors bring to the criminal justice system is that they provide a defendant with "an inestimable safeguard against the corrupt or overzealous prosecutor and against the compliant, biased, or eccentric judge."[6] Once summoned, these ordinary citizens are placed on a venire, or panel, from which the petit jury is selected. The venire is supposed to be drawn from "a fair cross section of the community."[7] This requirement comes from the Supreme Court's interpretation of the Sixth Amendment to the U.S. Constitution.[8] The Supreme Court has held that under the Sixth Amendment a criminal defendant is entitled to an impartial jury. One meaning of an impartial jury is that it has been fairly drawn from a venire from which no group has been systematically excluded.[9] Congress has since extended the fair-cross-section requirement to the civil jury. According to federal statute, the venire in a civil or criminal case must be randomly drawn from a fair cross section of the community.[10]

The fair-cross-section requirement, though difficult to achieve in practice, reinforces the notion that the jury is a democratic institution. This requirement reassures the criminal defendant that he or she is being tried by a jury that has not been stacked against him or her. As long as the venire is drawn from a fair cross section, meaning that no group has been systematically excluded, the defendant knows that the government will not be able to fill the jury with jurors who are sympathetic only to the government. This requirement also reassures the community, however diverse it is and however much some members may disagree with the verdict, that the selection of jurors was fair and that the verdict, however distasteful, should be accepted. Finally, the requirement makes it more likely than not that a range of viewpoints will be available to jurors during their deliberations. One limitation, however, is that the Supreme Court has never said that the petit jury must consist of a fair cross section of the community, largely because it believes that such a requirement would be unworkable.[11]

The hope is that a venire drawn from a fair cross section will lead to a petit jury that is diverse. To the extent that it is, the jury serves as a free school in democracy, teaching citizens who come from different backgrounds, classes, and occupations, and who are of different generations, religions, and races, that they can work together as peers to reach a verdict.

As part of this democratic endeavor, jurors are summoned and physically present in the courtroom for the purpose of hearing a case. One reason they have been selected for a particular case is that they have no connection to it. Thus they learn about the case by sitting together in the courtroom, observing the witnesses, and hearing the testimony and arguments. In this way, all of the jurors, regardless of their training or education, are treated as equals. They will be educated about the case together through the trial process.

The courtroom geography reinforces the notion of juror equality and juror participation in a democratic institution.[12] The jurors are seated together in the jury box. They are the ones to whom the lawyers and witnesses will address their comments. In some courtrooms, as a show of respect to the jury, everyone in the courtroom, including the judge, rises when the jury enters and leaves. In addition, the jury box is clearly demarcated from the other courtroom seats, which will be occupied by members of the public and press. Thus, from the beginning, the jurors are treated the same, and they are separated from everyone else in the courtroom so that they are not tainted by others' comments, so that they begin to conceive of themselves as a jury, and so that they begin to take seriously their responsibility.

1.2 The Jury as a Deliberative Body

The jury embodies not only democratic ideals but also deliberative ideals. At the close of the trial, the jury is led to the jury room, where, behind closed doors and in secret, it is expected to deliberate and to reach a verdict. In federal court, whether in criminal or civil cases, the verdict must be unanimous.[13] In criminal cases in most state courts, the verdict also must be unanimous.[14] To reach unanimity, jurors must recall evidence and testimony, exchange viewpoints, challenge mistaken notions, and be open to persuasion by other jurors.

The only guidance the court gives the jury about deliberations is that the jury must have a foreperson—a member of the jury who has responsibility for administrative tasks during deliberations, who sends notes to the judge should the jurors have questions, and who announces the verdict in open court. In some courtrooms, the foreperson is simply the first juror seated in the jury box; in others, the jurors select a foreperson. The judge, in his or her instructions to the jury, also may tell the jurors that they are to treat each other with respect, but other than that general admonition, the jury structures its own deliberations.

The goal of deliberation is to reach consensus. The jurors try to do this by recalling evidence and testimony, assessing the credibility of witnesses, and deciding which of the lawyers' arguments they find most persuasive. Kassin and Wrightsman describe two ways in which jurors persuade each other.[15] When jurors exert normative pressure on a dissenting juror, that juror may acquiesce and vote in a manner consistent with the others even though he or she may not be privately persuaded.[16] Or the other jurors may provide informational influence such that the dissenting juror actually changes his or her mind as a result of their arguments.[17] The latter is preferable to the former, but either may take place during deliberations. In fact, deliberations may not be limited to civil discussion. Some jurors report having felt bullied, coerced, or even threatened during deliberations.[18] Although such behavior is far from ideal, courts are reluctant to interfere. Indeed, it is hard to disturb a jury verdict even when deliberations fall short of the ideal. In federal court, judges will inquire into alleged juror misconduct only if there is a claim that a juror introduced outside evidence into the deliberations.[19]

The jury deliberations are integral to the jury decision-making process for several reasons. First, a discussion among twelve jurors, all of whom can recall different pieces of evidence, correct mistakes, and challenge assumptions,[20] is more likely to lead to an accurate verdict than an individual deciding on his or her own. Second, the verdict reached by the jury is made in the name of the community; thus, it is appropriate that it should be a group decision, with all the benefits that it provides and without placing the responsibility for that community decision on the shoulders of an individual. Third, the community is more likely to accept a verdict reached in its name if the decision was the result of deliberation by a jury drawn from a broad swath of the community. Even members of the community who disagree with the verdict are less likely to think it was the result of bias or self-interest if a diverse group engaged in discussion and reached consensus. Finally, a verdict reached through group deliberation is likely to leave the defendant with the hope that one of the jurors will understand the defendant's situation and be able to explain it to the other jurors; the defendant is less likely to have that reassurance when there is a single decision maker or when there are multiple decision makers but they do not deliberate.

While the trial and announcement of the verdict take place in the public eye, one of the defining characteristics of the jury's deliberation is that it takes place in secret. One reason secrecy has been so carefully guarded[21] is because jurors are supposed to engage in candid deliberations.[22] Private deliberations permit jurors to advance unpopular views. This is important in every case, but none more so than when there is an unpopular defendant. The privacy of the deliberations also protects the jurors: they can disagree with each other, and their views will go no further than the jury room. If the jury reaches a verdict, individual disagreements are put aside, and only the jury's verdict, rendered as a corporate body,[23] is announced, though the jurors may be polled in open court to ensure that they agree with the verdict.[24]

2. What Are Cyberjuries?

Cyberjuries are Web sites that invite two parties with a dispute to resolve it by asking participants who serve as cyberjurors to vote on the matter. One such Web site is www.iCourthouse.com. This Web site has one form of cyberjury that is operational and another that is still in the planning stages.[25]

The existing cyberjury is called a "peer jury" and more closely resembles an opinion poll than a jury. Parties present their dispute in a trial book, in which they provide opening statements, supporting testimony, and a closing argument. Each of these sections consists of only a paragraph or two. Anyone who registers at the Web site can read a summary of the pending cases, choose a case of interest, and serve as a cyberjuror in that case. The cyberjuror's sole responsibility on a peer jury is to read the trial book and to vote for either the plaintiff or the defendant. The cyberjuror can submit written questions to the parties, which the parties can choose to answer or not. The cyberjuror also can give reasons for his or her vote. The votes appear as a running scorecard that each new cyberjuror sees when he or she selects the case. There is no limit to the number of cyberjurors who can participate on a peer jury, nor do there appear to be any qualifications.

The other form of cyberjury, still in the planning stages, is a "panel jury." According to iCourthouse, this cyberjury will consist of twenty cyberjurors, who are selected after a limited voir dire, or questioning, of prospective cyberjurors. However, the parties will not be permitted to ask cyberjurors about their race, gender, or ethnicity, just as lawyers striking prospective jurors from a traditional jury are not permitted to ask about or act upon these characteristics.[26] After reading the trial books, cyberjurors will enter a chat room, where they will deliberate. The parties will be permitted to observe this deliberation. The Web site explains that the parties will be required to pay a fee for a panel cyberjury.[27]

Although there are distinctions between panel and peer cyberjuries, both share several features. First, both consider only civil disputes. Second, the disputes need not be legal in nature. Some of the disputes currently heard by peer juries involve relationships gone awry or disputes between parties whose relationship the law does not recognize. Third, the parties can use the decision in any way they see fit: they may abide by it, ignore it, use it as a negotiating tool in trying to settle their case, or use it as a test run for a case they might ultimately bring in a traditional court. Fourth, with both types of cyberjuries, iCourthouse has no power of enforcement. Fifth, anyone can serve as a cyberjuror; there do not appear to be any qualifications. Moreover, unlike traditional jury duty, cyberjury participation is wholly voluntary. Finally, with both forms of cyberjuries, there is no role for lawyers or judges.

3. Can Cyberjuries Contribute to Deliberative Democracy?

3.1 The Cyberjury as a Democratic Institution

Although cyberjuries in their nascent form perform far more limited functions than traditional juries, there are several ways in which cyberjuries are democratic institutions and foster democratic goals, including some that have proven elusive for traditional juries. Whether cyberjuries are viewed from the perspective of the cyberjuror or that of the parties, they promote a number of democratic objectives.

3.1.1 From the Cyberjuror's Perspective. Cyberjuries are far more democratic than traditional juries in the sense that they are open to everybody. One need not be a citizen of any particular state or even of the United States to serve as a cyberjuror; rather, one simply can be a citizen of the world. Moreover, cyberjuries allow for direct citizen participation. A cyberjuror goes to the Web site, registers, and chooses his or her case. The case is presented in plain language. The cyberjuror reads the trial book, asks questions, and votes. Unlike with the traditional jury, the state is not involved; it does not summon a cyberjuror, assign him or her to a case, or select a judge for the case.

Cyberjuries, which draw cyberjurors from anywhere in the world, are more likely to achieve the fair-cross-section ideal than a traditional jury. Although traditional jury venires are supposed to be drawn from a fair cross section of the community, cyberjuries are likely to be drawn from a much broader array because there is no geographical limitation imposed on who can serve and no skewing as a result of peremptory challenges, which allow lawyers to remove a certain number of jurors during traditional jury selection, usually without any explanation.[28] In addition, cyberjurors can serve on a cyberjury at any time of the day or night without missing work. As a result, cyberjuries might achieve a fair cross section, including a fair cross section based on economic class, which traditional juries do not always do.

The diversity of a cyberjury is limited only by the need for access to a computer with a Web connection. The "digital divide," in which those with access to computers are more likely to be white men[29] from middle- or upper-class backgrounds[30] living in developed countries,[31] may affect the composition of cyberjuries. Yet the digital divide is closing, and even those who do not have access to a computer with an Internet connection at home may still find other public locations from which to participate.

Those who participate as cyberjurors are true equals; they are not identified by race, gender, or ethnicity. Although the U.S. Supreme Court has said that individuals should not be precluded from jury service because of their group identity,[32] there have been many barriers to jury service for African American men[33] and all women[34] in the past. Even today, when selection for the traditional jury is supposed to be color-blind, race, gender, and ethnicity still shape some lawyers' exercise of peremptories. However, cyberjuries, whether peer or panel, can achieve the color-blind ideal because in cyberspace, cyberjurors are anonymous and unseen. Upon registration, cyberjurors receive a number, and that is their sole form of identification.

Cyberjurors, unlike most traditional jurors, can be active rather than passive participants. If Tocqueville was right that jury service teaches jurors to participate in their own self-governance, then the active model of cyberjuror reinforces this lesson more effectively than the passive model of the traditional juror. Cyberjurors are permitted to select their case, unlike traditional jurors. Cyberjurors can readily understand the case because it is described in plain language written by the parties. In addition, if cyberjurors have questions, they can ask the parties directly, whereas in only a few courtrooms throughout the country are jurors permitted to ask questions by submitting them in writing to the judge, who decides whether the parties should answer them.[35] Cyberjurors are even told that they are free to do research.[36] The active model of the cyberjuror could serve in some ways as a blueprint for reform of the passive model of the traditional juror.

3.1.2 From the Parties' Perspective. From the parties' perspective, cyberjuries provide a form of dispute resolution that is readily available to rich and poor alike. Whereas a traditional jury trial requires the parties to invest financial resources and time, a cyberjury is free and quick. The parties simply prepare a trial book and submit it. There is no need to consult a lawyer. Once both sides' trial books are posted, cyberjurors can respond.

If the parties do not want to be bound by the vote of the cyberjury, they can still use the cyberjury to prepare their case for trial before a traditional jury. When used in this way, the cyberjury still helps to lessen the gap between rich and poor by providing a focus group for the masses. In traditional litigation, only litigants with deep pockets can afford to test their case in front of a focus group or have the assistance of a jury consultant. Cyberjuries, even when they do not actually resolve the dispute for the parties, can still provide less affluent parties with a means of testing their case before they proceed in a traditional court.[37] Cyberjurors, through their questions to the parties and their reasons for their votes, can provide the parties with insights about the case. The panel cyberjuries, as envisioned by iCourthouse, will provide the parties with even more information by allowing them to observe the deliberations. Thus, cyberjuries can help to diminish the gap between rich and poor litigants in the traditional courtroom, where disparities in resources often result in advantages for one side.

3.2 The Cyberjury as a Deliberative Body

For cyberjuries, deliberation continues to remain elusive. Peer cyberjuries do not engage in deliberation, and panel cyberjuries, which will include some deliberation, do not yet exist. Thus, cyberjuries fall short as a deliberative model, and this is one aspect in which cyberjuries should emulate traditional juries more closely. However, traditional jury deliberation includes face-to-face discussion, and this aspect will be a challenge to replicate in cyberspace.

For cyberjurors to have any meaningful deliberation, there needs to be a limited number of cyberjurors on a cyberjury. Although there is nothing magical about the number twelve, it is a number that is small enough for the discussion to be manageable, yet large enough to provide a diversity of viewpoints.[38]

There are several ways in which cyberjurors could deliberate in cyberspace. Admittedly, the technology is ever-changing. One available method, as iCourthouse envisages, is for cyberjurors to deliberate in a chat room. However, my suggestion is that the parties not be able to observe this deliberation for the same reasons that traditional juries deliberate in private. If the parties want to learn about the deliberations afterward, they can consult the cyberjurors. During deliberations, however, cyberjurors, like traditional jurors, need to engage in candid discussion.

Even with a private discussion in a chat room, cyberjurors might need a more structured format to distinguish this discussion from other, more casual chat room conversations. One way to create a more structured deliberation is with software such as Unchat.[39] Unchat would allow cyberjurors to be seated around a representation of a table and would allow one person to be the foreperson or facilitator of the deliberations. Unchat is software specially created for sustained discussion among a limited number of people. Although its designers, mainly academics, hoped it would foster serious political debate in cyberspace, it also could encourage serious deliberation among cyberjurors.

One feature that Unchat does not provide, at least not yet, is for participants to see and hear each other as they deliberate. Currently they can only read each other's comments. However, much information is conveyed by body language, including one's facial expressions, tone of voice, inflection, and gestures.[40] Some, though not all, of this information could be captured if cyberjurors had webcams or video cameras that allowed them to see each other as they deliberated. However, this technology is still at an incipient stage. Today it is used mainly for business meetings by people who would otherwise have to travel great distances to meet.[41] The technology has its limitations: there is often a lag when people speak, the picture can be unsteady, most people do not own the necessary cameras and software, and good-quality equipment is expensive.[42] In the context of cyberjuries, while it would allow cyberjurors to see and speak to each other, it also would mean that they would no longer be anonymous, with the added safety that provides, and that cyberjuries would no longer be colorblind, with the loss that entails. Given how important anonymity is for many Internet users, the use of cameras would likely deter cyberjurors from participating on cyberjuries and therefore should not be required.

4. Conclusion

The introduction of the ancient institution of the jury to the new technology of the Web has led to the appearance of cyberjuries. Cyberjuries, however, are at an early and formative stage: they can become an integral part of our justice system or just a passing fad. The challenge is whether cyberjuries, which have the advantages of being inexpensive and accessible to a vast number of people, can develop into a dispute resolution mechanism that is respected, at least for settling certain types of disputes.

Cyberjuries, though a new development in cyberspace, build upon a long-standing institution that is a model of deliberative democracy. Although cyberjuries cannot and should not adopt all of the expensive and time-consuming protections of traditional juries, they should borrow some safeguards of traditional juries to improve their decision making and to enhance the regard in which they are held. At the very least, a cyberjury should consist of a limited number of cyberjurors who engage in deliberation. These modest reforms would not add unduly to the time or expense of cyberjuries and would enable them to serve as a model of deliberative democracy in cyberspace.

Notes

1. Alexis de Tocqueville, 1*Democracy in America*, ed. Jacob Peter Mayer and Max Lerner (New York: Harper and Row, 1969).
2. Id. at 252.
3. 28 U.S.C. sec. 1865(b)(2)(2000).
4. See, e.g., *Taylor v. Louisiana*, 419 U.S. 522, 530 (1975).
5. 391 U.S. 145 (1968).
6. Id. at 156.
7. Taylor, 419 U.S. at 530.
8. U.S. Constitution, Sixth Amendment ("In all criminal prosecutions, the accused shall enjoy the right to a speedy and public trial, by an impartial jury of the State and district wherein the crime shall have been committed.").
9. Taylor, 419 U.S. at 530.
10. 28 U.S.C. sec. 1861 (2000).
11. See, e.g., *Holland v. Illinois*, 493 U.S. 474, 480–84 (1990).
12. Cf. Patricia Ewick and Susan Silbey, "The Architecture of Authority: The Spatial Nexus of Law and Science," in Austin Sarat, Lawrence Douglas, and Martha Merrill Umphrey, eds., *The Place of Law* (Ann Arbor: University of Michigan Press, 2003).
13. Fed. R. Civ. P. 31; Fed. R. Crim. P. 48.
14. See Nancy S. Marder, "The Interplay of Race and False Claims of Jury Nullification," *University of Michigan Journal of Law Reform* 32 (1999): 285, 319 n.160 (listing states requiring unanimous verdicts).
15. Saul Kassin and Lawrence Wrightsman, *The American Jury on Trial* (New York: Hemisphere, 1988, 185).
16. Ibid.
17. Ibid.
18. See, e.g., "Woman Juror: Men Bullied Her to Convict," *Los Angeles Daily Journal*, January 4, 1994, 3.
19. Fed. R. Evid. 606(b).
20. See, e.g., Phoebe C. Ellsworth, "Are Twelve Heads Better Than One?" *Law and Contemporary Problems*, Autumn 1989, 205, 218.
21. See *United States v. Thomas*, 116 F.3d 606, 618 (2d Cir. 1997).
22. See *In re Globe Newspaper Co.*, 920 F.2d 88, 94 (1st Cir. 1990).
23. See Nancy S. Marder, "Deliberations and Disclosures: A Study of Post-Verdict Interviews of Jurors," *Iowa Law Review* 82 (1997): 465, 470–74.
24. Fed. R. Crim. P. 31(a)(d).
25. See FAQs at http://www.iCourthouse.com.
26. See, e.g., *J.E.B. v. Alabama ex rel. T.B.*, 511 U.S. 127 (1994); *Georgia v. McCollum*, 505 U.S. 42 (1992); *Edmonson v. Leesville Concrete Co.*, 500 U.S. 614 (1991); *Powers v. Ohio*, 499 U.S. 400 (1991); *Batson v. Kentucky*, 476 U.S. 79 (1986).
27. See FAQs at http://www.iCourthouse.com.
28. An explanation needs to be given only when one side has established a prima facie case that the other side has exercised a peremptory challenge based on the race, ethnicity, or gender of a prospective juror. The burden then shifts to the other side to provide a nondiscriminatory reason for the peremptory.
29. See Amy Harmon, "Computing in the '90s: The Great Divide," *Los Angeles Times*, October 7, 1996, D1.
30. See, e.g., John Owens, "Helping Close the Digital Divide," *Chicago Tribune*, August 7, 2000, B1.
31. See, e.g., John Markoff, "High-Tech Executives Urge Action on World's Digital Divide," *New York Times*, July 20, 2000, A6.
32. See, e.g., *Thiel v. S. Pac. Co.*, 328 U.S. 217, 220 (1946).

33. In 1880, the U.S. Supreme Court declared unconstitutional state statutes barring African American men from serving as jurors. See *Strauder v. West Virginia*, 100 U.S. 303 (1880). However, lawyers still found ways to keep African American men from serving on juries. See *Batson v. Kentucky*, 476 U.S. 79, 104 (1986) (Marshall, J., concurring) (describing methods).

34. In state courts, women could serve on juries only if the state permitted women jurors, and each state could decide. In federal courts, women could serve on juries only if the federal court sat in a state that permitted women jurors. In the Civil Rights Act of 1957, P.L. 85-315, sec. 152, 71 Stat. 634, 638 (codified as amended at 28 U.S.C. sec. 1861 (1988)), Congress finally created federal jury service qualifications independent of state jury qualifications. However, in some states women were still excluded by having to register affirmatively for jury service. See, e.g., *Hoyt v. Florida*, 368 U.S. 57 (1961).

35. Arizona is one state that permits jurors in criminal and civil cases to submit written questions to the judge. See, e.g., B. Michael Dann and George Logan III, "Jury Reform: The Arizona Experience," *Judicature* 79 (1996): 280, 281.

36. iCourthouse invites cyberjurors to "type in the URLs of sites containing legal resources." FAQs at http://www.iCourthouse.com.

37. Barbara Babcock identified voir dire as a means of levelling the playing field. See Barbara Allen Babcock, "Voir Dire: Preserving 'Its Wonderful Power,'" *Stanford Law Review* 27 (1975): 545, 549. Today, cyberjuries provide another way for poor litigants to gain additional information about their case before presenting it in a traditional court.

38. See *Williams v. Florida*, 399 U.S. 78, 102-03 (1970).

39. Beth Simone Noveck, "Unchat: Democratic Solution for a Wired World," in Peter M. Shane, ed., *Democracy Online: The Prospects for Political Renewal through the Internet* (New York: Routledge, 2004).

40. See, e.g., Note, "The Appearance of Justice: Judges' Verbal and Nonverbal Behavior in Criminal Jury Trials," *Stanford Law Review* 38 (1985): 89.

41. Julie Flaherty, "A Patch for Family Bonds Put Asunder," *New York Times*, May 10, 2001, D10. The Virtual Agora project at Carnegie Mellon University is currently developing software called Delibera that will provide a "high telepresence" platform for online citizen consultation, including video, audio, graphic, and text-based cues. Principal investigators are Peter Shane, Peter Muhlberger, and Robert Cavalier. Brief descriptions of this work appear at http://www.digitalgovernment.org/search/projects/project.jsp?ID=127 (accessed October 31, 2003) and http://communityconnections.heinz.cmu.edu/picola/index.html (accessed October 31, 2003).

42. Daniel R. Mintz, "For a Dad, Videoconference Ties That Bind," *New York Times*, June 10, 2001, 13.

References

"The Appearance of Justice: Judges' Verbal and Nonverbal Behavior in Criminal Jury Trials." *Stanford Law Review* 38: 89.

Babcock, Barbara Allen. 1975. "Voir Dire: Preserving 'Its Wonderful Power.'" *Stanford Law Review* 27: 545–65.

Dann, B. Michael, and George Logan III. 1996. "Jury Reform: The Arizona Experience." *Judicature* 79: 280–81.

De Tocqueville, Alexis. 1969. *Democracy in America*. Ed. Jacob Peter Mayer and Max Lerner. New York: Harper and Row.

Ellsworth, Phoebe C. 1989. "Are Twelve Heads Better Than One?" *Law and Contemporary Problems*, Autumn: 205–18.

Ewick, Patricia, and Susan Silbey. 2003. "The Architecture of Authority: The Spatial Nexus of Law and Science." In Austin Sarat, Lawrence Douglas, and Martha Merrill Umphrey, eds., *The Place of Law*. Ann Arbor: University of Michigan Press.

Flaherty, Julie. 2001. "A Patch for Family Bonds Put Asunder." *New York Times*, May 10, D10.

Harmon, Amy. 1996. "Computing in the '90s: The Great Divide." *Los Angeles Times*, October 7, D1.

Kassin, Saul, and Lawrence Wrightsman. 1988. *The American Jury on Trial.* New York: Hemi-sphere.

Marder, Nancy S. 1997. "Deliberations and Disclosures: A Study of Post-Verdict Interviews of Jurors." *Iowa Law Review* 82: 465–546.

Marder, Nancy S. 1999. "The Interplay of Race and False Claims of Jury Nullification." *University of Michigan Journal of Law Reform* 32: 285–321.

Markoff, John. 2000. "High-Tech Executives Urge Action on World's Digital Divide." *New York Times,* July 20, A6.

Mintz, Daniel R. 2001. "For a Dad, Videoconference Ties That Bind." *New York Times,* June 10, 13.

Noveck, Beth Simone. 2004. "Unchat: Democratic Solution for a Wired World." In Peter M. Shane, ed., *Democracy Online: The Prospects for Political Renewal through the Internet.* New York: Routledge.

Owens, John. 2000. "Helping Close the Digital Divide." *Chicago Tribune,* August 7, B1.

"Woman Juror: Men Bullied Her to Convict." 1994. *Los Angeles Daily Journal,* January 4, 3.

CHAPTER 4

Expanding Dialogue: The Internet, Public Sphere, and Transnational Democracy

JAMES BOHMAN

New technologies are often greeted with political optimism. The Internet was thought to herald new possibilities for political participation, if not direct democracy, even in large and complex societies, as "electronic democracy" might replace the mass-media democracy of sound-bite television. However, the high hopes for electronic democracy seem to have faded, as critics such as Sunstein and Shapiro have come to argue that central features of the Internet and computer-mediated communication generally undermine the sort of public sphere and political interaction that are required for genuine democratic deliberation (Sunstein 2001; Shapiro 1999). Whatever the empirical merits of such criticisms, they do point to an as yet unclarified problem in discussions of electronic democracy: we still lack a clear understanding of how the Internet and other forms of electronic communication might contribute to a historically new kind of public sphere and thus to a potentially new form of democracy.

Both the optimistic and pessimistic positions in the debate suffer from clear conceptual problems. Optimists take for granted that the mode of communication or technological mediation itself is constitutive of new possibilities. Pessimists make the opposite error of holding institutions fixed, here the institutions of the sovereign nation-state (Held 1995; Poster 2001). In a period when the political context has shifted and a broader array of institutional alternatives is now opening up to include transnational public spheres, it seems likely that electronic and computer-mediated network communication may well expand the scope of certain features of communicative interaction across space and time. Expanding the scope of communicative interaction should help to solve some of the problems of scale and the cultural limitations inherent in the literary public sphere as well as overcome some of the limitations on deliberation in the institutions of representative democracy. A proper assessment then not only will have to consider new possibilities; it will also have to take more fully into consideration the fact that public spheres, technologies, and democratic institutions exist not independently of one another but in ongoing and shifting historical relations.

Such an open-ended historical and pragmatic approach, with its emphasis on possibilities and interrelatedness, leads to somewhat optimistic conclusions about the public sphere and democracy under conditions of computer-mediated communication, although not unreservedly so. My argument has four steps. First, I undertake the conceptual clarification of the necessary conditions for a public sphere with the requirements of deliberative democracy in mind. This conception of democracy and of the public sphere is dialogical, where dialogue becomes public only if it is able to expand and transform the conditions of communicative interaction. Second, I then consider the potentials of computer-mediated communication on the Internet in light of these necessary conditions. If it is true that dialogue is public only when it is expansive and transformative, then the Internet is a public sphere only if agents make it so, if agents introduce institutional "software" that constructs the context of communication. This context is transnational rather than national, distributive rather than unified in form. Here the role that Internet-mediated publicness could play in specific institutions is examined through the experiences of governance in the European Union. Finally, I consider whether the novel public sphere that is created in transnational politics might itself feed back upon democratic institutions and help to promote new institutional forms that address problems of space and time that are inherent in considering global democracy, including issues of collective identity and citizenship. Participants in transnational public spheres could become transnational citizens if they have the technological means and public sphere at their disposal to make normative claims upon each other in a dialogical and deliberative fashion. First, however, the conception of the public sphere must be unhooked from its typical modern forms: the print medium and the institutions of the state.

1. Some Preliminaries: Technology and the Public Sphere

In order to adopt this pragmatic approach, it is first necessary to set aside some misleading assumptions that guide most conceptions of the public sphere and complicate any discussion of electronic democracy. These assumptions are normatively significant precisely because they directly establish the connection between the public sphere and the democratic ideal of deliberation among free and equal citizens. They can be misleading when the suggested connection is overly specific and leaves out an essential condition for the existence of a public sphere in large and highly differentiated modern societies: the technological mediation of public communication. In this section, I argue that if we consider this technological condition of possibility for any modern public sphere, we must relax the requirements of the public sphere as a forum realized in face-to-face communication. There are other ways to realize the public forum and its multiple forms of dialogical exchange in a more indirect and mediated manner, even while preserving and rearticulating the connection to democratic self-rule.

Once the concept is seen in a properly historical way, the public sphere (or *Öffentlichkeit* in the broad sense) is not a univocal normative ideal. It nonetheless still have necessary conditions. First, a public sphere that has democratic significance must be a forum, that is, a social space in which speakers may express their views to others, who in turn respond to them and raise their own opinions and concerns. Second, a democratic public sphere must manifest commitments to freedom and equality in the communicative interaction. Such interaction takes the specific form of a conversation or dialogue, in which speakers and hearers treat each other with equal respect and freely exchange their roles in their responses to each other. This leads to a third necessary feature for any public sphere that corrects for the limits of face-to-face interaction: communication must address an indefinite audience. In this sense, any social exclusion undermines the existence of a public sphere. Expansive dialogue must be indefinite in just this sense, and with the responses of a wider audience, new reasons and forms of communication may emerge. Communication is then "public" if it is directed at an indefinite audience with the expectation of a response. In this way, a public sphere depends upon repeated and open-ended interaction and as such requires technologies and institutions to secure its continued existence and regularize opportunities and access to it.

If this account of the necessary features of public communication is correct, then the very existence of the public sphere is always dependent on some form of communications technology to the extent that it requires the expansion of dialogue beyond face-to-face encounters. Historically, writing first served to open up this sort of indefinite social space of possibilities with the spatial extension of the audience and the temporal extension of uptake or response. Taking the potentials of writing further, the printed word produced a new form of communication based on a one-to-many form of interaction. Television and radio did not essentially alter this one-to-many extension of communicative interaction, even as they eased entry requirements of literacy for hearers and raised the costs of adopting the speaker role in a mass audience.

Computer-mediated communication also extends the forum by providing a new, unbounded space for communicative interaction. Its innovative potential lies not just in its speed and scale but also in its new form of address or interaction: as a many-to-many mode of communication, it has radically lowered the costs of interaction with an indefinite and potentially large audience, especially with regard to adopting the speaker role without the costs of the mass media. Moreover, such many-to-many communication with newly increased interactivity holds out the promise of capturing the features of dialogue and communication more robustly than the print medium. This network-based extension of dialogue suggests the possibility of reembedding the public sphere in a new and potentially larger set of institutions. At present, there is a lack of congruity between existing political institutions and the wider potential for public communicative interaction. Hence, the nature of the public or publics is changing.

A specifically egalitarian expansion of the public sphere requires a more elaborated institutional structure to support it (such as that achieved by the modern democratic state but not identical with it), as the social contexts of communication are enlarged with the number of relevant speakers and audience. Contrary to misleading analogies to the national public sphere, such a development hardly demands that the public sphere be "integrated with media systems of matching scale that occupy the same social space as that over which economic and political decision will have an impact" (Garnham 1993: 265). But if the only effective way to do this is through multiple communicative networks rather than the mass media, then the global public sphere should not be expected to mirror the cultural unity and spatial congruence of the national public sphere; as a public of publics, it permits a decentered public sphere with many different levels. Disaggregated networks must always be embedded in some other set of social institutions rather than an assumed unified national public sphere. Once we examine the potential ways in which the Internet can expand the features of communicative interaction using such distributive and network forms, the issue of whether or not the Internet can support public spheres changes in character. It depends on the political agency of those concerned with its public character.

2. The Internet as a Network and as a Space of Publics

The main lesson from the preliminaries of the last section is that discussions of the democratic potential of the Internet cannot be satisfied with listing its positive or intrinsic features—for example, its speed, its scale, its "anarchic" nature, its ability to facilitate resistance to centralized control as a network of networks, and so on. The same is true for its negative effects or consequences, such as its well-known disaggregative character or its anonymity. Taken together, both these considerations weigh against regarding the Internet as a variation of existing print and national public spheres. Rather, the space opened up by computer-mediated communication supports a new sort of distributive rather than unified public sphere with new forms of interaction. By distributive, I mean that computer mediation in the form of the Internet decenters the public sphere; it is a public of publics rather than a distinctively unified and encompassing public sphere in which all communicators participate. Rather than simply offering a new version of the existing public sphere, the Internet becomes a public sphere only through agents who engage in reflexive and democratic activity. For the Internet to create a new form of publicness beyond the mere aggregate of all its users, it must first be constituted as a public sphere by people whose interactions exhibit the features of dialogue and are concerned with its publicness. In order to support a public sphere and technologically mediate the appropriate norms, the network form must become a viable means for the expansion of the possibilities of dialogue and of the deliberative, second-order features of communicative interaction. These features may not be the same as manifested in previous political public spheres, such as the bourgeois public sphere of private persons.

If the Internet communication has no intrinsic features, it is because, like writing, it holds out many different possibilities in its transformation of the public sphere. Here it is useful to distinguish between hardware and software. As hardware, the World Wide Web is a network of networks with technical properties that enable the conveyance of information over great distances with near simultaneity. This hardware can be used for different purposes, as embodied in software that configures participants as "users." Indeed, as Lawrence Lessig notes, "an extraordinary amount of control can be built in the environment that people know in cyberspace," perhaps even without their knowledge (Lessig 1999: 217). Such computer programs depend on "software" in a much broader sense: software includes not only the variety of programs available but also the ways in which people improvise and collaborate to create new possibilities for interaction. Software in this sense includes both the modes of social organization mediated through the Net and the institutions in which the Net is embedded. For example, the indeterminacy of the addressees of an anonymous message can be settled by reconfiguring the Internet into an intranet, creating a private space that excludes others and defines the audience. This is indeed how most corporations use the Web today, creating inaccessible and commercial spaces within the networks by use of firewalls and other devices for commercial and monetary interactions among corporations and anonymous consumers. The Web thus enables political and social power to be distributed in civil society, but it also permits such power to be manifested less in the capacity to interfere with others than in the capacity to exclude them and alter the freedom and openness of its public space. This same power may alter other mediated public spheres, as when the *New York Times* offers to deliver a "personalized" paper that is not identical with the one that other citizens in the political public sphere are reading.

The fact that social power is manifested in technological mediation reveals the importance of institutions in preserving and maintaining public space, and the Internet is no exception. Saskia Sassen shows how the Internet has historically reflected the institutions in which it has been embedded and configured. Its "anarchic" phase reflected the ways in which it was created in universities and for scientific purposes. While the Web still bears the marks of this phase as possibilities of distributed power, it is arguably entering a different phase, in which corporations increasingly privatize this common space as a kind of *terra nullia* for their specific purposes, such as financial transactions. "We are at a particular historical moment in the history of electronic space when powerful corporate actors and high performance networks are strengthening the role of private electronic space and altering the structure of public electronic space" (Sassen 1998: 194). At the same time, it is also clear that civil society groups, especially transnational groups, are using the Web for their own political and public purposes, where freedom and interconnectivity are what is valued. We are now in a period of the development of the software and hardware of the Internet in which the nature of the Web is now at issue. At the same time, politics as such is at issue, with similar processes of political decentralization and social contestation in both domains. Those concerned with the publicness, freedom, and openness of the Internet as a public space may see features of the Internet that extend dialogical interaction threatened by the annexation of the Internet by large-scale economic enterprises. Such a concern requires that civil society actors not only contest the alterations of public space but place themselves between the corporations, software makers, access providers, and other powerful institutions that often enjoy an immediate and highly asymmetrical relation to individuals as "users" who enter into public spaces as the institutions configure them in the literal and institutional software they create for those who enter their private cyberspaces. "Users" can reflexively configure themselves as agents.

This suggests a particular analysis of threats to public space. It is now commonplace to say that the Internet rids communication of intermediaries, of those various professional communicators whose mass-mediated communication is the focus of much public debate and discussion and political information. Dewey lauded such a division of labor to the extent to which it can improve deliberation not merely in creating a common public sphere but also in "the subtle, delicate, vivid and responsive art of communication." This task is at least in part best fulfilled by professional communicators who disseminate the best available information and technologies to large audiences of citizens. Even with this dependence on such art and techniques of communication, the public need not simply be the object of techniques of persuasion. Rather than a "mass" of cultural dopes, mediated communication makes a "rational public" possible, in the sense that "the public as a whole can generally form policy preferences that reflect the best available information" (Page 1995: 194). If we focus upon the totality of political information available and this surprising empirical tendency (as noted by Benjamin Page and others) for the public to correct media biases and distortions as stories and opinions develop and change over time, it is possible to see how mediated communication can enhance the communication presupposed in public deliberation. In complex, large-scale, and pluralistic societies, mediated communication is unavoidable if there are to be channels of communication that are broad enough to address the highly heterogeneous audience of all of its members and to treat issues that vary with regard to the epistemic demands on speakers in diverse locales who can discuss them intelligently.

Given their attachments to various institutions and technologies, proponents of deliberation often claim there is a net normative loss in the shift to networked communication, further amplified by the "control revolution," by which various corporations and providers give individuals the capacity to control who addresses them and to whom they may respond (Shapiro 1999: 23). Or, to put this criticism in the terms that I have been using here, the mass public sphere is not replaced by any public sphere at all; rather, communicative mediation is replaced by forms of control that make dialogue and the expansion of the deliberative features of communication impossible. In the terms of economic theory, agents whose purpose it is to facilitate individual control over the communicative environment replace intermediaries. Such a relation, though, inevitably leads to the "reversal of agency," where the direction of control shifts from principals to the agents they delegate. It is false to say that individuals possess immediate control; they have control only through assenting to an asymmetrical relationship to various agents who structure the choices in the communicative environment of cyberspace.

There is more than a grain of truth in this pessimistic diagnosis of the control revolution. But this leaves out part of the story concerning how the public exercises some control over intermediaries, at least by those concerned with publicness. As with the relation of agent and principal, the problem here is to develop democratic modes of interaction between expert communicators and their audience in the public sphere. Citizens must now resist the mediaization of politics on a par with its technization by experts. The challenge is twofold. First of all, the public must challenge the credibility of expert communicators, especially in their capacities to set agendas and frames for discussing issues. Second, as in the case of cooperating with experts, the public must challenge the reception of their own public communication by the media themselves, especially insofar as the media must report, represent, and even construct the "public opinion" of citizens who are distant strangers. This self-referential aspect of public communication can be fulfilled only by interactions between the media and the public, in which public intermediaries challenge the ways in which publics are both addressed and represented.

Such problems are exacerbated as the mediated interaction becomes predominant in modern political and public spheres, creating new forms of social interaction and political relationships that reorder in space and time and become structured in ways less and less like mutually responsive dialogue (Thompson 1995: 85). Analogous considerations of agency and asymmetries of access to the norms that shape communicative interaction are relevant to the Internet. It is clear that corporations could function as the main institutional actors in developing electronic space and exert an influence that would restrict communication in ways even more impervious to corporate media and political parties. Just as all public spheres have technological mediation of features of communicative interaction, all public spheres require counterintermediaries and counter–public spaces of some kind or another to maintain their publicness. The sustainability of such spaces over time depends precisely upon the agency of those concerned with the character of public opinion and thus with influencing the construction of the public space by whatever technical means of communication are available. The Internet and its governance now lack the means to institutionalize the public sphere, especially since there are no functional equivalents to the roles played by journalists, judges, and other intermediaries who regulated and protected the publicness of political communication in the mass media.

Who are their replacements once the technology of mediation changes? The Internet has not yet achieved a settled form in which intermediaries have been established and professionalized. As in the emerging public spheres of early modernity, the potential intermediary roles must emerge from those who organize themselves in cyberspace as a public sphere. This role falls to those organizations in civil society that have become concerned with the publicness of electronic space and seek to create, institutionalize, expand, and protect it. Such organizations can achieve their goals only if they act self-referentially and insist that they may exercise communicative power over the shape and appropriation of electronic public space. Thus, contrary to Shapiro and Sunstein, it is not that the Internet gets rid of intermediaries as such; rather, it operates in a public space in which the particular *democratic* intermediaries have lost their influence. This is not a necessary structural consequence of its form of communication.

With the development of the Internet as a public sphere, we may expect its "reintermediarization," that is, the emergence of new intermediaries who counter its privatization and individualization brought about by access and content providers for commercial purposes and who construct the user as a private person. Actors can play the role of counterintermediaries when they attempt to bypass these narrow social roles on the Internet—more specifically, the role of a "user" in relation to a "provider" who sets the terms of how the Internet may be employed. The first area in which this has already occurred is in Internet self-governance organizations and their interest in countering trends to annexation and privatization. Here institutions such as the Internet Corporation for Assigned Names and Numbers (ICANN) have attempted to institute public deliberation on the legal and technological standards that govern the Internet (Fromkin 2003). This and other examples of a deliberative process through multiple intermediaries bears further examination.

Given that what is needed are alternatives to the current set of intermediaries rather than the absence of them, civil society organizations have distinct advantages in taking on such a responsibility for publicness in cyberspace. They have organizational identities, so they are no longer anonymous; they also take over the responsibility for responsiveness, which remains indeterminate in many-to-many communication. Most of all, they employ the Internet, but not as "users"; they create their own spaces, promote interactions, conduct deliberation, make information available, and so on. For example, a variety of organizations created a forum for the debate on the Multilateral Agreement on Investment (MAI), an issue that hardly registered in the national press. Not only did they make the MAI widely available, they held detailed online discussions of the merits of its various provisions (Smith and Smythe 2001: 183). As a tool for various forms of activism, the Internet promotes a vibrant civil society; it extends the public sphere of civil society but does not necessarily transform it. The point is not simply to create a Web site or to convey information. It becomes something more when sites are public spaces in which free, open, and responsive dialogical interaction takes place. This sort of project is not uncommon and includes experiments among neighborhood groups, nongovernmental organizations, and others. Hence, the organization acts as an intermediary in a different way: not as an expert communicator but rather as the creator and facilitator of institutional software that socializes the commons and makes it a public space. Such software creates a cosmopolitan political space, a normed communicative commons of indefinite interaction.

As long as there are cosmopolitan actors who will create and maintain such transnational communication, this sort of serial and distributed public sphere is potentially global in scope. Its unity is to be found in the general conditions for the formation of publics themselves and in the actions of those who see themselves as constituting a public against this background. Membership in these shifting publics is to be found in civil society, in formal and informal organizations that emerge to discuss and deliberate on the issues of the day. But while the creation of publics is a matter of the agency of citizens, the sustaining of general conditions that make such a process possible is a matter for formal institutionalization, just as sustaining the conditions for the national public sphere was a central concern of the democratic nation-state. In the case of such shifting and potentially transnational publics, the institutions that sustain publicness and become the focus of the self-referential activity of civil society must also be innovative if they are to have their communicative basis in dispersed and decentered forms of publicness. At the same time, these institutions must be deliberative and democratic. Because they become the location for second-order reflexive political deliberation and activity, these institutions are part of the public sphere as its higher-order and self-governing form of publicness transforms the Internet from a commons to an institutionally organized and embedded democratic space.

3. From Publics to Public Sphere: The Institutional Form of Transnational Democracy

In the previous section, I argued that reflexive agency of actors within cyberspace was required to create the "software" that could transform networks into publics that make use of its many-to-many distributive processes of communication. While such publics establish positive and enabling conditions for democratic deliberation, they are not themselves democratic (even if they are transnational and cosmopolitan rather than national). The public must itself be embedded in an institutional context, not only if it is to secure the conditions of publicness but also in order to promote the interaction among publics that is required for deliberative democracy. Thus, both network forms of communication and the publics formed in them must be embedded in a larger institutional and political context if they are to be transformed into public spheres in which citizens can make claims and expect a response.

There are several reasons to think that current democratic institutions are insufficient for this task. States have promoted the privatization of various media spaces for communication, including not only the Internet but also broadcast frequencies. Even if the Internet is not intrinsically anarchic and even if states were willing to do more in the way of protecting the public character of cyberspace, it remains an open question whether this form of communication escapes the way in which state sovereignty organizes space and time, including public space and the temporality of deliberation. It is precisely its potentially aterritorial character that makes it difficult to square with centralized forms of authority over a delimited territory. This sort of process, however, does not require convergence, especially since Internet use may reflect inequalities in the access to rule-making institutions as well as other, older patterns of subordination at the international level. It is also true that people do not as yet have patterns of communication sufficient to identify with each other on cosmopolitan terms. Nonetheless, new possibilities that the Internet affords for deliberation and access to influence in its distributive and network forms do not require such strong preconditions to have opened up new forms of democratization.

It is certainly not the case that states are now entirely ineffective, nor is it true that national public spheres are so culturally limited that they serve no democratic purpose. Rather, what is at stake is that such public spheres will cease to be politically important. If the Internet escapes territoriality, then there is no analogue at the institutional level for the particular connections and feedback relations between the national public sphere and the democratic state. Whatever institutions could promote and protect such a dispersed and disaggregated public sphere will represent a novel political possibility that does not "merely replicate on a larger scale the typical modern political form" (Ruggie 1996: 195). This access to political influence through mediated communication will not be attained once and for all, as in the unified public sphere of nation-states in which citizens gain influence through the complex of parliamentary or representative institutions. Currently Internet publics are "weak" publics, which exert such influence through public opinion generally. But they may become "strong" publics when they are able to exercise influence through institutionalized decision-making procedures with regularized opportunities for input (Fraser 1989; Habermas 1996). Thus, transnational institutions are adequately democratic if they permit such access to have influence distributively across various domains and levels, rather than merely aggregatively in the summative public sphere of citizens as a whole. Because there is no single institution to which strong publics are connected, the contrast between weak and strong publics is much more fluid than the current usage presupposes.

While the whole range of possible forms of institutionalization cannot be considered fully here, the European Union provides an interesting case study for a transnational policy, precisely because it obviously lacks the unitary and linguistic features of previous public spheres. I will consider only one aspect of institutionalization across multiple levels and centers of power: practices of decision making that are suggestive of how a polycentric form of publicness would permit a more rather than less directly deliberative form of governance, once we abandon the assumption that there is a unified public sphere connected to a single set of statelike authority structures that seem to impose uniform policies over its entire territory. As Charles Sabel has argued, a "directly deliberative" design in many ways incorporates epistemic innovations and increased capabilities of economic organizations, in the same way as the new regulatory institutions of the New Deal followed the innovations of industrial organization in the centralized mass production they attempted to administer and regulate (Dorf and Sabel 1996: 292). Roughly, such a form of organization uses nested and collaborative forms of decision making based on highly collaborative processes of jointly defining problems and setting goals already typical in many large firms with dispersed sites of production.

Such a process requires a design that promotes a great deal of interaction within the organization and across sites and locations. Within the normative framework established by initial goals and benchmarks, the process of their application requires deliberation at various levels of scale.

At all levels, citizens can introduce factors based on local knowledge and problems, even as they are informed by the diverse solutions and outcomes of other planning and design bodies. Local solutions can also be corrected, as these solutions can be tested by the problem solving of other groups. Thus, while highly dispersed and distributed, various levels of deliberation permit public testing and correction, even if they do not hierarchically override decisions at lower levels. Such a collaborative process of setting goals and defining problems produces a shared body of knowledge and common goals, even if the solutions need not be uniform across or within various organizations and locations. Sabel calls this "learning by monitoring" and proposes ways in which administrative agencies could employ such distributive processes even while evaluating performance at lower levels by systematic comparisons across sites. Innovations are not handed down from the top, since collective learning does not assume that the higher levels are epistemically superior.

The European Union implements such a decentralized process of regulation in its Open Method of Coordination (OMC). Such deliberative processes provide a space for ongoing reflection on agendas and problems, as well as an interest in inclusiveness and diversity of perspectives. These enabling conditions for democracy can take advantage of the intensified interaction across borders that is a by-product of processes of the thickening of the communicative infrastructure across state borders. Regulatory but still decentralized federalism provides for modes of accountability in this process itself, even while allowing for local variations that go beyond the assumption of the uniformity of policy over a single bounded territory typical of nation-state regulation. Sabel and Cohen argue that the European Union already has features of a directly deliberative polyarchy in the implementation of the OMC in its economic, industrial, and educational standards (Sabel and Cohen 2003). The advantage of such deliberative methods is that the interaction at different levels of decision making promotes robust accountability; accountability operates upward and downward and in this way cuts across the typical distinction of vertical and horizontal accountability (O'Donnell 1999). Thus, directly deliberative polyarchy describes a method of decision making in institutions across various levels and with plural authority structures.

The question still remains: who is the public at large at the level of implementation and democratic experimentation in directly deliberative processes? Sabel provides no answer to this question, asserting only that the process must be open to the public (Sabel and Cohen 1998). The problem for institutional design of directly deliberative democracy is to create precisely the appropriate feedback relation between disaggregated publics and such a polycentric decision-making process. As my discussion of the Internet shows, there is a technology through which this form of publicness is produced and which expands and maintains the deliberative potential of dialogue. Thus the European Union, at least in some of its decision-making processes, could seek the marriage of directly deliberative decision making and computer-assisted, computer-mediated, and distributive forms of publicness. Most of all, it would require experimentation in reconciling the dispersed form of many-to-many communication with the demands of the forum. Rather than providing some institutional formula, such direct and vigorous interaction among dispersed publics at various levels of decision making creates new forums and publics around locations at which various sort of decisions are debated and discussed. This sort of Internet counter–public sphere is potentially transnational, as is the case in the public that formed around the MAI. Appropriately designed decision-making processes such as those in the EU and the existence of a suitable form of publicness at least show how dialogue could be technologically and institutionally extended and democratically secured in a transnational context.

4. Conclusion

My argument here has been two-sided. On one hand, I have developed the innovative potential of electronic public space for democracy, especially when applied to a deliberative transnationalism. This potential transformation of democratic institutions shows the fruitfulness of thinking about cyberspace in political terms that are related to the sort of publicness that it generates. On the other hand, such a potential public sphere can be secured only through innovative institutions. In each case, new circumstances suggest rethinking both democracy and the public sphere outside the limits of their previous historical forms. Rethinking publicness allows us to see that some critical diagnoses of the problems of electronic democracy are short-circuited by a failure to think beyond what is politically familiar. For example, it is argued that communication over the Internet leads to "disintermediation," all the while ignoring the emergence of new intermediaries (Shapiro 1999: 55). The same is true of positive diagnoses that see the Internet as inherently democratic and dialogical. Critical analyses of the potential of the Internet and of the globalization of communication are better served neither by pessimism nor by optimism but by understanding potential gains and costs of these transformations for the public sphere. If my argument is correct that the Internet preserves and extends the dialogical character of the public sphere in a potentially cosmopolitan form, then a deliberative transnational democracy can be considered a "realistic utopia" in Rawls's sense; it extends the range of political possibilities for deliberative democracy.

I have argued that the Internet and other contemporary public spaces permit a form of publicness that results in a public of publics rather than a unified public sphere based in a common culture or identity. Nonetheless, speakers and their audience still stand in the essential normative relation of dialogical interaction, addressing each other in the normative attitude in which all may propose and incur mutual obligations. If the obligation-constituting elements of dialogue are preserved and extended in a new form of a deliberative public sphere, then a further essential democratic element is also possible: that the public sphere be a source of agency and social criticism, offering a space for those whose critical claims expose the limitations of its technological and institutional intermediaries. In either adopting the role of the critic or taking up such criticism in the public sphere, speakers adopt the standpoint of the "generalized other," the relevant critical perspective that opens up a future standpoint of a larger and more inclusive community. As Mead put it: "The question whether we belong to a larger community is answered in terms of whether our own actions call out a response in this wider community, and whether its response is reflected back into our own conduct"(Mead 1934: 270–71). This sort of mutual responsiveness and interdependence is possible only in a democratic form of communication that accommodates multiple perspectives. To the question of the applicability of such norms and institutions internationally, Mead is optimistic: "Could a conversation be conducted internationally? The question is a question of social organization" (Mead 1934: 271). Organization requires agency, and the social organization of technology begins with the interventions of democratic agents and intermediaries. If the Internet ultimately enables dialogue across borders and publics, it does so only if there are agents who make it so and if they eventually create transnational institutions whose ideals seek to realize a transnational public sphere as the basis for a realistic utopia of citizenship in a complexly interconnected world.

References

Dorf, Michael, and Charles Sabel. 1996. "The Constitution of Democratic Experimentalism." *Columbia Law Review* 98, 2: 267–443.

Fraser, Nancy. 1989. "Rethinking the Public Sphere." In C. Calhoun, ed., *Habermas and the Public Sphere*, 109–42. Cambridge, MA: MIT Press.

Froomkin, Michael. 2003. "Habermas@discourse.net: Towards a Critical Theory of Cyberspace." *Harvard Law Review* 116, 3: 751–873.

Garnham, Nicolas. 1993. "The Mass Media, Cultural Identity, and the Public Sphere in the Modern World." *Public Culture* 5, 2: 243–71.

Habermas, Jürgen. 1996. *Between Facts and Norms*. Cambridge, MA: MIT Press.

Held, David. 1995. *Democracy and Global Order*. Stanford: Stanford University Press.

Lessig, Lawrence. 1999. *Code and Other Laws of Cyberspace*. New York: Basic Books.

Mead, George Herbert. 1934. *Mind, Self, and Society*. Chicago: University of Chicago Press.

O'Donnell, Guillermo. 1999. "Delegative Democracy." In *Counterpoints*, 162–73. South Bend: Notre Dame University Press.

Page, Benjamin. 1995. *Who Deliberates?* Chicago: University of Chicago Press.

Poster, Mark. 2001. *What's the Matter with the Internet*. Minneapolis: University of Minnesota Press.

Ruggie, Gerald. 1996. *Constructing the World Policy*. London: Routledge, 1996.

Sabel, Charles, and Joshua Cohen. 1998. "Directly-Deliberative Polyarchy." In Christian Joerges and Oliver Gerstenberg, eds., *Private Governance, Democratic Constitutionalism and Supranationalism*, 1–26. Florence: European Commission.

Sabel, Charles, and Joshua Cohen. 2003. "Sovereignty and Solidarity: EU and US." In J. Zeitlin and D. Trubek, eds., *Governing Work and Welfare in a New Economy: European and American Experiments*. Oxford: Oxford University Press.

Sassen, Saskia. 1998. *Globalization and Its Discontents*. New York: New Press.

Shapiro, Andrew. 1999. *The Control Revolution*. New York: Century Foundation Books.

Smith, Peter, and Elizabeth Smythe. 2001. "Globalization, Citizenship and Technology: The Multilateral Agreement on Investment (MAI) Meets the Internet." In Frank Webster, ed., *Culture and Politics in the Information Age*, 183–206. London: Routledge, 2001.

Sunstein, Cass. 2001. *Republic.com*. Princeton: Princeton University Press.

Thompson, John. 1995. *Media and Modernity*. Stanford: Stanford University Press.

PART 2

Electronic Democracy and Democratic Revitalization

The Electronic Federalist: The Internet and the Eclectic Institutionalization of Democratic Legitimacy

PETER M. SHANE

Since the emergence of the Internet began to give rise to hopes for democratic revitalization through new information and communications technologies (ICTs), predictions and preferences have varied with regard to the anticipated trajectory of democratic renewal. Cyberdemocrats have urged on various grounds, both theoretical and pragmatic, that designers of electronic democratic initiatives focus on improving existing institutions of representative government (Clift 2000), creating the infrastructure for new forms of deliberative democracy (Dahlberg 2001), or accelerating the disintermediation of politics by enabling more direct, plebiscitary forms of democratic governance (Becker and Slaton 2000). The argument of this essay is that if new ICTs are truly to enable a revitalization of democratic practice, then they must be institutionalized in ways that enhance the underpinnings of democratic legitimacy in a multifaceted way. At the very least, this means a conscious program of designing and deploying ICTs to enhance both what I call election-centered democratic practice and practice associated with deliberative democracy. Cyberdemocrats should not focus their inventive energies solely on any one model of democratic legitimacy, or anticipate significant democratic renewal simply through a spontaneous flowering of online political practices, without regard to their design or whether any are linked formally to governmental outcomes.

The inspiration for this position is *The Federalist Papers*, the contemporary defense by Alexander Hamilton, James Madison, and John Jay of the then newly proposed Constitution of 1787. Their collection of essays, less a philosophical statement about politics than a set of arguments about the institutionalization of politics, is still generally regarded as our greatest native work of political theory. Two aspects of their work ought to be central to our own efforts to revitalize democratic legitimacy in the twenty-first century. The first is their commitment to the notion that the quality of political life depends upon the successful translation of sound political ideals and normative commitments into working political institutions. Democratic sentiments count for little without well-designed institutions to act upon them. The second is the brilliant institutional eclecticism they advocated with regard to the new constitution. To make the system work, the framers not only envisioned national executive, legislative, and judicial branches, each structured differently and each with different authorities, capacities, selection mechanisms, and internal decision-making processes; they also imposed federal constitutional roles explicitly on state judges and legislators, and authorized a future Constitution-amending role for popular conventions in the states (Shane 1999). The government so organized was intended to embody and carry forward a revolutionary ideal of "popular sovereignty," a wholly novel understanding of the nature of political legitimacy (Wood 1969). The founding generation had hardly worked out all details of how popular sovereignty was to work or how, in principle, it would function to confer legitimacy on the exercise of political power. But what the framers realized, and what the essays in *The Federalist Papers* demonstrate, is that robust democratic legitimation can effectively occur only through an eclectic amalgam of different kinds of political institutions. That is because the legitimating character of democracy derives from more than one attribute of democratic life and practice, and democracy will prove most vital where each legitimating attribute enjoys a healthy institutional life (Farina 1997).

The first part of this essay considers the nature of democratic legitimacy and explicates how different models of democratic organization seek to realize legitimacy in practice. Next, it explains why the only program of ICT-enabled democratic revitalization that can hope to succeed is a program that seeks to implement models of both election-based and deliberative democracy. Finally, it considers what an ambitious, self-consciously eclectic program of institutionalized ICT-enabled democratic practice might look like.

1. Three Models of Democratic Legitimacy

At the most general level, the goal of any project of democratic renewal would presumably be to deepen the legitimacy of a particular system of democratic governance. Allen Buchanan has helpfully defined "political legitimacy" as the moral entitlement of an entity to wield political power. He offers an elegant argument "that where democratic authorization of political power is possible, only a democratic government can be legitimate" (Buchanan 2002: 689). Buchanan does not define in any precise way what counts as democratic government; he says only that any such government must take as fundamental the equal consideration of all persons subject to its putative authority. Buchanan's view implies that the legitimacy of a democratic system is rooted in its objective success at achieving such equal consideration.

This perspective, however, is incomplete. It offers an objective standard by which to assess the legitimacy of democratic rule, but it does not take explicit account of the subjective experience of those who live in a putatively democratic regime. Democracy is a system of collective self-determination and is thus justifiably evaluated according to its contribution to the collective good. Democratic collective self-determination cannot be sensibly divorced, however, from the experience of individual self-determination. In the words of Robert Post: "[W]e could not plausibly characterize as democratic a society in which 'the people' were given the power to determine the nature of their government, but in which the individuals who made up 'the people' did not experience themselves as free to choose their own political fate" (Post: 71995). In short, if cyberdemocrats are to pursue a version of legitimacy likely to elicit enthusiastic public support, it is unhelpful to speak of a system's "democratic legitimacy" as something that can be established without consulting the experience of actual people subject to that system.

Following the insights of Buchanan and Post, I would therefore define a project of democratic renewal as one aimed at deepening democratic legitimacy. To deepen democratic legitimacy, we must intensify both the experience of autonomous political citizenship that democracy affords and the likelihood that binding decision-making processes will provide equal consideration for the interests of all persons. Any such project, in turn, must logically be based on one or more models of democratic legitimacy, that is, on one or more narratives that explain how particular prescriptions for democratic government or citizen practice yield regimes of equal consideration and the experience of autonomous citizenship.

There are three models of democratic legitimation that have deep roots in American political culture and that remain essential to democratic legitimacy in information age America—the models of election-centered, direct, and deliberative democracy. The boundaries between these models are porous; a democratic system can easily incorporate elements of all three, as ours does. But each of them rests on a different account of how citizens and institutions combine to afford democratic legitimacy. The accounts differ especially in the relative importance they ascribe to individual citizens versus government officials in arriving at decisions of public policy.

The most familiar model of democratic legitimacy rests on the election of public officials to make and enforce the laws. For virtually all observers, elections are the sine qua non of modern democracy in any sizable community. Elections presumably stand out for Americans as the most obvious source of a democratic government's moral authority to rule. The most conspicuous trend of the past century in democratic practice has been the momentum toward the inclusion of all adults in the franchise (Keyssar 2000).

In the election-centered model, however, the experience of autonomous citizenship is limited to the selection of candidates and the electoral choice among them. When it comes to actually deciding the content of public policy, elected representatives are centrally important, but individual citizens only indirectly so. The system's claim to legitimacy thus rests on twin pillars. One is the hope that autonomous electoral participation will afford citizens a sufficient experience of self-determination to warrant their allegiance to the outcome. The second is the presumption that representatives' accountability to the people who elect them will yield equal consideration for the interests of all persons, providing democratic government with its moral foundation. As to the latter point, elections supposedly maximize the incentive for those who exercise political power to internalize a sense of accountability to those they represent. Because those who govern can continue in office only upon reelection, office holders will presumably undertake meaningful efforts to justify publicly whatever official actions they take in representing their constituents. The fact of accountability and the hoped-for internalization on the part of rulers of a sense of genuine obligation to constituents increase the likelihood that a representative's actions will respect the equality of all persons.

The sense of accountability will also be intensified by an ongoing system of communication between elections that elections, in turn, help to motivate and energize. Legal scholar Robert Bennett has given an account of what he calls "conversational democracy," the sum total of the unbounded, free-floating, but meaningful political talk in which citizens, public officials, and journalists jointly engage (Bennett 1997). Under his model, the phenomenon of elections results in a system through which "the entire electorate is engaged on an ongoing basis by meaningful public conversation about public policy" (ibid.: 500). This conversation perhaps represents the most significant experience of political self-determination for individual citizens engaged in the electoral process, and it deepens the value of elections in achieving broad-based accountability by maintaining the attention and engagement of office holders on a permanent basis. The fact of ongoing conversation maintains the spotlight on office holders and requires them to confront the contending views of their constituents throughout their terms of office.

An alternative account of democratic legitimacy is typically called direct democracy (Cronin 1999). The practices that actualize the ideal of direct democracy are generally thought to come in two forms. One is "assembly democracy," typified by the New England town meeting, in which every adult citizen residing within the relevant jurisdiction is entitled to attend the meeting, help shape the agenda, and vote on public measures. More common, for obvious reasons of scale, are practices that, like candidate elections, are dependent on voting: the referendum and the initiative.[1]

The referendum and the initiative are elections focused on issues, not representatives. A referendum works in combination with a legislative process, typically as a prerequisite to a legislature-adopted measure becoming law. For example, every state but Delaware requires a vote of the people before a legislative proposal for a state constitutional amendment can become law (ibid.: 3). The legislature proposes, but the people must decide. Similarly, local referenda are often prerequisite to issuing bonds or raising certain taxes. By contrast, through the initiative, individual citizens place measures on a public ballot without any imprimatur from elected officials. Assuming some qualifying number of supporters, the initiative is presented for a vote of the electorate. The conclusions of citizens, rather than of their representatives, determine whether the proposal becomes law, and thus the initiative represents the purest form of direct democracy available on a large scale.

Direct democracy locates the moral entitlement of democratic government to rule in the capacity of citizens to determine for themselves the content of the laws that constrain their freedom. Because citizens experiencing these mechanisms are more likely to "experience themselves as free to choose their own political fate" than those who engage only in candidate elections, direct democracy has obvious appeal as a model of democratic legitimacy. It is not surprising that direct democracy ideas are generally popular with the American public; polls usually show support among Americans for direct democracy mechanisms at somewhere between 70 and 80 percent (McKay, Houghton, and Wroe 2002: 91).

It is difficult to see, however, how direct democracy promotes the equal consideration of the interests of all persons. There is no strong linkage between the opportunity for self-actualization through direct democracy and any assurance that the outcome of a referendum or an initiative will actually afford equal consideration. Nothing in the structure of "issue elections" gives any promise that citizens who participate in the vote have become informed of the contending positions or given any thought to the vote's potential impact on the interests of others. There is no way to hold any voter to account for championing a position that is not in the public interest, conscientiously determined (Hamilton 1996–97).

Nor can it be said persuasively that the outcomes of initiatives and referenda are legitimated by popular "consent" to their outcome. Champions of the losing position have not explicitly consented to be governed under the winning position, and theories of "tacit consent" are too acontextual to bear much moral weight. For example, continued residence within a jurisdiction hardly seems persuasive evidence of actual consent when exit costs are enormous and locating better circumstances elsewhere may be problematic (Buchanan 2003). It thus seems unsurprising, in retrospect, that of all the narratives of democratic legitimacy, direct democracy played the least notable role in the framing of our Constitution. The direct role of the people was enshrined, to be sure, in the capacity of popular conventions to ratify and later amend the Constitution.[2] Beyond that, however, our framers seemed to regard accountability to the public interest as the key to republican legitimacy. Direct democracy, being the least accountable form of self-governance, was given virtually no role in the day-to-day operation of American government.

The third model of democratic legitimacy has come to be called deliberative democracy. Under this model, democratic legitimacy is rooted in the position, as articulated by James Bohman and William Rehg, that "legitimate lawmaking issues from the public deliberation of citizens" (Bohman and Rehg 1997: ix). Deliberation, in theories of deliberative democracy, is a special form of rational communication operating in formal arenas and under specified norms (which, pursuant to deliberation, may become further specified). Mere political talk, although it may create a richer environment for deliberation, is not deliberation.

Deliberation was a core aim of the framers in designing a government of multiple branches, and even in envisioning the structure of those branches. In *The Federalist* no. 73, Alexander Hamilton underscored the value of an institutional design that would demand the concurrence of multiple institutions prior to the implementation of public policy: "The oftener [a] measure is brought under examination, the greater the diversity in the situations of those who are to examine it, the less must be the danger of those errors which flow from want of due deliberation, or of those missteps which proceed from the contagion of some common passion or interest" (Hamilton, Alexander, and Jay 1961: 443). He thought the multiple perspectives of the different branches of government were a critical virtue of the deliberative system: "It is far less probable that culpable views of any kind should infect all the parts of the government at the same moment and in relation to the same object than that they should by turns govern and mislead every one of them" (ibid.). This view of the new government carried forward what Hamilton believed was the critically deliberative character of the new nation's constitution-forming experience. "[I]t seems," Hamilton wrote in *The Federalist* no. 1, "to have been reserved to the people of this country, by their conduct and example, to decide the important question, whether societies of men are really capable or not of establishing good government from reflection and choice, or whether they are forever destined to depend for their political constitutions on accident and force" (Hamilton, Alexander, and Jay 1961: 33).

The new governmental design promoted deliberation in part by requiring the concurrence of multiple institutions for government action to move forward. Thus, the president needs Senate approval to ratify treaties or appoint the principal officers of the United States. No legislation may be enacted without the concurrence of the House and Senate and either the signature of the president or extraordinary consensus within the legislature—a two-thirds vote of each chamber. The president has virtually no capacity for domestic initiatives without congressionally enacted authority and appropriations. Each elected branch, because subject to judicial review, is open to the scrutiny of an unelected court. The unelected judiciary, at least in its exercise of criminal adjudication, is subject to review pursuant to the president's pardon power. Lest there be any doubt that such interactions would implicate different institutional perspectives, the Constitution provides that no executive or judicial office holder may be a member of Congress while in office. Thus, when Congress speaks to the executive, the courts to Congress, and so on, the conversation is guaranteed to involve distinctly different voices.

Even where deliberation is not mandatory, the Constitution invites it. It contemplates, for example, that the president will initiate legislative deliberation. He is authorized to "require the opinion, in writing, of the principal officer in each of the executive departments, upon any subject relating to the duties of their respective offices."[3] In addition to our bicameral legislative design and the patent implication that the executive branch will involve multiple departments interacting with the president, the judiciary is also envisioned as a multitiered branch, in which the Supreme Court exercises a limited amount of original jurisdiction but is primarily an appellate court to review the work of other tribunals.

As embodied in our original Constitution, however, the commitment to deliberation falls short of what contemporary theorists mean by deliberative democracy. The Constitution does not connect the deliberations of our government officials to the "public deliberation among citizens" to which Bohman and Rehg refer; our constitutionalized deliberation is chiefly among office holders alone.

In contrast, deliberative democrats of the twenty-first century seek to engage individual citizens in public deliberation. According to virtually all theorists of this model, deliberation under this model should ideally meet five criteria. The first is that the relevant deliberations must be open to all, and all who participate must be able to do so free of coercion. Second, each participant must be treated as an equal. Everyone can speak. Everyone has a voice in shaping the agenda. Everyone can raise questions, debate, and vote on outcomes. The third condition is rationality. Everyone who deliberates agrees to advance positions either by appealing to the common interest or by making arguments of a sort that all participants could accept. The fourth is reflexivity. Anyone can raise questions to the group about whether foundational norms are being respected. Speakers are encouraged to reflect on their own biases. Finally, the reasons for ultimate decision must be public. They must be open to the scrutiny of all, in order that they can again become the subject of yet further deliberation (Cohen 1997).

Given these criteria, the most familiar institutional framework that seems to fit deliberative democracy commitments is the New England town meeting, at least in its ideal form. Indeed, although often cited as an example of direct democracy, the town meeting would seem to draw its legitimating role at least equally from the deliberative democracy model. That is, the town meeting, as direct democrats prefer, offers a special opportunity for citizens to experience themselves as autonomous political actors. A town meeting, however, that is conducted according to the criteria of the deliberative democracy model also offers the promise of overcoming what would otherwise be direct democracy's critical shortcoming: the lack of any mechanism to ensure equal consideration for the interests of all who are affected by the group's decision making.

Deliberative democracy contributes to the equal consideration aspect of legitimacy in two critical ways. First, while the procedures of election-centered or direct democracy take the individual citizen and his or her preferences as given, it is accepted—even intended—that the processes of deliberative democracy will transform the perspective of the individuals who participate. In the words of Arthur Applbaum, "A usable definition of deliberative democracy refers to processes and institutions that aim at changing motivations, and consequently outcomes, for the better" (Applbaum 2002: 24). Thus, although also directly participatory in nature, deliberative democracy rests on ideas of self and identity distinctly different from those associated with initiative and referenda processes. Second, and relatedly, while the deliberative model resembles election-centered models in promising equal regard for the interests of all, such equal regard is achieved not in the accountability of decision makers to the governed, but in the very process of citizen deliberation. That is, the fundamental accountability in deliberative democracy does not run from the governor to the governed, but from each citizen to every other. It is the phenomenon of mutual regard among citizens, with consequent impacts on each citizen's sense of self and collective political identity, that is the key instrument under deliberative democracy for ensuring the equal consideration of all persons' interests.

Beyond the town meeting, this may not sound much like modern American government. But the deliberation-centered account actually resonates, at least to a degree, with a critical aspect of the modern administrative state, namely, federal administrative rule making. Administrative rule making, though hardly a perfect manifestation of ideal deliberative conditions, respects the criteria of deliberative democracy to a significant degree. Anyone can petition a federal agency for the issuance of or change in a rule. Once an agency proposes a rule, anyone can offer comments, which, if at all significant, cannot altogether be ignored by the agency. Should the agency decide to move from proposal to actual promulgation of a rule, its handiwork is subject to judicial review, which is broadly available, even if not exactly to everyone. The agency action may be rebuffed in court if its ultimate reasoning proves irrational, the agency lacked a rational factual basis for its conclusions, or the agency simply failed to account in a rational way for significant objections raised by commentators to the course of action the agency followed. The structure of rule making thus, in at least a modest way, positions the agency in a deliberative dialogue with citizens that links direct citizen input to official government decision making.

The two tables below encapsulate the foregoing analysis of the three models of legitimacy. Table 5.1 links the different models of democratic legitimacy to the degree of importance they attach to individual citizens and elected representatives, respectively, in deciding the content of public policy. Table 5.2 summarizes the primary mechanisms through which each model offers to support the pursuit of democratic legitimacy as I have defined it.

2. The Importance of Thinking Big: The Eclectic Institutionalization of Democratic Legitimacy

The foregoing review of the three models of democratic legitimacy implies, almost without further elaboration, why a project of democratic renewal incorporating elements of each model would be desirable. Each model offers strengths that complement weaknesses in how the others link political practice to democratic legitimacy. The point I want to make is more ambitious, however: ICT-enabled democratic initiatives cannot succeed in revitalizing democracy unless they actually help institutionalize both election-centered and deliberative democracy in a more robust way. There are two straightforward reasons. One is that the causes of contemporary democratic discontent require ambitious efforts to attend to both critical aspects of democratic legitimacy, that is, both the experience of

TABLE 5.1 The Key Actors in Three Models of Democratic Legitimacy

		How important are individual citizens in deciding the content of public policy?	
		Not very important	Central
How important are representatives in deciding the content of public policy?	Central	Election-centered democracy	Deliberative democracy (on other than a small-town scale)
	Not very important	Not a democratic system	Direct democracy

TABLE 5.2 Mechanisms of Legitimation in Three Models of Democracy

	Mechanisms Intended to Ensure the Two Key Components of Democratic Legitimacy	
	Supporting the experience of individual citizens as actors free to choose their own political fate	Fostering the equal consideration of the interests of all persons
Election-centered	Equal suffrage and unlimited participation in democratic conversation	Accountability of government officials to those who elect them
Direct democracy	Equal suffrage, unlimited participation in democratic conversation, and a direct role in framing the content of public policy	No structural mechanism
Deliberative democracy	Participation in civic dialogue under conditions of freedom, equality, reciprocity, reflexivity, and publicness	Development of mutual self-regard among citizens who engage in democratic deliberation

individual political autonomy and the achievement of equal consideration. The second is that any pragmatic democratic program must work on a broad scale, not simply on the level of small towns. Deliberative democracy, while attending ambitiously to both the experiential and fairness sides of democratic legitimacy, cannot be scaled to populations larger than small towns unless elected representatives play a central role. Moreover, on any level, there is no plausible amount of deliberative activity that could address the entire domain of government decision making that is critical to the public interest. On the other hand, deliberative democracy must be part of the reform package because election-centered democracy has not shown itself to be a sufficient guarantor of either the experience of political autonomy or the conscientious consideration of the interests of all persons to counter our current democratic malaise.[4]

Given the limits of this essay, I am going to assume a point that has few dissenters: ours is a time of widespread democratic discontent. In the United States, rates of political knowledge and participation are notoriously low; a sense of helplessness and inability to effect meaningful change is common. To quote Kettering Foundation president and former cabinet secretary David Mathews, many Americans feel as though they have been "forced out of politics by a hostile takeover."[5] The primary causes most often cited for the democratic malaise that seems to pervade the West involve a complex set of interlocking phenomena. These include globalization (which is itself not one thing but many), the marketization or privatization of ever larger aspects of our social and economic life, challenges to the vitality of national political identities supportive of democracy, a pervasive sense that government is increasingly driven by special interests rather than a genuinely public interest, and the alienation of the ordinary citizen from governments that seem increasingly remote and indifferent (Castells 1997). In the wake of these trends, it is not hard to imagine why people feel both that they have no control over their political fate and that their interests are not being seriously considered in the balancing act that produces public policy.

Undemocratic structural features of American politics exacerbate these sources of frustration. The electoral college, as we witnessed in 2000, amplifies the role of our least populous states in choosing the chief executive. We have a legislative upper house in Congress in which the ten most populous states, including over half the U.S. population, elect only 20 percent of the membership, while fifty of the one hundred senators represent states that, in total, contain just over 16 percent of the population of the United States.[6] The fact that we have geographically districted, plurality-winner, first-past-the-post elections for virtually all offices likewise impedes the goal of equal regard for the interests of all citizens (Guinier 1991). The system virtually ensures that the views and values represented in a legislative assembly will not be proportional to the distribution of those views and values in the population at large. The inability of District of Columbia residents to choose voting members of either house of Congress and the postconviction disenfranchisement by many states of felons even after their terms of punishment—a practice that has very substantially diminished the electoral power of African American men—also illustrate antidemocratic tendencies in our political institutions that substantially impede the capacity of elections, directly and indirectly, to sustain a sense of official accountability to "the people." It is altogether plausible that existing structures so entrench the political preferences of a relative few that no procedural changes that leave these structures intact can provide meaningful assurance that all affected interests will be effectively attended to in political discussion. So long as the deck is stacked in these ways, it is hard to see that forms of political participation, off- or online, that are only superficially inclusive will purvey any genuine sense of individual political autonomy for people whose participation never actually appears to affect political outcomes.

On the other hand, opportunities for ICT-enabled advances in political practice in support of both election-centered and deliberative democracy are so numerous, even within existing constraints, that the prospect of their possible transformative impact cannot be dismissed. Let me mention just a few of the innovative practices that are already gaining acceptance, and then offer some thought experiments in which these innovations might be brought to bear on alleviating antidemocratic aspects of current American politics.

Digital ICTs are currently enhancing democratic practice on a global basis. Cellular telephones played a critical role in democratic mobilization during recent elections in Kenya and South Korea.[7] Small handheld computers—personal digital assistants or PDAs—facilitate political organization and data gathering.[8] Most ambitiously, activists have been designing and implementing applications on the World Wide Web to facilitate information sharing, issue advocacy and debate, and the monitoring of elected officials and the candidates seeking to replace them. Web sites provide potential voters with much more easily accessible information about polling places and ballots.[9] New ICTs enable parties, candidates, and advocacy groups to organize volunteers and raise money more readily. We even witnessed in the 2000 presidential election the use of online tools for pledging votes across state lines to help overcome antidemocratic features of our arcane electoral college system (Manjoo 2000).

A wide variety of nongovernmental, nonprofit organizations have undertaken Web-based initiatives to bring citizens, within the confines of single Web sites, a set of useful functionalities for obtaining public information and discussing topics both among themselves and with public officials. The pioneering and arguably most mature effort in this regard is Minnesota E-Democracy (www.e-democracy.org), which hosts discussion forums on state and municipal issues and provides access to a wide range of public policy information (Dahlberg 2001). Interested readers can sign up for e-mail notification of public policy developments within self-identified areas of interest.

At Carnegie Mellon University, a team of e-democracy researchers is developing and testing software involving video, audio, and text-based tools to facilitate online deliberation.[10] An early usability test of the software in January 2004 created an online environment to emulate Deliberative Polling, a form of structured conversation pioneered by political scientist James Fishkin. If successful, such software could be used to assemble groups of citizens online who are chosen to be a statistically sound representative sample of a larger population, groups of representatives selected because of the organizations or interests they stand for, or any other group specifically designated to conduct an online deliberation around public policy. Given that significant experimentation with online consultation is already a global phenomenon (Coleman and Gøtze n.d.), it seems likely that software design will continue to evolve online environments that will emulate and perhaps even surpass many of the virtues linked to face-to-face deliberation.

With this range of existing innovation in the background, let me suggest as a kind of thought experiment the contours for at least one eclectic program for institutionalizing ICT-enhanced democratic practice that would advance legitimacy along both election-based and deliberative dimensions.

On the electoral dimension, three objectives should predominate in government-sponsored efforts to enhance representative accountability through ICTs: improving voter education, enlarging the electorate, and increasing the information available to voters regarding the performance of individual officials. Every jurisdiction that conducts candidate elections should provide accurate ballot information online. It should be possible, by typing one's address, to get accurate information about polling locations and hours. Voter registration should be available online, perhaps in combination with an offline mechanism for authentication and verification. (For example, a voter might register conditionally online, subject to the requirement to return by mail a verification form mailed to the putative voter by the relevant registration authority.) Most important, it should be possible to monitor the actual political conduct of the people for whom we vote. Citizen access to draft legislation, congressional research reports, and the voting records of members of Congress and other legislative bodies would make it far more plausible for nonspecialists to determine whether the people seeking our votes were behaving as advertised during their political campaigns (Corn 2000). None of these objectives would require innovative technology, nor even new institutions. At the federal level, the Congressional Research Service, adequately budgeted, could accomplish all of it.

What would require more creativity is the institutionalization of ICT-enhanced citizen deliberation. Around the world, as in the United States, the "citizen jury" has become an increasingly familiar institution to consult on particular issues facing town, city, and county councils. Imagine putting such an institution online. The relevant authority might employ statistical sampling techniques to qualify an online jury that is representative of the relevant jurisdiction. Jurors might be summoned to public policy jury duty in a manner akin to ordinary jury duty. The hosting agency could enable online access to background information, facilitate deliberation among jurors regarding the contents of specially prepared briefing reports, and survey the participants for the views that develop through that deliberation. Because the governing authority would presumably be bound in some degree to take account of the jury's deliberations in the form of official policy making, the citizen jury would institutionalize a form of direct democracy as well.

Even this sketchy a portrait of a fairly straightforward direct and deliberative e-democracy initiative highlights issues that would themselves have to be resolved by trusted, accountable public institutions—a fact that underscores the importance of pursuing enhanced electoral democracy and enhanced deliberative democracy simultaneously. In order for an online citizen jury to work, decisions would have to made on all of the following subjects, at least:

1. The range of topics on which citizen juries could be made available or that would be legally required, the range of persons authorized to request them, and a process for reviewing such requests
2. The process for identifying and "processing" jurors
3. The functionalities available online for juror education, deliberation, and opinion aggregation
4. The nature and content of background information for jurors and the processes for developing that information
5. The norms for the conduct of actual online deliberation, including how, if at all, it would be moderated and the length and quantity of permissible juror "posts"
6. The forms in which public officials would be bound to take jury results into account in actual decision making, and the opportunities, if any, for formal review of such actions

The questions thus posed of software design, information provision, norm setting, and official response are all politically sensitive and cannot themselves be legitimately addressed except by electorally accountable processes.

Imagine now scaling such an institution to the national level. We can consider a hypothetical congressional effort to create some national deliberative institution that might be designed to help overcome some of the antidemocratic features of our current government structure. Both the House and the Senate might decide to adopt adjunct deliberative institutions with some formal role in the legislative process, for example, providing citizen reports on certain classes of proposed legislation or entitling deliberative participants to place legislative proposals on the floor of either House that each respective chamber would be legally obligated to vote upon within a specified period. The Senate might decide on an institution whose participants were chosen through random sampling techniques but which would allow each state a delegation that corresponded in size to the size of the state's population. Such a scheme could help compensate for the Senate's dramatic malapportionment. Alternatively, the House might decide on a sampling technique designed to provide proportional representation to all political parties, including third parties that meet certain threshold criteria. Such an assembly might help overcome the antidemocratic character of our geographically districted, first-past-the-post, winner-take-all elections. In both cases, enabling the groups to deliberate online would make possible a breadth of inclusion that could not possibly be mustered with an institution whose members meet only face-to-face.[11]

Designing any such institution, face-to-face or otherwise, would entail the same kinds of decisions we could anticipate at the local level concerning systems for representative sampling, the qualifications for participation, and the expectations of participants. Quintessentially political decisions would have to be made about the range of topics eligible for discussion, the degree of consensus necessary to report group "conclusions," the norms governing discussion, appropriate forms of moderation or discussion management, and the trade-off between participant privacy and accountability in terms of the sharing of personal information about participants. The use of ICTs to enable such institutions would entail additional issues of design that implicate political choices in subtle but important ways. The manner in which issues would be presented and discussed online could easily, as deliberation skeptics point out, either privilege or devalue different forms and styles of communication. For example, could participants communicate via text, audio, or video, and in what combination and at which stages of their discussions? The design of the user interface and of the documents supporting discussion would entail choices of rhetoric and symbolism with political significance.

The point is, however, that these advances are technologically feasible. The only "wrong answers" to the question of how best to pursue democratic revitalization through ICTs are to think small, focus exclusively on existing practices, and pursue ICT-enhanced versions of only a single model of democratic legitimacy.

3. Conclusion

The genius of the American constitutional system lay in its blending of eclectic legitimating structures and processes, some resting on the model of election-centered accountability, others on the importance of deliberation to achieving the public interest through governmental action. If any program of electronic democracy is to address significantly the democratic discontents that now beleaguer our constitutional system, that program must also seek to revitalize our politics in both its election-centered and deliberative democratic aspects. Only a combined effort can hope to improve both the experience of political self-determination for American citizens and the likelihood that collective political choices will take fair and consequential account of the interests of all.

It will be noted that I am not making the case that a successful program of ICT-enabled democratic renewal must embrace direct democracy. This may seem surprising, since early e-democracy enthusiasts were especially hopeful about the disintermediating effects of online democratic practices. I believe, however, that the deliberative democracy model, institutionalized ambitiously, might well seem to most citizens to provide so satisfying an experience of individual self-determination—especially in combination with augmented opportunities to participate in electoral politics—that direct democracy would not seem to have all that much to offer in terms of a special or additional legitimating role. This does not mean that including ICT-enabled forms of direct democracy in a program of democratic renewal is necessarily a bad thing, only that it ought not have the same priority as the innovative pursuit of deeper legitimacy along both election-centered and deliberative lines.

The issue of scale would be sufficient, by itself, to require that cyberactivists concern themselves with the revitalization not only of the deliberative aspects of our democratic system but also of our mechanisms of electoral representation. The quality of our political life will always be significantly dependent on the responsiveness of public officials, and there is no democratic mechanism other than elections that can promote accountability as efficiently. But there are two perhaps less obvious reasons for the importance of electoral reform to deliberative democracy. First, the institutionalization of deliberative democracy involves numerous issues of design, control, and interconnection with formal policy making in ways that will inexorably be dependent on public officials. Their oversight of the process will be critical because of substantial concerns that deliberative forums will likely fall short from time to time in being completely hospitable to the interests of all persons and all groups. This is the second reason elections will remain critically important. As political scientists Iris Young and Lynn Sanders have cautioned, efforts (in Sanders's words) to elevate "expertise, moderation, and communal orientation" as norms of public decision making may interfere with "more basic problems of inclusion and mutual recognition" that confront historically underrepresented groups in the United States (Sanders 1997: 370; see also Young 2000). In other words, structural problems of race, class, and gender discrimination may prevent consensus-oriented assemblies from genuinely internalizing the full force of arguments made on behalf of traditionally excluded groups if representatives of those groups are limited to advancing their positions according to norms of deliberation that fail to counter bias. Elections will inevitably remain a critical focus for organizing efforts on behalf of such groups.

The availability of technology to enrich our political life does not guarantee success. But improving democratic legitimacy for twenty-first-century America surely seems a less daunting goal than deciding the issues of institutional design that confronted the original framers in Philadelphia in 1787. If we begin to focus ambitiously on how our existing governmental authorities might promote the institutionalization of new forms of ICT-enabled democratic practice under multiple models of legitimacy, the prospects for linking technological innovation with democratic renewal seem considerable. The discontents as well as the opportunities of our time make the pursuit of that promise an imperative.

Notes

1. The mechanism of recall, often categorized as a form of direct democracy, is more sensibly regarded as part of the election-centered model of democratic legitimacy. Like the referendum and the initiative, it was part of the Progressive Era's agenda of expanding popular control over state legislative processes, especially in the West, South, and Midwest. Progressives argued that state legislatures in these parts of the country had been significantly captured by railroads, banks, utilities, and other economic "special interests," whether

through back-room cajolery or outright bribery, and that democracy could be repurified only by giving voters more direct control over the legislators and their policy agenda (McKay, Houghton, and Wroe 2002). The prospect of recall, at least in principle, offers this potential. But it does not expand the direct power of citizens to set a legislature's policy agenda in any meaningful way. Even if a recall is prompted by voter discontent on a single issue and thus functions as a sort of quasi-referendum, the replacement of an individual legislator will not ensure a different collective legislative resolution. Moreover, given the bundle of issues on which every legislator must express a view, the generalized threat of recall seems unlikely to constrain a legislator very substantially. Thus, the recall possibility can do little to elevate individual participation in political decision making on specific issues. A more reasonable expectation of the recall possibility is that it could strengthen the internalization of accountability that underlies election-centered narratives of democratic legitimacy.

2. U.S. Constitution, Articles V and VII.

3. Ibid., Article II, sec. 2, par. 1.

4. Of course, this could be the result, in a large part, of contingent social, economic, and political conditions. Perhaps it is only with our electoral rules, or because of current patterns of economic and social inequality, that U.S. elections do not provide enough pressure on public officials to ensure genuinely equal consideration for the interests of all persons. One can imagine elections doing somewhat better in this regard if far more Americans voted far more regularly, and there might be yet more considerable improvement if all elections were publicly funded. There seems little immediate prospect of the latter, however, and the salience of special-interest money is exacerbated by antidemocratic structural features in our electoral rules and institutional structures, which are discussed in the text below. In summation, it seems dubious, even at higher levels of electoral activity, to expect that elected officials will become conscientiously accountable to all their constituents' interests while the scope of political participation for most citizens remains limited to their episodic role as voters.

5. Mathews is quoted at the Kettering Foundation Web site, http://www.kettering.org/Who_We_Are/who_we_are.html (accessed March 2004).

6. State population figures appear at http://www.census.gov/population/www/cen2000/phc-t2.html (accessed April 20, 2003).

7. Geoffrey York, "In South Korea, It's the Mouse That Roars: New Breed of Politician Taps the Country's Love Affair with High Tech," in Steven Clift, "[DW] South Korea—THE Net Election—New DO-Korea E-List," posting to Democracies Online Newswire, December 30, 2002, available at http://www.mail-archive.com/do-wire@tc.umn.edu/msg00588.html (accessed March 2004); Steven Clift, "[DW] Role of ICTs and Kenya Elections," posting to Democracies Online Newswire, December 30, 2002, available at http://www.mail-archive.com/do-wire@tc.umn.edu/msg00587.html (accessed March 2004).

8. Steven Clift, "[DW] Net and the Elections, News Links, Politics Online Analysis," posting to Democracies Online Newswire, November 4, 2002, available at http://www.mail-archive.com/do-wire@tc.umn.edu/msg00560.html (accessed March 2004).

9. Hamilton, Madison, and Jay would be proud that a leading example can be found at http://www.publius.org.

10. For additional background, see "Pittsburgh's By the People Citizen's Deliberation," available at http://caae.phil.cmu.edu/caae/dp/ (accessed March 2004).

11. This does not at all exhaust the possibilities. One can imagine a network of small deliberative bodies throughout the United States, operating online at least in part, that would fulfill Thomas Jefferson's vision of pervasive "ward" meetings. Each ward could assign representatives to yet higher-level virtual meetings, until a national "Web congress" molded the various positions into something approaching a consensus framework on an important issue. Philosopher Howard DeLong has imagined a congressionally authorized Court of Common Reason, which would draw a representative sample of Americans to use as an advisory jury on public policy issues. ICT-enabled citizen juries could thus be used at every

level of government to provide advice or even to place proposals mandatorily on the government's decision-making agenda.

References

Applbaum, Arthur. 2002. "Failure in the Cybermarketplace of Ideas." In Elaine Ciulla Kamarch and Joseph S. Nye Jr., eds., *Governance.Com: Democracy in the Information Age*. Washington, DC: Brookings Institution.

Becker, Ted, and Christa Daryl Slaton. 2000. *The Future of Teledemocracy*. Westport, CT: Praeger.

Bennett, Robert W. 1997. "Democracy as Meaningful Conversation." *Constitutional Commentary* 14: 481–533.

Bohman, James, and William Rehg. 1997. *Deliberative Democracy: Essays on Reason and Politics*. Cambridge, MA: MIT Press.

Buchanan, Allen. 2002. "Political Legitimacy and Democracy." *Ethics* 112, 4: 689–722.

Castells, Manuel. 1997. *The Power of Identity*. Oxford: Blackwell.

Clift, Steven. 2000. *The E-Democracy E-Book: Democracy Is Online 2.0*. Available at http://www.publicus.net/ebook/edemebook.html.

Cohen, Joshua. 1997. "Deliberation and Democratic Legitimacy." In Robert Goodin and Philip Pettit, eds., *Contemporary Political Philosophy: An Anthology*. Oxford: Blackwell.

Coleman, Stephen and John Gøtze. n.d. "Bowling Together: Online Public Engagement in Policy Deliberation." Available at http://www.bowlingtogether.net/.

Corn, David. 2000. "Filegate.gov." *Wired*, November. Available at http://www.wired.com/wired/archive/8.11/govdocs.html.

Cronin, Thomas E. 1999. *Direct Democracy: The Politics of Initiative, Referendum and Recall*. Cambridge, MA: Harvard University Press.

Dahlberg, Lincoln. 2001. "Extending the Public Sphere Through Cyberspace: The Case of Minnesota E-Democracy." *First Monday*, 6. Available at http://www.firstmonday.dk/issues/issue6_3/dahlberg/.

Farina, Cynthia R. 1997. "The Consent of the Governed: Against Simple Rules for a Complex World." *Chicago-Kent Law Review* 72: 987–1037.

Guinier, Lani. 1991. "The Triumph of Tokenism: The Voting Rights Act and the Theory of Black Electoral Success." *Michigan Law Review* 89, 5: 1077–54.

Hamilton, Alexander, James Madison, and John Jay. 1961. *The Federalist Papers*. Ed. Clinton Rossiter. New York: New American Library.

Hamilton, Marci A. 1996–97. "The People: The Least Accountable Branch." *University of Chicago Law School Roundtable* 4: 1–16.

Keyssar, Alexander. 2000. *The Right to Vote: The Contested History of Democracy in the United States*. New York: Basics Books.

Manjoo, Farhad. 2000. "Vote Trade: The Democratic Way?" *Wired News*, October 31. Available at http://www.wired.com/news/politics/0,1283,39860,00.html.

McKay, David, David Houghton, and Andrew Wroe. 2002. *Controversies in American Politics and Society*. Oxford: Blackwell.

Post, Robert C. 1995. *Constitutional Domains: Democracy, Community, Management*. Cambridge, MA: Harvard University Press.

Sanders, Lynn M. 1997. "Against Deliberation." *Political Theory* 25, 3: 347–76.

Shane, Peter M. 1999. "Reflections in Three Mirrors: Complexities of Representation in a Constitutional Democracy." *Ohio State Law Journal* 60: 693–709.

Wood, Gordon S. 1969. *The Creation of the American Republic, 1776–1787*. New York: W. W. Norton.

Young, Iris. 2000. *Inclusion and Democracy*. Oxford: Oxford University Press.

CHAPTER 6

Global Governance and Electronic Democracy: E-Politics as a Multidimensional Experience

 OREN PEREZ*

The globalization process has created a new realm of governance, which takes place outside the traditional boundaries of the state system. This new realm is led by multiple and highly diverse institutions—from the World Bank to the World Trade Organization and the new governance body of the Internet, the Internet Corporation for Assigned Names and Numbers (ICANN)—which enjoy increasing levels of autonomy. These new institutions hold vast influence over the life of the global citizenry. However, their legitimacy is deeply contested. The persistent protests against globalization provide a powerful indication of the depth of the opposition to these transnational bodies.[1] This opposition is based on two principal lines of critique: the first focuses on the nondemocratic nature of these global institutions, the second on their insensitivity to social and humanitarian concerns.

*I am grateful to the organizers of the conference "Prospects for Electronic Democracy," hosted by the Institute for the Study of Information Technology and Society, H. J. Heinz III School of Public Policy and Management, Carnegie Mellon University (September 20–21, 2002), and to the Florence Unger and Samuel Goldstein, M.D., Interdisciplinary Center for Law, Rationality, Ethics, and Social Justice for financial support. I would like to thank Nancy Marder, Tom Beierle, and Yoram Egosi for comments on an earlier draft of this essay.

The critiques of globalization use the notion of legitimacy both in a procedural sense, as a measure of consent and control, and in a more substantial sense, as a measure of moral adequacy. This chapter focuses on the first perspective.[2] This perspective measures the legitimacy of a transnational regime in terms of its willingness to open up its rule-making processes to external critique and participation. It constructs the challenge of legitimacy as a problem of institution design: of creating institutional structures that will allow the (global) public to take part, in a meaningful way, in the game of global governance.

The current global legal-political universe does not come close, however, to this democratic ideal. First, the still highly fragmented structure of the global state system does not provide a suitable framework for deliberating and reflecting on global dilemmas. Neither is there any global political framework that could serve as an alternative forum to the state system. This "democratic deficit" reflects, among other things, the lack of a coherent democratic tradition at the global level, and a deep disagreement about the proper face of a future global democratic order. In practice the global public remains, to a large extent, detached from the institutional processes that produce global law. With the increasing encroachment of transnational legal structures into the nation-state, this detachment is becoming highly problematic—at least from the view of consent-based legitimacy.[3]

The question this chapter seeks to explore is whether the Internet, as a new kind of communicative arena, can contribute to the development of more inclusive (global) decision-making structures. The capacity of the Internet to transcend barriers of distance and time makes it, at least prima facie, an ideal forum for hosting border-crossing political dialogue. Indeed, the Internet already serves as a host to substantial flows of (global-oriented) political communication. Web sites such as Protest.Net (http://www.protest.net), the Independent Media Center (http://www.indymedia.org), WebActive (http://webactive.com), and CorpWatch (http://www.corpwatch.org) operate as international hubs of political communication.[4] These sites serve not just as forums for deliberation but also as a means for coordinating political activity on the streets (e.g., protests at meetings of international organizations). This extensive political usage of the Net caused many commentators to argue that the Internet could revolutionize the face of global politics.[5] However, despite the impressive growth of civic protest on the Internet, and contrary to these revolutionary expectations, the influence of these electronically mediated activities has been quite limited; they remain tangential to the places in which governance is produced and exercised.[6]

I will argue that the Internet does have the potential to change the ways in which we both do and experience politics on the global level. In discussing the unique potential of the Internet, I will focus on one specific feature of the Internet, its multidimensionality—its ability to support multiple forms of deliberation and decision-making structures simultaneously. This feature opens new possibilities for structuring participatory processes. The main argument of this chapter is that the Internet can extend the universe of our democratic practices by enabling the development of multiple forms of deliberation and decision making. As such, it offers a way to cope with the difficult challenge of designing inclusive decision-making structures for a deeply pluralistic society (such as the world society). The introduction of the Internet thus can do more than merely reduce the various transaction costs that the political endeavor generates.[7] Indeed, I will argue that many contemporary projects of e-democracy miss the unique potential of the Internet by copying offline democratic practices "as is" into the Internet.

The first part of this chapter offers a review and critique of the unidimensional structure of contemporary democratic institutions. This critique leads to a first formulation of the multidimensionality thesis. The next section develops and extends the chapter's general argument with respect to the multidimensional potential of the Internet, elucidating the concept of multidimensionality and exploring how the Internet can contribute to the design of multidimensional democratic processes. The concluding section discusses several remaining dilemmas and challenges.

1. A Critique of the Unidimensional Structure of Contemporary Democratic Institutions

The idea of democracy is based on two underlying principles: a respect for the autonomy of the citizen and a belief in the value of equality. A democratic regime that realizes these principles should be based, I will argue, on a multidimensional model of deliberation and decision making. Contemporary democratic processes do not satisfy this requirement. In making this claim, I do not mean to argue that contemporary democratic governance structures—international or national—are completely unidimensional.[8] Rather, my argument concentrates on certain focal points of the democratic process, such as voting and public participation in rule making, that are fundamental to the democratic enterprise.

How do the notions of equality and autonomy (or freedom) fit into the concept of democracy? Equality requires that each member of the community should be given an equal opportunity to participate in a meaningful way (i.e., in a way that would provide him or her with some influence) in the decision-making process that produces the norms by which this community is governed. Autonomy requires that participants in a democratic process be able to express their independent and uncoerced judgment over the debated issue. These two notions play a key role in the characterization of democracy as a fair system of governance.[9] The way in which these two ideals have been translated into concrete institutional practices in Western societies and in international institutions reflects a highly uniform conception of the democratic process, calling into doubt its fairness and legitimacy.

A good example of this uniform conception involves the act of voting, which still constitutes the principal form of collective decision making in today's democracies. As the quintessence of democratic life, voting is expected to fulfill the dual requirements of autonomy and equality. These conditions require that "votes reflect voters' independent, uncoerced judgments, and that all votes are weighted equally" (Ansolabehere 2001). To achieve these requirements, voting is usually structured in a deeply uniform fashion, reflecting an attempt to ensure equal participatory conditions. Thus, the voting process usually takes place in highly uniform spatiotemporal conditions. Citizens vote at a specified time interval (identical for all), in highly comparable spaces (voting booths), and in a similar fashion (using the same voting technology).[10] Similar formalism characterizes the legal treatment of voting. Thus, for example, the Fifteenth Amendment of the U.S. Constitution provides that the "right of citizens of the United States to vote shall not be denied or abridged by the United States or by any State on account of race, color or previous condition of servitude." This negative formulation of the right to vote, which seeks to ensure both the equality and the autonomous character of voting, reflects a shallow understanding of these notions. Thus, for example, this provision disregards the important question of the capacity of citizens to participate in the democratic process. This question has practical consequences: should the procedures of voting be sensitive to the uneven capacities of various citizens? Should the government develop programs—such as educational initiatives—to ensure that citizens have the knowledge and necessary competencies to participate in democratic processes?[11] The design of the voting act was influenced by this legal formulation.

This procedural uniformity, which permeates the practice and discourse of "democracy," is not compatible with the reality of social and individual pluralism that characterizes the global society.[12] This incompatibility undermines the capacity of our contemporary democratic institutions to offer a fair system of collective governing. Let me explain first what I mean by "social pluralism." The notion of social pluralism designates two types of diversity, or double diversity: the first at the level of society, the second at the level of the individual. The first type of diversity is based on a vision of society as an amalgam of multiple discourses, none of which enjoys a privileged status. This worldview questions the possibility of reaching agreement with respect to social dilemmas. If the participants in a collective conversation can invoke different but equally valid discourses (each employing different criteria for validation) and, further, have highly different innate structures, the prospects for reaching consensual agreement seem very small (Luhmann 1996; McCarthy 1996: 1121).

The second form of diversity refers to the human profile of the demos; it depicts people as having distinct innate structures. This diversity has many features. It refers to cultural imprint ("baggage"), cognitive capacities, psychological profile, level of interest in public activities and concerns, and financial resources. These differences influence the way in which people respond to external perturbations; more generally, they influence the way in which people lead their lives (Hamburger 2002). Diversity at the individual (personality) level can influence the way in which people react to the Internet. These potential influences have only recently started to be investigated by psychologists. One such influence concerns people's differing needs for "closure" (ibid.: 6). People who have a high need for closure are motivated to avoid uncertainties. They tend to "freeze" the epistemic process. People with a low need for closure, in contrast, cope better with multiple choices and uncertain situations (ibid.). This difference can influence the way in which these distinct types react to the structure of Web sites: "people who have a high need for closure, namely, a need to have a structured and defined process of decision making, will find the mass of hyperlinks distracting and unnecessary; whereas those people with a low need for closure will feel better in an Internet environment surrounded by hyperlinks" (ibid.). Other personality traits that can influence Internet use, and thus contribute to the exclusion of some user types, are gender differences (Dahlberg 2001; Herring 1993), levels of extroversion and neuroticism, capacity for innovation, and attitudes toward risk and self-control (Hamburger 2002: 6–8).

If this two-fold diversity of human society is taken seriously, then the taken-for-granted uniformity of the democratic process should be reexamined. If people have diverse capacities and, further, can invoke distinct and equally valid discursive modules, there is no reason to assume that they can be fitted—as members of a democratic order—into a unidimensional decision-making process. This is particularly true when we move from the national to the international level. A decision to adopt an invariant decision-making framework is, therefore, necessarily discriminatory; it will usually have the effect of favoring a particular discursive perspective and a particular citizen profile.[13] To the extent that the idea of equality is interpreted as an instrument for constructing a fair system of governance, it should not lead, then, to an identity of form, but rather to a diversity of deliberative or decision-making structures. It is only by constructing governance as a multiform experience that we can hope to create the conditions for fair participation, which will enable the members of a community, despite their innate differences, to participate in the joint management of their lives. Creating fair conditions for participation is an essential step in the attempt to achieve legitimate governance.

This argument exposes a dialectical tension between the ideas of autonomy and equality. To respect the autonomy of your fellow citizens means to accept them as potentially different. A strict interpretation of equality (in the context of democratic procedures) is inconsistent with this requirement because it does not allow your fellow citizens to express themselves as fully autonomous members of the community. A formalistic under-standing of equality could lead, then, to a de facto denial of autonomy.[14]

2. The Internet as a Multidimensional Medium

To the extent that democracy is seen as an attempt to forge a legitimate system of governance for a pluralistic society, it should be able to deal fairly with the multiplicity of personalities and worldviews that coexist within that society. Achieving this requires a multidimensional framework of deliberation and decision making, which will transcend traditional democratic practices.[15] The Internet constitutes a space in which this mul-tidimensional vision can be realized.

This argument seeks to go beyond current uses of the Internet, which merely copy offline democratic practices onto the Internet. Before present-ing my argument about the multidimensional potential of the Internet, I would like to make two preliminary comments. The first seeks to make more explicit what I mean by "electronic democracy" or "electronic par-ticipation." The second adds another layer to the critique of current demo-cratic practices.

The argument here is based on a conception of democracy as a compre-hensive political framework that permeates all aspects of governance. Elec-tion-based democracy does not fit this definition because its principal participatory mechanism—election for office—does not offer the citizenry a real opportunity to influence the day-to-day administration of gover-nance. A comprehensive political regime should offer its citizenry, then, more than a right to influence the composition of certain decision-making bodies; it should incorporate its citizenry into the multiple decision-making structures through which political power is realized. This means an opportunity to take part in important policy decisions, decisions over resource allocation, and the legislation of new norms.[16] In the trans-national context, this vision calls for allowing the public to take an active and direct part in the work of international organizations. Indeed, if democracy is interpreted just as giving the public an opportunity to elect certain office holders, there is not much room for variation at the user interface level (there are not that many ways to present a choice between several candidates).[17]

How does the Internet fit into this democratic vision? I will distinguish in this context between three different forms of electronic democracy. The argument with respect to the multidimensional potential of the Internet applies, I believe, to each of these different forms. First, the Internet con-stitutes an efficient mean for achieving transparency. Transparency is a necessary condition for the evolution of meaningful deliberation. Second, the Internet can be used by a government or an international organization (henceforth referred to collectively as political agencies) to elicit public comments or votes on its normative output. Here, the Internet is used to facilitate unidirectional communication: the political agency, placed at the receiving end, is responsible for collecting, interpreting, and judging the comments of the public or, in the case of voting, for aggregating the public votes. The process of deliberation and voting is controlled by the political agency. Finally, the Internet can be used also to facilitate wide-ranging dialogue between the institution and the public (and within the public), that is, multidirectional communication. Under this model, none of the communicators has exclusive control over the timing and content of communications. Only this last option comes near the ideal picture of directly deliberative democracy.

The procedural uniformity of our contemporary democratic institutions is not just a product of political choices. It is also a reflection of certain spatiotemporal constraints. Using multiple formats for voting or deliberation can be highly demanding in terms of spatial and temporal resources. To understand these limitations, imagine that in the pluralistic society of Ersilia half of the community can think freely only when they are surrounded by green walls, while the other half can function properly only in an environment of total whiteness. To fulfill the special needs of the citizens of Ersilia, the elections would have to be conducted in parallel buildings, half of them painted green, half painted white. And if these distinct individual types are equally distributed across Ersilia, this unique demand will require either a doubling of voting space or conducting the voting over a longer period of time (e.g., two days), changing the color of the voting space midway through. However, since time and space are scarce resources, this solution could be highly expensive. Thus, if the green types do not constitute half of the community but instead are a minority group, it might be tempting to succumb to the taste of the majority, leaving all rooms white and hoping that the green types could somehow cope.[18] This social scarcity in time and space has influenced the design of democratic practices both in theory and in practice.

The emergence of the Internet frees us (to some extent) from these limitations. It allows us to simultaneously offer multiple forms of deliberation and decision-making structures, which could cater to different individual profiles and utilize varied discursive frameworks. Thus, the Internet can allow us to maintain and operate simultaneously different voting environments (e.g., different colors) that might appeal to different voters (as long as these voters can be identified—for example, through a process of self-selection).[19] Note that this argument applies equally to each of the three forms of e-democracy. The Internet can support multiple formats of presentation, which can cater to different types of users (transparency). In the case of unidirectional communication, the Internet can support multiple forms of soliciting comments from the public. Finally, the Internet can support varied environments for conversation among multiple individuals. Constructing these multiple formats does not depend on scarce spatial resources (e.g., meeting halls), since the Internet, which is a highly malleable medium, can be divided into distinct forums at a much lower cost. Furthermore, the Internet allows us to operate these diverse political forums or decision-making structures simultaneously. In contrast, constructing pluralistic procedures in the offline world would require either expansive investment in spatial (or other tangible) resources or a sequential use of the same spatial resource. The Internet enables us, therefore, to bring the democratic process—in spite of any procedural diversity—to a conclusion at a single (common) point in time.

To appreciate the foregoing argument, it might be useful to consider an example of an e-democracy initiative: Dick Morris and Eileen McGann's Web site, Vote.com. Vote.com is presented by its founders as "a fully interactive web site designed to give Internet users a voice on important public issues and other topics."[20] This is achieved by giving the visitors to the site an opportunity to vote on an issue (picked by the site managers) by choosing between two competing answers to a question put by the site-managers. Recent debates focused on the question of George Bush's attendance at the Earth Summit in Johannesburg, on whether the international community should introduce mandatory limits on greenhouse gases, and on whether the State of Florida should repeal a law that bans gays from adopting children.[21] The voters are offered a short exposition (forty to fifty words) of two competing views on the debated question and are asked to cast their votes on the basis of this information plus any prior knowledge. This scheme merely copies the usual polling technique into the Web, offering a uniform experience to all its users.

It should be emphasized, finally, that the argument with respect to the multidimensional capacity of the Internet holds true even if the assumption of double diversity is relaxed. Thus, even if one believes in the existence of a common discursive framework, which could ensure that any public debate will be resolved through rational deliberation (thus rejecting the thesis of discursive multiplicity), one might still find the multidimensional thesis appealing. This will be the case if one accepts the argument that a uniform decision-making or discursive framework necessarily discriminates against certain types of people due to cultural, psychological, or other personal differences (remember Ersilia). Thus, even if there is social agreement on the substantive criteria that should guide the decision-making endeavor, one can still make a strong argument for the need for multidimensional decision-making schemes.

3. Conclusion

The argument of the preceding sections raises a difficult challenge: is it possible to design a decision-making scheme that will be pluralistic—in the procedural sense suggested in this chapter—but, at the same time, be able to produce binding decisions? These conflicting demands—functionality and pluralistic sensitivity—create a difficult dilemma. If the decision-making scheme utilizes different discursive frames—each employing different criteria for validation—it is not clear on what basis the decision maker (whether the community or a single agent) can reach a decision in cases in which the distinct criteria lead to conflicting results. Designing a process that would be both fair (in terms of its sensitivity to various discourses and individual types) and reasonably efficient (in terms of its ability to generate conclusive results) might be an impossible task.

However, the fact that a complete solution to the tension between functionality and pluralistic sensitivity is probably not attainable does not mean that we should abandon the effort to improve the governance practices of our global institutions. It calls, rather, for a different constitutional strategy, which will replace the search for unitary governing structures with a polycentric and experimental approach.[22] The multidimensional thesis thus calls for a reorientation of our democratic intuitions; for exchanging the aspiration for consensual coexistence with a more modest hope—to build a society that can accommodate perpetual disagreements (McCarthy 1996; Teubner 1996).[23] Achieving this accommodation requires imagination, willingness to experiment, and an attitude of tolerance toward the other.

The argument of this essay follows this path; it does not seek to offer a complete resolution to the challenge of legitimate governance. Rather, it seeks to offer new paths for experimentation by focusing on the unique capacities of the Internet as a political medium. Using the Internet can enrich the participatory horizon of global institutions to the extent that they are willing to experiment with democratic ideas. Developing e-democracy initiatives does not necessarily require a radical departure from current constitutional structures; it could be implemented at the micro (operational) level of the organization, achieving still-significant results on the ground. The lack of an entrenched democratic tradition at the transnational level suggests that at this micro level one should find substantial space for experimentation. A good example is the administrative process of environmental impact assessment.[24] In contrast, the continued disagreement about the proper form of global democracy means that it would probably be quite difficult to change the constitutional core of many of the more established global institutions.[25]

The Internet opens new ways for imagining politics. These new paths could be especially important at the transnational level because of the deeply pluralistic nature of the global domain. To utilize this potential, however, we must free ourselves from the conventions of the offline world and from the temptation to transplant the practices of the offline world unchanged onto the Internet.

Notes.

1. For a detailed account of the antiglobalization movement, see the special report on globalization at the *Guardian* Web site, http://www.guardian.co.uk/globalisation (accessed September 1, 2003).

2. Substantive or nonprocedural accounts of legitimacy associate the term with a certain understanding of the common good. The main problem with this view is that it depends on the existence of an agreed-upon definition of the "common good." Without such shared understanding—commonly missing in pluralistic societies—it is hard to achieve legitimacy in this sense.

3. See, e.g., Mark C. Gordon, *Democracy's New Challenge: Globalization, Governance, and the Future of American Federalism* (New York: Demos, 2001).

4. Other leading Web sites include those of Fairness and Accuracy in Reporting (http://www.fair.org), IV Ciranda (http://www.ciranda.net), and Eurostep (http://www.eurostep.org). All of these Web sites include details of protests around the world, action alerts, and links to other protest Web sites.

5. See, for example: "The Changing Face of Protest," *Financial Times*, July 31–August 1, 1999, 12; Guy de Jonquie, "Network Guerrillas," *Financial Times*, April 30, 1998.

6. See, e.g., Oren Perez, "The Many Faces of the Trade-Environment Conflict: Some Lessons for the Constitutionalization Project," *European Integration Online Papers* 6, 11 (2002), available at http://eiop.or.at/eiop/texte/2002-011a.htm (accessed September 1, 2003).

7. These include the cost of individual participation (e.g., in the case of voting, the time a voter needs to become informed about the alternatives and the time it takes to actually cast a vote) and the cost of group mobilization (e.g., coordinating support for a certain cause or candidate).

8. Thus, for example, one can refer to the following elements in any governance or rule-making regime: the election of legislators, the lobbying of legislators, the independent work of administrative agencies that were endowed with certain powers by the legislating body (which are again subject to lobbying), the work of advisory committees, processes of public notice and comment on draft rules, and judicial review of rules and their application. Note, however, that to the extent that these elements create a multilayered system of governance, this multidimensionality is a product of temporal and spatial differentiation.

9. See further on this point Stephen Ansolabehere, "The Search for New Voting Technology," *Boston Review* October-November 2001, available at http://www.bostonreview.net/BR26.5/ansolabehere.html (accessed March 2004).

10. The term "voting technology" refers to the way in which the various alternatives are presented to the voter, the method in which the voter is supposed to cast a vote, and the way in which the votes are counted.

11. The right to informed participation (e.g., voting) was interpreted, traditionally, as a "social right" (rather like the right to education) and not as a constitutional right; social rights are still seen, however, as an "inferior" category of rights. For a more detailed treatment of the right to vote and the issue of social rights under U.S. law, see William Cohen and David J. Danelski, *Constitutional Law: Civil Liberty and Individual Rights* (Westbury, NY: Foundation Press, 1997).

12. One can find echoes of this uniform conception of the democratic act in the writings of prominent political theorists such as Jürgen Habermas and John Rawls. See, e.g., John Rawls, *A Theory of Justice.* (Cambridge, MA.: Harvard University Press, 1971), and Jürgen Habermas, "Paradigms of Law," *Cardozo Law Review* 17 (1996): 771–84.

13. For an empirical analysis of patterns of exclusion in a real-world e-participation scheme, see Lincoln Dahlberg, "Extending the Public Sphere Through Cyberspace: The Case of Minnesota E-Democracy," *First Monday* 6, available at http://www.firstmonday.dk/issues/issue6_3/dahlberg/ (accessed September 1, 2003).

14. For a similar argument, see Daniel R. Ortiz, "Democratic Values?" *Boston Review* October-November 2001, available at http://www.bostonreview.net/BR26.5/ortiz.html. The debate about the "proper" place and interpretation of the idea of equality is an old debate and has been examined in numerous articles. For two recent contributions, see Christopher J. Peters, "Equality Revisited," *Harvard Law Review* 110 (1997): 1210–64. and Kenneth W. Simons, "The Logic of Egalitarian Norms," *Boston University Law Review* 80 (2000):

693–771. I do not intend to review in this chapter the various manifestations of this debate. However, it might be worthwhile to note in brief in what way the perspective of this chapter differs from the traditional frame of this debate. The question of equality is usually invoked in the context of the distribution of treatments or resources within society. My argument, however, focuses on what is usually considered an unproblematic application of the notion of formal equality—the homogenous structure of the procedures of democracy.

15. Further support to this thesis can be found in recent attempts to develop new and varied participatory mechanisms in the offline world. See, e.g., in the environmental context: U.S. Environmental Protection Agency, "Engaging the American People: A Review of EPA's Public Participation Policy and Regulations with Recommendations for Action" (Washington, D.C.: EPA, 2000), and David M. Konisky and Thomas C. Beierle, "Innovations in Public Participation and Environmental Decision Making: Examples from the Great Lakes Region," *Society and Natural Resources* 14 (2001).

16. For a more detailed explication of the idea of directly deliberative democracy, see, e.g., Joshua Cohen and Charles Sabel, "Directly-Deliberative Polyarchy," *European Law Journal* 3 (1997): 313–42.

17. The question of user interface should be distinguished from the question of counting or preference aggregation. Even in the simple case of voting on candidates (simple in the sense of being a highly structured choice dilemma), there are many ways of aggregating voters' choices: plurality voting, Borda counting, Condorcet's pair ranking, and others. See Jonathan Levin and Barry Nalebuff, "An Introduction to Vote-Counting Schemes," *Journal of Economic Perspectives* 9 (1995): 3–26. The problem of aggregation becomes more difficult as the choice dilemma becomes less structured. I return to this question below.

18. The case of blind voters creates a similar dilemma. Is it enough just to grant blind citizens the right to be assisted in voting by someone of their choice; or should society develop voting technologies that will enable them to vote without help—which is more compatible with the interpretation of equality and autonomy suggested above? In the United States, many jurisdictions believe that providing blind people with assistance exhausts their equality obligations to the blind, and they make no effort to support technologies that would enable blind people to vote in secret without assistance. See Ortiz, "Democratic Values?" Would we accept such a position if the blind were not such a small minority? This dilemma raises interesting questions with respect to the proper scope of the Americans with Disabilities Act.

19. Another example concerns the difficulty of holding elections in a multilingual society. See Ortiz, "Democratic Values?" Under the Voting Rights Act, every jurisdiction in the United States must make voting materials available in the appropriate language to any minority language group that accounts for at least 5 percent of the jurisdiction's voting-age population. This law means that highly pluralistic counties have to provide voting materials in a large number of languages. Ortiz notes that in the next decade Los Angeles County, for example, will have to provide voting materials in more than ten different languages. This problem has clear technological implications. Traditional and optically scanned paper ballots make satisfying this requirement very difficult. If every ballot (and supporting materials) has to be printed in more than ten different forms, the expense quickly becomes unsustainable and paper management becomes highly complicated. In view of this problem Los Angeles and Riverside Counties, which are both linguistically diverse, have chosen to use punch card machines and direct-recording electronic devices. Neither requires expensive preparation of physical materials to make the ballot accessible to minority language groups. Internet voting should allow similar flexibility.

20. "What Is Vote.com?" available at http://www.vote.com/about_us.phtml?cat'4075633 (accessed September 1, 2003).

21. A detailed description of the debates and their results can be found at the Web site of Vote.com through the search function. The Earth Summit debate was posted on August 15, 2002, the debate on mandatory limits on greenhouse gases was posted on June 04, 2002, and the debate on the Florida statute was posted on March 26, 2002.

22. For a similar argument, see Elinor Ostrom, "The Danger of Self-Evident Truths," *Political Science* 33 (2000): 33–44.

23. Maturana similarly argues that living in a "multiversa" means that we, as observers, live "in many different, equally legitimate, but not equally desirable, explanatory realities, and that

in it an explanatory disagreement is an invitation to a responsible reflection of coexistence, and not an irresponsible negation of the other." Humberto R. Maturana, "Reality: The Search for Objectivity or the Quest for a Compelling Argument," *Irish Journal of Psychology* 9 (1988): 25–81.

24. A interesting attempt to design innovative environmental assessment mechanism is the Urban Lifestyles, Sustainability and Integrated Environmental Assessment (ULYSSES) project—a European research project on public participation in integrated assessment. See http://zit1.zit.tu-darmstadt.de/ulysses/index.htm (accessed September 1, 2003).

25. This constitutional core is very much influenced by the Westphalian tradition, which emphasizes the role of the state as the exclusive representative of the people and gives little credit to the idea of direct deliberation. Newly established institutions—such as ICANN—should probably be more willing to experiment with democratic models even at the basic constitutional level.

References

Ansolabehere, Stephen. 2001. "The Search for New Voting Technology." *Boston Review,* October-November. Available at http://www.bostonreview.net/BR26.5/ansolabehere.html.

Cohen, Joshua, and Charles Sabel. 1997. "Directly-Deliberative Polyarchy." *European Law Journal* 3: 13–42.

Cohen, William, and David J. Danelski. 1997. *Constitutional Law: Civil Liberty and Individual Rights.* Westbury, NY: Foundation Press.

Dahlberg, Lincoln. 2001. "Extending the Public Sphere through Cyberspace: The Case of Minnesota E-Democracy." *First Monday* 6. Available at http://www.firstmonday.dk/issues/issue6_3/dahlberg/.

Gordon, Mark C. 2001. *Democracy's New Challenge: Globalization, Governance, and the Future of American Federalism,* New York: Demos.

Habermas, Jürgen. 1996. "Paradigms of Law." *Cardozo Law Review* 17: 771–84.

Hamburger, Y. A. 2002. "Internet and Personality." *Computers in Human Behavior* 18: 1–10.

Herring, Susan C. 1993. "Gender and Democracy in Computer-Mediated Communication." *Electronic Journal of Communication* 3: 1–17.

Konisky, David M. and Thomas C. Beierle. 2001. "Innovations in Public Participation and Environmental Decision Making: Examples from the Great Lakes Region." *Society and Natural Resources* 14: 815–26.

Levin, Jonathan, and Barry Nalebuff. 1995. "An Introduction to Vote-Counting Schemes." *Journal of Economic Perspectives* 9: 3–26.

Luhmann, Niklas. 1996. "*Quod Omnes Tangit*: Remarks on Jürgen Habermas's Legal Theory." *Cardozo Law Review* 17: 883–900.

Maturana, Humberto R. 1988. "Reality: The Search for Objectivity or the Quest for a Compelling Argument." *Irish Journal of Psychology* 9: 25–81.

McCarthy, Thomas. 1996. "Legitimacy and Diversity: Dialectical Reflections on Analytical Distinctions." *Cardozo Law Review* 17: 1083–126.

Ortiz, Daniel R. 2001. "Democratic Values?" *Boston Review,* October-November. Available at http://www.bostonreview.net/BR26.5/ortiz.html.

Ostrom, Elinor. 2000. "The Danger of Self-Evident Truths." *Political Science* 33: 33–44.

Perez, Oren. 2002. "The Many Faces of the Trade-Environment Conflict: Some Lessons for the Constitutionalization Project." *European Integration Online Papers* 6, 11. Available at http://eiop.or.at/eiop/texte/2002-011a.htm.

Peters, Christopher J. 1997. "Equality Revisited." *Harvard Law Review* 110: 1210–64.

Rawls, John. 1971. *A Theory of Justice.* Cambridge, MA: Harvard University Press.

Simons, Kenneth W. 2000. "The Logic of Egalitarian Norms." *Boston University Law Review* 80: 693–771.

Teubner, Gunther. 1996. "*De Collisione Discursuum*: Communicative Rationalities in Law, Morality, and Politics." *Cardozo Law Review* 17: 901–18.

U.S. Environmental Protection Agency. 2000. "Engaging the American People: A Review of EPA's Public Participation Policy and Regulations with Recommendations for Action." Washington, D.C.: EPA.

CHAPTER 7

Interactivity, Equality, and the Prospects for Electronic Democracy: A Review

LORI M. WEBER AND SEAN MURRAY*

While some studies support the high hopes for the Internet and democracy in the United States (Blanchard and Horan 1998; Klein 1999), other studies have questioned its potential (Kraut et al. 1998; Wilhelm 1998). Nevertheless, since about the mid-1990s a scholarly research agenda has emerged on the subject of the Internet and its democratic potential, which some scholars refer to as "electronic democracy." While the bulk of this literature remains theoretical and speculative, there is also a budding area of empirical research. Because the research on electronic democracy is quite "eclectic" (Groper and Wu 1996: 247), this paper will review a selection of this emerging literature on electronic democracy from scholarly journals.[1] Overall, this review will focus upon two themes that are significant for an understanding of the prospects for electronic democracy: equality and interactivity.

1. Conceptualizing and Assessing "Electronic Democracy"

A study of the Internet and its potential to affect democratic processes or "electronic democracy" must begin with a conception of this abstract term. We submit that to conceptualize electronic democracy, one must first identify the political actors and institutions likely to use the Internet.

*We would like to gratefully acknowledge Jason Barabas, Gary Podesto, and Christopher Weare for their assistance with earlier drafts of this paper.

These actors are the following: government, political parties, media, and citizens, either directly or vis-à-vis interest groups and civic associations.

For purposes of this paper, we limit our conception of electronic democracy to these political actors and their utilization of the Internet.[2] We maintain that research in electronic democracy examines the actors who have created a presence in cyberspace and who have begun to take advantage of the Internet's informational and/or interactive capabilities. Furthermore, we argue that in this conception the themes of equality and interactivity are central for the assessment of electronic democracy.

1.1 Equality

First, an assessment of electronic democratic arrangements should examine and emphasize the value of equality. The proponents of electronic democracy advocate the Internet as a way to address inequalities in offline participation. Research in the United States has shown that voters are historically more likely than the general population to be white, educated, and of a moderate income level (Wolfinger and Rosenstone 1980). Moreover, when it comes to political activities beyond voting, an even more skewed demographic profile emerges (Verba, Schlozman, and Brady 1995).

The best-known way that inequality is perpetuated online is now known as the "digital divide." In his 1999 Department of Commerce study on the digital divide, titled "Falling Through the Net," former assistant Secretary of Commerce Larry Irving said that this issue "is now one of America's leading economic and civil rights issues" (1999, xiii). The digital divide issue entails that electronic democracy researchers begin with the question of who participates online.

1.2 Interactivity

Second, an assessment of electronic democratic arrangements must pay attention to the utilization of interactive capabilities on the Internet. The accessibility, convenience, and affordability of the Internet led early theorists such as Dutton (1994), Ogden (1994), and Negroponte (1995) to claim that the potentially interactive nature of the Internet will draw an increased proportion of society into the political realm. However, technology does not exist in a vacuum (Norris and Jones 1998). The influence of politics and human nature alter the processes and implications of technology and society (Samoriski 2000). The result is a society where access, influence, and voice are unequally distributed. This relationship has been true for past innovations such as the printing press, radio, and television and will continue to influence the evolution of the Internet (Buchstein 1997). Therefore, scholars such as Westen (2000) and Becker (2001) advocate long-term policies that allow for the development of interactive technologies.

In order to address the role of interactivity, we must first clarify the conception of the term used for purposes of this paper. Scholars of the Internet admit that the concept of interactivity, when used to describe the advantages of the Internet, "is proving to be an elusive concept" (Stoney and Wild 1998: 46). Wills (1996) writes that interactivity is best conceptualized as a form of engagement. The conception of interactivity as engagement is underscored by scholars such as Newhagen and Rafaeli (1996) when they assert that interactivity is the "extent to which communication reflects back on itself" (quoted in Weare and Lin 2000). Moreover, interactivity as engagement can be "defined in terms of *conversationality*, or the degree to which communication resembles human discourse" and in terms of "*Interpersonal Communication* [that] examines the capacity of the information systems to enable communication between two people or among a small group of people" (McMillan 1999: 378; see also Heeter 1989). We submit that studies that describe the online public as those who merely have access to the Internet fail to capture this conception of interactivity as engagement.

Interactivity has implications for equality because, even as the digital divide appears to close, access without interactivity provides only a partial picture of the online public. By emphasizing the role of interactivity, it is possible to ascertain how democracy in cyberspace may or may not be different from an offline conception of democracy that prioritizes the importance of two-way communication and political discussion (see, for example, Mutz 2002). We address interactivity by asking what political actors can and do accomplish online.

2. The Digital Divide: Who Participates Online?

The leading empirical research on the digital divide combines census data with surveys of Internet users to identify patterns of online activity. The Pew Foundation's Internet and American Life Project uses telephone surveys and census data to gauge how the profile of the American Internet user is evolving. Moreover, Norman Nie, director of the Stanford Institute for the Quantitative Study of Society (SIQSS), used his company, InterSurvey, Inc. (now Knowledge Networks) and their WebTV survey format to develop an updated picture of Internet users.

The continuing studies by both Nie and the Pew Foundation reveal some societal inequalities being perpetuated in cyberspace, especially with regard to income and education. There is also reason for optimism, however, as more recent surveys suggest that the digital divide may be shrinking, at least with regard to race and gender.

Affordability is one advantage that the Internet is supposed to provide. While the cost of personal computers does continue to become more reasonable, income still provides a barrier to Internet access. In the report "Who's Not Online" (Lenhart 2000), the Pew Foundation found that households earning more than $75,000 are three times more likely to have Internet access than those earning less than $30,000. Comparing 1999 median incomes of $42,504 for whites to $27,910 for African Americans, the income inequality of the digital divide becomes apparent. Tied into this is the factor of education: those with less education tend to earn less money and also may not have the computer skills to feel comfortable with the Internet.

While the offline inequality of income and education is mirrored online, recent research by Nie and Erbring (2000) found that race and gender were both statistically insignificant, each accounting for less than 5 percent of the difference in access to the Internet. Similarly, the Pew report "African Americans Online" (Spooner and Rainie 2000) revealed that the size of the black online population had nearly doubled over the previous year. Moreover, the rate of growth of the African American online population has been greater than that of whites over the last two years. Similarly, this Pew study revealed that African Americans and whites have both used the Web in similar proportions to get news about politics. This report leads Spooner and Rainie to assert that "eventually the proportions of each group online could be equal" (2000: 3).

However, if the news is true and the digital divide is indeed shrinking, this begs a further question: what are the causes and implications of a shrinking digital divide? The optimism that a shrinking digital divide entails should be guarded, since the demographics of access provide a fairly crude measure of democracy. Access to the Internet does not equate with use, and mere use does not equate with the deeper needs that a healthy democracy has for interactivity and political discussion. What the Pew and Nie studies fail to reveal is whether the Internet is mobilizing new citizens into politics. Moreover, these studies focus upon issues of access rather than the deeper need for interactivity that is prerequisite to forms of online political participation. Hence, a shrinking digital divide does not necessarily mitigate inequality, at least as far as political participation is concerned.

3. What Can and Do Political Actors Do Online?

The question of what political actors do online should be preceded by the question of what they *can* do online. The invention of the printing press, telephone, radio, and television have all had important implications for democracy. However, greater hope has been expressed for the Internet and democracy than for television, partly due to the Internet's interactive potential. But how much more will the Internet advance democracy beyond the printing press and telephone? It has the possibility to do more if political actors take full advantage of its possibilities, which combine and add (due to space, time, and cost) to the possibilities of the printing press and the telephone. The Internet, in short, has the potential to be an additional public space.

3.1 Government

The potential for using Internet technology for facilitating government operations and communications between citizens and officials drives much of the research on the government's role on the Internet. The cost-saving possibilities entailed by the provision of government services online makes this the most likely utilization of cyberspace by governmental actors. However, the true potential for electronic democracy, as argued earlier, lies in the interactivity that can take place between government officials and citizens in cyberspace. It is the latter service that research shows government has yet to utilize fully. Most research instead shows government, particularly local government, employing the Internet for the provision of services and information rather than for its interactive potential (Alexander 1999; Musso, Weare, and Hale 2000; Steyaert 2000; Watson and Mundy 2001).

Musso, Weare, and Hale (2000) and Steyaert (2000) point out that research into the effects of the Internet on governance exhibits an over-reliance on individual case studies. As of 1999, there had been no systematic studies of the adoption of municipal Web sites. In an attempt to alleviate this methodological shortcoming, Musso, Weare, and Hale conducted a content analysis of 270 municipal Web sites in California to answer several questions.

The first question Musso and colleagues addressed was whether or not city governments are creating Web sites. In 1997, they found that 210 of 454 cities, 46.3 percent, had sites containing organized information regarding local government. This was an increase from 25.8 percent only a year earlier. The second issue they examined was the characteristics of communities likely to adopt Web sites. This is an important approach in studying the equality of access to the Internet. They found that cities that have adopted Web sites tend to have significantly higher levels of expenditures and revenues. Residents of these cities also have higher median income and are more likely to have a college education. Steyaert (2000), using data collected from December 1998 through January 1999, also found that cities with Web sites are likely to be wealthier. While these results reflect the early research on the digital divide, it remains to be seen if there will be a similar increase in access for the less wealthy cities.

Finally, Musso, Weare, and Hale as well as Steyaert examined the interactive capabilities of municipal Web sites. Both research projects underscore that these sites tend to lack the resources necessary for two-way communication. Instead, the quality in the sites was found to lie in economic and commerce-related information. In addition, there was little emphasis on community involvement. Watson and Mundy (2001) agree that the potential for interactive governmental operations has been far from realized.

Similarly, there is literature that examines what is called the "community networking movement." Community networks are computer systems that allow citizens in particular geopolitical locations free access to the Internet and Internet communication (Alexander 1999; Schuler 1996). However, as Alexander argues, a central question for the "community networking literature is whether or not this movement enhances the *quality* of civic engagement" (1999: 279). Alexander's research along with others' (Beamish 1995; Gygi 1996) underscores the idea that enhancing civic engagement and interaction with government officials is rare among such networks. Overall, whether for financial, technological, or political reasons, the lack of development of interactive capabilities means that the full potential of the Internet has not been utilized by government Web sites.

3.2 Political Parties

According to Mancini (1999), the arrival of the Internet coincides with political parties becoming more machines of communication than bodies of organization. Driving party interest in the Internet is its ability to facilitate more rapid and efficient communication of political news directly to information seekers as well as to coordinate interactive online contacts between politicians and their constituents.

In the offline world, the two major parties battle for dominance of established channels of communication. With the introduction of the Internet, minor parties see an opportunity to take advantage of its economies in an attempt to compensate for the lack of coverage they receive in the traditional media. An early example of this occurred during the 1996 election cycle, when Browning (1997) says that the biggest victory for grassroots organizations on the Internet came in the form of widespread Net-based support for third-party candidates.

Given these possible points of access to political parties provided by the Internet, research in this area should have two points of focus: first, whether parties have developed an online presence, and second, whether the presence of minor parties on the Internet differs significantly from the coverage they receive from traditional media. By focusing on these two points, it is possible to gauge whether or not the Internet is countering some form of inherent inequality between major and minor parties.

Though in 1992 the Internet was not even a factor in political campaigns, by 1996 Senator Bob Dole was announcing his Web site at the end of a nationally televised presidential debate (Browning 1997). Though the electoral impact of the Internet was minimal in 1996, consultant Phil Noble noted, "This is the last election where that will happen" (Browning 1997: 55). With such a vital resource now at hand, there is little doubt that parties will continue to expand their presence on the Internet.

Margolis and Resnick (1999) provide one of the few systematic attempts to quantify the presence of specific parties on the Web. Noting that minor parties in the United States once had the jump on major parties online, Margolis and Resnick confirm that by 1996 the major parties had recovered and had largely taken over. Margolis and Resnick describe this evolution in terms of their "normalization hypothesis," which states that normal offline political and market inequalities are mirrored in cyberspace. This hypothesis contradicts the more optimistic alternative, the "inherent-equalization hypothesis." In this scenario, the nature of the Internet inherently invites equal exposure and access for all parties.

Margolis and Resnick found that while the major parties have more links on the Web, the minor parties are not far behind. For example, the Libertarian party has nearly 80 percent as many links as the Democratic National Committee and the Republican National Committee. In addition, the minor parties were found to have complex sites made up of many Web pages, and they also manage to keep their sites as updated as the major parties do. The final results of their study, while defying a simple acceptance or rejection of either the normalization or equalization hypotheses, show that there is some evidence that the Internet offers an improvement over offline political coverage. Minor parties do appear more frequently on the Internet than they do in traditional media.

Overall, both major and minor political parties have found the Internet advantageous in several ways. One use is to improve the speed of organizational communications. This involves e-mail and other instant messaging capabilities. Another use is soliciting donations. However, probably the most anticipated use of the Internet by parties is the dissemination of campaign and issue information directly to constituents, without the filter of the traditional media.

Of all the uses of the Internet by political parties, it is the direct communication with voters that has received the most scholarly attention. In 1996, the year of the first Internet-era election, Resnick (1997) wrote that so far campaigns on the Internet had relied on the same methods as real-world campaigns, such as literature tables, pictures, and solicitations for funds and volunteers. In that same year, Browning observed that many Web sites offered only one-way communication. Of that year's campaign she wrote: "A number of scholars saw the failure of interactivity in last year's campaign as irrefutable evidence that the Net won't become a tool of participatory democracy any time soon" (1997: 3). While this may be a hasty judgment, it does indicate that interactivity fails to be utilized to its full potential by political parties. Nonetheless, in a recent study of campaign use of the Internet, Kamarck and Nye (2002) found that in 1998, nearly three-quarters of candidate Web sites were partially interactive, at least offering the opportunity to send e-mail. Only two sites attempted to be fully interactive, with online chats with the candidate.

The change indicated here in just two years demonstrates the dynamic nature of the Internet.

Margolis and Resnick (1999) have also researched how parties are using the Internet in campaigns. In testing their normalization and equalization hypotheses with regard to the quality of features offered online, the evidence is again inconclusive. The party officials whom Margolis and Resnick interviewed indicated that the Web sites' primary value lay in enhancing the capacity of activists to get information useful for organizing, defending, or otherwise promoting a party and its candidates. These functions had previously been the domain of television, newspapers, and mailings but now are supplemented by the Internet. Several officials pessimistically described their use of the Internet as a symbolic commitment to technological advancement or else a preemptive move to ensure their party's presence in the new medium. More optimistic officials predicted that when the numbers of Internet users become a majority of the electorate, it would then make more sense for parties to make increased use of Web sites for persuading and mobilizing the electorate directly, as opposed to organizing and communicating with party activists. Overall, Margolis and Resnick (1999) observed that the emphasis for the future remains on communicating to the party faithful rather than developing more democratic procedures for conducting government and party business.

Given the direction pointed to by Margolis and Resnick, Kamarck and Nye, and others, future studies into how parties are using the Internet need to examine several issues. First, central to further development of the Internet's potential is gauging whether the interactive capabilities of Web sites are improving. Second, it is central to examine if party presence on the Internet is changing as a result of the noticeable success, or lack thereof, of online efforts.

3.3 Media

The role of the traditional media in the relationship between politics and citizens has been long established. The Internet has the potential to alter this relationship by providing a direct link between citizens and candidates. Mancini (1999) argues that the largest impact to be anticipated from any such alteration is in how it may change the dynamics of political agenda setting. Rather than competing as equals in the agenda-setting game, the media may see their role reduced in introducing salient issues. On the other hand, the media may adjust to the altered dynamics of agenda setting by adapting their methods to the new technologies available. Althaus and Tewksbury (2002) found that the media format used to read the news can affect which issues are salient on the individual level.

According to Tumber and Bromley (1998), mainstream media may change their role to that of providing secondary analysis and directing Internet users to other informational sites. Aufderheide (1998) and

Bardoel (1996) see the role of journalists as evolving into that of information guide, changing the traditional view of how the media provide public service. What these scholars call "service journalism" involves connecting Internet users with other useful Web resources. In this way, the media can become facilitators of responsible public discussion.

Research in this area so far is largely theoretical and anecdotal, but it is laying the foundation for the ways in which the evolution of the media can be studied. The results of this evolution will have a significant impact on the dynamics of the Internet. Tumber and Bromley (1998) argue that an important development that is relatively unexplored is the concern in the media, particularly newspapers, that their future is being rendered insecure by direct electronic communications between government and the public. In addition, there is a general lack of empirical studies about the relationship of journalism to the new technologies and the future of news in relation to the information society (Tumber 2001).

3.4 Citizen Groups, Associations, and Civil Society

Probably the greatest prospects for electronic democracy lie in citizen-to-citizen activity. Instead of relying upon governmental institutions and political parties to arrange meaningful spaces for interactivity, citizens may do so themselves. Moreover, the Internet has the potential to avoid many of the high costs of more traditional participation (Klein 1999). Consequently, citizen-initiated participation on the Internet may not suffer from the same inherent bias of inequality seen in the offline world of political participation.

Of course, in order for the Internet to exhibit potential in the political world, it must first be clear that it exerts positive influences in the social world or civil society. The inherent links social capital and interactivity have with political participation have been clearly demonstrated in political research (see Putnam 2000). While some studies of the Internet have questioned its ability to foster social connectedness (notably Kraut et al. 1998), much of the research has provided affirmative results (though some research remains neutral; see, for example, Uslaner 2000). Using survey data from the Pew Foundation, Howard (2001) and Howard, Rainie, and Jones (2001) argue that e-mail reinforces social networks. Similarly, based upon a random U.S. national survey, Robinson and colleagues (2000) find that Internet users exhibit more active social lives than their offline counterparts. Hampton and Wellman (1999), in a case study of Netville, a Toronto community network, found that the Internet supports social ties. However, they add that these ties are typically maintained through both online and offline interactivity.

Beyond interactivity, research has suggested that the mere informational aspect of the Internet builds social capital and can exhibit a positive influence on political participation. In a pooled data set from the 1998 and

1999, DDB Needham Life Style Studies (see Putnam 2000), Shah, McLeod, and Yoon (2001) find that the informational use of the Internet positively reinforces interpersonal trust and civic participation. Similarly, in a recent study using Survey 2000, a U.S. national survey data set collected in 1998 (see Witte, Amoroso, and Howard 2000), Weber, Loumakis, and Bergman (2003) find that Internet use contributes not only to civic participation but also to more overt political participation. On the other hand, Bimber (2001), using survey data on Internet use collected from 1996 to 1999, finds no support for the relationship between informational use of the Internet and political participation except in donating money.

A possible explanation for such divergent findings is an issue addressed earlier in this paper: conceptualizing the online public as those who merely have access to the Internet rather than interactivity. The studies that found a positive correlation between the Internet and civic and political participation used more extensive measures of Internet use (such as e-mail use and chat rooms). Bimber's study operationalized the online public—the independent variable—as access. Consequently, Bimber's research is highly instructive concerning the supposed shrinking digital divide, which also is limited by measures of access rather than use. In fact, all of the studies above consistently find that the inequalities of education, income, race, and gender that are present in political participation among nonusers are reflected in political participation among Internet users. In short, with regard to politics, the digital divide remains.

Nonetheless, the hope for electronic democracy persists. Blundo and colleagues (1999) present a case study that examines a group of low-income, predominantly African American women who went online in early 1992 to address the needs of their deteriorating public housing. The experience of going online, the researchers argue, "transformed the consciousness of these few residents forever and, importantly, moved them to action" (24). Similarly, McKenna and Bargh (1998), in surveys of participants of three Internet newsgroups, argue that membership in newsgroups dealing with marginalized sexual and ideological identities can be a central part of identity formation and can mitigate estrangement and social isolation.

In addition to bringing marginalized groups into cyberspace, electronic democracy must alter the ways in which citizens participate if the Internet is ever to alleviate inequality. If a healthy democracy entails an environment of political discussion, then Bimber's (2001) finding that Internet use increases monetary donations is instructive. Activities other than donating money are clearly needed. Moreover, with regard to research that finds a positive influence on political discussion, deliberative democratic theorists (Dryzek 2002; Habermas 1981, 1989; Gutmann and Thompson 1996) argue that only a special type of discussion, called deliberation, will do. To be deliberative, political discussion must be aimed toward cooperation, mutual respect, equality, and diversity among participants (see Gutmann and Thompson

1996). Research into the Internet is just beginning to address this important issue (see Buchstein 1997). Benson (1996) examines Usenet/Netnews bulletin boards and finds mixed results. Discussions on these bulletin boards exhibit both aggressiveness and formality and both angry assertion and attention to opposing arguments. In a similar study of political Usenet groups, Wilhelm (1998) finds that deliberation is rare and that instead these forums tend toward short-lived conversations among like-minded individuals. In addition, according to Gastil (2000), future research should be directed toward examining the similarities and differences between face-to-face deliberation and computer-mediated deliberation.

4. Conclusion: Directions for Future Research

As the study of electronic democracy is just in its early stages, it is an appropriate time to assess the quality and direction of research in this area. Given our value-based conception of electronic democracy, the issues of equality and interactivity provide one basis for a critique. The other basis for examining the research is in making sure that scholars are asking the right questions as they search for evidence of electronic government's potential.

Inequality and interactivity are themes that appear to be inherently linked when considering the prospects for electronic democracy. If the Internet is to improve the processes of democracy, citizens must have access to interactive channels and to the quality information necessary to utilize such capabilities fully. In turn, these abilities and knowledge must encourage offline interactivity and discussion if democracy is to be transformed. If the Internet were to be successful in altering the ways that citizens participate, then electronic government optimists could see their visions realized.

An assessment of electronic democracy made upon these two themes reveals that it continues to fall short of its potential. There is a divide in access to the Internet in our society, and this must be addressed to improve equality. In addition, research has shown that the interactive political and governmental functions of the Internet are not being satisfactorily implemented. Much electronic democracy falls short of taking full advantage of the interactive capabilities of the Internet and instead opts for the passive provision of information. While information provision is an important component of democracy, the inherent inequalities of democracy offline appear to be reflected in the online world, especially when interactivity fails to be utilized in tandem with information provision.

Notes

1. This paper reviews journal articles because we concluded that much of the current research presented in books is largely theoretical and limited in empirical scope. In order to find more empirically focused journal articles, the first step was to search the available electronic databases to determine which emphasized the relevant disciplines. The databases searched were EBSCO, JSTOR, International Political Science Abstracts (IPSA), and Ingenta. The

Project Muse database was considered but found to be of limited assistance. Deciding on which search terms to use was an important means of ensuring that each database was examined in a uniform manner. The relevant terms were divided into the categories of technology, discipline, and methods. Each database used provided some measure of success. EBSCO proved useful, especially by utilizing its peer-review option. Searching with the terms *Internet* and *democracy* yielded the most relevant results. JSTOR provides an emphasis on political science, sociology, and economics. Results from this database provided mostly social theory and economic discussions of technology. This is not surprising given the lack of political science research in this field. Ingenta also provided useful communication and social theory references by searching for *electronic democracy*. The IPSA database contains most of the political science literature.

2. We recognize that a complete conception of democracy entails an analysis of the interrelationship of political actors. However, the empirical literature in electronic democracy is still in a nascent stage and hence, tends to deal with various political actors one at a time. Consequently, this essay is also missing this component, and we submit that this is a necessary step for future research.

References

Alexander, Jason Hansen. 1999. "Networked Communities: Citizen Governance in the Information Age." In Gwenn Moore and J. Allen Whitt, eds., *Research in Politics and Society: Community Politics and Policy.* Greenwich, CT: JAI Press.

Althaus, Scott L., and David Tewksbury. 2002. "Agenda Setting and the 'New' News: Patterns of Issue Importance Among Readers of Paper and Online Versions of the *New York Times*," *Communication Research* 29: 180–208.

Aufderheide, P. 1998. "Niche-Market Culture, Off- and Online." In D. L. Borden and K. Harvey, eds., *The Electronic Grapevine: Rumour, Reputation and Reporting in the New Online Environment.* London: LEA.

Bardoel, J. 1996. "Beyond Journalism." *European Journal of Communication* 11: 283–302.

Beamish, A. 1995. "Communities On-line: Community Based Computer Networks." Master's thesis, Massachusetts Institute of Technology, Cambridge, MA. Available at http://loohooloo.mit.edu/arch/4.207/anneb/thesis/toc.html.

Becker, Theodore L. 2001. "The Comprehensive Electronic Town Meeting and Its Role in 21st Century Democracy." *Futures* 33: 347–50.

Benson, Thomas W. 1996. "Rhetoric, Civility, and Community: Political Debate on Computer Bulletin Boards." *Communication Quarterly* 44: 359–78.

Bimber, Bruce. 2001. "Information and Political Engagement in America: The Search for Effects of Information Technology at the Individual Level." *Political Research Quarterly* 54: 53–68.

Blanchard, Anita, and Tom Horan. 1998. "Virtual Communities and Social Capital." *Social Science Computer Review* 16: 293–307.

Blundo, Robert G., et al. 1999. "The Internet and Demystifying Power Differentials: A Few Women On-Line and the Housing Authority." *Journal of Community Practice* 6: 11–26.

Browning, Graeme. 1997. "Updating Electronic Democracy." *Database* 20: 47–50.

Buchstein, Hubertus. 1997. "Bytes That Bite: The Internet and Deliberative Democracy." *Constellations* 4: 248–63.

Buchstein, Hubertus, and Alexander Staudacher. 1996. "Bitter Bytes: Cybercitizens and Democratic Theory." *Deutsche Zeitschrift für Philosophie* 44: 583–607.

Dutton, William H. 1996. "Network Rules of Order: Regulating Speech in Public Electronic Forums." *Media, Culture and Society* 18: 269–90.

Gastil, John. 2000. "Is Face-to-Face Citizen Deliberation a Luxury or a Necessity?" *Political Communication* 17: 357–61.

Groper, Richard, and Wei Wu. 1996. "Political Participation and the Internet: A Review Essay." *Political Communication* 13: 247–57.

Gutmann, Amy, and Dennis Thompson. 1996. *Democracy and Disagreement.* Cambridge, MA: Harvard University Press.

Gygi, K. 1996. "Uncovering Best Practices: A Framework for Assessing Outcomes in Community Computer Networking." *Community Networking.* Available at http://www.laplaza.org/cn/local/gygi.html.

Habermas, Jürgen. 1981. *The Theory of Communicative Action,* vol. 1. Trans. Thomas McCarthy. Boston: Beacon Press.

Habermas, Jürgen. 1989. *The Structural Transformation of the Public Sphere.* Cambridge, MA: MIT Press.

Hampton, Keith N., and Barry Wellman. 1999. "Netville Online and Offline." *American Behavioral Scientist* 43: 475–93.

Heeter, C. 1989. "Implications of New Interactive Technologies for Conceptualizing Communication." In Jerry L. Salvaggio and Jennings Bryant, eds., *Media Use in the Information Age: Emerging Patterns of Adoption and Consumer Use.* Hillsdale, NJ: Lawrence Erlbaum.

Howard, Philip. 2001. "Can Technology Enhance Democracy? The Doubters' Answer." *Journal of Politics* 63: 949–56.

Howard, Philip, Lee Rainie, and Steve Jones. 2001. "Days and Nights on the Internet: The Impact of a Diffusing Technology." *American Behavioral Scientist* 45.

Irving, Larry. 1999. "Falling Through the Net." National Telecommunications and Information Administration, Washington, D.C.

Kamarck, Elaine C., and Joseph S. Nye, Jr. 2002. *Governance.com: Democracy in the Information Age.* Washington, D.C.: Brookings Institution Press.

Klein, Hans K. 1999. "Tocqueville in Cyberspace: Using the Internet for Citizen Associations." *The Information Society* 15: 213–20.

Kraut, Robert, et al. 1998. "Internet Paradox: A Social Technology That Reduces Social Involvement and Psychological Well-being." *American Psychologist* 53: 1017–31.

Lenhart, Amanda. 2000. "Who's Not Online." Pew Internet and American Life Project. Available at http://www.pewinternet.org/reports/index.asp.

McKenna, Katelyn Y., and John A. Bargh. 1998. "Coming Out in the Age of the Internet: Identity 'Demarginalization' Through Virtual Group Participation." *Journal of Personality and Social Psychology* 75: 681–94.

McMillan, Sally J. 1999. "Health Communication and the Internet: Relations Between Interactive Characteristics of the Medium and Site Creators, Content, and Purpose." *Health Communication* 11: 375–90.

Mancini, P. 1999. "New Frontiers in Political Professionalism." *Political Communication* 16: 231–45.

Margolis, Michael, and David Resnick. 1999. "Party Competition on the Internet in the United States and Britain." *Harvard International Journal of Press/Politics* 4: 24–48.

Musso J., C. Weare, and M. Hale. 2000. "Designing Web Technologies for Local Governance Reform: Good Management or Good Democracy?" *Political Communication* 17: 1–19.

Mutz, D. 2002. "Cross-cutting Social Networks: Testing Democratic Theory in Practice." *American Political Science Review* 96: 111–26.

Negroponte, Nicholas. 1995. *Being Digital.* New York: Knopf.

Newhagen, John E., and Sheizaf Rafaeli. 1996. "Why Communication Researchers should study the Internet: A Dialogue." *Journal of Communication* 46: 4–13.

Nie, Norman H., and Lutz Erbring. 2000. "Internet and Society: A Preliminary Report." Stanford Institute for the Quantitative Study of Society, Stanford University, Stanford, CA. Available at http://www.stanford.edu/group/siqss/Press_Release/Preliminary_Report.pdf.

Norris, Pippa, and David Jones. 1998. "Virtual Democracy." *Harvard International Journal of Press/Politics* 3: 1–5.

Ogden, Michael R. 1994. "Politics in a Parallel Universe." *Futures* 26: 713–29.

Pew Research Center. 2000. "Internet Election News Audience Seeks Convenience, Familiar Names." Available at http://www.pewinternet.org/reports/index.asp.

Putnam, Robert. 2000. *Bowling Alone: The Collapse and Revival of American Community.* New York: Simon and Schuster.

Resnick, David. 1997. "Politics on the Internet: The Normalization of Cyberspace." *New Political Science* 41–42: 47–67.

Robinson, John P., et al. 2000. "Mass Media Use and Social Life among Internet Users." *Social Science Computer Review* 18: 490–501.

Samoriski, J. H. 2000. "Private Spaces and Public Interests: Internet Navigation, Commercialism and the Fleecing of Democracy." *Communication Law and Policy* 5: 93–113.

Schuler, D. 1996. New *Community Networks: Wired for Change*, New York: Addison-Wesley.

Shah, Dhavan V., Jack M. McLeod, and So-Hyang Yoon. 2001. "Communication, Context, and Community: An Exploration of Print, Broadcast, and Internet Influences." *Communication Research* 28: 464–507.

Spooner, Tom, and Lee Rainie. 2000. "African Americans and the Internet." Pew Internet and American Life Project. Available at http://www.pewinternet.org/reports/index.asp.

Steyaert, Jo. 2000. "Local Governments Online and the Role of the Resident: Government Shop Versus Electronic Community." *Social Science Computer Review* 18: 3–16.

Stoney, S., and M. Wild. 1998. "Motivation and Interface Design: Maximising Learning Opportunities." *Journal of Computer Assisted Learning* 14: 40–50.

Tumber, H. 2001. "Democracy in the Information Age: The Role of the Fourth Estate in Cyberspace." *Information, Communication and Society* 4: 95–112.

Tumber, Howard, and Michael Bromley. 1998. "Virtual Soundbites: Political Communication in Cyberspace," *Media, Culture and Society* 20: 159–68.

Uslaner, Eric. 2000. "Trust, Civic Engagement, and the Internet." Paper prepared for the Joint Sessions of the European Consortium for Political Research, Workshop on Electronic Democracy: Mobilisation, Organisation, Participation via New ICTs, University of Grenoble. Available at http://www.pewinternet.org/papers/paperspdf/UMD_Uslaner_Trust.pdf.

Verba, Sidney, Kay Lehman Schlozman, and Henry E. Brady. 1995. *Voice and Equality: Civic Voluntarism in American Politics*. Cambridge, MA: Harvard University Press.

Watson, Richard T., and Bryan Mundy. 2001. "A Strategic Perspective of Electronic Democracy." *Communications of the ACM* 44: 27–31.

Weare, Christopher, and Wan-Ying Lin. 2000. "Content Analysis of the World Wide Web: Opportunities and Challenges." *Social Science Computer Review* 18: 272–93.

Weber, Lori, Alysha Loumakis, and James Bergman. 2003. "Who Participates and Why? An Analysis of Citizens on the Internet and the Mass Public." *Social Science Computer Review* 21: 26–42.

Westen, Tracy. 2000. "E-Democracy: Ready or Not, Here It Comes." *National Civic Review* 89: 217–22.

Wilhelm, Anthony G. 1998. "Virtual Sounding Boards: How Deliberative Is On-Line Political Discussion?" *Information, Communication and Society* 1: 313–38.

Wills, S. 1996. "Interface to Interactivity: Technologies and Techniques." In C. McBeath and R. Atkinson, eds., *Proceedings of the Learning Superhighway: New World, New Worries? 3rd International Interactive Multimedia Symposium*. Perth, Australia: Promaco Conventions.

Witte, James, Lisa Amoroso, and Philip Howard. 2000. "Method and Representation in Internet-based Survey Tools- Mobility, Community, and Cultural Identity in Survey2000." *Social Science Computer Review* 18: 179–95.

Wolfinger, Raymond E., and Steven J. Rosenstone. 1980. *Who Votes?* New Haven, CT: Yale University Press.

CHAPTER 8

Online Deliberation: Possibilities of the Internet for Deliberative Democracy

TAMARA WITSCHGE*

Within every "healthy" democracy, differences of opinion and conflicts on public issues should exist. Moreover, for theories of deliberative democracy, difference of opinion is central to political or public-spirited talk. Rather than viewing democracy as the process of expressing preferences and registering them in a vote, democracy is viewed as a "process that creates a public, citizens coming together to talk about collective problems, goals, ideals, and actions" (Young 1996: 121). Public communication is needed to come to mutual understanding, and for some scholars, even to obtain consensus. For that to come about, a free and open exchange of information and arguments should take place, and different voices should be present in the debate.

Empirical research, however, shows that citizens mostly discuss politics with people who hold the same views and have the same background. Given the difficult nature of political conflict, people tend to avoid it. Also, political power structures ensure that particular voices dominate public discourse, eliminating further oppositional or alternative voices. Moreover, current practices and attitudes in Western democracies correspond mostly to the interest-based type of democracy, where citizens do not need to leave their own subjective point of view or discuss and reason about their private interest in terms of the common good (Young 1996).

*This research is funded by the Dutch Science Foundation (NWO), grant number 425.42.008.

Given this situation, where political talk, if conducted at all, almost never meets the requirements established by democratic theorists, much hope has been pinned on the Internet. Not only could the Internet encourage more people to discuss politics by freeing them of psychological barriers, but it could do so by offering a (partial) solution to the problems that deliberative democracy is confronted with—problems previously seen as insurmountable. The Internet "makes manageable large-scale, many-to-many discussion and deliberation" (Coleman and Gøtze 2001: 17). It also seems to bring us closer to the solution of four problems that have made full participation in modern democracies difficult, if not impossible: time, size, knowledge, and access (Street 1997).

The aim of this chapter is to examine whether or not the Internet holds possibilities for deliberative democracy in terms of meeting the criteria of difference and disagreement. I will confront the theoretical focus on difference and disagreement with empirical studies into political talk, which show that theory and practice diverge at this point. Next, I will look at the potential of the Internet to overcome this tendency to avoid difference and disagreement by giving an overview of the empirical studies in this field. Last, I will look critically at these studies in order to see what still needs to be done in this field in order to gain insight into the Internet's potential for democracy.

1. "Ordinary" Political Conversation Versus Deliberation

To meet the requirements of deliberative democracy, and for political discussions to have the outcomes it is valued for, not just any type of discussion suffices. The general idea of deliberative democracy is that political conversation does not serve democracy if it is not deliberative and among a heterogeneous group of people. The fundamental criteria of deliberative democracy include the presence of difference between and disagreement among participants with regard to their opinions and arguments. Public conversation should air disagreements and include a variety of perspectives and views (Fishkin 1995; Gutmann and Thompson 1996).

It is not the fact that people talk about political issues (or the frequency with which they do so) that makes deliberation serviceable for democracy (Schudson 1997). Rather, the virtues of the public sphere, where deliberation takes place, originate from the fact that a group of people with different opinions and different backgrounds engage in a public debate. The idea of the public sphere is that this is a space where public opinion is formed, but only after "exposure to a sufficient amount of information, and also to an appropriately wide and diverse range of options" (Sunstein 2001).

As MacKuen states, only interactions between individuals with differing views, as opposed to interactions between those who hold similar views, "allow genuine debate and an exchange of ideas" (1990: 60). Such interactions will give the participants the opportunity to "choose from a broader menu," and this would ultimately lead to a growing social awareness, as it would result in the decline of self-interest.

Empirical research, however, gives an altogether different picture; studies about the frequency with which citizens engage in political discussions, and with whom they are likely to talk, have shown that most political conversations occur among family, friends, and people whose political views are similar (e.g., Bennet, Flickinger, and Rhine 2000; Conover, Searing, and Crewe 2002; Berelson 1952; Wyatt, Katz, and Kim 2000; Stromer-Galley 2002). It is because of the existence of difference and disagreement that the norms that govern deliberation differ from the more comfortable forms of conversation that people normally seek. People have a tendency to look for like-minded individuals with whom to discuss politics because this is less threatening and more enjoyable (e.g., Schudson 1997). Deliberation serves democracy, however, because differences of opinion are addressed and these opinions are put to the test in order to move society forward. "The deliberative process forces citizens to justify their decisions and opinions by appealing to common interests or by arguing in terms of reasons that 'all could accept' in public debate" (Bohman 1996: 5).

Given this demanding nature of deliberation, it should come as no surprise that when opportunities present themselves, people do not usually "jump at the chance to become active participants" (Warren 1996: 266).

2. Why People Avoid Contested Conversations

Why is it that people avoid the conversations in which a diverse range of (contesting) viewpoints could arise? Over the years, many theorists have tried to explain this phenomenon and political apathy in general. I will here give an account of the most central arguments in this field, without claiming to be comprehensive. I start with the more general theories on political apathy, which include more specific explanations on difference and disagreement, and work toward the theorists who focus specifically on the latter.

Though written down fifty years ago, the determinants of political apathy that Rosenberg (1954) identified still are being employed in current studies. The factors identified by Rosenberg are explanations for political indifference and inactivity, but most are equally applicable to political talk in particular. First, like many other scholars, Rosenberg sees the threatening nature of politics as an explanation for why people avoid it. "In a democratic society, politics are *controversial*, and controversiality, while it may encourage interest, also has potential interpersonal consequences which may foster political inactivity" (Rosenberg 1954: 354). Second, although political participation is aimed at getting one's will translated into political action, most people think activity is futile and do not believe they can influence political forces (Rosenberg 1954: 354–60). Third, group norms may encourage political apathy, or at least withhold people from action.

Aversion to the controversial nature of politics is also central to the theory of the spiral of silence (Noelle-Neumann 1989). Although this theory was originally developed to give an account of how public opinion comes into being, it provides reasons to avoid speaking up and for avoiding difference of opinion. There are four assumptions that underlie the spiral of silence (Noelle-Neumann 1989: 299):

1. Society uses threats of isolation toward deviant individuals.
2. Individuals experience fear of isolation at all times.
3. Out of their fear of isolation, individuals try to estimate the general opinion at all times.
4. The result of the estimates influences the behavior of all individuals in the public sphere, specifically through showing or hiding opinions—that is, by speaking up or keeping silent.

Fearing isolation, people do not feel free to speak up if they believe they hold dissenting views. This means people restrict themselves to having conversations with like-minded people or have no political conversation whatsoever.

Contrary to the suggestion of an innate fear of the contested political realm, Eliasoph (1998) maintains we are *not* born apolitical. Apathy is caused by the obstacles that "lie in the path of any group that tries to express publicly-minded sentiments in public contexts," obstacles such as groups not encouraging talking in meetings, individuals silencing themselves in group meetings, groups ignoring members who insist on talking about politics during meetings, or groups silencing their public-spirited speech in front-stage contexts (Eliasoph 1998: 256–57).

Other reasons for avoiding politics are feelings of inadequacy, ignorance, apathy, alienation, unwillingness to challenge group norms, and fear of contradicting a majority (Wyatt, Kim, and Katz 2000: 101). Hollander identifies the following impediments to free speech: "the risk of disapproval, the lack of perceived alternatives, the fear of disrupting an event, misperceptions of the extent to which others share one's opinions, the unwillingness to take responsibility, and a sense of impotence" (in Wyatt et al. 1996: 230).

Empirical studies of the reasons for avoiding conflict show that some of the elements of the spiral of silence indeed can be used as explanations for political apathy and the unwillingness to express one's opinions publicly (Taylor 1982; Glynn 1984; Glynn, Hayes, and Shanahan 1997; Scheufele 1999). The strongest predictors in this are fear of isolation and perceptions of present public support. Other empirical studies have shown that "fear of harming others is a greater inhibitor than fear of disapproval or rejection" (Wyatt et al. 1996: 243; Wyatt, Kim, and Katz 2000: 101). Whether it is fear of harming others or fear of being harmed oneself, there are obviously factors that inhibit people from speaking freely. This results in a nonideal type of discussion, as neither diversity nor equality of participants and viewpoints can arise. The question is, does the Internet indeed free people from the psychological barriers to engage in politics?

3. Does the Internet Ease Difference and Disagreement in Discussions?

Several aspects thus contribute to a general avoidance of "genuine" politics—politics that revolves around conflict, difference, and disagreement. In this section, I will explore the potential of the Internet to overcome the tendency to avoid difference and disagreement. Features of the Internet may take away, or at least lessen, the uncomfortable feeling people have when confronted with conflict, disagreement, or difference. The Internet could become a space where political conversation takes place in a context of diversity, in terms of both the participants and the range of opinions held.

First, I will look into the question of heterogeneity. Can, and does, the Internet draw a more diverse group (compared to the offline conversations) of people into conversation, and do we encounter a greater diversity of voices? Second, I will discuss the main features of the Internet that are endorsed as enabling it to meet the criteria of deliberation: anonymity and the supposedly equalizing effect of reduced social cues.

3.1 Heterogeneity

The nature of the Internet facilitates the participation not only of *more* people but also of a more *heterogeneous* group of people; cyberspace "is a place where difference is not hard to find" (Dahlberg 2001a). "The onward rush of electronic communications technology will presumably increase the diversity of available ideas and the speed and ease with which they fly about and compete with each other" (Page 1996: 124).

Robinson, Neustadtl, and Kestnbaum (2002: 300) try to answer the question whether "Internet use may mean that the American public is becoming less or more diverse politically." Based on earlier descriptions of Internet users, they expected it to be a place with people open to and tolerant of deviant or nonconforming individuals in society. The results of the study made them conclude that Internet users were more supportive of diverse and tolerant points of view than nonusers. Schneider, in his study of the online newsgroup talk.abortion, states that when diversity is measured by the introduction of new participants talk.abortion can be considered a diverse arena and a dynamic conversational environment (Schneider 1997).

So the Internet seems to be a perfect place to find different views expressed by a diverse group of people who are at the same time open to such difference and to the disagreement needed for deliberation. The

Internet is an ideal space for individuals to expand their horizons and to meet, or at least encounter, tens, hundreds, or thousands of new people and be confronted with a range of new topics and views. The question is, however, do all these different people also actually find each other on the Internet, or do they seek the like-minded all the same? Wallace finds that disagreement does take place on the Internet; indeed, it becomes "very heated and contentious," even when everyone in the exchange conforms to the group's written and unwritten norms (Wallace 1999: 74).

However, as Dahlberg notes, although the conversations on the Internet feature disagreements, "virtual communities are often based upon people getting together with similar values, interests, and concerns" (Dahlberg 2001a: 10). Similarly, Wilhelm finds that most participants within a discussion group hold the same views on a political topic or candidate (Wilhelm 1999: 172). This finding is congruent with Davis's findings from a study into Usenet. He concludes that Usenet becomes "more than anything a forum of reinforcement" (Davis 1999: 162), dominated by like-minded participants who limit the diversity of opinions by not tolerating dissenting views.

Should we then conclude that Sunstein's fear is justified—that new technologies are polarizing society—because people's ability to hear echoes of their own voices and to wall themselves off from others has increased? As Sunstein (2001) argues, like-minded people can deliberate with greater ease and frequency with one another over the Internet. Although this is true, we cannot conclude from this possibility alone that the Internet is actually having a polarizing effect. First, there are contradictory findings, due to major differences in methodology. We need to answer the questions of what diversity and heterogeneity on the Internet mean and how these could be measured. Second, we need to go beyond comparing what is happening on the Internet with the ideal of (deliberative) democracy; we need to examine whether what is happening on the Internet is an improvement with regard to the existing offline situation. As O'Hara states, "It is clear reasonable access to opposing views can generally be found" (O'Hara 2002). The ease with which search engines can be used to find like-minded people is equal to the ease with which one can use them to find different and disagreeing voices—probably much more easily than in offline life. And third, the Internet is just *one* medium people use to get their information, to discuss politics and exert influence. We would have to see how the online world interacts with the offline one in order to see its real potential to do harm or good for democracy. Looking at its features, anonymity, and reduced social cues, let us see if it at least has the potential to create an environment where people would not avoid difference and disagreement.

3.2 Anonymity

Whether people's fears are of isolation, humiliation, harming others, not being liked, or disapproval, it could easily be argued that in an anonymous setting such fears would be reduced. After all, the actions of those engaging politically would not be as easily ascribed to them, and immediate pressures from others would be lessened because no one would be physically present. As Wallace (1999: 124–25) recognizes, "when people believe their actions cannot be attributed to them personally, they tend to become less inhibited by social conventions and restraints." The ability of a group to pressure a dissenting individual is lessened on the Internet, and in this way the tendency to conform could weaken. Wallace summarizes a number of empirical studies that do find that dissenters feel more liberated to express their views online than offline, which might result from the fact that the "dissenter would not have to endure raised eyebrows or interruptions by members of the majority, or be made to feel uncomfortable about the failure to agree with the others" (Wallace 1999: 82).

However, other studies find, on the contrary, that dissenting views are not tolerated online. Dissenters are ignored, with the result that they become frustrated and finally give up and leave the discussion group (Davis 1999). Not only are dissenters ignored, there is also a risk of "vigorous attack and humiliation." Davis states that "Usenet political discussion tends to favor the loudest and most aggressive individuals" (ibid.: 163). In accord, Barber, Mattson, and Peterson (1997) admit that anonymity can help promote safer and open discussion, but they argue that it is precisely anonymity that undermines the deliberative potential of the Internet, as it seems to cause a "general lack of civility." Streck (Streck 1998) compares the Internet with a "shouting match," which results, as he argues, from the freedom from sanction and the power of anonymity and untraceability. Dahlberg (2001a) also states that flaming is attributed to the disinhibiting effects of computer mediated communication—feeling freer to express oneself as one wishes. Although there are differences in estimates of the frequency of flaming, it is clear flaming occurs quite often, and single flames can easily escalate into real flame wars.

So it seems that anonymity and the absence of social presence, which seemed so promising for democracy, can instead work against a genuine democratic exchange. However, all is not lost. First, one can increase civility by setting up forum rules and guidelines. An example that has been relatively successful is Minnesota E-Democracy (Dahlberg 2001b). This does mean, however, that careful consideration has to be given to the extent to which restriction and moderation of posting are needed in order to keep the discussion civil, and to what extent this undermines freedom of expression.

Second, I do not want to draw premature conclusions, as we do not know how the participants themselves feel about this. Most of the conclusions on flaming are based on content analyses. We cannot conclude from this that people really feel restricted about giving their view, dissenting or not. We do not know whether these online uncivil behaviors have the same effect as the offline ones would have. Only when we know how participants feel about issues such as misconduct, group pressure, and flaming can we try to grasp the potential of this specific feature of the Internet for democracy.

3.3 Reduced Social Cues

An important issue in obtaining heterogeneity in discussions is equal access to and equality in the discussion for all the participants. Though access to the Internet and the problem of the digital divide are issues of major import, I will not discuss them here; rather, I focus on equality *within* the discussion. Perceived ignorance, incapability, and inequality are impediments to participation in political conversations. When people do decide to participate in conversations, their participation might be overruled by dominant others, or their contribution might be valued less or more depending on their status.

The Internet is often praised for its possibility to liberate us from the social hierarchies and power relations that exist offline. "[T]he 'blindness' of cyberspace to bodily identity . . . [is supposed to allow] people to interact as if they were equals. Arguments are said to be assessed by the value of the claims themselves and not the social position of the poster" (Dahlberg 2001c: 14). Gastil (2000: 359) sees this feature as one of the strongest points of the Internet: "If computer-mediated interaction can consistently reduce the independent influence of status, it will have a powerful advantage over face-to-face deliberation." In a discussion forum, your words would carry more weight than your socioeconomic position. When status cues are difficult to detect, stereotyping and prejudice lessen. This would result in more participation and greater influence for lower-status members (Wallace 1999: 99).

The absence of social cues thus bodes well for equality in discussion groups. But although participants in an online discussion group in theory have equal opportunity to post and equal opportunity to be heard, in practice this is often not the case. "[O]nline status is often directly reinforced by the revelation of offline identities that are . . . readily brought into cyberspace" (Dahlberg 2001a: 15). By abusive postings, monopolization of attention, and control of agenda and style of discourse, some participants are able to make their voices heard more than others. Schneider concludes that participation in talk.abortion is not equal, but rather "dramatically unequal." More than 80 percent of the postings are posted by fewer than 5 percent of the participants (Schneider 1997: 85).

Herring moreover states that although more and more women are getting online, research on online interaction does not support the claims of widespread gender anonymity (Herring 2000). Users are sometimes not even interested in exploiting the potential for anonymous interaction. The use of one's real name can give more weight to a posting because it "lends accountability and a seriousness of purpose to one's words that anonymous messages lack" (Herring 2000: 2). But even when gender is not being expressed voluntarily, there are differences in ways of expression, for instance, in civility and length of message.

The absence of social cues, in short, does not seem to lead to the equality it was valued for. But again, we do not know how participants perceive this issue themselves. It may be that people do feel more equal in online forums than they feel offline. It does seem clear that racism, ageism, and other kinds of discrimination against outgroups seem "to be diminishing because the cues to outgroup status are not as obvious" (Wallace 1999: 99). Moreover, the Internet has rapidly and dramatically increased the capacities to develop, share, and organize information (Warren 2001: 78), realizing more equality of access to information (Gimmler 2001: 31). This might in time lead to more equally informed citizens with more equal capacities to deliberate.

4. Discussion: How Gloomy Is Democracy's Future?

The apparent message of studies of the potential of the Internet for deliberation is that the democratization process some scholars expected is not taking place. Should we really conclude from this that the online discussion forums "have not achieved a nirvana of direct democracy, where all participate equally in a substantive exchange of ideas," as Davis (1999: 165) does? No. These investigations do not enable us to fully evaluate the democratic prospects of the Internet.

First, there are a number of methodological problems. It has been shown that different researchers report opposing findings. The difficulty with complex notions such as the public sphere, deliberation, and even difference and disagreement is that the step from theory to data is not straightforward. The difficulties lie, on one hand, in the quantitative studies that operationalize the normative notions in such a way that the measurements do not lead to any insights into the complex matter of deliberation.[1] Often the dimensions of deliberation are reduced to quantitative indicators in a manner that allows very few conclusions to be drawn.

On the other hand, we have the qualitative studies, which are much more embedded in the theory and in this way do more justice to the complexity of the relevant issues. The trouble with these studies, however, is that they lack a clear connection between theory and data, leaving us with a seemingly arbitrary evaluation of the public sphere. We need a method that does not reduce "normative principles for reasonable discussion to anthropologically relative characterizations, and likewise without prefiguring the categories and principles of descriptive inquiry in a way that makes them immune to empirical disconfirmation" (Van Eemeren et al. 1993: 1–2). Dahlberg (2000: 120) shares this concern, stating that we need to find a balance between the concept of the public sphere as a "discrete variable (as in 'pure' quantitative research) and a sensitizing concept (as in 'pure' qualitative research)."

Moreover, the Internet is still a rather new medium; although it has existed for quite some time now, its usage is still in flux. Empirical research conducted up to now does not provide enough understanding to permit us to rely solely on quantitative study. Most studies into the effect of the Internet on democracy, however, "reflect the unfortunate trend in political science to jump right into new fields of inquiry with quantitative analysis" (Howard 2001: 951).

Second, we have to realize that content analyses or discourse analyses alone will not do the job. If we really want to grasp the democratic potential of the Internet, we need to look beyond what actually can be found on the Internet, whether through the more quantitative content analysis or through the more qualitative discourse analytic and ethnographic approaches, as there is the problem of observability: "potential interactants who choose to remain silent, and potential authors who fail to write, are lost to the analysis" (Hine 2000: 54).

Third, we do not gain much insight if we look only at what people produce on the Internet and do not know the intentions of the producers. As Bimber (1999: 425), for instance, states, "floods of e-mail from citizens acting without lasting convictions about public problems or lasting interests do not add to democratic discourse." We need to look beyond mere flows of communication. "What makes opinion deliberative is not merely that it has been built upon careful contemplation, evidence, and supportive arguments, but also that it has grasped and taken into consideration the opposing view of others" (Price, Cappella, and Nir 2002: 97).

In order to comprehend the democratic possibilities of the Internet, we need to concentrate on trying to understand the users of the Internet. What drives people to discuss politics on the Internet instead of or in addition to discussing it offline? What are the outcomes of online deliberation?

Fourth, we need to keep in mind that the Internet is a complex space used by many different kinds of people and for many different reasons. The Internet is not a more stable social space than offline spaces are. "The Internet is so fluid as to be rendered meaningless as a storage medium; it is never constant, never fixed, no matter that the textual traces left there seem to give it form" (Jones 1999: 12).

Not only is the Internet itself a complex space, but it also interacts with yet another complex space, the offline world (Kendall 1999). Or, as Dahlgren puts it:

> The rampant intermeshing of the Net with so many social institutions, organizations, and everyday settings invites us to consider

how this technology is concretely used and integrated in these various contexts, where people are repeatedly moving between on- and off-line activities within the practical circumstances they have at hand. So while one could conceivably analyze some aspects of civic culture by focusing purely on the Net, I would instead choose to see how the Net is used in conjunction with other, off-line activities. (2000: 339)

This connection between offline and online holds methodological implications that have not been taken sufficiently into consideration thus far. We need to see how spaces such as offline and online media outlets or offline and online political talk interact, and how they constitute civic engagement together.

Last, I do not think it is enough to compare online discussions with the ideal of deliberation. Instead, to evaluate democratic potential, we need to compare them with offline discussions as well. As stated above, studies have shown that online discussions do not meet the requirements of the ideal public sphere. We can state whether the Internet is enhancing democracy only when we compare it with the offline situation. However small the contribution of online discussion to the political process might be, democracy *can* benefit from it.

5. Conclusion

I began this essay by discussing the difficult nature of "genuine" politics—difficult because genuine politics, as advocates of deliberative democracy note, involves difference and disagreement. But it is exactly this difference and disagreement that make people avoid deliberative politics. As empirical studies show, people would rather seek like-minded others with whom to talk politics because this is less threatening and more enjoyable. I have discussed a number of explanations for political apathy and the avoidance of politics. Aspects such as fear of the consequences of politics and its controversiality, fear of isolation, feelings of inadequacy, perceived lack of knowledge, unwillingness to challenge group norms, fear of harming others, and the fear of contradicting a majority all contribute to a general avoidance of politics.

Features of the Internet such as reduced social cues, a lowered sense of social presence, and the possibility of remaining anonymous have generated renewed interest in political conversation and deliberative democracy. I have tried to answer the question whether the Internet indeed holds potential for deliberative democracy through increasing heterogeneity. More specifically, I have looked into the potential of anonymity and reduced social cues to create an environment where people would not avoid difference and disagreement a priori.

Empirical studies, although sometimes reporting opposing findings, are not as optimistic about democracy on the Internet as the cyberoptimists were in the medium's early days. The Internet does not seem to generate diversity in voices and viewpoints in the way that was anticipated. Anonymity does not liberate us of all the fears we have about encountering conflict. Rather, anonymity seems to result in a risk of vigorous attack and humiliation and other forms of incivility. Nor does the absence of social cues lead to the discursive equality it was valued for.

All in all, the empirical studies present a gloomy picture for democracy. However, it remains far too early to conclude that the Internet is not enhancing and cannot enhance democracy. As I have argued, many gaps in the empirical research need to be bridged before we can draw any conclusions on the Internet's potential.

Note

1. For an attempt to deal with this problem, see Graham and Witschge 2003.

References

Barber, Benjamin R., Kevin Mattson, and John Peterson. 1997. "The State of Electronically Enhanced Democracy: A Report of the Walt Whitman Center." Available at http://wwc.rut-gers.edu/markleproj.htm (accessed November 10, 2001).

Bennet, Stephen E., Richard S. Flickinger, and Staci L. Rhine. 2000. "Political Talk Over Here, Over There, Over Time." *British Journal of Political Science* 30, 1: 99–119.

Berelson, Bernard. 1952. "Democratic Theory and Public Opinion." *The Public Opinion Quarterly* 16, 3: 313–30.

Bimber, Bruce. 1999. "The Internet and Citizen Communication with Government: Does the Medium Matter?" *Political Communication* 16, 4: 409–28.

Bohman, James. 1996. *Public Deliberation: Pluralism, Complexity, and Democracy.* Cambridge, MA: MIT Press.

Coleman, Stephen, and John Gøtze. 2001. "Bowling Together: Online Public Engagement in Policy Deliberation." Available from http://bowlingtogether.net/about.html (accessed December 2001).

Conover, Pamela Johnston, Donald D. Searing, and Ivor M. Crewe. 2002. "The Deliberative Potential of Political Discussion." *British Journal of Political Science* 32, 1: 21–62.

Dahlberg, Lincoln. 2000. "The Internet and the Public Sphere: A Critical Analysis of the Possibility of Online Discourse Enhancing Deliberative Democracy." Ph. D. dissertation, Massey University.

Dahlberg, Lincoln. 2001a. "Computer-Mediated Communication and the Public Sphere: A Critical Analysis." *Journal of Computer-Mediated Communication* 7, 1.

Dahlberg, Lincoln. 2001b. "Extending the Public Sphere Through Cyberspace: The Case of Minnesota E-Democracy." *First Monday* 6, 3. Available at http://www.firstmonday.dk/issues/issue6_3/dahlberg/ (accessed March 2004).

Dahlberg, Lincoln. 2001c. "The Internet and Democratic Discourse." *Information, Communication and Society* 4, 4: 615–33.

Dahlgren, Peter. 2000. "The Internet and the Democratization of Civic Culture." *Political Communication* 17, 4: 335–40.

Davis, Richard. 1999. *The Web of Politics: The Internet's Impact on the American Political System.* Oxford: Oxford University Press.

Eemeren, Frans H. van, Rob Grootendorst, Sally Jackson, and Scott Jacobs. 1993. *Reconstructing Argumentative Discourse.* Tuscaloosa: University of Alabama Press.

Eliasoph, Nina. 1998. *Avoiding Politics: How Americans Produce Apathy in Everyday Life.* Cambridge: Cambridge University Press.

Fishkin, James S. 1995. *The Voice of the People: Public Opinion and Democracy*. New Haven: Yale University Press.

Gastil, John. 2000. "Is Face-to-Face Citizen Deliberation a Luxury or a Necessity?" *Political Communication* 17, 4: 357–61.

Gimmler, Antje. 2001. "Deliberative Democracy, the Public Sphere and the Internet." *Philosophy and Social Criticism* 27, 4: 21–39.

Glynn, Carrol J. 1984. "Public Opinion Du Jour: An Examination of the Spiral of Silence." *Public Opinion Quarterly* 48, 4: 731–40.

Glynn, Carrol J., Andrew F. Hayes, and James Shanahan. 1997. "Perceived Support for One's Opinions and Willingness to Speak Out: A Meta-Analysis of Survey Studies on the 'Spiral of Silence.'" *Public Opinion Quarterly* 61, 3: 452–63.

Graham, Todd S., and Tamara Witschge. 2003. "In Search of Online Deliberation: Towards a New Method for Examining the Quality of Online Discussions." *Communications* 28, 2: 175–204.

Gutmann, Amy, and Dennis Thompson. 1996. *Democracy and Disagreement*. Cambridge, MA: Belknap Press.

Herring, Susan, C. 2000. "Gender Differences in CMC: Findings and Implications." *Computer Professionals for Social Responsibility Newsletter* 18, 1.

Hine, Christine. 2000. *Virtual Ethnography*. London: Sage.

Howard, Philip E. N. 2001. "Can Technology Enhance Democracy? The Doubter's Answer." *The Journal of Politics* 63, 3: 949–55.

Jones, Steve, ed. 1999. *Doing Internet Research: Critical Issues and Methods for Examining the Net*. Thousand Oaks, CA.: Sage.

Kendall, Lori. 1999. "Recontextualizing 'Cyberspace': Methodological Considerations for On-Line Research." In Steve Jones, ed. *Doing Internet Research: Critical Issues and Methods for Examining the Net*, 57–74. Thousand Oaks, CA: Sage.

MacKuen, Michael. 1990. "Speaking of Politics: Individual Conversational Choice, Public Opinion, and the Prospects for Deliberative Democracy." In John A. Ferejohn and James H. Kuklinski, eds., *Information and Democratic Processes*, 59–99. Urbana: University of Illinois Press.

Noelle-Neumann, Elisabeth. 1989. *Öffentliche Meinung: Die Entdeckung Der Schweigespirale*. Frankfurt: Ullstein.

O'Hara, Kieron. 2002. "The Internet: A Tool for Democratic Pluralism?" *Science as Culture* 11, 2: 287–98.

Page, Benjamin I. 1996. *Who Deliberates? Mass Media in Modern Democracy*. Chicago: University of Chicago Press.

Price, Vincent, Joseph N. Cappella, and Lilach Nir. 2002. "Does Disagreement Contribute to More Deliberative Opinion?" *Political Communication* 19, 1: 95–112.

Robinson, John P., Alan Neustadtl, and Meyer Kestnbaum. 2002. "The Online 'Diversity Divide': Public Opinion Differences among Internet Users and Nonusers." *IT and Society* 1, 1: 284–302.

Rosenberg, Morris. 1954. "Some Determinants of Political Apathy." *Public Opinion Quarterly* 18, 4: 349–66.

Scheufele, Dietram A. 1999. "Deliberation or Dispute? An Exploratory Study Examining Dimensions of Public Opinion Expression." *International Journal of Public Opinion Research* 11, 1: 25–58.

Schneider, Steven M. 1997. "Expanding the Public Sphere Through Computer-Mediated Communication: Political Discussion About Abortion in a Usenet Newsgroup." Ph.D. dissertation, Massachusetts Institute of Technology.

Schudson, Michael. 1997. "Why Conversation Is Not the Soul of Democracy." *Critical Studies in Mass Communication* 14: 297–309.

Streck, John M. 1998. "Pulling the Plug on Electronic Town Meetings: Participatory Democracy and the Reality of the Usenet. "In Chris Toulouse and Timothy W. Luke, eds. *The Politics of Cyberspace: A New Political Science Reader*, 18–48. New York: Routeledge.

Street, John. 1997. "Remote Control? Politics, Technology and 'Electronic Democracy.'" *European Journal of Communication* 12, 1: 27–42.

Stromer-Galley, Jennifer. 2002. "New Voices in the Political Sphere: A Comparative Analysis of Interpersonal and Online Political Talk." *Javnost/The Public* 9, 2: 23–42.

Sunstein, Cass R. 2001. *Republic.com*. Princeton, NJ: Princeton University Press.

Taylor, D. Garth. 1982. "Pluralistic Ignorance and the Spiral of Silence: A Formal Analysis." *Public Opinion Quarterly* 46, 3: 311–35.

Wallace, Patricia. 1999. *The Psychology of the Internet.* Cambridge: Cambridge University Press.

Warren, Mark E. 2001. *Democracy and Association.* Princeton, NJ: Princeton University Press.

Warren, Mark E. 1996. "What Should We Expect from More Democracy? Radically Democratic Responses to Politics." *Political Theory* 24, 2: 241–70.

Wilhelm, Anthony G. 1999. "Virtual Sounding Boards: How Deliberative Is Online Political Discussion?" In Barry N. Hague and Brian D. Loader, eds., *Digital Democracy,* 154–78. London: Routledge.

Wyatt, Robert O., Elihu Katz, and Joohan Kim. 2000. "Bridging the Spheres: Political and Personal Conversation in Public and Private Spaces." *Journal of Communication* 50, 1: 71–92.

Wyatt, Robert O., Elihu Katz, Hanna Levinsohn, and Majid Al-Haj. 1996. "The Dimensions of Expression Inhibition: Perception of Obstacles to Free Speech in Three Cultures." *International Journal of Public Opinion Research* 8, 3: 229–47.

Wyatt, Robert O., Joohan Kim, and Elihu Katz. 2000. "How Feeling Free to Talk Affects Ordinary Political Conversation, Purposeful Argumentation, and Civic Participation." *Journalism and Mass Communication Quarterly* 77, 1: 99–114.

Young, Iris Marion. 1996. "Communication and the Other: Beyond Deliberative Democracy." In Seyla Benhabib, ed., *Democracy and Difference,* 120–37. Princeton, NJ: Princeton University Press.

CHAPTER 9

Hacktivism and the Future of Democratic Discourse

ALEXANDRA SAMUEL

The phenomenon of hacktivism demonstrates the extent of the challenge of translating democratic discourse to the Internet. Hacktivism is, as the name suggests, the marriage of computer hacking and political activism. The first widely acknowledged example was a 1998 virtual sit-in against the Mexican government, in solidarity with the Zapatista rebels. The sit-in consisted of a simple script that participants could use to direct their Web browsers to constantly reload the government's main Web page, overloading the site with traffic in the hope that it would slow or crash. This event, dubbed Floodnet, was created by a New York–based group of activists who called themselves the Electronic Disturbance Theater (EDT).

In the years since the EDT's Floodnet, the term *hacktivism* has been applied to a wider range of transgressive, network-enabled forms of activism. The realm of hacktivism now includes:

- Site defacements: hacking into a Web server and replacing the home page with a political message, usually a criticism of the organization that has been hacked, or of some other cause or organization with which it is associated.
- Site redirects: hacking into a Web server and changing its addressing so that would-be visitors to the site are instead redirected to an alternative site, usually one that is critical of the hacked site.
- Information theft: hacking into a private network and stealing information. The hack is publicized (and proof offered) with the goal of

embarrassing the organization with the laxness of its information security, not distributing the stolen information.

- Information theft and distribution: hacking into a private network, stealing information, and publishing that information online.
- Site parodies: creating parody sites that spoof a target organization, often by imitating the appearance of its Web site, and by locating the spoof at a URL (Web address) that is likely to be confused with the address of the original (spoofed) site.
- Virtual sabotage: online activities designed to damage the information technologies of the target.
- Viruses: creating self-executing software programs that propagate and distribute messages or sabotage.
- Software development: creating software tools that serve specific political purposes, usually created and distributed as open-source software.
- Virtual sit-ins or denial-of-service attacks: creating code that allows protesters to rapidly reload Web pages on targeted servers, overloading them with traffic until they crash.

The heterogeneous forms of hacktivism are mirrored by the heterogeneity of causes, groups, and individuals who take part in hacktivist activities. Chinese hackers, possibly with government backing, protested NATO's bombing of the Chinese embassy in Kosovo with attacks on U.S. Web sites. Political party sites from Australia to the United Kingdom have been hacked and defaced during election campaigns. The Arab-Israeli conflict has spawned an online war between hacktivists on each side. The Nike Web site has been hacked and replaced with a link to an antiglobalization organization. More recently, the Cult of the Dead Cow, a leading hacker group, launched Hacktivismo, a software project intended to break down barriers to the free flow of online information in countries with authoritarian regimes.

Hacktivism raises a number of challenges for visions of online civic deliberation. In the broadest terms, it draws our attention to the fact that the Internet's political impact may not be neatly contained by tidily structured participatory opportunities. But it also raises more particular challenges to a number of the specific issues posed by deliberative democracy.

This essay will examine two of these challenges: the challenges to deliberative concepts of free speech and accountability. Each of these concepts is to some degree contested, with different deliberative theorists arguing for different formulations. Yet hacktivism challenges the very terms of debate on each issue, encouraging us to reformulate each concept for the purposes of envisioning online deliberation.

Before approaching each of these challenges in turn, I begin with a brief discussion of the notion of online deliberation as it has been formulated by others. I then introduce a taxonomy of hacktivism that will be crucial to understanding the lines of division among hacktivists on the issues of free speech and accountability. For each of these problems I demonstrate how the divisions among hacktivists translate into larger problems for conceptualizations of online deliberative discourse. I conclude by suggesting that the problems raised by hacktivism are symptomatic of larger phenomena in the online world, demanding a more fundamental review of our vision for online deliberative discourse.

1. Envisioning Digital Deliberation

Much of the debate over the Internet's potential as a home for democratic discourse has been framed by the theories of Jürgen Habermas. Authors including Froomkin (2003), Poster (1995), and Thornton (2002) draw attention to the parallels between the conditions for democratic discourse outlined by Habermas and the potential conditions of online deliberation. Habermas's vision for deliberative democracy is fundamentally communicative, resting on a notion of deliberation as a perpetual conversation among citizens. The purpose of this conversation is "to generate a 'rationally motivated consensus' on controversial claims" (Benhabib 1986: 284). Habermas specifies the conditions of the "ideal speech situation" necessary to enable this kind of conversation:

1. Participation in such deliberation is governed by the norms of equality and symmetry; all have the same chance to initiate speech acts, to question, interrogate, and to open debate.
2. All have the right to question the assigned topics of conversation.
3. All have the right to initiate reflexive arguments about the very rules of the discourse procedure and the way in which they are applied or carried out. (Mouffe 1999, citing Benhabib 1996)

Dahlberg discerns the characteristics of the ideal situation in his study of Minnesota E-Democracy, a prominent example of online citizen-to-citizen political debate. Dahlberg describes Minnesota E-Democracy as a successful example of structuring online dialogue "to stimulate reflexivity, foster respectful listening and participant commitment to ongoing dialogue, achieve open and honest exchange, provide equal opportunity for all voices to be heard, and maximize autonomy from state and corporate interests" (Dahlberg 2001: 627–28).

Despite the theoretical congruity between Habermas's ideal speech situation and some of the apparent characteristics of online dialogue, there are concerns about whether theory can translate into practice. Dahlberg himself qualifies the longer-term prospects of Minnesota E-Democracy, which he believes "may largely be following the course of what Habermas described as the bourgeois public sphere, a narrowly defined rational-critical public increasingly marginalized by the commercialization of the medium and by more populist forms of political participation" (Dahlberg

2001: 628). Streck raises similar concerns about the Well, a widely praised online community that he describes as "a computer-based instance of Jürgen Habermas's bourgeois public sphere, in which the educated and affluent come together outside both home and state for critical discussion of art, literature and politics" (Streck 1998: 28).

While Habermas thus provides some useful frameworks for considering the challenge of online deliberation, his work by no means resolves how the Internet could house democratic deliberation. Perhaps for that reason, some authors have been tempted to go beyond Habermasian models, or to use Habermas's work more loosely in their examinations of online discourse. Hale, Musso, and Weare are among those who draw on Barber's notion of "strong democracy" to consider possibilities for "more thoughtful, civic-minded and deliberative patterns of communication" (1999: 104). Coleman and Gøtze frame their examination of policy deliberation with Dewey's vision of "improvement of the methods and conditions of debate, discussion, and persuasion" (Dewey, quoted in Coleman and Gøtze 2001: 11). Witschge, in this volume, synthesizes a range of deliberation theorists (including Dryzek, Bohman, and Cohen) in order to formulate requirements for online deliberation (Witschge 2004).

Both the Habermasian and non-Habermasian variants share some common preoccupations, however. Each assumes that some sort of free speech principle must be in operation—although the boundaries of legitimate speech may be conceived differently. Each also addresses the problem of anonymity, although there are significant differences as to whether it is seen as constructive or destructive to democratic discourse. Before examining how hacktivism challenges the way each of these debates has been formulated, let me briefly turn to the core lines of debate within the hacktivist community itself.

2. Forms of Hacktivism

The various forms of hacktivism fall into three clusters, which I have termed *political cracking, performative hacktivism,* and *political coding.* Political cracking consists of illegal or nebulous hacktions, undertaken by hacktivists from hacker backgrounds, aimed at protesting or influencing policy. Performative hacktivism consists of hacktions aimed at policy protest or influence, conducted by hacktivists from artist-activist backgrounds. Political coding is undertaken by hacktivists with hacker backgrounds and consists of hacktions aimed at circumventing public policy. These three clusters reflect covariation on a range of crucial dimensions, such as the objectives of particular hacktivists, the legality of their tactics, and their patterns of collaboration. The clusters also reflect profound divisions among hacktivists on the issues of free speech and accountability—divisions that shed light on some of the core claims of those envisaging deliberative democracy online.

2.1 Political Cracking

Political cracking consists of hacktions aimed at public or policy influence, undertaken by hackers. This encompasses the vast majority of hacktivist activity to date and spans a wide range of issues and nations. It also encompasses a wide range of tactics, including site defacements, redirects, denial-of-service attacks, information theft, and sabotage.

Calling these activities "political cracking" draws on a distinction that is maintained by many members of the hacker community. Among early computer enthusiasts, a "hack" was a technical "feat . . . imbued with innovation, style, and technical virtuosity," and people "called themselves 'hackers' with great pride" (Levy 1984: 23). Hackers from that generation "prefer to call their progeny 'crackers' in order to differentiate themselves from what they perceive as their younger criminal counterparts" (Thomas 2002: ix). Many younger hackers also use the distinction between hacking and cracking to separate criminal activity from exploration.

Yet political cracking is the strand of hacktivism that remains closest to its hacker roots. Indeed, political cracking can be seen as a direct outgrowth of the informal "hacker ethic" that has guided many first- and second-generation hackers. Most discussions of the hacker ethic refer to the six tenets summarized by Levy:

- Access to computers—and anything which might teach you something about the way the world works—should be unlimited and total. Always yield to the Hands-On imperative!
- All information should be free.
- Mistrust authority—promote decentralization.
- Hackers should be judged by their hacking, not bogus criteria such as degrees, age, race, or position.
- You can create art and beauty on a computer.
- Computers can change your life for the better. (Levy 1984: 39–49).

The hacker ethic both drives and justifies much of the activity of political crackers—and of political coders, too. Many of the issues that have been embraced by hacktivists are direct outgrowths of this hacker ethic. Issues such as Internet censorship, privacy, security, access to encryption, and intellectual property rights are all organically linked to the beliefs that information should be free and authority mistrusted. These are the issues that have inspired much of the activity of political crackers, particularly in the early days before the term *hacktivism* was even in play.

The fact that political crackers have directed so much of their activity toward online issues makes it hard to draw a line between hacking and hacktivism. When Kevin Mitnick was arrested and prosecuted for his hacking, thousands of hackers mobilized to support him—in many cases by defacing sites to add "Free Kevin" messages. Was this hacktivism or plain old hacking? According to the hacker ethic, it's a false distinction because hacking is an inherently political act, the liberation of information.

The line becomes sharper when we look at the more recent activities of political crackers. What started out as a phenomenon of cracking on hacker-specific issues has broadened to encompass a much broader range of causes, from gun control (pro and con) to globalization and corporate power. Today the greatest concentration of political cracking incidents occurs in the context of transnational cyberwars: between Israelis and Palestinians, Indians and Pakistanis, Chinese and Americans. Each of these cyberwars has seen hundreds or even thousands of Web sites defaced in a campaign that pits political cracker against political cracker.

While it has been credibly argued that governments have sponsored some of this cyberwar cracking, the majority of political cracking activities are illegal in the jurisdiction of the target, the cracker, or both. As a result, political cracking is almost always anonymous, or more often pseudonymous. Precisely because hacker culture puts so much value on technical prowess, crackers like to build their reputations by taking credit for their hacktions under handles (pseudonyms).

The fact that the activities of political crackers are generally illegal does not mean they are necessarily destructive. Indeed, the "hacker ethic" is widely seen as precluding destructive activity:

> It is against hacker ethics to alter any data aside from the logs that are needed to clean their tracks. They have no need or desire to destroy data as the malicious crackers. They are there to explore the system and learn more. (Mizrach n.d.)

Unlike other forms of hacktivism, engaging in any form of political cracking requires at least a minimal knowledge of code and/or hacking techniques, which is still almost unheard of outside the hacker community. Political cracking is thus almost entirely confined to hacktivists who come from hacker backgrounds or who have spent enough time on hacker sites to acquire the necessary skills. These crackers can work alone or in small groups (sometimes called hacker gangs) in undertaking their various hacktions.

Like their nonpolitical counterparts, most political crackers seem to be quite young—if not teenagers, then not far into their twenties. While there are some women involved in political cracking, most of these teenagers are boys. As Douglas Thomas points out, hacking is very much a "boy culture" in its emphasis on notions of mastery, competition, and subordination (Thomas 2002: xvi). That carries over to the world of political cracking, in which political site defacements will bear comments such as "all those wannabe unicode kiddies who are defacing thinking they have joined us can DREAM ON cuz all they are doing is making themselves more GAY" (listserv.gao.gov COMPROMISED 2001).

As that kind of language suggests, political cracking is all about getting attention—in other words, pursuing influence rather than a direct effect on outcomes. Indeed, political crackers make a point of noting that, however rude or irritating their defacements are, "[i]t's just a machine we use to do what we do, not a gun or missile or something" (Domina Security 2002).

2.2 Performative Hacktivism

Performative hacktivism consists of hacktions aimed at public or policy influence, undertaken by hacktivists with artist-activist backgrounds. It draws heavily on the tradition of political theater in its adaptation of hacking for political purposes. The term *performative* encompasses not only the broad notion of hacktivism as performance—which these hacktions most certainly are—but also the more particular idea of political protest as a "speech act." The notion of politics as spectacle that has informed performative hacktivism also characterizes a wider array of "carnivalesque" protest tactics popularized by the antiglobalization movement (Boje 2001).

Most performative hacktivists come from theater or art backgrounds and see hacktivism as a new form of political art. Many performative hacktivists produce other forms of Internet or digital art in addition to their hacktivism. No doubt because of these roots, performative hacktivism comes disproportionately from the left. It has addressed such issues as globalization, liberation struggles (especially that of the Zapatistas, in Mexico), and corporate power. Many performative hacktions have been coordinated, or at least timed to coincide, with simultaneous street protests.

The most visible groups of performative hacktivists are the Electronic Disturbance Theater (EDT), ®™ark, and the electrohippies. The Electronic Disturbance Theater is a group of four U.S.-based activists who banded together in 1998 to create a digital protest in solidarity with the Zapatistas. ®™ark (http://RTMark.com) is a U.S.-based activist "mutual fund" that sponsors acts of "anticorporate sabotage"—including a number of hacktions. It uses its status as a legal corporation to both spoof and benefit from limitations on corporate liability. The UK-based Electrohippie Collective was created in July 1999 with the intention of using the Internet to challenge the commercialization of cyberspace; until it disbanded in July 2002, it focused its activities on anticorporate hacktions such as its virtual sit-in against the World Trade Organization (WTO).

The members of the EDT consciously decided to abandon the anonymity that was usual among computer hackers. Their members are thus identifiable as Ricardo Dominguez, a New York–based performance artist;

Stefan Wray, a Texas-based journalist then working on a graduate degree at New York University; and Carmin Karasic and Brett Stalbaum, both programmers and Internet artists. Participants in the virtual sit-ins that are organized by EDT usually remain anonymous, but leaders of other performative hacking groups are also, for the most part, visible under their own names.

Performative hacktions have encompassed a wide range of issues but usually focus on offline issues such as globalization and human rights. They almost always engage a multinational coalition of activists, even if the sites are assembled by hacktivists in one country who then solicit sit-in participation from a broader cross-national population.

Performative hacktivism mostly takes the form of virtual sit-ins or site parodies—forms of hacktivism with clear precedents in the traditions of street protest and political theater. This area of hacktivism has also made some moves into the field of software development, but only as a way of facilitating the primary tactics of sit-ins and site parodies. The EDT developed an open-source version of its sit-in tools, and a group called the Yes Men have created software that automates the creation of Web site parodies.

While performative hacktivist tactics are carefully constructed to avoid clear legal jeopardy, they are not without legal risk. The virtual sit-in tactic is essentially a less illegal version of the denial-of-service attack; since actual people are loading the pages that overload a server, it is not clearly illegal. But at least one virtual sit-in (conducted by the EDT in 1998) was counterattacked by the U.S. military, and a site parody (of the WTO's Web site) faced the threat of legal challenge.

The intensity of the reaction that these hacktivists have provoked attests to the success of their hacktions as performance. Performative hacktivists are very much oriented to the public eye and see their activities as a way of challenging corporate and media domination of public discourse. Their hacktions are aimed not at directly affecting outcomes but at shifting that discourse by raising awareness and creating public pressure.

As this may suggest, performative hacktivism is more theory-driven than other forms of hacktivism. Performative hacktivists often cite French critical theorists as sources of intellectual inspiration in their efforts to comprehend the political or performative dimensions of cyberspace. Different performative hacktivists offer different theoretical takes on the nature of hacktivism, but a common theme is the way the Internet has changed the relationship between the human body and human identity. Performative hacktivists use the Internet as a way of exploring the new virtual body and its relationship to the corporeal world; they sometimes argue that power has shifted altogether into the virtual world and thus needs to be challenged within cyberspace itself. (Critical Art Ensemble 1994: 3)

2.3 Political Coding

Political coding consists of hackers applying their technical skills to the creation of code that circumvents, ignores, or supersedes policy. These hackers are metaphorically (and perhaps literally) the older brothers of political crackers. Many of the hackers who participate in political coding started out as nonpolitical hackers, programmers, or crackers and came to political coding as an outgrowth of that activity. They typically adhere to the hacker convention of using handles (pseudonyms), though the real names that correspond to most of these handles are relatively easy to ascertain.

Political coding so far reflects the cyberlibertarian world view described by Barbrook and Cameron (1995), Katz (1997), Norris (2001), and others. This cyberlibertarian ideology emphasizes individual rights, especially online rights, as the most important political good. This viewpoint explains why political coding has focused entirely on issues that are directly related to the hacker community. Some hacktivists argue, as did Oxblood Ruffin when I interviewed him in September 2002, that this focus on Internet-oriented issues is core to the notion of hacktivism—that hacktivism is, by definition, activism related to the Internet.

Several political coding projects have facilitated the distribution of DeCSS, a piece of software that decrypts DVDs for playback on Linux machines. The software has been banned at the behest of the Motion Picture Association of America (MPAA), which objected to the cracking of its CSS encryption, meant to prevent the copying of DVDs. The DeCSS coding projects have been undertaken by solo or small-group actors, working anonymously or pseudonymously.

Another strand of political coding focuses on Internet censorship, particularly as it affects democracy activists in authoritarian regimes. Internet censorship has been the chief target of the Hacktivismo project, sponsored by the Cult of the Dead Cow (cDc). The Hacktivismo project has rapidly become the center of the political coding scene and has received a great deal of media attention.

Hacktivismo was the brainchild of Oxblood Ruffin, the cDc's "foreign minister," who began working on the Hacktivismo project in the summer of 1999 (Cult of the Dead Cow 2000–01). The goal of Hacktivismo's first project, named Peekabooty, was to "create a product that can bypass the nation-wide censorship of the World Wide Web practiced by many countries" (Peekabooty 2002). Peekabooty broke off from Hacktivismo in 2001 before finally releasing its first operational software in 2002.

Meanwhile, the Hacktivismo project expanded to include other anticensorship tools, such as Camera/Shy, a steganography tool that lets activists encrypt their messages by hiding them in an image. Hacktivismo has also expanded to include a range of activists from outside the cDc, many of them Toronto-based coders personally recruited by Ruffin. Other

Hacktivismo volunteers have joined the team from as far away as Germany, Taiwan, and China, using the Internet to collaborate on software development. It can thus be characterized as multinational hacktivism.

All of these projects—DeCSS, Peekabooty, Camera/Shy—aim not at policy influence but at policy circumvention. The various programs aimed at disseminating DeCSS are not trying to change the legal rulings on DeCSS decryption; they are trying to make those rulings unenforceable and meaningless. Peekabooty doesn't try to change the Chinese government's Internet censorship policy; it provides a way of evading that censorship, regardless of the government's policy.

Political coding thus constitutes a focused but potentially significant erosion of state sovereignty. Hacktivists use code to sidestep governmental authority. Instead of pursuing new policies or legal rulings, coders circumvent existing law and regulation by providing ways of evading the law that have few or no consequences for the end user of the software.

In the process of circumventing policy, these projects may also have some policy impact by raising awareness of the issues they focus on. The Hacktivismo team, in particular, takes care to publicize its activities in order to increase media coverage of the censorship issue. But awareness and influence are useful by-products, not the primary goal.

The ability to circumvent policy depends on hacktivists committing the time to develop and complete a software product. The software that political coders develop is virtually always open-source, which means it can be freely distributed, modified, and improved by other coders. The open-source model lessens the burden on any one developer or team, but software development is still a time-intensive form of hacktivism compared with defacing a Web site.

It is also skill-intensive, since it demands a core team of coders. But not all political coders are programmers: a number of people involved in the Hacktivismo project contribute other kinds of skills, such as writing or Web site design. While this suggests that political coding does not necessarily require a high level of programming knowledge, even nonprogrammers tend to have some background in Internet-oriented activities. Although they may not be hackers per se, they are certainly conversant in hacker culture.

The Hacktivismo project is very much a collective endeavor. While single hackers may take the lead on one project, writing most or even all of the code, the success of each piece of software depends on its dissemination to a larger community of users. The project Web site, which is collectively produced and maintained (again, with a couple of lead designers and writers), is thus crucial to the project's larger mission of promoting awareness of Internet censorship and of ways to evade it.

The legal risks associated with political coding vary from project to project. Jon Johansen, the Norwegian teenager who created the original DeCSS software, has been indicted in Norway and cannot travel to the

United States for fear of prosecution there. Hacktivismo's board of directors includes Cindy Cohn, a lawyer for the Electronic Frontier Foundation, specifically to guard against the potential legal ramifications of Hacktivismo's various activities.

Ultimately the success of political coding seems to lie in the high perceptions of efficacy among its practitioners. Hacktivists who have started out in other forms of hacktivism may be drawn in by the promise of direct effect. The creator of thehacktivist.com, known by the name metac0m, comes from an activist background, but as he noted in my interview with him in September 2002, he has moved his energies into political coding because it "produces something tangible, rather than just protest" and is "something people can use."

3. The Problem of Free Speech

Identifying these three types of hacktivist helps us understand the internal hacktivist divisions on key questions of free speech and accountability. Both issues are hotly debated in the hacktivist community as well as among deliberative democrats.

Free speech is essential to any model of democratic discourse, and some even argue that the very purpose of free speech is "to ensure that it is possible for people to engage in the discussion and deliberation necessary for the successful use of democratic institutions" (Nickel 2000: 3). As Cohen has pointed out, free speech is especially crucial to deliberative democracy, and for this reason, free speech protection in a deliberative democracy must extend beyond specifically political speech to encompass the full range of "conscientious expression" (Cohen 1998: 208, 210).

But the Internet may make protecting free speech more difficult and more complicated, as the case of hacktivism suggests. Many forms of hacktivism—most notably Web site defacements and virtual sit-ins—involve jamming or altering someone else's speech. Web site defacements replace one online message with another. Virtual sit-ins temporarily silence (or muffle) a message as a way of drawing attention to another. Are these actions forms of free speech or a rebuke to it?

Political coders argue that freedom of speech is absolute and that any form of hacktivism that interferes with the publishing rights of its target—such as defacements or virtual sit-ins—is thus illegitimate. They argue that freedom of speech is what hacktivism is all about:

> I think hacktivism should be about delivering a message, just like good old grass roots activism. It shouldn't be about doing damage to someone else network, or taking away their right to express their views. We just want to make a fuss so people will pay attention to what the message is we wish to deliver. (Bronc Buster in a message on the hacktivism.ca listserv, August 27, 1999)

Or as Hacktivismo leader Oxblood Ruffin put it when I interviewed him, "Don't try to deny anyone the right of speech or the right of publishing."

To that end, political coders put much of their energies into protecting freedom of speech online. The Hacktivismo/Peekabooty projects focus on extending online free speech protections to jurisdictions that have limited speech rights. The DeCSS projects, too, represent a commitment to free speech rights for code—consistent with coders' view of software as a form of speech. "I believe that code does have consciousness," said Ruffin. "Cindy Cohn [a lawyer for the Electronic Frontier Foundation, and a Hacktivismo advisor] has established that code is speech."

In contrast, performative coders argue that freedom of speech is relative, and that inequalities of communications access mean that some have more speech than others. Defacements and sit-ins thus level the playing field. This perspective is explicitly juxtaposed with the hacker/coder preoccupation with protecting the flow of information online. For example, when I interviewed him in May 2002, Ricardo Dominguez described the reaction to one of his virtual sit-ins this way:

> As we were about to start the action, we were surrounded by a group of hackers called Hart. Dutch hackers. And they said, Ricardo, Stefan, what you're about to do will destroy infrastructure. And if you guys do it, we will take you down. It was our first encounter with what I call the "digitally correct" community. Those who believe that bandwidth is above human lives.

Performative hackers (and their supporters) sometimes justify their actions with a "level playing field" argument:

> Which law are hacktivists to adhere to anyway, when they are trying to support an oppressed group of indigenous peoples in another country? Isn't the law one of the prime obstacles in any activist's path? Isn't activism always a way of challenging institutionalised power without going through accepted channels? (xday-dreamx in a message on the hacktivism.ca listserv, August 27, 1999)

While political crackers tend not to get into these debates over principle, their comments reflect a similar "ends over means" attitude. They consistently deflect questions about their methods, and instead draw attention to the methods of their targets:

> We would call ourselves as people who're trying to make a difference and showing the true faces of the countries like Israel, India or any other country doing unjustice. We don't mind what people call

us, our work speaks for itself. (Electronic interview with m0r0n
and nightman, October 2002)

The challenge posed by political crackers and performative coders is
an interesting one for deliberative democrats. Whereas much of the discussion over the bounds of legitimate speech focuses on freedom of
expression, the hacktivist problem does not derive, in a strict sense, from
any limitations on the ability to speak.[1] After all, any hacktivist has the
alternative of publishing his or her views on a Web page. The motivation
for hacktivism lies not in unequal access to speech but rather in inequality
in the ability to be heard. The problem thus stems from the very virtue
that so many deliberative theorists see in the advent of the Internet: the
universal availability of a platform for self-expression. By providing a very
widely accessible tool of mass communication, the Internet has made the
ability to communicate much less scarce. Instead, it is the availability of
audience that is scarce.

The problem of limited audience is described by Goldhaber's work on
the "attention economy." As Goldhaber notes, "attention . . . is an intrinsically scarce resource." Yet where Goldhaber anticipates that "individual
attention getters of all sorts will find it ever easier to get attention directly
through the Web" (Goldhaber 1997), the hacktivist case suggests that even
skilled Internet users may find it ever harder to command an audience in
an atmosphere with so many competing for attention. Hacktivism provides a way of addressing inequalities of audience access, even when ave-
nues of expression are widely available.

The challenge for deliberative democrats is that acknowledging
audience scarcity (and inequality of access) makes freedom of expression
look like a relatively hollow basis for deliberation. If participants cannot be
satisfied with the opportunity for speech but instead demand the
opportunity to be heard, how are we to constitute procedural principles
for online deliberation?

3.1 The Problem of Anonymity

Perhaps no aspect of online communications poses as great a challenge to
our aspirations for meaningful democratic discourse as the ready availability of anonymous speech. Anonymity has been only a rare feature of
speech in the "real" world, but in cyberspace it is routine.

The role of anonymity in public life has been subject to much debate.
The debate can be distilled to two contradictory positions. One sees anonymity as a necessary and valuable part of political life. This position ties
anonymity closely to free speech, holding that total privacy—anonymity—is sometimes necessary to free speech. Anonymity "encourages the
free flow of ideas" (Judge Kenneth C. MacKenzie, quoted in Amis 2001),
allowing people to make unpopular statements that nonetheless enrich

public debate. Anonymity allows speech in which the focus is on the speech, not the speaker. Anonymity allows people "to avoid persecution" (Marx 2001) even as they speak their conscience freely.

The opposite extreme sees anonymity as a danger to democracy and public life. This position focuses on accountability as the root of responsible behavior and responsible politics. Anonymity brings out the worst in people by allowing them to evade the consequences of their speech or actions. Anonymity precludes meaningful speech because it makes it impossible to judge the interests or motives of the speaker. Some also argue that "anonymity—like the myth of Gyges's ring that makes the wearer invisible—leads inexorably to immoral and even illegal behavior" (Saco 2002: 117).

This debate is crucial to our assessment of the prospects for electronic democracy. If anonymity is congenial to democracy, online deliberation may be, if anything, *more* robust than its offline predecessors. If, on the other hand, anonymity is destructive to democracy, either our hopes for electronic democracy must be constrained or our laws and technologies of identity verification must be greatly strengthened.

Yet until now the debate over anonymity has been largely a theoretical one. The two extreme positions in the anonymity debate represent normative beliefs about anonymous speech, not empirical claims about how anonymity actually works. As long as anonymity was constrained to "bathroom walls and prank calls" (Hilden 2001), this was by necessity a hypothetical discussion. But the rapid expansion in anonymous speech facilitated by the Internet allows us to examine these competing principles against a richer field of anonymity practices.

Hacktivism offers a particularly interesting array of anonymity practices. First, it offers three very distinct positions on anonymity, represented by the political cracker, performative hacker, and political coder clusters. Second, the very extremism of hacktivist practices make them appear similar to the best- and worst-case scenarios envisaged by anonymity advocates and opponents: if we fear that anonymity facilitates injurious or even criminal behavior, then hacktivism may be a case in point. Political crackers deface Web sites, slow, block, or damage Web servers, distribute viruses, and wreak other kinds of havoc. Their actions could be seen as just the type of antisocial behavior feared by anonymity opponents. On the other hand, political crackers could be seen as vindicating the hopes of anonymity advocates, in that crackers use anonymity to express unpopular or challenging opinions. Their destructiveness is usually limited and is always in service to some form of political communication or action. And both political crackers and political coders detach their message from the identity, nationality, or location of the messenger—again, as envisioned by some anonymity proponents.

But the actual practices of hacktivists do not fit neatly into the expectations of either camp—perhaps because the two camps represent idealized extremes. As Gary Marx has observed, anonymity is not a binary phenomenon. Rather, "identifiability at one extreme can be contrasted with anonymity at the other. Describing a variety of kinds of identity knowledge and approaching these as distinct continua brings us closer to the messiness of the empirical world" (Marx 2001). And the actual practices of hacktivists offer all the messiness we could want, with different types of hacktivists using anonymity in very different ways.

Political crackers usually use what Marx refers to as "pseudonyms that can not be linked to other forms of identity knowledge—the equivalent of 'real' anonymity (except that the name chosen may hint at some aspects of 'real' identity, as with undercover agents encouraged to take names close to their own)" (Marx 2001). This reflects the fact that crackers are engaged in activities that could entail significant legal consequences if they were caught.

In contrast, political coders most frequently use "pseudonyms that can be linked to legal name and/or locatability—literally a form of pseudo-anonymity" (Marx 2001). Coders vary somewhat in their use of pseudonymity: the participants in Peekabooty are identified by their legal names on the project's Web site, while Hacktivismo participants use their pseudonyms in their work with the project but are mostly forthcoming with their real names in face-to-face interactions, and DeCSS authors sometimes use traceable pseudonyms or real names and sometimes use untraceable pseudonyms or remain anonymous.

Performative hackers, in contrast, are generally known by their real names. The names of the Electrohippies, the ®™ark team, and the members of the EDT are all publicly available. The EDT consciously rejected anonymity when it got the hacktivism ball rolling, as Dominguez noted when I interviewed him, and others have followed suit.

How are we to interpret this variation in "nymity" practices? Not in the terms afforded by democratic theory's debate over anonymity—with the possible exception of the pseudonymity and anonymity practiced by political crackers. Their use of pseudonymity and anonymity as a shelter from legal consequences fits the argument that "anonymity supports the mischievous, the petty vandalisms against each other and authorities that give us room to mock perceived hegemonies and to release 'incorrect' but genuine feelings" (Smith 1997: 42).

But the variation in hacktivist nymity practices is ultimately ill-predicted by the scholarship on offline anonymity. These various practices are better understood as decisions about the construction of a digital identity than as statements of offline accountability. As Diane Saco argues, "Electronic pseudonymity—anonymity through the adoption of an alias—can have the parallel effect of constructing a kind of public voice even as it protects personal identity" (Saco 2002: 119). Hacktivists clearly construct "public voices" in their deliberate and strategic use of real names, anonymity, and pseudonymity.

Political coders and political crackers create online public voices through their consistent use of a pseudonym online. If crackers were interested only in escaping the legal consequences of their hacktions, they would be better off leaving their Web defacements unsigned. But the use of digital pseudonyms allows the creation of a cumulative body of work—a digital manifesto—for which they are both identifiable and accountable within the virtual community.

Being able to take digital credit for one's hacktivism is only part of the attraction of pseudonymity, however. As the United States Supreme Court observed in the 1995 case *McIntyre v. Ohio Campaign Commission,* "Anonymity . . . provides a way for a writer who may be personally unpopular to ensure that readers will not prejudge her message simply because they do not like its proponent." This dimension of electronic pseudonymity is particularly in keeping with the tenet of the hacker ethic that holds that "[h]ackers should be judged by their hacking, not bogus criteria such as degrees, age, race, or position" (Levy 1984: 43). This is explicit in political crackers' rejection of questions about their age or nationality, as m0r0n and nightman noted in an electronic interview: "Dividing people according to country is not our style, as mentioned earlier. 'DIVISION' is not a word in our lexicon." Pseudonymous and anonymous hacking is a statement about separating the virtual body from the physical body and all the criteria (such as nationality, race, and gender) that we use to judge physical personae.

Performative hackers' use of real names is an explicit rejection of that separation. Performative hacktivists argue for a reunion of virtual and real politics and criticize, as Dominguez did, the hacker fantasy of "having the data body leave the real body, the electronic body uploading itself." Using real names in cyberspace is a way of rejecting the hacker separation between the virtual and real, and instead affirming real-world accountability for virtual acts.

These different nymity choices thus translate into different kinds of accountability claims. Political crackers use robust pseudonymity or anonymity to declare that they are accountable to no one (although either coder carelessness or government intelligence work may sometimes put the lie to that claim). Political coders embrace (generally weak) pseudonymity as a hacker convention. While they thus construct a digital persona—a public voice—that is accountable to the digital community, it is accountable only in terms that divorce the judgment of the digital body from the characteristics of its fleshy analogue. Performative hackers explicitly reject the pseudonymity and anonymity of the hacker world and embrace accountability to the physical world instead.

The idea of nymity as a sort of accountability claim is a significant challenge to democratic theories that treat nymity as an issue of principle. Hacktivist practices suggest that rather than framing the question of anonymity as a principled debate over accountability in public speech, nymity should be seen as one of the kinds of claims that speakers make when participating in deliberative discourse.

4. Conclusion

The challenges that hacktivism has posed to the notions of freedom and accountability in democratic discourse are likely the first wave of a larger transformation. Hacktivist tools are being distributed to a widening audience that will find lower and lower barriers to entry. The purpose of these tools is to take the decision to monitor or regulate speech out of the hands of the state. Instead of collective decisions (or authoritarian decisions) about how speech should be regulated, individuals create their own speech regimes by choosing tools that provide them with a greater degree of privacy. By creating these tools, hacktivists and other Internet users preserve the Internet as a space for self-regulating speech.

That may be a challenge for proceduralist visions of deliberative democracy that seek to establish structures for discourse—including ground rules for free expression and accountability. But the impossibility of enforcing rules of discourse may be the ultimate victory for the Habermasian vision of the public sphere as deliberation without coercion, its only goal "a consensus brought about by coercion-free communication" (Habermas 1983: 173).

Note

1. See, for example, Cohen 1998; Nickel 2000; Charney 1998.

References

Amis, D. 2001. "Net Anonymity: Free Speech or Cheap Words?" Available at http://www.spiked-online.com/Articles/0000000054A7.htm (accessed November 19, 2002).

Barbrook, R., and A. Cameron. 2002. *The Californian Ideology* Alamut: Bastion of Peace and Information, 1995 Available from http://www.alamut.com/subj/ideologies/pessimism/califIdeo_I.html. (accessed October 7 2002).

Benhabib, S. 1986. *Critique, Norm, and Utopia: A Study of the Foundations of Critical Theory.* New York: Columbia University Press.

Benhabib, S. 1996. Toward a Deliberative Model of Democratic Legitimacy. In *Democracy and Difference*, edited by S. Benhabib. Princeton: Princeton University Press.

Bennett, W. L. 1998. "The UnCivic Culture: Communication, Identity, and the Rise of Lifestyle Politics." Available at http://www.apsanet.org/PS/dec98/bennett.cfm (accessed September 7, 2002).

Boje, D. M. 2001. "Carnivalesque Resistance to Global Spectacle: A Critical Postmodern Theory of Public Administration." Available at http://cbae.nmsu.edu/~dboje/papers/carnivalesque_resistance_to_glob.htm (accessed October 6, 2002).

Buster, B. "Target?" [e-mail]. hacktivism.ca listserv, August 27, 1999 (accessed November 25, 2001).

Chambers, S. 2000. "A Culture of Publicity." In S. Chambers and A. N. Costain, eds., *Deliberation, Democracy, and the Media*, 193–208. Lanham, MD: Rowman and Littlefield.

Charney, E. 1998. "Political Liberalism, Deliberative Democracy, and the Public Sphere." *American Political Science Review* 92, 1: 98–110.

Cohen, J. 1998. "Democracy and Liberty." In J. Elster, ed., *Deliberative Democracy*, 195–231. New York: Cambridge University Press.

Coleman, S., and J. Gøtze. 2001. "Bowling Together: Online Public Engagement in Policy Deliberation." Available at http://bowlingtogether.net/bowlingtogether.pdf (accessed March 1, 2002).

Critical Art Ensemble. 1994. *The Electronic Disturbance.* Brooklyn, NY: Autonomedia.

Cult of the Dead Cow. 2000–01. The Hacktivismo FAQ v1.0. Available at http://www.cultdead-cow.com/cDc_files/HacktivismoFAQ.html (accessed March 22, 2004).

Dahlberg, L. 2001. "The Internet and Democratic Discourse." *Information, Communication and Society* 4, 4: 615–33.

Domina Security. 2002. Interview with AIC (Anti India Crew). Available at http://www.dominasecurity.com/hackerz/aic.htm (accessed September 27, 2002).

Fischer, F. 2001. *Citizens, Experts, and the Environment.* Durham, NC: Duke University Press.

Froomkin, A. Michael 2004. "Technologies for Democracy." In Peter M. Shane, ed., *Democracy Online: The Prospects for Political Renewal Through the Internet.* New York: Routledge.

Goldhaber, M. H. 1997. "The Attention Economy and the Net." First Monday 2, 4. Available at http://www.firstmonday.org/issues/issue2_4/goldhaber/index.html (accessed March 22, 2004).

Habermas, J. 1983. *Philosophical-Political Profiles.* Cambridge, MA: MIT Press.

Hale, M., J. Musso, and C. Weare. 1999. "Developing Digital Democracy: Evidence from Californian Municipal Web pages." In B. N. Hague and B. Loader, eds., *Digital Democracy: Discourse and Decision Making in the Information Age,* 96–115. New York: Routledge.

Hilden, J. 2001. "The Legal Debate Over Protecting Anonymous Speakers Online." Available at http://www.gigalaw.com/articles/2001-all/hilden-2001-02-all.html (accessed November 19, 2002).

Katz, J.E., and P. Aspden. 1997. A nation of strangers? *Communications of the ACM* 40:81–86.

Levy, S. 1984. *Hackers: Heroes of the Computer Revolution.* New York: Penguin Books.

"Listerv.gao.gov COMPROMISED." Mirrored at http://www.safemode.org/mirror/2001/12/09/ftp.gao.gov/mirror.html (accessed July 20,2002).

Marx, G. T. 2001. "Identity and Anonymity: Some Conceptual Distinctions and Issues for Research." In J. Caplan and J. Torpey, eds., *Documenting Individual Identity.* Princeton: Princeton University Press. Available at http://web.mit.edu/gtmarx/www/identity.html (accessed May 3, 2004).

Mizrach, S. n.d. "Is There a Hacker Ethic for 90s Hackers?" Available at http://www.fiu.edu/~mizrachs/hackethic.html (accessed October 7, 2002).

Mouffe, C. 1999. "Deliberative Democracy or Agonistic Pluralism?" *Social Research* 66, 3: 745–58.

Nickel, J. W. 2000. "Free Speech, Democratic Deliberation, and Valuing Types of Speech." In S. Chambers and A. N. Costain, eds., *Deliberation, Democracy, and the Media,* 3–9. Lanham, MD: Rowman and Littlefield.

Norris, Pippa. 2001. *Digital Divide: Civic Engagement, Information Poverty, and the Internet Worldwide.* New York: Cambridge University Press.

Peekabooty. 2002. "About the Peekabooty Project." Available at http://www.peek-a-booty.org/pbhtml/modules.php?name=Content&pa=showpage&pid=1 (accessed October 7, 2002).

Poster, M. 1995. "CyberDemocracy: Internet and the Public Sphere." Available at http://www.hnet.uci.edu/mposter/writings/democ.html (accessed November 22, 2002).

Putnam, R. D. 2000. *Bowling Alone: The Collapse and Revival of American Community.* New York: Simon and Schuster.

Saco, D. 2002. *Cybering Democracy: Public Space and the Internet.* Minneapolis: University of Minnesota Press.

Smith, J. M. 1997. *Private Matters: In Defense of the Personal Life.* Reading, MA: Addison-Wesley.

Streck, J. M. 1998. "Pulling the Plug on Electronic Town Meetings: Participatory Democracy and the Reality of the Usenet." In C. Toulouse and T. W. Luke, eds., *The Politics of Cyberspace.* London: Routledge.

Thomas, D. 2002. *Hacker Culture.* Minneapolis: University of Minnesota Press.

Thornton, A. 2002. "Does Internet Create Democracy." Available at http://www.zip.com.au/~athornto//thesis_2002_alinta_thornton.doc (accessed November 21, 2002).

Wilhelm, A. G. 2000. Democracy in the Digital Age: Challenges to Political Life in Cyberspace. New York: Routledge.

xdaydreamx, 2001. "Re: filling its 404 error logs with the names of the men, women and" [e-mail]. hacktivism.ca listver, August 27, 1999 (accessed July 20, 2001).

CHAPTER 10

ICANN and Electronic Democratic Deficit

DAN HUNTER

Any number of idealized conceptions of democracy have been projected onto cyberspace. Direct democracy advocates have suggested that cyberspace reduces political transaction costs to zero, and thus we can at last have genuine self-government, with everyone voting on every issue all the time. Deliberative democracy theorists embrace the Internet because it offers the opportunity to engage the demos, informing each and every one of its members, providing them with a costless way of debating and deliberating. Advocates of participatory democracy envision a vast sea of committed, electronically connected citizens directly engaging with their government—indeed, like the ancient Greek ideal, actually supplanting government and becoming it. It seems that cyberspace is like Coke: any democratic theory goes better with it.

Unfortunately, theory and practice are slightly different. In this essay, I argue that there is a vast gap between theoretical conceptions of democracy and the reality that operates within online institutions. The particular institution I want to focus on is the Internet Corporation for Assigned Names and Numbers (ICANN). This body is unusual but, I think, characteristic of the types of online institutions we will see emerge as cyberspace matures. It is not tied to any specific physical place or jurisdiction and so cannot rely on geographical partitions of the demos. Its constituents come from multiple arenas, with divergent policy interests, so it cannot rely on homogeneity of interests to generate acceptable political outcomes. Most of what it does is published online, analyzed in detail, and criticized endlessly. As such, ICANN is an excellent case study in whether genuine online institutions can meet our expectations of democracy. In the first part of this essay I sketch the structural features of ICANN and explain its attempts to be more democratic and why they failed.

There are two possible views why online democracy and ICANN have been such a disastrous mix. The received wisdom is that the problem is with ICANN: through ineptitude, foolishness, or rampant power mongering by its administrators, it fails to meet its democratic obligations. My view is that the problem is with our understanding of democracy. Democracy is an empty concept that describes few, if any, of our genuine political commitments. In the second part of the essay, I examine the contested and contestable features of democracy. I begin by focusing on the embedded implications of the word *democracy* and how these generate a series of arguments against the nature of modern politics and the rise of the administrative state. Following Rubin (2001), I argue that this focus distorts the account of the way that modern political institutions relate to their citizens. Instead, I suggest that we look at how and whether institutions actually meet the political commitments which we consider important. The third part of the essay then examines the nature of democracy and political commitments in online institutions. Within the context of ICANN, I examine whether and how these political commitments are met, and conclude that they may be, even if we would consider the process to be antidemocratic. I discuss whether our political commitments can be, and have been, met by online institutions such as ICANN, and conclude that if they have not been met to date, then it has been as a result of deferring to the impoverished idea of democracy, not because of some systemic problem with online political institutions.

1. ICANN and Representative Democracy

ICANN came into being in 1998 as a result of a number of events, most notable of which was a U.S. white paper on the domain name system (U.S. Department of Commerce 1998). The white paper outlined the U.S. government's attitude toward governance of these issues; rather than continue to be the de jure and de facto controller of names and addresses on the Internet, the United States wanted a private entity to take over control. Within a remarkably short time (four months), ICANN was formed and began accreting the powers necessary to undertake this job.

Formed as a nonprofit corporation, it has a typical corporate structure: a CEO, a board of directors, various lower-level workers with responsibility for certain parts of the business, and so forth. Given that its ostensible mandate is to oversee the domain name space and Internet protocol addresses, there is nothing odd in its being a corporation. Many standards-setting and technical administration organizations operate in corporate form. Unlike a corporation, however, ICANN undertakes significant regulatory functions, which make it look much more like a governmental actor of some kind or another. For example, any changes to the domain name system involve some effect upon business interests in domain names. Thus the addition of new name spaces, or the creation of a mechanism to resolve disputes between trademark holders and domain name holders, would involve making decisions that most people would understand as both regulatory and political.

It was therefore recognized immediately that ICANN could not operate just as a typical corporate entity and that it needed some concession to democracy. Thus it has a large board of directors, whose members initially were to be drawn from various interested constituencies. These constituencies—domain name registrars, other Internet bodies concerned with technical matters such as protocols and addresses, and so on—were represented at board level, and also within their own lower-level advisory groups, called "supporting organizations" or "advisory committees." There was also specific consideration given to the interests of sovereign countries, which was recognized as important given that ICANN has responsibility for country-code top-level domains such as .au for Australia, .se for Sweden, and .cc for the Cocos Islands.

What was not initially anticipated was the idea that any part of ICANN should be accountable to the Internet community as a whole. That is, the idea of popularly elected representatives within ICANN was initially ignored and then resisted. However, the pressures in favor of popularly elected representatives was too great, and eventually ICANN blinked. It announced that five of its nineteen directors were to be elected from the Internet community "at large." These positions have been a source of consternation ever since, both for those within ICANN who oppose populist elections and the specific results of the elections and those outside ICANN who argue that the power of the people has been watered down to the point of being purely symbolic. Two of the directors were elected on a platform that promised constant criticism and oversight of the board, and they have made good on the promise ever since. ICANN now presents the unedifying spectacle of a house divided against itself, with increasingly rancorous exchanges between the directors played out on a global stage.

These internal structural features aside, other aspects of ICANN attract fire. Most notable has been the creation of the Uniform Domain Name Dispute Resolution Policy (UDRP), a private adjudication mechanism that seeks to resolve some types of disputes between real-world trademark owners and online domain name registrants. The introduction of the UDRP was controversial in part because it was seen as bypassing national court systems. More importantly, the UDRP privileged trademark owners over domain name owners under most conditions. Since then, the UDRP has become more controversial, as studies by Mueller (2000) and Geist

(2001, 2002) suggest that the application of the policy is biased in favor of trademark owners.

ICANN has since wallowed in the mire of its own creation, with its decisions attracting ongoing criticism and its decision-making processes bogging down in the mud of accountability and transparency concerns. In order to forestall inevitable U.S. governmental intervention, ICANN recently undertook a process of structural reform. The reform proposals include the removal of the at-large directors, changes in oversight processes, and suggestions to use national governments as proxies for popular representation. Since many of the reforms seek to facilitate decision making and consequently involve a reduction in direct accountability to an electorate and the removal of some oversight controls, the changes have stoked the already glowing fires of criticism.

For all the attacks on its integrity, ICANN is not a remarkably secretive or tyrannical organization. It shares many of the features of democratically constituted institutions existing in the real world. Its decisions are announced after notice is given of proposals, and time for comment is allowed. It operates discussion lists for interested parties to have a say in both the process and outcome of its decision making. It has formal representation for the community at large. Its decision making is, at least in principle, based on the notion of consensus, an entirely unobjectionable (if unworkable) democratic principle. The dispute resolution mechanism it created abides by all of the formal requirements for both the rule of law and natural justice—stated laws, neutral arbiters, opportunity for pleading one's case, and so on. We may argue that the outcomes of this process are structurally biased against one set of interests (as Mueller and Geist argue, though see Kur 2002), but this is the same criticism that is regularly made of national laws and courts that conform to our expectations of democracy.

In short, ICANN is a reasonably open and responsive organization. It is more transparent and accountable than, say, the vast majority of nonprofit organizations, publicly traded corporations, universities (whether public or private), or indeed almost any other type of private organization that one can imagine. Why, then, is it accused of being such an intolerable organization? Many people, even ICANN itself, see the body as a governmental actor; moreover, they see it as a governmental actor that has a commitment to direct democracy. The problems with ICANN then have something to do with its strange quasi-corporate, quasi-governmental nature and the high-handed character of its actions, but perhaps more interestingly have a great deal to do with our lack of understanding of what it means to be an online democratic institution. The question, then, is whether online institutions such as ICANN can be "democratic" in the way usually assumed by critics.

2. Getting Past Democracy

Among other criticisms, ICANN is routinely accused of lacking legitimacy and behaving without a mandate from its constituents. Modern Western conceptions of political legitimacy are, of course, grounded in expectations that derive from our understanding of democracy. Hence, direct democracy advocates favor direct mandates from the demos on issues of varying generality, generated through plebiscites or referenda. Madisonian representative democracy relies on elected representatives who are responsible to their constituents. And the modern theories of deliberative democracy focus on the legitimacy gained by inclusive rational debate on political issues. Whatever your favorite flavor of democracy, our conception of the modern Western state relies in large part on the assumption of democracy for its legitimacy. As a result, criticisms of ICANN's legitimacy stem essentially from assumptions about the nature of democracy within our political system.

This seems to be a reasonable approach, and one might first consider it to be a bad thing that ICANN is "undemocratic." However, when we examine the nature of the modern Western state we find that it too suffers from a series of "democratic deficits" that call into question either the nature of the state or the nature of our understanding of the concept of democracy.

Aristotle's original conception of a democracy was of a direct democracy, with the by now familiar requirement that all citizens vote on all substantive issues and that all citizens were obliged to serve within the Athenian senate. The notion of rule by assembly was common to many city-states, and it was particularly pronounced within Athens. With the translation of his *Politics*, Aristotle's views on the nature of democracy became a model for democracy thinking from the thirteenth to the eighteenth century. However, as Rubin (2001) notes, the problem with direct democracy, and certainly the version preferred by the Athenians, is that we have never seen it in any Western political system since the classical period. Though some other medieval political systems such as the Italian city-states or the Swiss cantons bore a superficial similarity to this type of organization, they turned out to be a dead end of Western political development.

Democratic thinking abandoned its assumption of direct voting and revolving assemblies and turned instead to the concept of representation. The development of representative democracy as the dominant form of Western political systems was not due to the imposition of a theory of democracy, but reflected the rise of collective organizations such as guilds, the Church, and universities, among others. The two characteristic features of representative democracy, the view that "what touches all similarly is to be approved by all" and the idea that another could act in one's stead, owe nothing to initial conceptions of democracy and everything to the emergence of medieval corporate entities.

The purpose of this overview is not to provide simply a historical account of the development of democratic thinking and theorizing. Instead, its purpose is to articulate some of the assumptions that are built into our understanding of the term *democracy*. Rubin suggests that premodern conceptions of democracy infect any theory or argument that uses democracy as a normative standard against which an institution is judged. The worst thing that one can say of a government or its institutions is that it is "undemocratic." But the term carries with it the implications from the premodern, simpler era, and so modern political institutions cannot help but be found wanting. Rubin's focus is on criticisms made of the rise of the vast, credentialed, "undemocratic" administrative arm of Western political systems (specifically the executive in the U.S. system). He suggests that the focus on the concept of democracy makes us "overlook or underestimate features that are central to that government's operation and to imagine or overemphasize other features that are of minimal importance" (Rubin 2001: 725).

The obvious example is the extended attack on judicial review by the legal-process school. This school characterized judicial review—specifically the role of the Supreme Court during its opposition to the New Deal legislation—as antidemocratic. The same criticism is reflected perhaps more strongly with discussions and criticisms of online democracy, and specifically within the analysis made of ICANN. ICANN is routinely accused of failing to be democratic. I suggest that these accusations are unhelpful, for as Rubin suggests, to label something "undemocratic" is not a valid criticism of institutions within modern Western political systems.

Rubin's account is tremendously helpful in explaining that there is a problem with our understanding of democracy, which in turn leads to unhelpful criticisms of modern political institutions. However, the issue then arises as to the nature of the political commitments we hold, if democracy is not a good description of them. Rubin's method is to follow on from Habermas and use microanalysis, the positive analysis of the political institution at the level of the interaction between citizen and organization. The idea is, simply, that individuals create social systems. In describing the social system we should, therefore, focus first on the aggregate of individual interactions, in order to understand the higher-level process that emerges. For example, consider elections. According to many democratic theories, voting holds the preeminent role in the political system. However, in microanalysis, voting is merely a political signal that is controlled by the government: in terms of timing, choice, capacity of persons, information granted about the parties, and so forth. Thus, elections are not an autonomous signal from the individual, but rather a government-generated signal that elicits a response from a government-generated populace. Why, then, have elections? Rubin suggests that we have elections to deal with our commitments to ensure a stable succession in government (one without bloodshed or intractable rivalry), to provide periodic opportunities to review the competence of government members, and to ensure some (though not absolute) responsiveness of the representatives. Focusing at this level, therefore, provides a better definition of the commitments we hold than the notion of democracy.

For the purposes of this essay, there are a number of difficulties with applying this approach. Not only is microanalysis a positive methodology without external normative grounding, it also has only really been applied to real-world political activities. Moreover, it can be seen as generating a series of conclusions ("elections are to handle succession") that are as susceptible to criticism as the concept of democracy. Finally, democracy has a wonderful concreteness and solidity as a concept that appears to be invariant across times and cultures. Microanalysis, being descriptive, is necessarily a partial account dependent on the individuals being examined at any one point.

I am going to leave these concerns aside here. I do not defend this decision, except to say that this essay seeks to remove democracy as the basis of analysis of electronically constituted organizations. In the end, we may come back to democracy as the only appropriate way of understanding and critiquing online institutions, but for my purposes it is enough to show how an exclusive focus on democracy is damaging.

3. ICANN and Electronic Democracy: Hippogriffs, Shareholders, and Citizens

In this part, I explain how the premodern implications inherent in democracy theories are applied to new entities such as ICANN. I endeavor to demonstrate how reliance on democracy to criticize online institutions is a counterproductive way of criticizing these institutions. If we are concerned about changing these organizations to reflect our genuine political commitments, then we need a better understanding of these commitments. ICANN deserves condemnation if it fails to meet genuinely held political commitments. It does not deserve to be criticized for being "undemocratic" when that term embodies political commitments that are unrealistic, not held by relevant constituencies, or irrelevant.

ICANN is a curious institution. One is tempted to characterize it as neither fish nor fowl. But perhaps it is better to suggest that, like medieval monsters such as the griffin or the more outlandish hippogriff, it is a curious grafting of multiple animal parts: head and claws of an eagle, body of a lion, back legs of a horse. The grafting in ICANN's case is between a corporate entity operating within the purview of a sovereign government and a transnational governmental entity that is relatively autonomous. ICANN is a private, nonprofit California corporation and subject to the usual strictures of corporate entities. However, one of its fundamental functions is that of transnational regulator, and in this sense it appears much more like an executive or legislative agency.

The reason for building a quasi-governmental corporate hippogriff is by now well known. By the mid-nineties, the United States realized it was faced with an international diplomatic problem and a regulatory nightmare. It effectively owned the Internet, by virtue of the Department of Commerce's control over IP address and domain name allocation. This included effective control over the allocation of registry functions within country-code top-level domains. Though Internet takeup in other countries was sketchy at the time, it was not hard to foresee a period when diplomatic issues would emerge over U.S. control of the name spaces of other sovereign countries. There was also the problem that the "netizens" of the day were broadly libertarian, and committed to Internet self-governance based on "rough consensus and running code." Thus, the United States wanted an entity interposed between itself and the day-to-day decision making over addresses and name spaces. Its hand was forced by the actions of Jon Postel, the creator and "real" owner of the domain name system, who conjured ICANN out of whole cloth and anointed it as ruler. Though the process may have occurred in a way not envisaged by the U.S. administration the creation of ICANN was in keeping with the aims of the U.S. and U.S. regulators were no doubt relieved that they did not have to intervene directly.

ICANN's combination of corporate and governmental features is interesting for a number of reasons. Like the hippogriff and unlike, say, a mule, ICANN does not combine the characteristics of its parents uniformly. Whole body parts of one animal are grafted onto parts of other animals. Some parts of ICANN operate like a corporation, while others are much more like governmental instrumentalities. For example, in dealing with disclosure of some sorts of information, it resolutely maintains that it is a corporation and sees no need to engage in the kind of disclosure requirements assumed by agencies. In relation to determining the appropriate relationship between intellectual property interests that arise online and offline, it operates like a government agency. Not only did it convene hearings on the appropriate balance to strike, it received a report from a prominent international body—the World Intellectual Property Organization—promulgated a law as a consequence of the report, and created an entire adjudication system to deal with disputes pursuant to this new law.

The dual character of ICANN leads to alternative views of the kinds of political commitments we should expect. One view, most recently expressed by Frankel (2002), is that ICANN needs to conform with corporate governance expectations. The other approach, most obviously identified with Froomkin (2000) and Weinberg (2000), is to demand that ICANN comply with the usual democratic expectations we have for governmental institutions. Models stemming from corporate governance and democratic theory are not irreconcilable, but they do tend to focus on different features of an institution. Corporate governance models are concerned with responsible management and disclosure of meaningfully relevant material to stakeholders. Political democracy models look to the features discussed above: voice, citizenship, representation, control over representative by constituents, and so on. In essence, these models advance differing political commitments, and an examination of the requirements of the legislative and executive models of ICANN casts useful light on the question of its democratic legitimacy.

3.1. ICANN as Executive Agency

This view that ICANN lacks democratic legitimacy assumes that it is some sort of governmental actor, though accounts differ as to what government we might be talking about here, and what type of actor within that government ICANN might be. Froomkin (2000), perhaps ICANN's most plangent and well-informed critic, assumes that the government at issue is that of the United States, and ICANN is in fact assuming the mantle of one of the administrative agencies. Since ICANN is not a formally constituted executive agency, he argues, it falls afoul of both U.S. administrative law and the U.S. Constitution.

While these may be relevant considerations within a U.S. constitutional environment, it is hard to see any broader political commitment that is implicated by ICANN's actions. Indeed, Froomkin (2002) subsequently noted that this was a criticism not of ICANN but rather of the federal government's end run around its obligations. As other commentators have suggested, ICANN itself avoids an explicit connection with the U.S. government and instead sees itself (at times) as transnational and transgovernmental. However, it still adopts features of certain types of actors within Western governmental structures, especially actors within the U.S. system. Weinberg (2000) demonstrates that ICANN has appropriated features of both unrepresentative executive agencies and representative legislatures. Thus, ICANN adopts administrative features such as notices of proposed rule makings and comment periods for interested parties, reconsideration processes for parties affected by rule makings, the existence of an external review mechanism for decisions, and so on. As Weinberg notes, even the specifics of these features mimic U.S. administrative laws; aspects such as who is an affected party, timeliness of the reconsideration application, exhaustion of rights, and the concepts of interim relief and pleading are all familiar to the laws regulating U.S. executive agencies.

The issue that emerges here is whether there are political commitments that are implicated in agencies of this sort and which might be applied to ICANN. Indeed, since the rise of administrative agencies within the United States was the basis for many of the concerns about "democratic deficits" during the last century, ICANN's self-conscious invocation of

U.S. administrative approaches is interesting here. The criticisms of ICANN as an administrative agency focus on features such as those identified by Froomkin (2000), including the public's right to notice and comment, to accountable decision making, to due process, and so on.

Weinberg adopts similar concerns. We might consider each of these to be relevant and appropriate political commitments, but in fact they are little more than invocations of democracy at one remove. As Weinberg (2000) indicates, the reason we care about these issues is to reconcile administrative decision making with the agencies' insulation from direct democratic control. He goes so far as to say that any of ICANN's processes will be adjudged legitimate only to the extent that it constrains itself, just like a federal agency. As a result, ICANN can become legitimate only if it becomes democratic, and we're back to where we started.

3.2. ICANN as Legislature

At other times and places, ICANN specifically invokes features, such as legislatures, that are more common in democratic institutions. Various aspects of ICANN's structure and operational methods have been created with this type of implicit democratic model. For example, a number of committees and "supporting organizations" have been created to influence the overall direction of the organization. Not only are these committees and supporting organizations usually structured as representative democratic institutions, but they often also contain explicit geographical representation requirements. There are problems with these organizations, notably that they are not representative in the typical one-person-one-vote sense, and also that they display some elements of regulatory capture. However, these concerns pale in comparison with the nature of the board.

It is at the highest level that ICANN's reliance on representative democracy ideals has caused the most problems. ICANN's board of directors is constituted as a form of representative institution. There are nineteen seats that are divided up so that certain constituencies are represented. The constituencies are primarily technical groups with responsibilities for various engineering aspects, but they include members who are closely aligned with trademark owners, commercial operators of domain name registries, and others whose interest is primarily corporate.

Until the recent change, nine seats were given over to the at-large directors, who were supposed to represent the Internet community at large. This created huge problems. Initially these positions were, effectively, internal appointments. ICANN was forced to introduce elections for five of the positions, which were divided into geographical regions, and it has had a storied relationship with them ever since. The election was a disaster according to almost any metric of the effectiveness of representative elections. The constituency for each was huge but unresponsive. Of the hundreds of millions of people who might have voted for their one representative, fewer than one thousand votes was enough to secure the win for some representatives. This extraordinarily low voter turnout can be attributed to a number of factors: most of the world doesn't have access to the Internet, those who do have access don't know about ICANN, and those who do know about ICANN don't care about how it is run. However, another disincentive to vote was the sheer difficulty of doing so: though ICANN is the online institution par excellence, much of the election took place offline for security reasons, thus showing we are still dependent on physical indicators of the identity of the elector. So an elaborate and expensive physical mailing took place, sending user identification numbers and passwords to those who had initially registered online. Only then, armed with the physical slip of paper, was the elector allowed to vote online.

Apart from the practical problems with running an election of this sort, a number of obvious questions emerged. Weinberg (2000) suggests two: first, what does it mean to "represent" any community as ill-defined as the Internet community, and second, should a technical body such as ICANN be representative at all? Other questions might be added: first, why should a geographical distribution of regions be a meaningful division of the online demos, and second, why have representation at all?

In short, we are once again confronted with the question of whether the problems with ICANN's democratic approach, in this case its attempt at representation, are meaningful. The idea of representation itself does not appear, to me at least, as any kind of political commitment of any online community. And particularly within the kind of body that ICANN is, representation makes little sense at all.

4. Conclusion

I have asked whether our political commitments can be, and have been, met by online institutions such as ICANN. I think that if they have not been met to date, it has been as a result of deferring to the impoverished idea of democracy, not because of some systemic problem with the form of online political institutions we have seen so far.

However, to say that democracy is an inadequate grounding for criticisms of online institutions is not to say that these institutions should be immune from criticism. It has not been possible here to establish a normative theory of how best to meet our online political commitments, or even to explore more fully what those commitments would look like. The task has been here simply to make democracy seem less like an answer and more like a question in relation to institutions such as ICANN.

There is clearly significant work that must be done here: more and more transnational and cyberspace political actors such as ICANN are likely to emerge as the current geopolitical system is found unequal to online challenges. We must then start to define what amounts to appropriate political concerns and what amounts to mere vestigial appendages of a political system that never really existed. Cyberspace should not be ruled like the Athenian senate. But it is an open question how it should be ruled.

References

Frankel, Tamar. 2002. "Accountability and Oversight of the Internet Corporation for Assigned Names and Numbers." Report to the Markle Foundation. Available at http://www.markle.org/news/ICANN_fin1_9.pdf.

Froomkin, A. Michael. 2000. "Wrong Turn in Cyberspace: Using ICANN to Route Around the APA and the Constitution." *Duke Law Journal* 50: 17–184.

Froomkin, A. 2002. "Form and Substance in Cyberspace." 6 *Journal of Small and Emerging Business Law* 6: 93–124.

Geist, Michael. 2001. "Fair.com? An Examination of the Allegations of Systemic Unfairness in the ICANN UDRP." Available at http://aix1.uottawa.ca/~geist/geistudrp.pdf.

Geist, Michael. 2002. "Fundamentally Fair.com?: An Update on Bias Allegations and the ICANN UDRP." Available at http://aix1.uottawa.ca/~geist/fairupdate.pdf.

Kur, Annette. 2002. "UDRP: A Study by the Max-Planck-Institute for Foreign and International Patent, Copyright and Competition Law." Available at http://www.intellecprop.mpg.de/Online-Publikationen/2002/UDRP-study-final-02.pdf.

Mueller, Milton. 2000. "Rough Justice: An Analysis of ICANN's Dispute Resolution Policy." Available at http://www.acm.org/usacm/IG/roughjustice.pdf.

Rubin, Edward L. 2001. "Getting Past Democracy." *University of Pennsylvania Law Review* 149: 711–92.

U.S. Department of Commerce. 1998. "Management of Internet Names and Addresses." Docket number 980212036-8146-02. Available at http://www.ntia.doc.gov/ntiahome/domainname/6_5_98dns.htm.

Weinberg, Jonathan. 2000. "ICANN and the Problem of Legitimacy." *Duke Law Journal* 50: 187–260.

PART 3

The Lessons of Electronic Democracy Practice

CHAPTER 11

Digital Deliberation: Engaging the Public Through Online Policy Dialogues

THOMAS C. BEIERLE

Accompanying the last decade's enthusiasm for the Internet economy were equally extravagant expectations about information technologies' impact on democracy and governance. Most of these predictions were variations on the theme of a stodgy representative system overthrown by some form of direct online democracy. Clearly the more extreme versions of economic revolution and its analogue in government have not come to pass. However, a quiet evolution in public administration is taking place as rapid advances in information technology converge with an increasing interest in improving public involvement in government decision making.

A renewed interest in public participation—offline and on—can be seen in the increasing use of a broad array of public participation processes by public agencies. Policy dialogues, stakeholder advisory committees, citizen juries, facilitated mediations, and various other processes have joined traditional public hearings and public comment procedures as familiar components of the public participation mix. Most participation processes tend to fall into one of two categories. First are small group interactions that emphasize face-to-face deliberation focused on problem solving and consensus building. Second are processes designed to accommodate large groups in a much less interactive mode of discourse.

All too rare are participation processes that span the two categories by engaging large numbers of people in interactive dialogue. It is here that Internet-based approaches to public participation may offer something profoundly innovative. Moving participation to the Internet can increase the number of participants by breaking down barriers created by geography, daily commitments of work and family, social and psychological insecurities, and lack of information. Dialogues can also support dynamic communication in which participants don't just make statements for others to hear; they listen to, respond to, and question statements made by others, all with adequate time to formulate ideas and responses.

This essay examines online dialogues as an innovative form of public participation. It draws much of its insight from an online dialogue sponsored by the Environmental Protection Agency (EPA), which brought together 1,166 people for two weeks in the summer of 2001. Participants were mainly from the United States, but some joined in from Brazil, South Africa, and elsewhere. Designed to consider public participation policies at the agency, the National Dialogue on Public Involvement in EPA Decisions (the Dialogue) covered issues ranging from the information and assistance the public needs to be effectively involved in EPA decision making to the particulars of participation in rule making, permitting, and Superfund. EPA convened the Dialogue to obtain input on its draft Public Involvement Policy (PIP) and gather ideas on how best to implement the PIP.

1. A Niche for Online Dialogues

The most appropriate way to analyze government-led online public dialogues is as one of many processes available to agencies for involving the public in decision making. Such dialogues will be mainstreamed only to the extent that they offer agencies and the public a new way of achieving the many possible purposes of public participation. Some of these purposes are informational, such as eliciting better facts and ideas and providing insights into public values and opinion (Stern and Fineberg 1996; Beierle 1999). Others speak to benefits derived from the act of participating, such as citizens' learning and empowerment or the collective enhancement of civic capacity (Barber 1984). Still other purposes are instrumental, such as influencing agency decisions or resolving disputes and building trust so that decisions can be implemented (Beierle and Konisky 2001).

Different purposes necessitate different kinds of participation. Relatively unstructured processes open to all members of the public can be very useful for eliciting information and ideas. Such processes may be particularly useful in the early stages of policy making, when information is being gathered, ideas are being formulated, and the full range of opinions is being assessed (Walters, Aydelotte, and Miller 2000). More tightly structured small group processes may be more appropriate for resolving disputes over a narrow set of options as a policy process nears its end, as complexity puts high demands on participants, or in cases where participants' acceptance of a decision is crucial (Thomas 1995).

For analysts, a key issue is selecting the right kind of process for the purposes intended. To simplify, we can think of their choice as involving three dimensions: the breadth of participation, the nature of interaction, and the process's intended output. These three dimensions are illustrated in Table 11.1 by reference to four types of processes that cover much of the terrain of modern public participation: public comments, public hearings, advisory committees, and negotiations.

The four different types of processes involve quite different opportunities for members of the public to attend, from broad open access to a narrow selection of "representative participants." The nature of interaction among participants varies greatly among the different types of processes as well, from static one-way communication to reciprocal dialogues. And processes differ in the nature of their expected outputs, defined by EPA into three categories: information exchange, recommendations, and agreements (EPA 1998).

Missing among the four types of processes outlined above are those that engage a large number of people in interactive dialogue. From the perspective of agency-led participation, such processes offer a number of benefits. As Harter (1982) has asserted in the context of regulatory negotiations, interactive dialogue can support a more reasoned analysis of issues by reducing the incentives for opposing interests to hew to extreme views and by subjecting assertions to direct rebuttal. Broad participation in such processes allows agencies to move beyond hearing from their established interest group constituencies—the "usual suspects," according to one analyst's description—by helping to overcome asymmetries in access (Applegate 1998). Beyond their utility for agencies, broad-based interactive processes are those with the most potential to invigorate civic life through deliberative democracy—the "informed participation of citizens in the deliberative process of community decision making" (Weeks 2000).

Face-to-face processes that engage large groups in dialogue-based interaction are not unheard of, but they are rare and complex (Weeks 2000; ADSS 1999). Online dialogues can be a far easier way to bring these large

TABLE 11.1 Characteristics of Participation Processes

	Breadth of participation	Type of communication	Output
Public comments	Broad	Static	Information exchange
Public hearings	Broad, but geographically limited	Static	Information exchange
Advisory committees	Narrow	Dialogue	Recommendations
Negotiations	Narrow	Dialogue	Agreements

groups together and are therefore potentially easier to bring into the mainstream of agency activity. Online dialogues are characterized by a few basic features. They typically offer broad, open access—available to anyone who hears of the opportunity and is interested enough to participate. Participants are typically asked to post messages to a Web site, replying to other messages to create a "thread" or conversation. This threading feature encourages back-and-forth dialogue, and an asynchronous structure allows adequate time for considered reading and posting. Dialogues typically stay focused on a particular topic through a structured and time-limited design that often involves daily themes, the identification of roles for various participants, and some degree of facilitation.

To say that online dialogues possess the characteristics of a new form of public involvement is not to say that these dialogues in practice always work as intended. In fact, there are a number of examples where few participants showed up and back-and-forth interactions were quite limited (Finney 1999, 2000; Holt et al. 1997). However, a variety of guidance documents have sprung up to help practitioners design effective online dialogues (Clift 2002; Dahlberg 2001; Rosen 2001; Coleman and Gøtze 2001).

To understand the potential of online dialogues, we turn to the National Dialogue on Public Involvement in EPA Decisions. The evaluation framework is derived from the work of Weeks (2000), who views large-scale deliberative processes as a way to revitalize public life through deliberative democracy. Forums that encourage deliberative democracy have four characteristics. First is broad and representative participation. Second are informed participants. Third is deliberative interaction, meaning a group effort to reflect critically on available, and often competing, options and choose a course of action among them. Fourth is a credible forum whose process and results are considered legitimate by the public and the sponsoring agency.

2. The National Dialogue on Public Involvement in EPA Decisions

EPA convened the National Dialogue on Public Involvement in EPA Decisions as a vehicle for obtaining input on the agency's draft Public Involvement Policy and advice on how to implement that policy. It was used as an alternative to holding public meetings around the country, which EPA had originally planned to do. The Dialogue had a few key features:

- A vigorous advertising campaign to attract participants
- An electronic "briefing book" of background material
- The ability to create threaded online conversations of linked messages
- Features for sorting and filtering messages by date, subject, thread, or daily topic
- An agenda of daily topics

- Daily "hosts" from EPA and expert "panelists"
- Daily summaries

Much of the information for this evaluation comes from a survey conducted immediately after the Dialogue. The response rate on the survey was 35 percent of all those who agreed to take it when registering for the Dialogue and 47 percent of those who posted at least one message to the Dialogue.

3. Broad, Representative Participation

Online dialogues should involve more people than would be practical in an offline setting. Ideally, participants would be representative of the broader public in terms of both the diversity of interests and values they bring and demographics. In understanding breadth and representation, it is important to look not just at who registers for a dialogue but at the dynamics of actual participation, including how broad and representative the evolving content of a dialogue is.

When compared to alternatives, the EPA Dialogue involved many more participants than would have otherwise participated. A public comment process on the PIP that preceded the Dialogue attracted relatively few comments, mainly from state government. The series of public meetings originally envisioned for the program may have involved large numbers of people in aggregate, but not all in a single forum. An advisory committee would have involved only a handful of participants. In contrast, when the Dialogue began, 957 people had registered to participate. By the time it ended, that number was up to 1,166.

Those registered for the Dialogue were representative of the broader public in the sense of bringing a diverse set of interest affiliations, attitudes about EPA, and geographical locations. Roughly equal percentages (about 15 percent) of participants came from environmental or community groups and from industry, covering the two principal public constituencies in environmental debates. Attitudes toward EPA were fairly evenly divided as well, with 34 percent of survey respondents saying they felt very positive or moderately positive about the agency and its approach to public involvement prior to the Dialogue, 31 percent saying that they felt neither positive nor negative, and 28 percent saying they felt moderately or very negative. Reflecting geographic diversity, registrants came from every state in the United States as well as two territories.

Participants were not representative of the broader public, however, in terms of their use of the Internet and some of the demographic factors related to Internet use. The Dialogue engaged—almost exclusively—people who frequently used the Internet: 86 percent of survey respondents said they used the Internet at least ten times a week, and another 13 percent used it at least five times a week. By contrast, only 44 percent of the

U.S. population at that time used the Internet at all (U.S. Department of Commerce 2000). The fact that the Dialogue attracted people who were, by and large, frequent users of the Internet led to discrepancies in education and race that are characteristic of the digital divide. Demographic data from the survey suggested that participants were considerably older and better-educated than the general U.S. population and somewhat more likely to be female and white.

Registration data sketch an incomplete picture because actual activity in the Dialogue may not replicate the breadth and representativeness of the registrants. Not everyone who registered actively participated, and different people participated in different ways. Of the 70 percent of participants who registered as active participants (that is, with the intent to post messages), 320 actually posted at least one message, and they collectively produced 1,261 messages over the course of the Dialogue. Figure 11.1 shows the pattern of participation over the course of the Dialogue (note that the low period of activity was a weekend, July 14 and 15).

Not everyone who visited the EPA Dialogue site posted messages. Web site statistics indicated that between 150 and 310 individuals visited the site each day. This translates into one to four readers for each person posting a message. Based on how many messages people read during their site visits, it can be estimated that for each message someone posted, around seventy messages were being read.

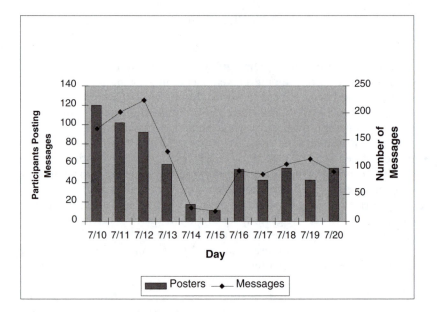

Figure 11.1 Pattern of Messages and Participants Posting Messages.

TABLE 11.2 Inner, Middle, and Outer Circles of Participation

	Number of participants	Percentage of participants	Percentage of messages
Inner circle	32	10	43
Middle circle	87	27	36
Outer circle	201	63	20

Participants posting messages demonstrated a range of activity, which can be defined in terms of three concentric circles: an inner circle of very active posters, a middle circle of moderately active posters, and an outer circle of infrequent posters. As shown in Table 11.2, 10 percent of participants—the thirty-two members of the inner circle—contributed fully 43 percent of the messages to the Dialogue.

Interestingly, the inner circle of thirty-two active participants shared the broad affiliations of the larger group, representing environmental organizations, community groups, university faculty, EPA staff, industry trade associations, and others. Reflecting the balance in affiliations among those who wrote much of the content of the Dialogue, just over half (51 percent) of survey respondents agreed or strongly agreed that the Dialogue was balanced among different points of view, and only 12 percent disagreed or strongly disagreed.

Although a small group of people contributed disproportionately to the Dialogue, it didn't turn into a small-group discussion among the inner circle. Most of the threads were initiated by the middle circle (45 percent of threads), not the inner circle (34 percent of threads). Even the outer circle gave a respectable showing, generating 21 percent of threads. In the survey, 48 percent of respondents agreed or strongly agreed that the Dialogue wasn't dominated by a few participants, 19 percent thought that a few participants did dominate, and 33 percent neither agreed nor disagreed.

4. Informed Participation

An educated citizenry has long been acknowledged as crucial to a well-functioning democracy: if the people are governing themselves, they should know what they are talking about. The main education tool for the Dialogue was the briefing book, which contained a variety of materials about the PIP and public participation at the agency. However, the survey suggests that the briefing book may not have been all that useful to many participants. When compared with other sources of information and expertise—the daily summaries, daily panelists, and EPA hosts—they rated the briefing book as the least important contributor to the overall quality of the Dialogue.

Part of the reason that the briefing book may have been less useful than other resources was that the majority of participants were already familiar with EPA and with public participation at the agency. Excluding those who worked at EPA, 40 percent of survey respondents said they were involved with EPA at least once a month, and 21 percent interacted with EPA at least once a year. Only 12 percent had not been involved with EPA in some way over the last five years. Seventy-six percent said they were either very or somewhat familiar with EPA public involvement policies, 48 percent knew that an EPA public involvement plan had been released for comment before the Dialogue, and 14 percent had already commented on it.

Interestingly, the very informed nature of the group led to charges that the Dialogue was simply another opportunity for the experts to talk to each other. Nonetheless, there were interesting examples of participation by self-identified average citizens with little direct experience with EPA. One such person posted seventeen messages overall, a few on nearly every day. She was an encouraging and supportive voice for others who were participating, and she drew on her own experiences with local pollution to highlight problems others were facing.

5. Deliberative Participation

The essence of deliberative democracy is, of course, deliberation. As defined here, deliberation involves moving from individual opinion to group choices and plans of action. A threshold condition for deliberation is reciprocity—the back-and-forth in a conversation as people engage with what others have said. Public comment processes are low in reciprocity; deliberative processes—such as policy dialogues, negotiations, or mediations—are generally high in it.

After the first day of the Dialogue, when most people were simply introducing themselves rather than replying to earlier messages, the volume of messages that were replies to previous messages leveled off at 50 percent to 75 percent of all messages each day. Eighty-three percent of all messages in the Dialogue were part of threads (i.e., series of messages and replies), and 25 percent of the threads consisted of six messages or more. These thread data actually undercount the degree of reciprocity because participants broke some conversations into two or more threads.

Deliberation is more than just reciprocity, however. It is a process of group decision making—of moving from personal opinion to group judgment and action. Holt and colleagues (1997) operationalize the concept of public deliberation by describing six steps through which it proceeds:

1. Participants make a personal investment in the process and begin by seeking to understand the issues, introducing themselves, and learning about each other.
2. Participants express how they feel about issues, begin to identify with those who hold similar beliefs, and build on messages submitted by others.

3. Participants analyze available alternatives by identifying and weighing pros and cons from diverse perspectives.
4. Participants move beyond their private interests and consider how the consequences of the choices affect others and the general public good.
5. Participants make choices based on the public good, although they may not all make the same choice (i.e., they may not reach consensus).
6. Participants discuss how to put their choices into practice, often by articulating what each can do.

There is ample evidence from the Dialogue of the first two steps and some evidence of the third and perhaps fourth, but there was little movement in the Dialogue toward group decisions and actions as reflected in steps five and six.

Step one was largely accomplished in the first few days of the Dialogue, when participants introduced themselves and described why they were interested in participating. Not only did they learn about each other, they learned about each other's views on the issues: 70 percent of participants either agreed or strongly agreed that they learned a great deal about how other participants viewed public participation. A sense of commitment to the process also developed. For example, as revealed in the survey, the second most frequent motivation for posting a message (after interest in the topic) was "a sense of responsibility to actively participate."

There is also ample evidence of the identification and interaction characteristics of step two. People often expressed how they felt about various issues and built on the contributions of others. Participants also appeared to identify with others of like mind. For example, 33 percent of survey respondents offered "others had already made my point" as frequently or very frequently their reason for not posting a message.

There is less evidence from the survey for steps three and four, in which participants weigh the pros and cons of different decisions and move toward a perspective of the public good. Certainly one could find some messages in the Dialogue that displayed these characteristics. Moreover, 81 percent of survey respondents agreed or strongly agreed that communication in the Dialogue was "constructive and useful for examining questions and ideas," suggesting some movement away from personal opinion to a weighing of options. However, for participants to analyze available alternatives—the essence of steps three and four—they need to know what they are deciding about, and there was little in the Dialogue to identify particular decision points. Moreover, the structure required to analyze alternatives may not have existed, as highlighted by one participant: "I thought it was chaotic—a lot of individuals firing single ideas from a lot of different directions—no way to carry on any kind of meaningful dialogue."

Not surprisingly, there was little movement in the Dialogue into steps five and six, where choices are made and actions defined. There were, however, a few points in the Dialogue where a group of participants considered mobilizing for actions offline. For example, in individual threads, participants encouraged each other to fight the proposed elimination of one of EPA's information provision programs, help develop plain-English regulatory and scientific guides, and develop a directory of public participation experts and a bibliography of the public participation literature.

The principal reason that the Dialogue overall didn't move into a decisional mode is that it was never intended to do so. All of EPA's language to participants about the Dialogue was expressed in terms of "sharing," "seeking," or "learning about" participants' thoughts, ideas, and concerns, not about making decisions regarding various aspects of the policy under discussion. The agenda was not set up to identify particular decision points or frame questions that needed resolution. With more active facilitation or other means, online dialogues may reach these last stages of group deliberation, but the EPA Dialogue provides little evidence of that possibility.

6. Credible Process and Results

Credibility refers to the perceived legitimacy of the Dialogue as a forum for public involvement as well as the utility and legitimacy of its outputs. It is quite clear that participants felt that the Dialogue was a credible process. Seventy-six percent of participants rated the Dialogue experience as very or somewhat positive, and 87 percent said EPA should definitely or probably conduct more in the future. When asked in the survey whether the Dialogue had changed their opinion about EPA and its public involvement processes, 43 percent of respondents said they felt more positive, and only 6 percent said they felt more negative.

One way that EPA reinforced the legitimacy of the forum was by being responsive, sending a signal that the agency was attentive and interested. Lead EPA staff replied quickly to all messages that they thought required an EPA response. When they could not answer a question directly, they forwarded it to contacts in appropriate EPA offices or other agencies. On some occasions, EPA staff acting as daily hosts did lapse into formulaic and bureaucratic language, raising the ire of participants and underlining their expectation that EPA too would engage in the free-flowing interactions that characterized much of the rest of the Dialogue. Such expectations created difficulties for some staff because they did not have enough decision-making authority to be able to "make policy" via the Dialogue and hence had to try to be responsive without officially committing the agency to do anything.

The question of how credible—or, more to the point, how useful—public input was to EPA is more difficult to ascertain. There is no question that the Dialogue gave EPA more input on the PIP and its implementation, ranging from explicit instructions to identification of the public's most frequent complaints, concerns, and questions. This input was forwarded to each of the EPA workgroups involved in PIP implementation. Lead EPA staff members also held internal briefings for higher-level EPA officials. Various EPA offices said they would continue to "mine" the Dialogue for information. In follow-up interviews, however, some of the EPA staff participating in the process said they liked the Dialogue but found little in the content of the messages that was new or surprising. Most of these EPA staff were deeply involved in public participation day to day, and results would likely be different if EPA staff less familiar with public participation had been more involved.

7. Conclusion

The EPA online dialogue demonstrates that such processes can fill a niche in the public participation tool box by bringing together large groups of people in an interactive process of exchanging information. Using an evaluation framework based on characteristics of deliberative democracy provides additional insights about the dynamics of such an approach to participation.

Participation in the Dialogue was broad and representative in terms of interest groups, if not in terms of demographics. Participants were informed, but mainly by their past experiences rather than by the briefing book provided along with the Dialogue. Communication in the Dialogue was reciprocal and characterized by commitment, identification, and learning, although it fell short of being truly deliberative. Finally, the Dialogue process was largely considered credible by participants and by EPA.

Future efforts that push electronic dialogues toward more sophisticated deliberation should pursue improvements in five areas. The first is dialogue format, which could be explicitly modeled on the six steps of deliberation and supported by an active moderator encouraging participants through those steps. Second is software design, which could improve people's ability to follow the evolving conversation through graphical representation and summarization. A third area of improvement is in fostering behavioral norms, such as asking participants to probe contentious voices for underlying issues or encouraging nonexperts to actively participate. Fourth are institutional issues, such as government agency outreach to those not normally represented in policy making. Finally are access issues that encourage broader online access across socio-economic groups. Conscious refinements in format, software, behavioral norms, institutional issues, and access—together with formal evaluation—need to be part of a long-term effort to test and refine online dialogues. Such an effort may well demonstrate the utility of this process for achieving some of the most ambitious goals of public participation in public policy making.

References

Americans Discuss Social Security (ADSS). 1999. *Americans Discuss Social Security: Final Report.* Washington, D.C.: ADSS.

Applegate, John S. 1998. "Beyond the Usual Suspects: The Use of Citizens Advisory Boards in Environmental Decisionmaking." *Indiana Law Journal* 73, 3: 1–43.

Barber, Benjamin. 1984. *Strong Democracy: Participatory Politics for a New Age.* Berkeley, CA: University of California Press.

Beierle, Thomas C. 1999. "Using Social Goals to Evaluate Public Participation in Environmental Decisions." *Policy Studies Review* 16, 3–4: 75–103.

Beierle, Thomas C., and David M. Konisky. 2001. "What Are We Gaining from Stakeholder Involvement? Observations from Environmental Planning in the Great Lakes." *Environment and Planning C: Government and Policy* 19, 4: 515–27.

Clift, Steven. 2002. "Online Consultations and Events—Top Ten Tips for Government and Civic Hosts." *Democracies Online Newswire.* Available at http://www.publicus.net/articles/consult.html (accessed February 9, 2003).

Coleman, Stephen, and John Gøtze. 2001. "Bowling Together: Online Public Engagement in Policy Deliberation." Hansard Society, London. Available at http://bowlingtogether.net/ (accessed March 2004).

Dahlberg, L. 2001. "The Internet and Democratic Discourse." *Information, Communication, and Society* 4: 615–33.

Environmental Protection Agency (EPA). 1998. *Better Decisions Through Consultation and Collaboration: A Manual on Consultative Processes and Stakeholder Involvement, Draft.* Washington, D.C.: Environmental Protection Agency.

Finney, Colin. 1999. "Extending Public Consultation Via the Internet: The Experience of the UK Advisory Committee on Genetic Testing Electronic Consultation." *Science and Public Policy* 26, 5: 361–73.

Finney, Colin. 2000. "Implementing a Citizen-based Deliberative Process on the Internet: The Buckinghamshire Health Authority Electronic Citizens Jury." *Science and Public Policy* 27, 1: 45–64.

Harter, Philip J. 1982. "Negotiating Regulations: A Cure for Malaise." *Georgetown Law Journal* 71, 1: 1–118.

Holt, M. E., F. Rees, J. D. Swenson, and P. B. Kleiber. 1997. "Evolution of Evaluation for Critical, Reflective, and Deliberative Discourse: National Issues Forums Online." Paper presented at the Special Interest Group on Assessment and Evaluation of the European Association for Research on Learning and Instruction, August 26–30, Athens, Greece.

Rosen, Tommy. 2001. *E-Democracy in Practice: Swedish Experiences of a New Political Tool.* Swedish Association of Local Authorities and Swedish Federation of County Councils and Regions, Joint Department of Democracy and Self-government.

Stern, Paul C., and Harvey V. Fineberg, eds. 1996. *Understanding Risk: Informing Decisions in a Democratic Society.* Washington, D.C.: National Academy Press.

Thomas, John C. 1995. *Public Participation in Public Decisions.* San Francisco: Jossey-Bass.

U.S. Department of Commerce. 2000. *Falling Through the Net: A Report on Americans' Access to Technology and Tools.* Washington, D.C.: U.S. Department of Commerce.

Walters, L. C., J. Aydelotte, and J. Miller. 2000. "Putting More Public in Policy Analysis." *Public Administration Review* 60: 349–59.

Weeks, E. C. 2000. "The Practice of Deliberative Democracy: Results from Four Large-scale Trials." *Public Administration Review* 60: 360–72.

CHAPTER 12

Participation, Deliberative Democracy, and the Internet: Lessons from a National Forum on Commercial Vehicle Safety

J. WOODY STANLEY, CHRISTOPHER WEARE, AND JULIET MUSSO*

The Internet is increasingly viewed as a means for including citizens in government policy making and administrative processes (Bimber 1998, 1999, 2001; Dahlberg 2001; Weare 2002). Despite the growing interest in electronic democracy, there is inadequate empirical work on applications of communications technology for this purpose (Weare 2002). An important question is whether the Internet medium will enable individuals to participate more equally and effectively in the processes of governing. As a new type of public space, the Internet may reduce barriers to participation of scale, proximity, and time. If so, it could promote democratic deliberation among individuals and enhance democratic practice by bringing values and interests under greater public scrutiny. On the other hand, the Internet may undermine participation by increasing inequalities of access, fragmenting public comment from the processes of government, and reinforcing divisiveness in public discourse.

*We thank Thomas Beierle, Tamara Witschge, and Nancy Marder for their helpful comments and suggestions. This research was funded in part by the National Science Foundation, Information Technology Research Program Award #0112899. This paper represents the views of the authors and not those of the U.S. Department of Transportation or any of its modal administrations.

This essay reports the results of an effort to create an Internet-based forum, which involved private citizens, interest group representatives, and agency managers in an online conversation about the role of the federal government in improving commercial vehicle safety. As part of a strategic planning exercise that also accepted public comment through a traditional docket, the Federal Motor Carrier Safety Administration (FMCSA) sponsored an Internet forum between August 2000 and June 2001. The forum was designed to encourage the exchange of policy information and foster two-way discussion among participants on this important issue.

This forum presented the opportunity to examine the influence of the Internet on aspects of the practice of democratic discourse in an actual agency setting. A comparison of the written comments in the public docket to the corpus of electronic messages in the Internet forum archives provides evidence that computer-mediated communication encourages public discussion and broadens the level of participation by individuals and groups previously uninvolved in the policy-making process. An analysis of the interactive, two-way communication in the online conversation also provides some support for the notion that the Internet can foster dialogic communication that may advance deliberative democratic practice.

1. Background and Need

The Internet is a multidimensional and global medium that supports a variety of uses, including information retrieval, multimedia, telephony, chat rooms, videoconferencing, and broadcast, as well as new ways for individuals to communicate in a decentralized and asynchronous manner. Because of these characteristics, the Internet holds the potential to change communication by creating entirely new forms of mediation and connecting widely dispersed communities of interest (Rheingold 1993; Grossman 1995; Negroponte 1995). During the past century, advances in communication technology have had profound effects on patterns of communication, including widening the scope of personal contacts, expanding political information gathering such as polling, accelerating movements toward more interactivity, and lowering the costs of reaching a wide audience (Pool 1977; Abramson, Arterton, and Orren 1988). Despite these trends, technology has had relatively less impact on group-based communication when compared to interpersonal conversation, information aggregation, and broadcast communication (Weare 2002). While conference calls and videoconferencing facilitate group communication, dialogue continues to be most successful when it occurs in small groups in a face-to-face setting. Developing an understanding of how groups communicate in an Internet-based setting is critical to understanding the potential of this medium as a public space for dialogue.

In face-to-face group settings, dialogue is advocated as a means to improve the quality of human interaction (Bohm 1996; Cissna and Anderson

1998; Ellinor and Gerard 1998; Saunders 1999; Tannen 1998; Isaacs 1999, 2001). Dialogue occurs when a conversation evolves from a debate, or dialectic, to a more self-reflective and generative state, through a suspension of one's assumptions and rules (Isaacs 1999). The qualities of this ideal state are consistent with the notion of free and equal discourse, which theorists associate with deliberative democratic practice. Isaacs defines dialogue as "a conversation among peers [in which] everyone is responsible equally" (1999: 332). This definition is remarkably similar to the view expressed by discourse theorists, including Dryzek (1990), Benhabib (1996), and Habermas (1996), that an ideal democratic discourse entails face-to-face communication among a wide range of equals prior to formal, collective decision making. Rather than simply registering and aggregating preferences as in a plebiscitary democracy, a deliberative democracy is based on a free discourse among political equals, in which interests and values are subject to scrutiny (Dryzek and Torgerson 1993). Deliberative democrats call for the use of new and more expansive spaces, which, in the ideal, can be construed as a type of public sphere in which rational individuals can meet to discuss their future (Habermas 1996). An Internet-based setting, if designed to foster communication within a group, offers the possibility of serving as such a public sphere for dialogue.

Communication theorists and social scientists alike argue that much of the public discussion that occurs in American society is predisposed to polarized discourse or debate, failing to generate the true benefits of dialogue. Yankelovich (1991) believes this situation is due, in part, to several common misperceptions about the political decision-making process. These include the assumption that decisions depend on specialized knowledge possessed only by experts, the view that Americans are apathetic and lack relevant knowledge, and an unfounded faith in the ability of elected officials to understand and represent the electorate's views well. These misconceptions overlook the central role that personal viewpoints play in decision making and the importance of "disciplined talk" for forging consensus around values and develop mutual understanding that promotes successful problem solving (Yankelovich 1999).

Usenet, a decentralized system enabling Internet users to post and read messages on a wide variety of topics, was the first such technology to be widely adopted for discussion purposes, and it continues to enjoy wide popularity. The empirical literature on Usenet discussions suggests that it has influenced the nature of communication. Baym (1996) concluded that the Usenet medium significantly influences communication and participation, leading to a hybrid of oral, written, interpersonal, and mass forms of communication. Similarly, Galegher, Sproull, and Kiesler (1998) observed that Usenet discussion groups combine many of the features of oral conversation and written text, as well as new features specific to the medium. Schneider (1997) found participation in a Usenet discussion to be highly diverse and inclusive but lacking in equality and quality because a few participants dominated the discussion.

There has been only limited empirical study of the potential for democratic discourse in Internet forums in a governmental setting (Dahl 1998; Spano 2001). Musso, Weare, and Hale (2000) concluded that most local municipal government Web sites in California do not provide the information and communication capabilities to support deliberative democratic practices adequately. However, in a case study of a forum sponsored by the Minnesota E-Democracy initiative, Dahlberg (2001) found online discourse to stimulate reflection, encourage respectful listening and on-going participation, facilitate an open and honest exchange between participants, and provide equality of opportunity to all participants. To build upon these findings, this essay considers the extent to which the FMCSA-sponsored forum broadened participation and supported democratic dialogue in a federal government agency setting. The primary questions that this research attempted to address were:

- Did the Internet forum allow broader participation by individuals, and groups they represent, in the policy-making process?
- To what extent did the two-way communication in the Internet forum setting foster democratic deliberation?

2. Forum Description

When Congress created the FMCSA within the U.S. Department of Transportation in 1999, the new agency was directed to develop a ten-year strategic plan. A committee of agency managers, including one of the authors, initiated a planning process in June 2000 (Stanley 2002). Agency decision making, primarily centered on rule making, traditionally relies on one-way, written communication to obtain public input. In this case, FMCSA managers decided to extend public involvement in the planning process by including an Internet-based forum, which was called the 2010 Strategy and Performance Planning (2010 Strategy) Web site. Both a public docket and a Web site were established and operated continuously from August 2000 to June 2001. Participation by interested parties through the public docket and Web site was solicited by personal invitation from agency managers, notices in the *Federal Register,* and a news release.

The Internet forum was designed to increase interaction among FMCSA managers and members of the traffic safety community, including those who are subject to federal motor carrier safety regulations. Agency managers anticipated that information about key issues and possible solutions, including nonregulatory approaches, would result from the two-way discussion at the Web site. They also hoped that awareness of the issues would improve by the sharing of technical information and personal views among participants.

The site was designed to solicit opinions and concerns from site visitors, who could either register or participate anonymously. Technical papers and related documents were posted at the forum Web site to provide a common understanding among participants of key commercial vehicle safety issues. Electronic links were established to reports and other information at additional Web sites, so that all participants would have the same access as agency managers to relevant information.

At the 2010 Strategy Web site home page, visitors could select from several options, including a hyperlink to the entire collection of messages and reference materials at the Information and Collaboration group area. At the group area page, which is illustrated in Figure 12.1, visitors could either create a new discussion topic or reply to a message in an existing discussion thread. They also had the option to submit an electronic message to the public docket through a link posted elsewhere at the Web site. A message from the "Stop killing people going under trailers in accidents" discussion thread is illustrated in Figure 12.2. The body of the message, with an identifying header, was provided with a respond option and a display of its position in the thread. In addition to the asynchronous discussion, participant interaction was encouraged through an e-mail notification feature used to broadcast new messages daily to all registered

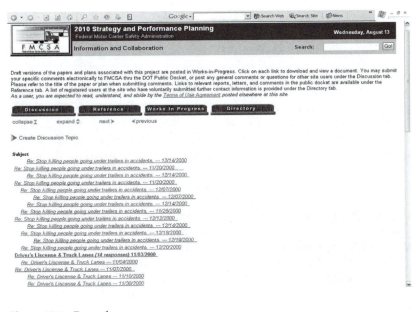

Figure. 12.1   Example group area page

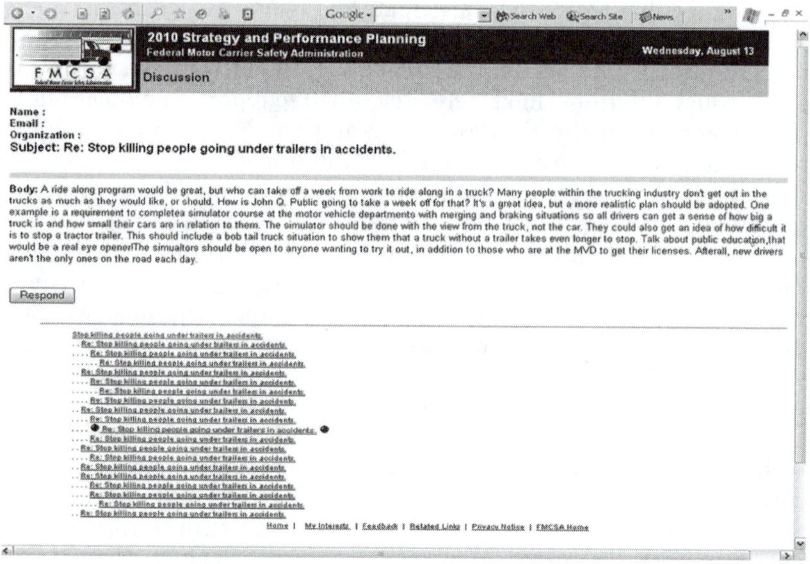

Figure. 12.2 Sample discussion thread message

visitors. Stanley (2002) provides further description of the operational features of the 2010 Strategy Web site.

3. Data and Methods

The public docket contained 102 letters or e-mail messages that were posted chronologically as received. One hundred and sixteen identifiable individuals contributed 339 messages to the 2010 Strategy Web site, and another 177 messages were contributed anonymously for a total of 516 messages. Of these, 65 were removed because they violated the terms-of-use agreement, leaving 451 messages that were organized in topical discussion threads. Messages embedded in a discussion thread were classified as one of three types: seed messages that began a new topic, reply messages that continued a discussion, and solo messages that elicited no response (Galegher, Sproull, and Kiesler 1998). There were seventy-four seed and twenty-three solo messages in the discussion forum. Including the messages that were removed, fifty-two of the seed messages elicited five or fewer responses, seven seeds received between six and ten responses, and fifteen seeds led to more than ten responses. The largest thread included twenty-nine messages.

Content and conversational analyses were employed to examine the written communication to the docket and Web site. The unit of analysis was the entire textual record of a letter sent in the docket or message posted to the Web site. Individual participants were classified by their organizational affiliation from among a list of targeted groups that were identified using agency mailing lists and other reference sources. Based on their group affiliation, it was possible to identify and count the frequency of participation by members of specific groups.

We analyzed message content to identify a number of distinct features. The first was the use of formal versus informal presentation styles. An earlier study in an electronic group discussion reported that the style of messages is more likely to be informal, direct, and engaged (Galegher, Sproull, and Kiesler 1998). Informal conversational devices used by writers included the use of first- and second-person pronouns, run-on sentences, parenthetical remarks, and exclamatory expressions. Informal style is also often associated with the use of personal narratives or stories. By contrast, a formal style of argument involves the use of the opposite conversational devices, such as use of third person, proper sentence structure, and correct grammatical responses. Each comment or message was coded as being written in either a formal or informal style.

The messages in a few discussion threads were selected for further interpretation using the Isaacs (1999) action model of dialogue. This model identifies four fields of a conversation that begins in a narrow space of politeness and civility, or Field I, in which discourse is constrained by prevailing rules and social norms. Conversation can then progress through breakdown, or Field II, where norms are examined and people begin to take positions. Next, conversation enters a stage of inquiry, or Field III, in which the dialogue is more reflective. The ultimate stage of conversation is flow, or Field IV, which exists when participants create new rules for interaction and each participant is personally included in the conversation.

4. Results

The number and range of individual participants increased as a result of the use of the Internet forum. While 100 individuals submitted comments by letter or electronically to the public docket, 116 individuals posted electronic messages in the forum discussion area. An additional 130 people registered at the Web site but did not post a message. The characteristics of participants suggest that the Internet forum attracted a new group of individuals to the planning process. While the docket and the Web site were both readily accessible, only four individuals commented through both communication media.

More important, the majority of individuals, approximately 85 percent, who provided docket comments had been invited to participate by FMSCA managers, either by letter or personally. Moreover, participation in the public docket was highest for individuals who were contacted more than once, supporting the notion that the existence of social ties among members of a group is an important influence on participation (Bimber

2001). In contrast, more than 90 percent of the participants in the Web site forum had not been contacted. However, a number of individuals with known interests and expertise who were invited to participate, including most FMCSA managers, did not submit messages in the forum discussion.

The Internet forum also expanded the range of participants and the groups they represent in the planning process. As illustrated in Table 12.1, 60 percent of the participants who contributed their comments to the public docket were representatives of government agencies or membership organizations. By contrast, 64 percent of the participants in the forum discussions were either commercial vehicle drivers, others employed in the commercial vehicle industry, or private citizens, including relatives of traffic crash victims.

The structure and style of communication differed between the public docket and the forum Web site. The docket communication was one-way and oriented primarily to agency officials. Even though it was possible to access and view the comments in the public docket electronically or in person at any time, there was only one reply to a previous comment.

In contrast, the structure of communication in the forum Web site discussion was frequently two-way. As noted earlier, seventy-four seed mes-

TABLE 12.1 Participants by group affiliation: docket versus web site.

	Percentage of participants in the Internet forum	Percentage of participants in the public docket
Commercial driver	27%	5%
Others, including private citizens	16%	14%
Industry/original equipment manufacturer or supplier	16%	14%
Unknown or anonymous	14%	1%
Government	13%	33%
Industry/shipper/receiver	5%	0%
Academic/research	3%	2%
Membership/trade association	3%	27%
Police/enforcement agency	3%	4%
Total	100%	100%

sages received at least one reply message. The ten most active participants accounted for almost a third of all messages. Nevertheless, over forty participants contributed at least two messages. In most cases, the messages were directed at other participants instead of agency officials. The difference in the orientation and structure of the messages clearly indicates that the Internet discussion features, which included e-mail notification, created opportunities for interactive discussion, not only between individuals and agency officials but also between individual participants.

The characteristics of the written responses differed between the two channels. Nearly all of the messages in the Web site were written in an informal style. They were abbreviated, focused on a single topic, and used the first person in the sentence structure. Of the comments to the public docket, 49 percent were more formally written, 47 percent were informal, and 4 percent were too ambiguous to characterize. These letters tended to address multiple issues and were more comprehensive in scope. In the informal comments, the style of communication appeared to be influenced more by the social experience of the participant rather than the medium of communication. For example, most private citizens who submitted comments used a personal narrative style in comments to both the docket and the Web site.

Although the forum Web site did facilitate more interactive, two-way discussion, the style of conversation in the messages was predominantly debate and dialectic, both of which might be termed Field II conversation styles using Isaacs's schema. These discussions for the most part remained on topic and were constructive, even if they were principally in a debating style. Another positive result was the relatively low incidence of flaming. In at least one discussion thread consisting of twenty-nine messages, titled "Big rig driving age," there was some evidence of a dialogic, or Field III, conversational style. Stanley (2002) provides a more detailed interpretation of the results and a discussion of how Isaacs's model was employed in this analysis.

5. Discussion and Conclusion

The communitarian view of democracy rests on the principle that citizens should be given more opportunity to participate in the processes of government. A central precept is that processes and institutions should be designed to allow citizens to consider issues, weigh alternatives, and express a judgment about which policy option is preferred (Barber 1984, 1995; Dryzek 1990; Matthews 1994). This view is expressed today by the term *deliberative democracy*, which is used for a broad and diverse set of perspectives, assumptions, and aims in recent thinking about democracy (Saward 2001). Deliberative democracy encompasses institutional contexts and practices that promote open dialogue and encourage the emergence of shared solutions through the creation of new knowledge and understanding (Gutmann and Thompson 1996).

The 2010 Strategy Web site offered a new public space for this purpose, but it achieved, at best, mixed results. Individual participation in the planning process broadened as a result of the Internet forum to include commercial vehicle drivers, employees in the commercial motor vehicle industry, and private citizens, including relatives of traffic crash victims. Many of these individuals would not ordinarily participate in FMCSA-sponsored policy-making discussions. At the same time, individuals representing the groups that are traditionally more informed about the issues and engaged in the policy-making process did not participate as widely in the Internet forum. With only a few exceptions, FMCSA managers with critical knowledge and expertise did not participate overtly. They were reluctant to comment on issues raised during the forum for a variety of reasons, including the fact that their public comments might influence ongoing rule-making actions. What is not known, however, is the extent to which they actively followed ongoing discussions or contributed comments anonymously. During the discussions, a few participants questioned why agency managers were not more active in the discussion, and Yankelovich (1991) argues that agency managers should play an active and constructive role in facilitating individual participation and greater sharing of the available information. The hurdles to eliciting the involvement of public officials in such forums and the benefits derived from their engagement are important areas for future research.

Based on the conversational analysis of the messages in selected discussion threads, it is apparent that the Internet forum was not typically a setting in which "the deliberations and persuasions [serve to] distinguish the democratic process and make participation in it a transformative lesson in the common good" (Abramson, Arterton, and Orren 1988: 23). Given the lack of affinity among participants, Bimber (2001) would argue that this result was to be expected. However, the result that the conversation in at least one discussion thread led to more reflective thinking and dialogue should be viewed positively. Further research is needed to understand what design features and processes of Internet-based forums best facilitate such democratic dialogue.

The Web site also served as a useful source of critical policy information to site users. During the busiest month, approximately 6,750 individuals visited the site to view information and download documents. While this was an important step toward informing participants, it was not readily apparent in the discussion forum that this information was utilized. The role of information provision in facilitating dialogue and the best methods for providing that information remain important topics for further research.

This research also leaves unanswered the question of the impact of Internet forums on agency decision making. FMCSA managers reviewed the comments and messages from the public docket and Internet forum during the development of the strategic plan. The opinion among most members of the agency committee was that the input provided by participants was valuable, primarily because it served to validate the scope and content of the plan. Comments that spoke directly to specific paragraphs or elements of the draft plan released midway through the planning process most likely had the greatest impact. In the final version of the strategic plan, FMCSA published a response that noted when suggestions and recommendations were included in the final plan but did not identify the comments of a particular individual or organization. The style and structure of the Web site discussions serves to reinforce Yankelovich's observation (1999) that citizens form judgments from interactions with other people. However, it was not readily apparent that many FMCSA managers recognized this form of judgment, at face value, as being a primary source of public opinion in formulating agency strategies and policies.

This study does suggest some tentative lessons for public administrators considering using similar Internet forums to increase participation and deliberation in the processes of government. Most importantly, the development of a forum should be considered as part of an overall agency effort to involve the public, rather than an isolated event or an alternative to an existing channel of communication. The use of the Internet should be integrated with existing processes and activities within social mechanisms and communities in which individuals, including agency officials, already participate. For example, an Internet forum could be held in conjunction with a workshop or public meeting, allowing more individuals to overcome the limitation of physical proximity to participate. Alternatively, a forum might serve as an extension to a workshop or public meeting, allowing participants to overcome the constraints of time by extending their face-to-face deliberations in an asynchronous fashion.

In addition, various means should be used to inform and enable all potential participants of the opportunity to participate in an Internet forum. As the results of this study suggest, there may be large numbers of individuals receptive to an Internet-based approach who represent member groups, such as commercial truck drivers and other frontline employees of organizations, that have traditionally been underrepresented in policy-making processes. These individuals may be reached through various traditional marketing mechanisms such as announcements and press releases, or nontraditional approaches such as e-mail lists, Usenet announcements, and direct links from other important Web sites, including portals that serve as government information gateways.

Because the perceived political legitimacy of the discussions is likely to be a critical determinant of who participates and how, public administrators play an important role in creating conditions for the success of an Internet forum. A primary way to legitimate the activity is for agency officials to directly participate in the discussions. They can assert themselves in a variety of ways, which would be aimed at ensuring that participation in the Internet forum is the behavioral norm, not the exception, within their own organizations. As an example, officials could lead and moderate discussions on a particular national issue or policy topic. At the nexus of much of the information, they are in a position to raise the public consciousness on an issue, as Yankelovich (1999) suggests, by condensing and explaining a complex policy issue or question into a set of choices, perhaps supported by an analysis of the pros and cons of each choice. More important, they can moderate discussions and keep participants informed when they feel that observations about agency actions are incomplete or incorrect. They can also encourage their peers and staff to participate directly in the forum discussions. Beyond their direct participation, agency officials can report the information and use the results from the Internet forum discussions in their follow-up decision making and actions, and further validate this result through communication of the results within and outside the agency to their colleagues and the public.

References

Abramson, J. B., F. C. Arterton, and G. Orren. 1988. *The Electronic Commonwealth: The Impact of New Media Technologies on Democratic Politics.* New York: Basic Books.

Barber, B. R. 1984. *Strong Democracy: Participatory Politics for a New Age.* Berkeley, CA: University of California Press.

Barber, B. R. 1995. "Searching for Civil Society." *National Civic Review* 84: 114–18.

Baym, N. K. 1996. "Agreements and Disagreements in a Computer-Mediated Discussion." *Research on Language and Social Interaction* 29: 315–45.

Benhabib, S. 1996. *Democracy and Difference: Contesting the Boundaries of the Political.* Princeton, NJ: Princeton University Press.

Bimber, B. 1998. "The Internet and Political Transformation: Populism, Community, and Accelerated Pluralism." *Polity* 31: 133–60.

Bimber, B. 1999. "The Internet and Citizen Communication with Government: Does the Medium Matter?" *Political Communication* 16: 409–29.

Bimber, B. 2001. "Information and Political Engagement in America: The Search for Effects of Information Technology at the Individual Level." *Political Research Quarterly* 54: 53–67.

Bohm, D. 1996. *On Dialogue.* London: Routledge.

Cissna, K. N., and R. Anderson. 1998. "Theorizing About Dialogic Moment: The Buber-Rogers Position and Postmodern Themes." *Communication Theory* 8: 63–104.

Dahl, R. A. 1998. *On Democracy.* New Haven, CT: Yale University Press.

Dahlberg, L. 2001. "The Internet and Democratic Discourse." *Information, Communication, and Society* 4: 615–33.

Dryzek, J. S. 1990. *Discursive Democracy: Politics, Policy, and Political Science.* New York: Cambridge University Press.

Dryzek, J. S., and D. Torgerson. 1993. "Democracy and the Political Sciences: A Progress Report." *Policy Sciences* 26: 127–37.

Ellinor, L. and G. Gerard. 1998. *Dialogue: Rediscover the Transforming Power of Conversation.* New York: John Wiley.

Galegher, J., L. Sproull, and S. Kiesler. 1998. "Legitimacy, Authority, and Community in Electronic Support Groups." *Written Communication* 15: 493–530.

Grossman, L. K. 1995. *The Electronic Republic: Reshaping Democracy in the Information Age.* New York: Viking.

Gutmann, A., and D. Thompson. 1996. *Democracy and Disagreement.* Cambridge, MA: Harvard University Press.

Habermas, J. 1996. *Between Facts and Norms: Contributions to a Discourse Theory of Law and Democracy*. Cambridge, MA: MIT Press.

Isaacs, W. 1999. *Dialogue and the Art of Thinking Together*. New York: Currency/Random House.

Isaacs, W. 2001. "Toward an Action Theory of Dialogue." *International Journal of Public Administration* 24: 709–48.

Matthews, D. 1994. *Politics for People: Finding a Responsible Public Voice*. Urbana: University of Illinois Press.

Musso, J., C. Weare, and M. Hale. 2000. "Designing Web Technologies for Local Governance Reform: Good Management or Good Democracy?" *Political Communication* 17: 1–19.

Negroponte, N. 1995. *Being Digital*. New York: Knopf.

Pool, Ithiel de Sola, ed. 1977. *The Social Impact of the Telephone*. Cambridge, MA: MIT Press.

Rheingold, H. 1993. *The Virtual Community: Homesteading on the Electronic Frontier*. Reading, MA: Addison-Wesley.

Saunders, H. H. 1999. *A Public Peace Process: Sustained Dialogue to Transform Racial and Ethnic Conflicts*. New York: St. Martin's Press.

Saward, M. 2001. "Making Democratic Connections: Political Equality, Deliberation, and Direct Democracy." *Acta Politica*, winter: 36.

Schneider, S. M. 1997. "Expanding the Public Sphere Through Computer-Mediated Communication: Political Discussion About Abortion in a Usenet Newsgroup." Ph.D. dissertation, Massachusetts Institute of Technology.

Spano, S. 2001. *Public Dialogue and Participatory Democracy: The Cupertino Community Project*. Cresskill, NJ: Hampton.

Stanley, J. H. 2002. "*Participation, Democratic Deliberation, and the Internet: Lessons from a National Forum on Commercial Vehicle Safety*." Ph.D. dissertation, University of Southern California.

Tannen, D. 1998. *The Argument Culture: Moving from Debate to Dialogue*. New York: Random House.

Weare, C. 2002. "The Internet and Democracy: The Causal Links Between Technology and Politics." *International Journal of Public Administration* 25: 659–92.

Yankelovich, D. 1991. *Coming to Public Judgment*. Syracuse, NY: Syracuse University Press.

Yankelovich, D. 2001. *The Magic of Dialogue: Transforming Conflict into Cooperation*. New York: Simon and Schuster.

CHAPTER 13

Internet-Based Political Discourse: A Case Study of Electronic Democracy in Hoogeveen

NICHOLAS W. JANKOWSKI AND RENÉE VAN OS

The amount of activity undertaken during the past few years to incorporate electronic networks into the information and communication systems of municipalities is, by all accounts, enormous. Community networks, sometimes called digital cities or public education networks, are mushrooming across North America and Europe. These networks are initiated in some cases by individuals and independent organizations, but frequently by local governments. Provision of governmental services via such networks is, as a consequence, expanding rapidly. In the Netherlands, for example, nearly two-thirds of the local governments maintain Web sites (Consumentengids 2002). Although most of these sites are static and concentrate primarily on relatively basic information provision, a growing number provide interactive services and forms of citizen-government discussion. A few are concerned with incorporation of electronic networks into the process of political deliberation.

This essay examines one initiative related to this last development: the conduct of Internet-based political discourse in the Dutch city of Hoogeveen. This initiative transpired within the virtual space of the electronic community network operating in that city—Digitale Stad Hoogeveen (see www.hoogeveen.nl). The Hoogeveen Digital City was established in May 1996 and serves as the formal Web site for this municipality of fifty thousand residents. The site has achieved national acclaim for its design and for the online discussions it has hosted. In many ways, the Hoogeveen Digital City can be considered one of the more advanced community networks in the Netherlands with regard to initiatives aimed at engaging citizens in politically oriented discussion.

A case study was conducted of this community network (van Os 2002), focusing on the political discussions organized prior to the municipal elections held in March 2002. One of the central issues in this study is the manner in which these online political discussions contribute to creation of a public sphere, considered essential to many forms of "electronic democracy." The first section of this essay elaborates the theoretical underpinnings of the study. The second section provides an overview of the three forms of online discussion hosted by Digitale Stad Hoogeveen. In the third section, findings from an analysis of different forms of online discussion are presented. The fourth and last section presents a number of conclusions and reflections on the value of such online initiatives for electronic democracy.

1. Theoretical Perspectives

Two intertwined theoretical discourses inform this study: notions of electronic democracy and considerations of the meaning of the public sphere within a computer-mediated communications (CMC) environment. Regarding electronic democracy, many scholars have been concerned with elaborating the features of this and similar terms (e.g., Tsagarousianou, Tambini, and Bryan 1998; Hague and Loader 1999; Hacker and Van Dijk 2000; Jankowski, van Selm, and Hollander 2001; Coleman and Gøtze 2001; Oblak 2001). Hacker and van Dijk (2000: 1) provide a compact—and consequently very general—formulation: "a collection of attempts to practice democracy with the limits of time, space and other physical conditions, using ICT (Information and Communications Technologies) or CMC instead, as an addition, not a replacement for traditional 'analogue' practices." Oblak (2001) points out that many of these discussions seem to place emphasis on innovations in communication technologies that facilitate such activities as televoting, electronically held referendums, and online discussions. She stresses, however, that such innovations do not unconditionally improve the democratic process. Achieving such improvement depends on the theory of democracy underlying adoption of a particular innovation in communication technology.

In this chapter, emphasis is placed on the deliberative component of democracy, particularly how the notion of the public sphere might be applied to an environment promoting online political discussion. Deliberation is often aligned with the notion of the public sphere and is considered by some (e.g., Habermas 1989; Keane 1991) as a prerequisite to the proper functioning of a democracy. A "strong" democracy is characterized by a form of participation, engaging citizens in those decisions concerning issues that impinge upon and are important to them (Barber 2000; Gimmler 2001: 24; Hague and Loader 1999: 7). The Internet provides new arenas where citizens can "meet" political representatives and discuss issues of collective concern. Hague and Loader remark, however, that, "if an enhanced form of digital democracy is to emerge, it would be reasonable to speculate that it is likely to be a hybrid democratic model containing elements of both participatory and representative forms of democracy" (1999: 7). Gimmler considers this as a "two-track model of democracy": on one hand, there is the constitutional democratic state and its parliamentary and legal institutions, and on the other hand there is the public sphere of civil society. Gimmler believes that "the legitimacy and functional capacity of a pluralistic democracy can be guaranteed only by a combination of both spheres: neither the existence of representative democracy and the rule of law alone, nor the simple fact of citizens participation in all political decisions, can produce the political process necessary to maintain a legitimate society" (2001: 24). In this vein, some of the online arenas for political discourse may have direct ties with the state, providing what Tsagarousianou (1999: 196) calls "citizen-to-authorities communication." Other arenas may emphasize citizen-to-citizen communication.

Schneider (1996, 1997) and Dahlberg (2000, 2001a, 2001b, 2001c) have contributed much to our understanding of the issues and problems related to incorporation of an Internet-based public sphere in a more general notion of civil society. Although both scholars have constructed models reflecting the central dimensions of the public sphere, the four dimensions proposed by Schneider—equality, diversity, reciprocity, and quality of the discourse—are employed, with some modification, in this study. In the first place, Schneider's study was based on a large-scale quantitative investigation, while this case study is small-scale and interpretative in character. Schneider does emphasize the need to achieve mutual understanding during discussions, and this aspect is considered in the small-scale investigation reported in this chapter. Situations in which participants act primarily out of self-interest or with intent to persuade other participants are detrimental to achievement of an ideal public sphere (Schneider 1997: 13). Further, reaching decisions based on such discussions is less important than the contribution of the discussions to the quality of political life through identification of the public interest and consideration of alternative formulations of the public good.

The operationalization of these dimensions for this case study may be found elsewhere (van Os 2002); here, only brief descriptions are provided.

- *Equality.* Everyone with interest in a particular issue (e.g., political actors, government officials, local residents) should have the possibility of contributing to an online discussion. Contributions made to a discussion are expected to be equally distributed among participants and without impairment through forms of domination or intimidation by other participants.

- *Diversity.* Online discussions are to reflect both the range of issues related to a particular topic and the range of participants representing standpoints on the topic. Such diversity is necessary to ensure broad public dialogue.

- *Reciprocity.* Participants in online discussions are obliged to acquaint themselves with the positions of other participants, as well as to exercise mutual understanding of the standpoints taken by others.

- *Quality.* An online discussion is considered of high quality when a rational-critical argument constitutes the basis of the discussion. With this aspect in mind, participants are expected to place their own values and interests within a wider social context. As a basic indication of quality, postings to online discussions are expected to be related to the topic of a particular discussion. Although consensus is not seen as the ultimate goal of a discussion, a debate of high quality is expected to reflect some degree of convergence of standpoints.

2. Online Discussions

As previously mentioned, the community network Digitale Stad Hoogeveen is an initiative of the local government of Hoogeveen, a city located in the eastern part of the Netherlands. The municipality launched a relatively conventional Web site for the city in May 1996 and a year later expanded it to include the Digital City Hall. This part of the Web site is the most developed and provides a range of information and registration services to residents. Resident access to other sources of online information is also considered important, and Hoogeveen Digital City is meant to serve as a gateway through provision of links to other Web sites maintained by organizations and businesses active in the city. One of the special features of this community network is the degree of online discussions made available to residents. In the past few years, Hoogeveen has experimented with three forms of online discussions: Digital Consultation Hour, Digital Debate, and Digital Discussion Platform.

The Digital Consultation Hour was initiated in 2001 as a real-time form of communication between local government representatives and residents. This type of online discussion provides opportunity for synchronous exchange in a question-and-answer format. During the first year of operation, six Digital Consultation Hours were organized on a bimonthly basis around a range of topics considered salient for the community, including recreational facilities for young people, parking, and the municipal budget. In a government report reviewing these initial experiences with the Digital Consultation Hour, the central objective is described as an effort to "reduce the distance between government and citizens" in Hoogeveen (Hansma 2002: 2). On average, some twenty-five people submitted questions during any one of the online discussions. A particularly active discussion was devoted to city recreational facilities, where forty-three people submitted a total of 104 questions during the hour-long period. In contrast, during a discussion on housing issues only five people visited the site and no questions were posed.

The second form of online discussion with which the community network experimented is called Digital Debate and was especially organized as part of the campaign for the 2002 municipal elections. Representatives from the political parties with candidates running in the election were invited to participate in this real-time two-hour event. Residents were asked to contribute to discussion threads that developed during the course of the Digital Debate. All participants, both residents and political candidates, had opportunity to initiate threads during this debate—in contrast to the previously described Digital Consultation Hour. Some twenty-nine different threads were initiated during this debate. Approximately a dozen postings were placed on each of these threads. Nearly three-quarters of these postings, however, originated from the political candidates; the rest came from individuals not involved in the organization of the event.

The third form of online discussion practiced in Hoogeveen is called the Digital Discussion Platform and resembles conventional Internet-based discussion lists. This form of online discussion is, in contrast to the other two forms, continuously available on the Hoogeveen Web site. The municipal government follows a laissez-faire policy regarding this online activity. For example, the webmaster is instructed to intervene in a discussion only when very general criteria of propriety, as specified on a code of conduct posted on the site, are violated. As of March 2002, twenty-two discussions were accessible on the site, dating back to September 2001. Some fourteen of these discussions had fewer than three postings and were not included in the analysis. Earlier discussions had been removed from the site by the webmaster, following the policy to periodically delete old material from the site. The duration of these discussions varied from a few weeks to several months. In the eight discussions with three or more contributions, twenty-eight people posted messages, with an average of five per discussion. The number of postings per participant varied in a manner similar to that reported in other studies of discussion lists (Schneider 1996; Jankowski and van Selm 2000; Hagemann 2003; Albrecht 2003): a small handful of people were responsible for a large percentage of the postings. In the case of these eight discussions, four individuals were responsible for nearly 50 percent of the ninety-five postings.

The city of Hoogeveen sees the Digital Consultation Hour as an arena where government officials can interact with residents. The Digital Debate is meant to be a space for exchange between politicians and elected representatives. Under consideration for the future is the possibility of a broader range of government employees (e.g., department staff members) taking part in this discussion form. Current policy regarding the Digital

Discussion Platform stipulates that government employees and elected representatives may take part as individuals, just like other residents of the city, but not as representatives of the city government.

3. Dimensions of the Public Sphere

The above three types of debate on the Hoogeveen Digital City, taken together, account for fifty-seven different online discussions. Of these, twenty-four were suitable for analysis and were examined with respect to the indicators of the four components of the public sphere previously elaborated. Regarding the component of equality, three facets of postings were examined: indications suggesting special treatment based on the status of a participant, indications of intimidating or denigrating language, and indications of domination within a discussion. Generally speaking, contributions to the Digital Discussion Platform generated the most instances of these three indicators, which probably can be attributed to the asynchronous nature of the discussion environment. The first facet, special treatment because of status, was recorded in 10 of the 95 postings on the Digital Discussion Platform; 5 of the 138 postings on the Digital Debate manifested this facet. These postings often involved a political candidate emphasizing his or her status as a politician, using such reference to terminate the discussion. In the Digital Consultation Hour no indication of inequality was found in the discussions examined.

The second facet, intimidating or denigrating language, also was observed in both forms of discussion. Of the 95 postings to the Digital Discussion Platform, 11 expressions of intimidation and 11 remarks that included denigrating language were noted. This kind of remark was less frequent in the Digital Debate: 2 were noted as intimidating and 4 as denigrating, out of the 138 postings to this discussion form. Based on comments from interviews with participants, these remarks, along with those alluding to the status of participants, often created a sphere in which some participants declined to be further involved in the discussions. In this sense, such remarks not only reflected an unequal distribution within the discussion but also may have played a negative role in overall access to the discussions.

The third facet, domination of the discussions, was recorded as the number of postings by participants.[1] In both the Digital Debate and Digital Discussion Platform, a relatively small number of participants contributed most of the postings. In the Digital Debate, four of the twenty-one participants contributed more than half of the postings; in the Digital Discussion Platform, five of the twenty-eight participants were responsible for this amount (see Table 13.1 and Table 13.2).

The diversity component of the public sphere was examined as variations in the topics of discussion and the participants. In the Digital Consultation Hour, slightly more than one topic per posting was included,

TABLE 13.1 Postings to Digital Debate

Postings (N = 138)	Participants (N = 21)	Percentage of total postings	Cumulative percentage
21 (15.2%)	1	15.2%	15.2%
18 (13.0%)	1	13.0%	28.2%
17 (12.3%)	1	12.3%	40.5%
16 (11.6%)	1	11.6%	52.1%
11 (8.0%)	1	8.0%	60.1%
10 (7.2%)	1	7.2%	67.3%
8 (5.8%)	2	11.6%	78.9%
6 (4.3%)	1	4.3%	83.2%
4 (2.9%)	1	2.9%	86.1%
3 (2.2%)	2	4.3%	90.4%
2 (1.4%)	4	5.8%	96.3%
1 (0.7%)	5	3.6%	100%

TABLE 13.2 Postings to Digital Discussion Forum

Postings (N = 95)	Participants (N = 28)	Percentage of total postings	Cumulative percentage
23 (24.2%)	1	24.2%	24.2%
9 (9.5%)	1	9.5%	33.7%
7 (7.4%)	1	7.4%	41.1%
6 (6.3%)	1	6.3%	47.4%
5 (5.3%)	1	5.3%	52.7%
4 (4.2%)	5	21.1%	73.8%
3 (3.2%)	2	6.3%	80.1%
2 (2.1%)	3	6.3%	86.4%
1 (1.1%)	13	13.6%	100%

compared to an average of nearly two topics per posting for the Digital Debate and Digital Discussion Platform. Postings were also progressively longer for those types of discussion, with fewer structural limitations. For the Digital Consultation Hour, resembling a question-and-answer session, the length of an average posting was no more than 30 words. The average posting for the Digital Debate was 46 words; for the Digital Discussion Platform the average posting was 179 words. The format for this last type of online discussion was, as previously mentioned, similar to asynchronous Internet discussion lists. As such, participants had more time to compose their postings, which probably accounts for the longer contributions. Both of the other discussions were held in real time, and participants were restricted to posting contributions during the relatively short period that the discussions were in operation.

Regarding the public sphere component of diversity in participants, the Digital Consultation Hour was structurally restricted to allowing only one participant to engage in exchange with a representative of local government at any point in time. As a consequence, the smallest number of participants was involved in these sessions as compared to the other two types of online discussions. The average number of topics on which these participants posted contributions did not differ substantially from the number of topics for participants involved in the other two forms of discussion.

For the component of reciprocity three patterns of interaction were examined in the two forms of discussion that allowed for extended interaction, the Digital Debate and the Digital Discussion Platform. In the first place, indications as to whether participants would ask for or would provide information were considered. Second, the presence of verbal attacks in postings, directed at other participants, were noted. Finally, the sequence of postings was monitored to determine the degree of reaction to previous postings.

Regarding the first indicator, no substantial difference was found between the two types of online discussion: about a fifth of all postings to the Digital Debate and to the Digital Discussion Platform posed questions, and about the same number of postings provided answers to previously formulated questions. One of the differences between these two types of discussions, however, is the degree to which the initial contribution to a particular discussion could be interpreted as initiating further deliberation through the manner in which information was provided or requested. In the thirteen discussions monitored in the Digital Debate, initiation of further discussion occurred about half of the time. In the eight discussions of the Digital Discussion Platform that were inspected, this feature was present in nearly all cases.

Regarding indications of verbal attack, the Digital Discussion Platform contained many more postings with this characteristic than did the Digital Debate. About half of the discussions on the Digital Discussion Platform contained examples of verbal attacks and denigrating comments. In the Digital Debate only two examples of denigrating comments were identified, which probably can be partially explained by the real-time presence of discussion partners, as compared to the asynchronous format of the Digital Discussion Platform.

As for the degree of reactions to postings, contributions to the Digital Debate were less frequently addressed by another participant than contributions to the Digital Discussion Platform. Put differently, 60 percent of the contributions to the Digital Debate and 44 percent of the contributions to the Platform sessions did not receive even one reaction.

The pattern of reciprocity in the Digital Discussion Platform seems more complex than that found in the Digital Debate. There is, for example, more interaction among participants involved in the Platform discussions as compared to the Digital Debate. Indications of mutual understanding, in contrast, occurred more often in the Digital Debate than in the Digital Discussion Platform. In the Platform sessions, it seemed as if participants focused on reacting to each other without providing any indication of understanding the position taken by others (see Table 13.3).

The component of discussion quality is composed, like the previous component, of a series of elements. First, aspects of rational-critical arguments are examined, such as providing support for a position through reference to illustrative material or to personal experience. References to political party statements, however, also require reflection on the reasons behind the statements. Second, the postings were examined as to whether reference was made to the initial discussion topic, as an indicator of continuity in the exchange. Third, the postings were examined for signs of convergence in the discussion through, for example, participants accepting argumentation from each other or expressing points of commonality.

The discussions conducted on the Digital Discussion Platform reflected more of these characteristics of rational-critical discourse than did the other two discussion types. More than half (57 percent) of the postings to the Platform sessions were supported with argumentation, compared to 39 percent of the postings to the Digital Debate and 40 percent of the postings to the Digital Consultation Hour. In a sense this is not surprising, since the Digital Discussion Platform was the only type of online discussion that provided extended time for developing such argumentation.

TABLE 13.3 Indicators of Reciprocity

Indicators	Digital debate	Digital discussion platform
Mutual understanding present	36 (32.5%)	15 (19.8%)
No mutual understanding present	48 (43.4%)	34 (45.5%)
Reference to posting of other participants, but no indication of either mutual understanding or no mutual understanding	27 (24.1%)	26 (34.7%)
Total	111 (100%)	75 (100%)

The absence of indicators of convergence of positions suggests limited effort to understand the position of the other discussants. Although personal positions may be well formulated and argued, the quality of the discourse, as defined in the context of this study, is limited. As suggested above, such discussions have the tendency to go nowhere and to be more a reflection of individual opinions than collective deliberation.

4. Conclusion

This case study, albeit of modest scope and intention, suggests a gloomy picture for the nature of political deliberation in online environments. Online discussions such as those practiced on Hoogeveen Digital City provide, it seems, a limited contribution to deliberative democracy and to the four components of the public sphere. The discussions examined were dominated by a small group of participants, were relatively narrow in the range of issues discussed, were limited in expression of mutual interest or reciprocity, and were low on the measures of quality employed.

In summary, the ideal public sphere as elaborated in the theoretical section of this chapter was found only in limited form among the online discussions analyzed in this case study. In the first place, the discussions reflected a relatively high degree of inequality among participants. Second, the discussions provided a degree of diversity in topics; participants were able, in principle, to initiate discussions on a wide range of topics. The structure of the online discussions, however, can negatively influence the degree of diversity through, for example, limitations in time and substantive focus. The structure of the Digital Consultation Hour was the most constrictive of the three forms of online discussion. Third, the level of reciprocity differed substantially between the Digital Debate and the Digital Discussion Platform. This component of the public sphere seemed to be influenced by the manner in which the discussions were organized: the asynchronous form of discussion seemed to provide more opportunity to read and react to the postings of other participants. This did not mean, however, that participants expressed more mutual understanding for the positions taken by others in the discussions. On the contrary, this component of the public sphere was not evident, which may have been related to the indirect form of discussion. Fourth, the quality of the discussions suffered from the same malaise as the reciprocity component: participants tended to express limited understanding for the positions taken by others in the discussions. Regarding convergence of positions, no indication was found in the discussions analyzed. Participants, instead, continued to maintain the initial positions taken in the discussions.

There were, of course, differences found between the three forms of discussion. The Digital Consultation Hour format provided the least opportunity for exchange; the Digital Debate, held in real-time and allowing for immediate interactions between participants, seemed to foster less understanding and reciprocity; the Digital Consultation Platform, essentially an Internet discussion list, provided more time and space for extended contributions and interactions. None of these differences, however, suggests a single form of discussion that clearly contributes more to deliberation than the others.

As to which of the three discussion forms seems to have the greatest potential of contributing to the four components of the public sphere, it appears as if asynchronous discussion forms, like that found in the Digital Consultation Platform, provide the most opportunity for equal input, diverse contributions, mutual exchange (reciprocity), and a quality form of rational-critical discourse. This potential is related to the basic characteristics of such discussions: participants may freely determine when they take part, can take the necessary time to compose their postings, may elaborate on their arguments as extensively as is required, and may incorporate the opinions of other participants into their postings. But it is precisely this discussion form in which the most difficulties were encountered in Hoogeveen, particularly through the language employed and verbal attacks by some participants. There are solutions to this kind of difficulty, however, such as assigning an independent moderator to these discussions with instructions to inhibit such attacks and to stimulate contributions at other phases in a discussion.

It is important to mention the limitations of this case study of Hoogeveen Digital City. To begin, no comparisons were made between the online deliberations and those conducted offline, in "real life." It may be that with such a comparison the online discussions would score better than the offline along the four public sphere components of equality, diversity, reciprocity, and quality of discourse. This is one of the many aspects not known on the basis of the findings emerging from this case study. It is also not known what contribution organizational features such as moderated discussions might have on the nature of the deliberations. Finally, we have no idea what long-term effect such discussions may have on the political awareness and actions of participants. For all we know, participants in such discussions may become more aware and active citizens than those not exposed to online deliberations.

Moreover, the nature of political deliberation, on- or offline, may be richer and more complex than can be captured by the operationalization of the public sphere employed in this case study. A rethinking of the ways in which the public sphere should be measured, particularly in a virtual environment, is one of the most immediate tasks for researchers concerned with investigating this concept. In sum, much work, theoretical and empirical, has yet to be done.

Still, the legacy of this modest initiative to introduce online political deliberation by means of the facilities made available through Hoogeveen Digital City remains, with all of the above qualifications and reservations, somber. This case study suggests that the potential of online discussions to contribute in a substantial manner to public discourse and, ultimately, to a more democratic form of political engagement may be very limited.

Portions of this chapter, *Internet-based Political Discourse: A Case Study of Electronic Democracy in Hoogeveen*, by Nicholas W. Jankowski and Renée van Os, appeared in the Dutch language *Jaarboek ICT & Samenleving 2004*, as "Digitale Democratie binnen de gemeente Hoogeveen" [Digital Democracy in the city of Hoogeveen], edited by J. de Haan & O. Klumper, (Boom, Amsterdam, The Netherlands).

Note

1. The six Digital Consultation Hour discussions could not be included in this part of the analysis because of the question-and-answer nature of this discussion form.

References

Albrecht, S. 2003 "Whose Voice Is Heard in a Virtual Public Sphere?" Conference paper, Oxford Internet Institute.

Arterton, C. F. 1987. *Teledemocracy: Can Technology Protect Democracy?* London: Sage.

Barber, B. R. 2000. "Which Technology for Which Democracy? Which Democracy for Which Technology?" *International Journal of Communications and Law* 6: 1–8.

Coleman, S., and J. Gøtze. 2001. "Bowling Together. Online Public Engagement In Policy Deliberation." Hansard Society, London. Available at http://bowlingtogether.net.

Consumentengids. 2002. "Gemeentehuis in cyberspace [City hall in cyberspace]." *Consumentengids*, 66–71.

Dahlberg, L. 2000. "The Internet and the Public Sphere: A Critical Analysis of the Possibility of Online Discourse Enhancing Deliberative Democracy." Ph.D. disseration, Massey University.

Dahlberg, L. 2001a. "Computer-Mediated Communication and the Public Sphere: A Critical Analysis." *Journal of Computer-Mediated Communication* 7, 1.

Dahlberg, L. 2001b. "Extending the Public Sphere Through Cyberspace: The Case of Minnesota E-Democracy." *First Monday* 6, 3. Available at http://www.firstmonday.dk/issues/issue6_3/dahlberg/index.html

Dahlberg, L. 2001c. "The Internet and Democratic Discourse." *Information, Communication and Society* 4, 4: 615–33.

Gimmler, A. 2001. "Deliberative Democracy, Public Sphere and the Internet." *Philosophy and Criticism* 27, 4: 21–39.

Habermas, J. 1989. *The Structural Transformation of the Public Sphere.* Cambridge, MA: MIT Press.

Hacker, K. L., and J. van Dijk. 2000. *Digital Democracy: Issues of Theory and Practice.* London: Sage.

Hagemann, C.P.M. 2003. "Complotten, sarcasme en bevestiging van de eigen identiteit: Analyse van een Usenet nieuwsgroep over de moord op Pim Fortuyn [Complot, sarcasm and realization of own identity: Analysis of a Usenet newsgroup regarding the murder of Pim Fortuyn]." *Amsterdams Sociologisch Tijdschrift* 30, 1–2: 110–39.

Hague, B., and B. Loader, eds. 1999. *Digital Democracy: Discourse and Decision Making in the Information Age.* London: Routledge.

Hansma, A. 2002. *Rapport voor Burgemeester en Wethouders gemeente Hoogeveen betreffende het digitaal spreekuur.* [Report for the mayor and members of the Hoogeveen city council regarding the digital consultation hour]. Hoogeveen: City Office of Information.

Jankowski, N., and M. van Selm. 2000. "The Promise and Practice of the Public Debate." In K. L. Hacker and J. van Dijk, eds., *Digital Democracy: Issues of Theory and Practice*, 149–65. London: Sage.

Jankowski, N., M. van Selm, and E. Hollander. 2001. "On Crafting a Study of Community Networks: Considerations and Reflections." In L. Keeble and B. Loader, eds., *Community Informatics: Community Development Through the Use of Information and Communication Technologies,* 101–17. London: Routledge.

Keane, J. 1991. *Media and Democracy.* Cambridge: Polity Press.

Oblak, T. 2001. "Images of Electronic Democracy: Communication Technologies and Changes in Participation and Communication Processes." Ph.D. dissertation, University of Ljubljana.

Os, R. van. 2002. "Digitale democracie: een case studie naar de rol van online discussies binnen het lokale politieke proces [Digital democracy: a case study regarding the role of online discussions within the local political process]." Master's thesis, University of Nijmegen.

Schneider, S. 1996. "A Case Study of Abortion Conversation on the Internet." *Social Science Computer Review* 14, 4: 373–93.

Schneider, S. 1997. "Expanding the Public Sphere Through Computer-Mediated Communication: Political Discussion About Abortion in a Usenet Newsgroup." Ph.D. dissertation, Massachusetts Institute of Technology, Cambridge. Available at http://www.sunyit.edu/nsteve/abstract.html.

Tsagarousianou, R. 1999. "Electronic Democracy: Rhetoric and Reality." *Communications: The European Journal of Communication Research* 24, 2: 189–208.

Tsagarousianou, R., D. Tambini, and C. Bryan. 1998. *Cyberdemocracy: Technology, Cities and Civic Networks.* London: Routledge.

CHAPTER 14

The League of Women Voters' DemocracyNet (DNet): An Exercise in Online Civic Engagement

JACKIE MILDNER WITH NANCY TATE

This essay seeks to present the League of Women Voters' DemocracyNet (DNet) program as a case study of an effort to foster meaningful and enduring online civic engagement and deliberation and to ascertain if the program is meeting this goal.

Civic engagement has many components and definitions. The League's DNet program provides thorough, nonpartisan information on candidates and ballot measures in thousands of communities across the country. This project engages three different groups: DNet volunteers, the public, and the candidates. The main focus of this chapter will be on the volunteers and their activity as an aspect of civic engagement.

The League of Women Voters' DemocracyNet program is a practical application of the League's overall mission to encourage an engaged and informed citizenry. The League was established more than eighty years ago to help women exercise their newly granted right to vote. Since that time, the League has addressed many issues, but its core expertise remains voting: helping citizens become more comfortable with the process, the issues, and the candidates so that they are more inclined to vote. As part of this core function, Leagues across the country have produced paper Voter Guides, a print forum in which the state or local Leagues pose questions to candidates and provide the public with each candidate's answers. With the rise of the Internet, the League saw the opportunity to combine its expertise in voter education with emerging technology. Through this medium, voter education and civic engagement could potentially be accomplished on a much larger, more thorough platform.

DNet is that platform. It is a nationwide, interactive online network of electoral information. The League has a long, well-earned reputation as a trusted source of objective, nonpartisan information. DNet provides citizens across the country with information on elections at the federal, state, and local levels. DNet covers offices from the president and members of the U.S. Congress to governor and state legislator and all the way down to mayor, school board member, and sheriff. No other online voter education service covers such an extensive range of candidates and ballot initiatives as DNet, making it a true grassroots service and giving it a presence that is both local and national.

Only the League, with its vast network of volunteers, could produce the comprehensive data provided on DNet. Local volunteers who agree to cover specific elections invite all candidates running for each office to participate. They create the election in the DNet system and load the candidates' names and contact information. Volunteers provide each candidate with a secure password and ID, provide training to candidates or their staffs, and assist them in uploading information, if necessary. Most importantly, the volunteers follow up with the candidates throughout the election cycle to answer any questions that may arise and to urge them to participate actively.

DNet's core feature is a unique grid (Figure 14.1). In each office covered, the names of all candidates running for office appear in a column on the left. When a candidate makes a statement, the name of the issue appears at the top of a new column and a check mark appears under that topic next to the candidate's name. Potential voters can see the candidate's full statement by clicking on the check mark.

DNet encourages interaction between candidates. Each time a candidate posts an issue statement, the DNet system automatically e-mails each of the opponents, alerting them that candidate X has posted a statement on topic Y. The e-mail includes the text of the statement and urges all opponents to respond. Candidates can address the same issue and post statements on any new topic they like.

Because the information provided is collected largely by volunteers working with candidates and government agencies, there is an interesting aspect to the civic involvement of providing the information in the first place. Through DNet these volunteers actively engage their communities, research election and voting information (too often not easily available to the public), and build the program infrastructure. These activists work to stimulate other members of their communities to increase their interaction with candidates, elected officials, and government agencies.

Content is the key ingredient of a good Web site. Who collects it, how is it collected, and where it comes from are factors that make a site legitimate

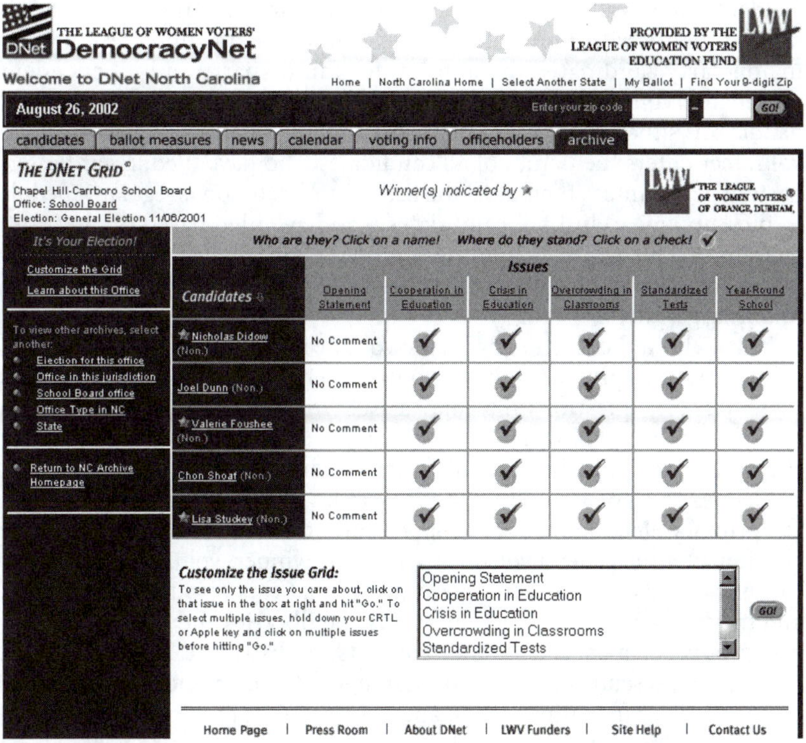

Figure 14.1

in the eyes of the public or not. The role of the League volunteers in gathering content for DNet may appear deceptively simple. It is actually a tremendous undertaking. Volunteers start with varying levels of knowledge or contact with the intricacies of the electoral process but by the end of an election cycle, they have become intimately familiar with the process and have actively interacted with every step.

The role of the volunteer begins with selecting the specific races she wishes to cover on DNet (e.g., the gubernatorial election in Texas). First the volunteer must locate the correct source for candidate filing deadlines, registration deadlines for the primary and general elections, the dates of the primary (or caucus) and general elections, and any runoff contingencies. The election must be created within DNet, and information needed for this step includes information about the nature of the relevant primaries or caucuses—for example, is there an open primary, or is candidate selection limited to party members? Volunteers locate and enter a description of the office covered. Once the candidate filing deadline has passed, the volunteer locates the official list of candidates and loads their names, party affiliations, and contact information into DNet.

Identifying candidate filing deadlines and entering candidate names is not a straightforward procedure. Many states have one filing deadline for major-party candidates and another for minor-party and independent candidates. Volunteers have several options and must decide how they will handle this situation. In many cases, once the first deadline has passed, the volunteer enters the names of all candidates who have filed, regardless of party. The volunteer then pulls the list of candidates on a regular schedule to pick up any additional candidates who have filed based on any later deadlines. This involves sending out candidate invitation letters, passwords and IDs, and training instructions over a period of time rather then in one large batch.

Throughout the election cycle, the volunteers follow up with candidates or their staffs to provide training, to urge them to participate actively, and to answer any questions that may arise. Other volunteer activity often includes entering information for candidates who are unable to do so for themselves, monitoring to make sure candidates are abiding by DNet guidelines and policies, removing the names of candidates who have lost the primary election or have dropped out of the race, and archiving the election after the general vote by marking the winner. Volunteers also work to get the word out to their communities that this resource is available, and they work with other organizations and libraries and attend community events, such as state fairs or concerts, to distribute DNet materials. Many Leagues send volunteers to local high schools to lead discussions on voting, register first-time voters, and present DNet as a resource for election information. Volunteers also work with local media to write op-ed pieces, facilitate articles on DNet and voting, and give interviews for print, radio, and TV.

The League has fought throughout its existence to improve our system of government and to encourage an informed, engaged citizenry. The enduring vitality and resonance of the League as a trusted force for change and good government comes from its unique decentralized structure: a national organization with nearly one thousand local and state Leagues, as well as Leagues in the District of Columbia, Puerto Rico, and the Virgin Islands. With Leagues in states and localities across the country, the League of Women Voters has more than 130,000 active members and supporters.

Throughout its history, the League has played a critical role in making sure voters are informed and in pressing candidates for public office to address the questions citizens want answered. League volunteers have long-standing relationships in their communities and an unparalleled track record of securing reliable information for voter use in local, state, and federal elections. As mentioned, this information has traditionally been provided in the form of written Voter Guides. DNet takes that work to a new level, putting the guides online and adding the benefit of interactivity made possible by new technology.

1. DNet History

DNet was originally created in the mid-1990s by the Center for Governmental Studies (CGS), a nonprofit organization located in Los Angeles that focuses on political communication and community involvement. In 1998, the League of Women Voters Education Fund (LWVEF) encouraged by a number of state leagues including those of California, Washington, and Pennsylvania, began exploring opportunities to establish a nationwide online voter education presence. The League selected DNet, primarily due to its interactive features and ability to be utilized across the country regardless of the technological capabilities of state and local election agencies. CGS and the LWVEF signed an agreement to partner on DNet with CGS providing technical support and the League providing content.

In 1999, the embryonic online political community began to see a new presence emerging. For-profit organizations (dot-coms) began establishing commercial Web sites focusing on civic engagement while making a profit. The League and CGS were approached by a number of such organizations, and ultimately CGS sold the DNet site to a new company named Grassroots.com (now Grassroots Enterprises). DNet's existing features were refined, new features were introduced, and the underlying support platform was overhauled, allowing for vastly more election coverage and viewer traffic. Grassroots.com signed a partnership agreement with the League, with the League maintaining its role as content provider.

As planned, the DNet site was launched nationwide in January 2000. The League implemented a concentrated training program for DNet volunteers in all fifty states plus the District of Columbia. Election 2000 saw an unprecedented number of political and election-related Web sites, partisan and nonpartisan, commercial and nonprofit. Market fragmentation and exaggerated expectations for advertising revenue were among the reasons many of these sites closed after just one year. In 2000, Grassroots.com's business focus shifted, and DNet was transferred to the LWVEF. Since February 2001, DNet has been fully owned and operated by the League.

Since its national launch, information on over 51,700 candidates in 16,180 elections has been posted on DNet, including information about their positions on important state and local issues. In 2000, all of the presidential candidates participated in DNet and actively updated their information as their campaigns progressed. Over 1,400 ballot measure questions have also been covered on DNet.

Election coverage can be broken down by year in several ways. Election 2000 had information on 17,051 candidates and 509 ballot measures. Election 2001 had information on 9,293 candidates and 288 ballot measures. Election 2002 had information on over 25,000 candidates and 600 ballot measures.

2. DNet Features

A viewer accesses DNet's election content in one of two ways, either by clicking on a map of the United States or by entering a zip code on the DNet home page. Voters are then shown a list of races currently being run in a specific area. Selecting an election takes voters to the candidates and issue grid for a particular race.

As previously mentioned, the grid lists the names of all ballot-qualified candidates vertically down the left side, and the issues on which candidates have made statements listed horizontally across the top. Each candidate's position statement on an issue can be read by selecting it from the grid. Selecting the issue heading from the grid brings up nonpartisan background information on that issue.

The League, widely recognized for its history of conducting live candidate debates, often refers to DNet as an online debate. Studies have shown that viewers want not only to see how individual candidates stand on the issues but also to be able to compare the candidates' positions easily, preferably on one page. DNet has a feature that makes this possible. Once a viewer has selected one candidate statement—for example, on school vouchers—the viewer can click on "Create a Virtual Debate" from a list of options. The viewer is then shown the first paragraph of all candidate statements posted on this issue. The statements are lined up, one below another, on the same screen. Viewers are easily able to compare the candidates head-to-head on the issues.

Selecting the name of a candidate brings up that candidate's biography, photograph, campaign address, and phone number, a hypertext link to the candidate's own campaign Web site, further links to campaign finance reports on that candidate, a calendar of campaign appearances, and a list of endorsers. Each candidate is able to list up to three different e-mail addresses.

Voters can interact with the candidates in a number of ways. Candidates may present their e-mail addresses under "General Information," allowing potential voters to contact them directly to ask questions not addressed in the grid or to request additional information. DNet allows candidates to list additional e-mail addresses under "Volunteer" and "Contribute." DNet fosters civic engagement by making it easy for individuals seeking to become more involved in the process, by contributing to a candidate or by actively working on a campaign, to do so.

There is another way the public can actively participate in DNet that involves the viewer, the League volunteer, and the candidate all working together. If the viewer wants to know one or all candidates' positions on an issue that is not being addressed in the grid, she can select "Submit a Question." This feature sends the question to the League volunteer who is monitoring that election. The volunteer can sort the questions coming from the public and send them to the candidates, urging them to respond in the grid so that the responses are available to everyone. This middle step of volunteer engagement gives more weight to the submission. The volunteer can gently pressure the candidates to respond publicly by pointing out that these questions are coming from their potential constituents and that these potential voters will wonder why the candidates do not want to respond.

In addition to candidate information, citizens find additional content provided on tabs that appear above the issue grid. These tabs direct the public to information on ballot initiatives in their area, location-specific news items, information about and links to elected officials, and thorough voting information. The voting tab provides citizens with important dates and deadlines, registration and absentee ballot procedures, information about the voting technology their jurisdiction uses, and directions for locating their polling place.

Ballot measures (or referenda) are covered on DNet. Volunteers identify state, county, or local ballot measure that will appear in the next election. These questions are often very confusing to voters, who may have difficulty determining how to indicate whether they support or oppose the issue, even if they can determine what the question really means. Volunteers are able to post information on these questions, including the full text of the referendum, analysis, pro and con arguments, and simplified-language versions. This information must be completely nonpartisan, and volunteers have to locate this content actively, sometimes drawing on the League itself if the League has done an analysis of the question, or from other sources such as the relevant secretary of state.

3. Case Studies

To facilitate a deeper examination of the role of League volunteers, four state Leagues (Arizona, Illinois, Pennsylvania, and Texas) filled out questionnaires and answered follow-up questions to establish brief case studies of our volunteers in action. These four Leagues were asked to give brief descriptions of their DNet activity and to state how long they had participated in the program, how many volunteers they had across the state, how many races and candidates they approached for 2002, and so on. They were asked to give a personal assessment of the DNet program itself.

The four states surveyed have all had DNet experience for at least two full election cycles. Three of them, Illinois, Pennsylvania, and Texas, have been involved with DNet since 1998. Arizona has participated since 2000. The four states tackled an ambitious number of races and candidates for the 2002 cycle. Arizona covered approximately 185 races involving approximately 925 candidates. Illinois covered approximately 200 races and some 600 candidates. Pennsylvania covered about 493 candidates in federal, statewide, and state legislative races. Texas covered 353 races involving approximately 925 candidates.

The four states utilize a varying level of volunteer support. Only one, Texas, currently employs a paid staff member who dedicates part of her time to working on DNet. Currently, the executive director of the League of Women Voters of Illinois coordinates Illinois DNet activities, but DNet is a very small part of her responsibilities. Arizona's level of volunteer support began with twelve to fifteen people working on DNet in 2000, then decreased to four people in 2001, when they focused on local elections. In 2002, they split the state coordinator role among four volunteer state coordinators who work with individuals in local Leagues, approximately ten volunteers in total. Illinois began with fifteen volunteers in 2000 and had twenty to thirty people working on DNet in both 2001 and 2002. Pennsylvania had a very small number of volunteers in 2000, peaked with seventeen to twenty people in 2001 (when they had a paid, full-time coordinator who focused much of her efforts on training volunteers), and had five volunteers participating in 2002. Texas shows the most consistent growth in the number of volunteers working on DNet. In 2000 there was one, in 2001 there were thirteen, and in 2002 there were twenty-eight. Several of the states point to high volunteer turnover from one year to the next as one of the challenges of the program. It appears that having a paid staff member helps a state League recruit and train more local volunteers who become engaged in the political process and in their communities.

The methods used to contact candidates were essentially the same in each of the four states; letters, e-mail, and phone calls. Typically, each state begins by sending the candidates an official letter introducing them to the program and inviting them to participate. Texas sends their letters out in packets that include information on their printed Voter Guides. They have found through experience that coordinating these two tools is an efficient way to engage in voter education. In early fall 2002, Texas also sent postcards to the candidates, reminding them to participate. Illinois includes a DNet brochure, a flyer, and a reply fax form with their letters. Arizona began the program in 2000 by sending out letters by mail but found that candidates often did not read this printed material, and in 2002 the volunteer state coordinators asked the local Leagues to e-mail the candidates rather than send a printed letter (a printed letter was used when the candidate had no e-mail).

In 2002, Texas and Pennsylvania produced a printed Voter Guide in which they asked candidates to answer specific questions and allowed them a very limited space—usually one paragraph or fifty words—to respond. Both Texas and Pennsylvania posted the candidate responses to the Voter Guide questions in the DNet grid but encouraged candidates to continue to participate actively by adding additional issue statements and, because DNet provides more space, adding additional text to explain their Voter Guide responses more fully.

Outreach efforts differed from case to case. Three of the states actively worked with local and school libraries to promote DNet as an election resource. Leagues also promoted DNet at live election events, debates, forums, and town halls. Several combined DNet outreach with their voter registration drives and distributed materials at concerts, fairs, supermarkets, rallies, and other community events.

The four states are unanimous in their belief that the public, once aware of the program, is very enthusiastic and positive about the amount and type of content that is available. Viewers have told them DNet is the best election resource available. But volunteers point out that public awareness of DNet remains limited. Much more effort needs to be put into getting the word out and letting the public know the site exists and where to find it. One state points out that the level of enthusiasm is very high when there is good content posted in the elections the viewer is interested in. But potential voters are quickly frustrated when they look up elections and find the candidates have not loaded any issue statements. Since the level of candidate participation increases dramatically in the weeks just prior to the general election, there is concern that people coming to DNet earlier in the election cycle could be disappointed and not return later, when more data are available. Arizona has been hesitant to "overpromise" what can be found on the site and, as a result, limits its outreach efforts. They report that 2002 was the first year they prominently promoted DNet in their other League activities and materials. One case study stresses the "chicken-and-egg effect." The public and the media become interested in DNet when candidates have begun to post information. Yet candidates often hold off until there is a demonstrated interest in the site from the voters and the media. The volunteers repeatedly confront this dilemma, simultaneously pursuing outreach and content.

The state coordinators were asked if they had learned anything new about voter education since implementing DNet. One state coordinator reported an increased understanding of the challenges faced by third-party candidates who are generally excluded from live debates. The DNet program is free and allows minor-party candidates an opportunity to "make a lot of noise" and potentially pressure the major-party candidates to respond in the DNet grid. But her volunteers have noted that even on a free platform, money still plays an enormous role in politics. Minor-party candidates may have the same access but usually have less staff and other resources that help a campaign participate actively in DNet. DNet has increased the contact this coordinator's League has with the minor parties and has provided a venue for more volunteer interaction.

Arizona reported that all who have worked on DNet have learned a great deal about the political process. The state coordinators specifically mention a young intern working with the League in 2000 who said that participating in the project completely changed her understanding of politics. Following different campaigns and working with candidates, particularly the candidates who didn't respond immediately or who failed to post information, gave her an understanding of what is important to candidates, where they will focus their time and resources, and how candidates view their potential constituents.

One state told us that although more candidates perceived the benefits to their 2002 campaigns and agreed to participate, they remained very resistant to the interactive features of the program. By interactive, they meant responding to viewer questions and responding to an opponent's statement and engaging their opponents in an ongoing debate in the DNet grid. The volunteers heard repeatedly that campaign staffs are stretched to the limit and lack time to keep up with activity within their grid. Candidates find DNet a valuable opportunity to connect with potential voters but are more interested in using the program as a way to attract viewers to their own Web sites. Younger candidates tend to take advantage of the interactive features. In their third year with the program, League volunteers still posted more information for the candidates than the candidates themselves did. Although this trend seems to be reversing, DNet depends heavily on its network of actively engaged volunteers to provide election information to the public.

Another League reported similar experiences. Each year more candidates post statements, but they still avoid interacting with each other or the public. Interestingly, a few local races covered in 2001 resulted in a lively online debate that showed the volunteers and the public the real potential of this tool, but this is still a rare occurrence.

Generally our case studies told us that DNet has had limited impact on the communities it aims to serve. Real penetration into public awareness occurs where dedicated League volunteers actively track down election information and pursue candidate involvement. When there is little content on the site, Leagues have hesitated to reach out to other organizations that would help increase the program's impact. Cooperation with other community groups, libraries in particular, has yielded the best results. An increasing number of libraries use DNet as their source of election information. Librarians display DNet flyers and posters and, more important, direct people to the site when asked for election resources. Librarians have been very receptive, often telling the volunteers that before DNet they didn't have a good source of information to which they could refer people. One state League saw the biggest impact in rural areas where recently trained volunteers participated for the first time. There is a dramatic difference in DNet's role as a part of the local election culture between places where volunteers are aggressively involved and in communities where they are not.

Finally, our four states were asked to draw upon their firsthand experience with the program and provide a personal assessment. In response, one state coordinator told us she believes that DNet is key to keeping League members engaged in the community and the League an active player in the evolving political process. The most challenging part of her job is one that can be overcome, convincing local Leagues that DNet is an easy way to serve voters and raise visibility for the League. One coordinator feels that DNet's real strength isn't the interactive features but its more basic informational functions, such as listing the names and contact information for candidates running for office.

Overall, even given the technical challenges, volunteer turnover, and some frustration, all case study subjects remain enthusiastic about the program. They see DNet as a program ahead of its time. One coordinator points to its potential as a resource for voters ages eighteen to twenty-four. Another feels personally that it is not yet as effective a voter education tool as live debates and Voter Guides, but firmly believes in the promise of what DNet could become—*the* clearinghouse for online election information, with rich content and useful links. Several believe that an online educational program such as DNet is the future of the League. The program's potential is unlimited.

4. Conclusion

The goal of this essay has been to examine the League of Women Voters' DemocracyNet to see if it qualified as a genuine online civic engagement program. Through a brief look at the activities of the three groups who must participate in the program in order for it to be a success, we have been able to answer some of the questions raised and draw some conclusions.

The role of the League volunteers who work on DNet has been examined. DNet engages potentially hundreds of volunteers in political activity across the country. Through their work researching election and voter registration information, filing deadlines and official candidate lists, ballot measure information and analysis, they are building the most comprehensive voter resources on the Internet. These data are often not easily accessible otherwise. Through phone calls and e-mail questions from the public, the League knows that voters have a difficult time finding it, and many give up in frustration. DNet volunteers often encounter the same frustration. Gathering this information and entering it into DNet is not only a tremendous public service but a challenging exercise. Beyond locating basic election information, volunteers must be active throughout the entire election cycle and beyond. As shown, candidates are contacted not once but repeatedly. Volunteers often establish relationships with candidates and their campaign staffs. They train candidates on how to use DNet and upload statements and bios when candidates cannot. Volunteers research official campaign materials to locate information that could be loaded into DNet. They identify "hot races" that generate public and media attention and often focus their attention where it can have the most impact. They monitor candidate activity on the site and step in when the rules of participation are broken. They try to facilitate debate among candidates and elicit answers to questions from viewers. All this activity results in a large group of citizens providing information to the public while also educating themselves.

The key to online civic engagement programs is the content that is offered online. If the goal is to have people become active offline, the public needs to see credible information that spurs them to action. DNet provides that content. Currently, most candidates do not post this information themselves, and until they do, the role of DNet volunteers is essential. A democracy is based on a public engaged in all parts of government. DNet is a project that allows people to go beyond simply voting on Election Day. It is a program that fosters the engagement of an ever-increasing number of people in the process of elections and voting.

PART 4

Social, Psychological, and Political Contexts for Electronic Democracy

CHAPTER 15

Virtual Distance and America's Changing Sense of Community

PAUL G. HARWOOD AND WAYNE V. MCINTOSH

Past technological advances have altered the fabric and character of American society. From the formation of the U.S. postal system in the eighteenth century and the proliferation of telegraph access across America in the mid-nineteenth century, information technologies have been increasing relational distance and shrinking the worlds of successive generations. Although the instruments of change are technological, the consequences are behavioral. Today, in this age of hyperindividualism, we are undergoing a period of further technological and social transformation with the development of computer-mediated communication (CMC). The Internet, through its myriad of different configurations of communication is shrinking our world (Morris and Ogan 1996: 46). CMC, however, is not merely a rerun of the past. It is a new phenomenon.

Unlike past technologies, CMC has not only made each of us part of yet a smaller "global village" (McLuhan 1964) but also created a new place—cyberspace. Cyberspace is not simply an array of communication devices, but a new, technologically determined location that can be populated by new communities and host extensions of current ones in electronic outposts (Rheingold 1993; Barlow 1995; Agre and Schuler 1997; Hill and Hughes 1997; Cherny 1999; Fernback 1999). With the Internet's annihilation of time and space, American society is again in flux. CMC has considerably diminished the role of physical location in social relations. Geographic proximity is no longer a necessity for the maintenance of close-knit relationships, and people are no longer bounded individuals but "networked individuals" (Wellman 2001).

In this chapter, using the Social Capital Benchmark Survey (2000), we examine what type, or sense, of community people are experiencing within this new boundless place of cyberspace. We investigate whether individuals' computer-mediated community experiences mirror or stand juxtaposed to their offline sense of belonging, gained through interactions in their physical neighborhoods and at their places of work. In the face of declining civic volunteerism and social participation offline (Putnam 1995b, 2000), arguably the products of our transitory postindustrial relationships, the boundless Internet provides opportunities for Americans to regain a sense of civic renewal. Thus, we investigate numerous sociobehavioral factors that may help us understand why an individual reports sensing community online. For example, the effect of an individual's geographic isolation from people of his or her own race is analyzed and found to be an important determinant to an individual's sense of community in the ether.

1. Senses of Community

The word *community*, like all language, is a social construct, which over time and through contextual changes has evolved to have multiple meanings. The notion of community is central to understanding social relationship structures and relational distance. The conceptual origins of *community* are derived from the Latin *communis* (common oneness), and early sociological usage was "based on the pedestrian notion of community as a geographical or spatial unit" (Hillery 1955; Howard 1997: 61). Even in the 1950s, an era of suburbanization, a survey of the uses of the word *community* in U.S. society reported some ninety-four definitions of the term, the most salient of which were "locality, social interaction and common tie" (Ishida 1999: 1), with "common territory over and above all others" emphasized in the conclusions as the most important prerequisite (Howard 1997: 64). Today, while most Americans may no longer physically live a small-town life, such a spatial definition and understanding of community still hold salience (Perry and Mackun 2001).

The contemporary resonance and importance of small-town values in America is quickly discerned by flicking through a *TV Guide* or by channel-surfing during prime time—catching glimpses of Smallville, to name but one stark example. The networks know what sells, and small-town life sells. Although, television programming is not the real thing, it reflects cultural preferences and an electronic window through which the audience might experience, by proxy, small-town life at eight o'clock Eastern, seven Central. While television visually illustrates small-town social relationships, the Internet, through its "netcast" architecture, may allow individuals to gain a sense of belonging rather than merely passively watching it (Bonchek 1997). The Internet may allow the individual actually to be "there" (Kosinski 1971).

However, can such a Mayberry USA experience be reproduced online and aligned with the "so-called virtual communities" (Davis 1999: 166)? After all, newsgroups and other online weak-tie social groups "undergo a process of continuous membership evolution" (Davis 1999: 166). Such groups do not embody the stability of social relationships depicted by the small-town image but instead, arguably, reflect suburbia, "communities of limited liability" (Fischer 1992: 80). Whether online *Gemeinschaft*—a feeling of being part of a communal life system—will be realized, therefore, is highly debatable.

The small town embodies more than mere social relationships—it involves politics, too. The small town is a social organism with the "capacity for unified volition and action" (Tönnies 1955: 25), a social form that tends not only to unify and bind but also to move its members toward conformity of action. It is a milieu that fosters an individual sense of belonging and mutual bond of commitment and responsibility. It is clearly not a single, embryonic social form. Thus, it can be asked whether online communities are the "social aggregations that emerge from the Net when enough people carry on public discussion long enough, with sufficient human feeling, to form webs of personal relationship in cyberspace" (Rheingold 1993), social organizations with the "capacity for unified volition and action" (Tönnies 1955: 25)? Or are "Netizens" (Hauben and Hauben 1997), although "networked individuals" (Wellman 2001) with an ability to form distributed global relationships, merely participating in transitory *Gesellschaft*-like social relationships online that lack "affective ties" (Galston 1999: 5)? Before conclusions can be drawn, it is important to recognize that there are other less stark, less polarized conceptual definitions of community to give meaning to our suburbanized, post-industrial lives.

Increasingly, Americans are understanding community in new nonspatial terms, most notably within Wuthnowian small groups, "the private, largely invisible ways in which individuals choose to spend a portion of their free time" (Wuthnow 1994: 2). Such groups "are not simply an informal gathering of neighbors and friends, but organized groups: Sunday school classes, Bible study groups, youth groups and singles groups, book discussion clubs, [and] sports and hobby groups" (Wuthnow 1994: 4). These clusters provide invaluable emotional support to individual participants. Although people join groups for a variety of reasons and needs, "community is what people say they are seeking when they join small groups" (Wuthnow 1994: 3). Wuthnowian small groups, while not geographically determined, as was characteristic of past voluntary associations, are a response, "an alternative" (Luke 1993), to America's highly mobile and transient society (Rosenblum 1999: 261; Wuthnow 1994: 4–5). They are what Beniger (1987) terms "pseudo-community"—fostered by "bridges" that connect the "weak ties" of each individual's self-interest with the collective passion or impulse expressed by the group (Granovetter 1973; Harwood and Lay 2001).

2. Studying a Sense of Community

The community concept has clearly evolved over time, and given the proliferation of CMC, we are likely to see further change in Americans' sense of community. Thus, community in the ether is destined to be socially constructed rather than technologically determined. It is salient, therefore, to ask how and for what goal will we shape cyberspace; and how will cyberspace come to shape us?

Sherry Turkle (1995: 233), having employed ethnographic techniques to study a specific population group, concluded that people have turned to "neighborhoods in cyberspace" to fill their offline community void. It is questionable, however, whether one could generalize Turkle's experience at Dred's Bar, the "watering hole on the MUD LambdaMOO" (Turkle 1995: 233), to explain America's sense of community out "there" in all of cyberspace (Barlow 1995). Probably not, or at least no better than if one spent every night at a bar in College Park, Maryland, in the hope of explaining America's offline sense of community. Moreover, such online "going native" research isolates the cyberexperience (Turkle 1995). The unit of analysis, for example, a multiuser dungeon (MUD), is placed within a cybervacuum, rather than, as in this research, situating individuals' online experience within the context of their offline lives. The Internet's technology has minimized physical distance and space as facilitators of social interaction. Thus, researchers must take care not to erect borders of convenience in cyberspace to facilitate their analysis of America's online experience.

Here, no such borders were erected to determine whether the Internet's netcast architecture affords mechanisms for seeking a *Gemeinschaft*-like sense of community online. Instead, our examination of individual-level evidence, in the form of a national survey, is theoretically guided by analogy. A contemplation of the new world of cyberspace can begin only if the new is seen as "both an extension and a transcription of the world we know" (Gunkel and Gunkel 1997: 124). Hence, to comprehend the new social interactions online, we must first understand conceptions of community and the individual-level factors that predict people's interactions offline.

One such factor we wish to study is an individual's confidence in others—succinctly, trust. "[A]n individual whom we know will inspire in us a certain confidence, however slight; a stranger, on the other hand, is likely to create in us a certain feeling, often quite strong, of mistrust" (Tönnies 1955: 6). In the physical world, this kind of confidence in others (as opposed to mistrust) is important in determining whether individuals experience a sense of community. We hypothesize that people who have developed a foundation of social trust in others are likely to experience a sense of community online. Building a general trust in others is an experiential phenomenon, and it should carry over into the more anonymous interactions online.

As discussed earlier, small-town life is more than social relationships; it is also politics. Thus, we hypothesize that political trust is significant to the concept of community. When present, individuals willingly conform to the collective will of the people around them. Therefore, political trust is an important component of geographically based social organization, with the ability to bind and constrain its members; however, due to the embryonic state of online groups and the ease of exiting them (one click and you're gone), such groups cannot instill such conformity. Political trust, therefore, should have no effect on whether an online sense of community is obtained.[1]

Other factors we consider are residential mobility, attitudes toward others within the community, and offline social networks. A relatively stationary residence is important because it anchors an individual to a particular locale. We measure this concept in two ways: first, by the length of time lived in a particular location; and second, by the individual's expectation of her place of residence five years hence. We hypothesize that residential mobility feeds into the development of meaningful attachments. An expectation of remaining in the same location for at least the next five years will enhance one's neighborhood sense of community. Likewise, we believe that residential mobility, irrespective of analogy, will not be a significant predictor of whether an online sense of community is developed.

With regard to community attitudes, as with trust, if an individual has a sense of belonging or feels she can exert even minimal influence on her local community, this will be predictive of her online attitudes. Those who have a negative image of their local community and/or the people within it will be more likely to seek surrogate communities online.

Turning to social networks, we believe that one's social connectedness—talking to neighbors, for example—will be positively associated with neighborhood sense of community. With regard to our school or workplace interaction, whether one talks with neighbors is expected to be irrelevant. However, we do expect the number of close friends an individual has to be predictive of feeling a part of things both on- and offline. Intuitively, people who are social in one environment are expected to be social in others.

3. Methods and Data

To test our hypotheses, we use the Social Capital Benchmark Survey (2000), which comprises a national sample of 3,003 respondents and representative samples in forty communities nationwide covering an additional 26,200 respondents. Here we use the national sample.

Because we do not seek to investigate within a cybervacuum, focusing exclusively on online activities, nor do we wish to forget the separation between home and work brought about by past technological annihilations of distance, we explore the sense of community individuals experience in their neighborhoods and their places of work as well as online.[2] In addition, we consider the anomaly in online behavior of America's youth (those ages eighteen to twenty-four). Today's young, the first digital generation, are the group to watch; the long-term effect of online community life for America's civil society is in the hands of their generation and those who follow them.

3.1. Bivariate Results

In exploring the contexts in which people report a sense of belonging, we find a distinction between neighborhood and work or school. Of those deficient in a neighborhood sense of community, 25 percent say that they acquire it instead from the people they encounter online. This compares with only 8.1 percent of individuals who experience no community feelings among the people with whom they work or attend school. Removing the youngest cohort (eighteen to twenty-four years old) from the analysis decreases those percentages to 11.5 percent and 7.6 percent, respectively. The 13.5 percent drop in neighborhood sense of community with the exclusion of the eighteen-to-twenty-four age cluster illustrates the uniqueness of their online social behavior and suggests differences among age groups in how people compensate for varying degrees of social isolation in the real world.

The role of today's youth as crafters of America's changing sense of community is indicated further as 41.5 percent of eighteen- to twenty-four-year-olds report a sense of community from their digital interactions, compared with only 8.3 percent of those ages forty-five to fifty-four. This is a very large difference. As a group, the young are among the least networked offline, with 31.4 percent reporting not being a member of any formal group, compared to 19.3 percent of the forty-five- to fifty-four-year-olds. They also spend a disproportionate amount of time in the ether; 28.4 percent of all respondents in the sample who are logged on for twenty hours or more per week are eighteen to twenty-four years of age. In addition, the young (eighteen to twenty-four), and not surprisingly their parents (forty-five to fifty-four), report the highest levels of home Internet access, reaching better than 61 percent. No doubt some of the young are Turkle's MUD dwellers, who create fanciful avatars and role-play with others for hours on end. Increasingly, the young are also heavy instant-messaging (IM) users, maintaining preexisting friendships long distance when away at college, and creating loose online networks of cyberfriends for real-time messaging sessions. The importance of the young and the type of community they find or create online must not be overlooked when probing America's changing sense of community.

Turning to our analysis of trust, we find that 24.6 percent of those who lack confidence in others find a sense of community online (declining to 15.8 percent when the young are excluded). No such age disparity is apparent, however, among those who think people can be trusted (13 percent and 12.1 percent, respectively). Thus, while "trusting people [may be] no more or less likely to go online than misanthropes" (Uslaner 2000: 21), a general mistrust of others offline is not an obstacle, especially among the youngest adults, for securing a feeling of community in cyberspace. In addition, the lack of trust required for community in the ether may be suggestive of the "limited-liability" nature of our youths' online lives, given the ease of entry and exit. Online interactions are often weak and lack stability (Cherny 1999; Harwood and Lay 2001). Thus trust in others, a necessity for building offline relationships, is not so essential online because people understand that they can enter and leave quickly and anonymously.

Our two residential mobility variables (how long a person has lived in the local community and whether she expects to be in the community five years hence) impart nothing conclusive concerning whether an individual realizes a sense of community online. However, despite the irrelevance of actual physical connectedness to it (i.e., residential mobility), a clear disparity exists between individuals who perceive they can have an impact in making their community a better place to live, and those who feel otherwise. Among those who feel ineffectual, 30 percent find community online, compared to just 16.3 percent of their neighbors who report an ability to exert moderate influence over their proximate, offline world. It is equally noteworthy that, when eighteen- to twenty-four-year-olds are omitted, only 15.8 percent of those who report having no impact on making their neighborhood a better place to live experience a cybersense of community. Therefore, the lack of perceived impact by today's youth on making their local physical environment a better place to live is an important determinant in their search for community online. The responsibility for their perception, however, must lie at least in part with their elders.

Our other community attitudinal variable also indicates some interesting differences. One-fourth of all respondents who believe their local leaders do not really care about them look to the digital world for a sense of community, compared to only 14.2 percent of those who say local leaders do care. Thus, the role that people can expect to play in their community life and the messages received from their leaders help to determine whether an individual seeks an alternative, virtual "home."

Perhaps even more important, we find that those who live the most isolated lives, who belong to no groups at all (32.4 percent) and who never (or only perhaps once a year) exchange verbal pleasantries with a neighbor

(37.9 percent), report that they gain a sense of community online. These figures drop to 23.4 percent and 27.5 percent, respectively, when the young are excluded from the analysis—still quite high. Thus for society's least connected (regardless of age), the digital world offers a surrogate sense of belonging that they do not find in their everyday lives. Such individuals find others online with similar outlooks and with whom they can interact from any distance. This group undoubtedly includes a mixture of the alienated, Uslaner's (2000) "misanthropes," and Kraut and colleagues' introverts (2002), as well as the socially inept, who can use the Net's text-based communication mode as an electronic lifeline to find collectivity among others.

Juxtaposed against these "anonymizers," we encounter Wellman and colleagues' "glocalizers" (Wellman 2001; Wellman et al. 2002). People who are the most well integrated into their physical community, those involved in more than eight groups (22.7 percent) and who talk to their neighbors every day (22.6 percent), report finding a sense of community online as well. In addition, an individual who senses community offline, whether in her neighborhood or at school or work, is more likely to find community online. Thus, the tools of the information revolution provide a convenient means for the already involved to complement their engagement when they are physically alone and at any hour of the day.

Turning to examine demographic differences, we find that fully one-third of all individuals earning $30,000 or less (23.4 percent when the young are excluded), compared with 14.4 percent (12.2 percent) in the $50,000–$75,000 income bracket, find a sense of community online. Thus, lower economic status, even when the young (who naturally skew the lower income level results) are excluded, is associated with finding community online. This result is consistent with Sherry Turkle's (1995) ethnographic findings that for some, notably the young and early adopters, cyberspace acts as a safety net by offering an electronic avenue by which they can mimic a middle-class life.[3] Indeed, some individuals can utilize the Net's architecture to hide otherwise stigmatizing influences, such as often accompany low income.

We also find that men (21.6 percent) are a bit more likely to obtain a sense of community online than women (15.5 percent) and, not surprisingly, single people (24.9 percent) more so than married folks (13.7 percent). More interesting is the apparent disparity between whites and nonwhites. More than one-quarter of nonwhites experience a sense of community online, even when the young are excluded, compared to only 15.4 percent (and 10.7 percent for ages twenty-five to ninety-two) among whites. This difference suggests that individuals are using the new electronic media not only to surmount personal introversion or social ineptness but also to overcome societal prejudices. Indeed, the online world can be color-blind, whereas the offline world clearly is not. Here we must acknowledge earlier studies that have shown that nonwhites, notably

African Americans, are among the late adopters of CMC technologies (U.S. Department of Commerce 1999, 2000; Novak and Hoffman 1998). For some, when the novelty value wears thin and individuals turn to e-mail, the Web, and to an increasing extent IM (like early adopters), the percentage reporting an online sense of community may be reduced.

However, when we consider the location of one's residence, race seems to be a clear factor. For example, one-fifth of white respondents living in a metro status area (MSA) center city find a sense of community online, compared to more than one-quarter of their nonwhite neighbors—not a huge difference. People living in rural, nonincorporated areas, though, report a starkly different use of the Internet. Indeed, only 14.6 percent of whites find community online, compared with 40.7 percent of nonwhites. This is significant because of the spatial distribution of races across urban and rural America (Perry and Mackun 2001). Thus, geographic isolation from others of one's race, combined with political isolation (being nonwhite in much of rural America), is important in determining the likelihood that people will gravitate to the electronic "village."

Although the location of an individual's residence is important when race is considered, the provision of home Internet access is not a prerequisite for the experience of an online sense of community, illustrating the Internet's involvement in all our offline environments. Thus, a sense of community online, meaningful or otherwise, is not entirely contingent on having home Internet access. In short, not having Internet access at home does not make you an online community have-not, but it probably does limit your opportunities.

Time is a valuable and limited resource, so it is important to ask, though difficult to discern from survey data, what social and civic activities (if any) are being displaced by high Internet use. For the anonymizers, particularly "misanthropes" (Uslaner 2000), arguably not much civic input is lost, although multitasking (watching television, playing online games, and instant-messaging digital friends) is a likely phenomenon. However, for other anonymizers, those utilizing the perceived anonymity of the Internet to overcome introversion or social ineptness, the medium provides an attractive alternative. By contrast, because of their online engagement and high levels of offline social participation, glocalizers are likely changing their mode of connection from the telephone to the computer, rather than supplementing actual face-to-face interaction with computer-mediated interaction. Such cyberinteractions, therefore, are merely the online migration of the instrumental, transitory relationships of their offline *Gesellschaft* lives. Thus while cyberspace is being populated by new communities, it is also hosting the extension of preexisting relational structures.

3.2. Multivariate Results

Placing the observations into a multivariate framework, we find a number of interesting relationships. Table 15.1 reports the results of two models, one in the context of respondents' feeling that their neighborhood represents a real community and the other including perceptions about the workplace or school environment. Each of these two models was run twice, once with the young included in the framework and once without. We ran each model twice to illustrate the anomaly of today's young.

Past research has suggested that high-trust individuals are no less and no more likely than others to go online (Uslaner 2000). However, according to our analysis, among those who express faith in others offline, their social trust negatively influences the development of an online sense of community (political trust is simply irrelevant). In fact, the greater an individual's social mistrust, the greater the likelihood that she will seek an electronic community. This is consistent across three of four models, the only exception being when the young are not included in the work and school analysis. Some people who have failed to make connections in their primary social spaces—work, school, neighborhood—are apparently using the Internet to locate a place where they gain a sense of belonging.

Although political trust has no predictive value with regard to the tendency to find online communities, perceptions about local leaders matter a great deal. Indeed, there is a consistently strong negative relationship: feeling alienated from community leadership significantly enhances the likelihood that one will search for an alternative communal experience online.[4]

Turning to residential mobility, longevity in one's local community fosters deeper connections to the neighborhood. This being the case, it is entirely reasonable to find that long-term residents of all ages are not likely to seek community online, whereas recent movers are more likely. At the same time, residential longevity has little impact within the context of the school or work environment. People who have recently moved no doubt use the Internet to maintain connections to the place they just left and/or to their established networks.

In light of recent social capital research (Putnam 1995a, 2000), we considered three indicators of offline social networks—number of formal group involvements, sociability with neighbors, and number of close friends—as predictors of an online sense of community. None is significant when the youngest cohort is excluded from the model; however, in the two models including the young, number of close friends has a strong positive association. Thus, it would appear that the young, unlike their elders, do have close online friends, who arguably provide emotional support and encouragement. Unfortunately, how meaningful such friendships actually are (i.e., the level of support and trust of online friends) cannot be ascertained from these data.

The importance of the time spent online can be gauged, however, and, as expected, digital time is statistically significant as a predictor of online sense of community. The level of association is greatest when the young are included in the model, but it is also fairly strong for the rest of the population as well. Finally, we consider a number of demographic indicators. Income, gender, and marital status have negligible effects. Race, however, shows statistically significant association with our online community observation in all models.[5] As an additional check on the race issue, we looked at the co-relationships between race and three of our model predictors: social trust, number of years lived in the community, and the local-leaders-don't-care responses.[6] Indeed, nonwhites demonstrate a strong proclivity to seek out a comfortable electronic social niche, perhaps to compensate for what is lacking in the world where they live and work. Thus as our bivariate analysis suggests, race is an important predictor in determining individuals' experiences online, possibly a direct consequence of experiences offline.

4. Implications of Findings

The Internet revolution for the already connected has not wrought vast changes. It has only enhanced already hyperinvolved lives. The real revolution involves America's socially isolated, for whom the Internet is a digital lifeline. Some may be the alienated—"misanthropes," as Uslaner (2000) calls them—who are able to find others online with similar outlooks and with whom they can interact from a safe distance. Others may simply find themselves disconnected for a range of reasons, such as job hunting, or because their political and/or demographic profile does not match that of their neighbors. The allegiances and bonds associated with the state (at whatever level of aggregation—local, state, regional, national) are geographically determined. To the extent that online communities exist independent of physical space, a general civic culture may not be enriched. For example, immigrants and regional transplants, if they are electronically connected, can easily remain in contact with home groups and delay (perhaps indefinitely) integration into civic life of their new locations. From their perspective, this might be an attractive strategy for dealing with a physical world in which they are a distinct minority. Indeed, if independent cybercommunities begin to thrive, traditional collective social capital may be diminished. Indeed, our analysis (Table 15.1) suggests that nonwhites utilize the Internet's community potential in more systematic and substantial ways than do members of the white majority. If the digital world provides solace to those who live a racially isolated existence (real or perceived), it is certainly significant. Our analysis suggests that when people feel marginalized by their community, they find community at the margins, and these questions warrant more extensive and thorough scrutiny.

TABLE 15.1 Predictors of Online Sense of Community

VARIABLES	The people in your neighborhood give you a sense of community		The people you work/go to school with, give you a sense of community	
	All ages G	Excluding 18–24-year-olds G	All ages G	W/o 18-24 yr olds G
SENSE OF COMMUNITY				
Neighborhood	.3454	1.0771 *	-	-
Place of work/school	-	-	1.2283***	1.3444 *
TRUST				
Social trust	-.5050****	-.4055 *	-.3744 **	-.1833
Political trust	.0744	.3230	-.0149	.1435
RESIDENTIAL MOBILITY				
Years lived in local community	-.0849	-.1421	-.2079 *	-.3227 *
Expect to leave community in five years	.0876	.6203	.0062	.4213
COMMUNITY ATTITUDES				
Perceived impact in making community a better	.1387	.0697	-.0351	-.0884
The leaders running my community do not care	-	-1.3995 *****	-1.1582	-1.6444
SOCIAL NETWORKS				
Number of formal group involvements	-.1255	-.2070	-.0459	-.0985
Frequency of talking to neighbors	.1012	-.0462	.1139	-.0442
Number of close friends	.2884*	-.0122	.2896 *	.0107
ONLINE				
Time spent online in typical week	.0616 ***	.0597 *	.0582 ***	.0498

DEMOGRAPHICS

Age (all, 18–92 years)	-.1214	-	-.2354 *	-
Age (>24 years)	-	.4162 **	-	.1926
Gender	-.3519	-.3128	-.2995	-.4346
Income	-.2077*	-.1391	-.1340	-.0853
Married	-.0710	-.2330	.0461	-.1560
Metro area status	.0434	.0326	.0609	.0797
Race	-1.0295	-1.6414 *****	-.9240 **	-1.3865 ****
Constant	-1.0474	-1.3128	-1.0553	-.2475
N	558	468	559	468
R^2 Cox & Snell (Nagelkerke)	.147 (.244)	.157 (.298)	.168 (.280)	.139 (.270)

Logistic regression. *Source:* Social Capital Benchmark Survey (national sample). Dependent variable = online sense of community, * p<.05 ; ** p<.01 ; *** p<.005 ; **** p<.0005 ; ***** p<.00005 (one-tailed test).

In closing, we would urge that the groups of people who say they find a sense of community on the Internet deserve much more extensive attention—particularly those who do not seem to find a zone of comfort and belonging in their everyday lives. The Internet revolution has probably only enhanced the lives of many among the hyperinvolved. Moreover, the young are a group to watch, to assess the socialization effects of living their formative years in an electronic-saturated world. Much depends on whether the cyberactivity of today's young is a product of their youth or of their generation. Community, starting with its Latin origins, has been and remains a social product, and it will be the experience of today's young that will shape our expectations for community in the years ahead. Will they find *Gemeinschaft*?

Notes

1. Political trust is constructed by using a combination of reported trust in local and national government and in the local police. These factors also load highly on only one factor, capturing 58.73 percent of the variance. Higher scores also indicate higher levels of political trust.
2. The questions were worked as follows:
   Neighborhood Sense of Community
   Q: People in your neighborhood give you a sense of community?
   School/Workplace Sense of Community
   Q: The people you work with or go to school with give you a sense of community?
   Online Sense of Community
   Q: People you have met online give you a sense of community?
3. See Turkle's (1995) account of Thomas, a twenty-four-year-old bellhop who is unable to live the middle-class life offline and who turns to cyberspace, notably MUDs, to get "back into the middle class" he knew as a child.
4. This variable is coded 0 for "leaders don't care" and 1 for "leaders do care."
5. The race variable is collapsed into two categories, nonwhite (0) and white (1).
6. We calculated a correlation coefficient for each of the pairs, and all are significant at the .01 level. Thus, race (0 = nonwhite, 1 = white) is correlated with the other variables as follows: our social trust index (r = .316), years lived in the local community (r = .110), and leaders do not really care (r = .094). We also assessed the relationships with cross-tabulations, and the cell entries indicate a clear relationship (chi-square is significant in all cases). Social trust is constructed by using components analysis. The variable is constructed by using indicators of trust in neighbors, religious group members, shop clerks, and coworkers. These questions load highly on one factor using the usual criteria (eigenvalues > 1). The factor scores explain 59.25 percent of the variance, suggesting a latent variable in which higher scores indicate higher levels of social trust.

References

Agre, Phil, and Douglas Schuler, eds. 1997. *Reinventing Technology, Rediscovering Community: Critical Explorations of Computing as a Social Practice.* London: Ablex.

Barlow, John. 1995. "There is a There There in Cyberspace." Available at http://www.eff.org/Publications/John_Perry_Barlow/HTML/utne_community.html (accessed July 15, 2002).

Beniger, James. 1987. "Personalisation of Mass Media and the Growth of Pseudo-Community." *Communication Research* 14: 352–71.

Bonchek, M. 1997. "From Broadcast to Netcast." Available at http://www.ai.mit.edu/msb/thesis (accessed December 2, 1998).

Cherny, Lynn. 1999. *Conversation and Community: Chat in a Virtual World.* Stanford: Center for the Study of Language and Information Publications.

Davis, Richard. 1999. *The Web of Politics.* Oxford: Oxford University Press.

Fernback, Jan. 1999. "There Is a There There: Notes Toward a Definition of Cybercommunity." In Steve Jones, ed., *Doing Internet Research*, 203–20. Thousand Oaks, CA: Sage Publications.

Fischer, Claude. 1992. "Ambivalent Communities: How Americans Understand Their Localities." In Alan Wolfe, ed., *America at Century's End*. Berkeley: University of California Press, 79–93.

Galston, William. 1999. "Does the Internet Strengthen Community?" Available at http://www.puaf.umd.edu/IPPP/fall1999/internet_community.html (accessed February 23, 2000).

Granovetter, Mark A. 1973. "The Strength of Weak Ties." *American Journal of Sociology* 78, 6: 1360–80.

Gunkel, David, and Ann Hetzel Gunkel. 1997. "Virtual Geographics: The New World of Cyberspace." *Critical Studies in Mass Communication* 14: 123–47.

Harwood, Paul G., and J. Celeste Lay. 2001. "Surfing Alone: The Internet as a Facilitator of Social and Political Capital?" Paper presented at the annual meeting of the American Political Science Association, San Francisco.

Hauben, Michael, and Ronda Hauben. 1997. *Netizens*. Los Alamitos, CA: IEEE Computer Society Press.

Hill, Keith, and J. Hughes. 1997. "Computer-Mediated Political Communication: The USENET and Political Communities." *Political Communication*. 14: 3–27.

Hillery, George A. 1955. "Definitions of Community: Areas of Agreement." *Rural Sociology* 20: 111–23.

Howard, Tharon W. 1997. *A Rhetoric of Electronic Communities*. London: Ablex.

Ishida, Toru. 1999. *Community Computing*. Chichester: John Wiley and Sons.

Kosinski, Jerzy. 1971. *Being There*. New York: Harcourt Brace.

Kraut, Robert, Sara Kiesler, Bonka Boneva, Jonathon Cummings, Vicki Helgeson, and Anne Crawford 2002. "Internet Paradox Revisited." *Journal of Social Issues* 58: 49–74.

Luke, Timothy W. 1993. "Community and Ecology." In S. Walker, ed., *Changing Community: The Graywolf Annual Ten*. St. Paul, MN: Graywolf Press.

McLuhan, Marshall. 1996. *Understanding Media*. New York: New American Library. Originally published 1964.

Morris, Merill, and Christine Ogan. 1996. "The Internet as Mass Medium." *Journal of Communication* 46, 1: 39–50.

Novak, Thomas, and Donna Hoffman. 1998."Bridging the Digital Divide: The Impact of Race on Computer Access and Internet Use." Available at http://elab.vanderbilt.edu/research/papers/html/manuscripts/race/science.html (accessed January 29, 2003).

Perry, Marc and Paul Mackun. 2001. "Population Change and Distribution." Washington, D.C.: U.S. Census Bureau. Available at http://www.census.gov/prod/2001pubs/c2kbr01-2.pdf (Accessed May 11, 2004).

Putnam, Robert. 1995a. "Bowling Alone: America's Declining Social Capital." *Journal of Democracy* 6, 1: 64–78.

Putnam, Robert. 1995b. "Tuning In, Tuning Out: The Strange Disappearance of Social Capital in America." *PS: Political Science and Politics* 28: 664–83.

Putnam, Robert. 2000. *Bowling Alone: The Collapse and Revival of American Community*. New York: Simon and Schuster.

Rheingold, Howard. 1993. *The Virtual Community: Homesteading on the Electronic Frontier*. Reading, MA: Addison-Wesley.

Rosenblum, Nancy. 1999. "The Moral Uses of Pluralism." In Robert Fullinwider, ed., *Civil Society, Democracy and Civic Renewal*, 255–71. Lanham, MD: Rowman and Littlefield.

Social Capital Benchmark Survey. 2000. Available at http://www.ropercenter.uconn.edu/scc_bench.html (accessed April 14, 2001).

Tönnies, Ferdinand. 1955. Community and Association. London: Routledge and Kegan Paul. Originally published 1931.

Tönnies, Ferdinand. 1957. Community and Society. East Lansing: Michigan State University Press. Originally published 1887.

Turkle, Sherry. 1995. "Virtuality and Its Discontents: Searching for Community in Cyberspace." *Life on the Screen*. New York: Simon and Schuster.

U.S. Department of Commerce. 1999. Falling Through the Net: Toward Digital Inclusion. Washington, DC: U.S. Department of Commerce.

U.S. Department of Commerce. 2000. Falling Through the Net: New Data on the Digital Divide. Washington, DC: U.S. Department of Commerce.

Uslaner, Eric. 2000. "Trust, Civic Engagement, and the Internet." Paper presented at the Joint Sessions of the European Consortium for Political Research. Workshop on Electronic Democracy: Mobilisation, Organisation, and Participation via New ICTS, University of Grenoble, April 6–11.

Wellman, Barry. 2001. "Little Boxes, Glocalization, and Networked Individualism." Paper presented at the Digital Cities Conference, Kyoto. Available at http://www.digitalcity.jst.go.jp/cosmos/symposium/3_barry2.pdf.

Wellman, Barry, Anabel Quan-Hasse, James Witte, and Keith Hampton. 2002. "Capitalizing on the Internet: Network Capital, Participatory Capital, and Sense of Community." In Barry Wellman and Caroline Haythornthwaite, eds., *The Internet in Everyday Life*. Oxford: Blackwell. Available at http://www.chass.utoronto.ca/~wellman/publications/index.html.

Wuthnow, Robert. 1994. *Sharing the Journey: Support Groups and America's New Quest for Community*. New York: Free Press.

CHAPTER 16

Access, Skill, and Motivation in Online Political Discussion: Testing Cyberrealism

PETER MUHLBERGER

Researchers, policy experts, and social activists employ the term *digital divide* to speak about an important concern—that new information and communication technologies (IT), particularly the Internet, might exacerbate existing social inequalities. Ultimately, the digital divide *is* the inequalities created by new information technologies. Because directly measuring such inequalities would be very challenging, research has generally focused on factors that inhibit the use of the Internet and thereby disadvantage various social groups. Digital divide research generally focuses on three broad factors: access, skill, and motivation. While access constitutes the chief focus of much research, skill and motivation are increasingly seen as a "second-level" digital divide that can disadvantage some groups even if they have access.

The notion of a "democratic digital divide" is about the more narrow concern that IT may aggravate political inequality—the unequal distribution of political power among population groups. Though political power is notoriously difficult to measure (Dahl 1961; Gaventa 1980), research can begin with an examination of the role of inequalities in access, skill, and motivation on the use of IT for political purposes. These factors can also shed light on subtle yet important features of the digital divide, such as motivational differences between online and offline political discussants.

Political inequality matters because, as Verba, Schlozman, and Brady (1995) show, there are high levels of demographic inequality in voting, donating money, and other types of political action in the United States. In addition, underlying political inequality are the low levels of political knowledge, sophistication, and participation of most Americans (Converse 1964; Gilens 2000; Kinder 1983, 2003; Luskin 1987; Neuman 1986; Putnam 2000). Low levels of knowledge and sophistication can result in poor public policy choices (Gilens 2000). Lack of participation can result in reduced community control over political institutions and public policy (Rothenberg 1992).

Norris (2001) has identified a variety of theoretical positions regarding the democratic digital divide. The cyberoptimist view holds that IT will appreciably reduce political inequality, ignorance, and apathy (Aikens 1996; Kirschner 1994; Rheingold 2000; Schwartz 1996). The cyberpessimist view suggests IT will further increase the influence and knowledge of the advantaged, exclude the disadvantaged, and introduce new possibilities of social control and manipulation by the powerful (McChesney, Wood, and Foster 1998; Schiller 1989). A cyberskeptic view suggests that political life with the Internet will be business as usual (Margolis and Resnick 2000; Webster 1995). In this view, the structural forces that make modern politics what it is do not change when people come online.

Finally, a cyberrealist view agrees that not much has visibly changed politically but that the new capacities created by the Internet represent a potential that can be tapped under the right circumstance and that do empower more peripheral groups (Bimber 1998, 2000; Norris 2001). By reducing the marginal cost of political information, communication, and organizing, at least the potential exists for IT to substantially mobilize political action. Structural factors resulting in a lack of political motivation prevent mobilization at the moment, but if an event of sufficient concern occurs, the Internet greatly increases the possibility of mobilization, as it already has in some countries (Watts 2003). Also, less visible forms of mobilization may occur, particularly of social movements comprising highly motivated people with nonmainstream political concerns. Finally, there may be subtle yet important effects of IT on political activity. For instance, political discussion online is often more public than in face-to-face settings, which may affect the motives and behavior of those involved.

This essay examines how the Internet affects one type of political activity—political discussion. Political discussion plays an important role in conveying political information, stimulating political participation, and helping people decide how to vote (Huckfeldt and Sprague 1991; Klofstad 2001; Lupia and McCubbins 1998). Thus, political discussion promotes both political action and political knowledge. This essay focuses on survey data from a random sample of a midsized American city, Pittsburgh, Pennsylvania, to clarify the relative roles of demographics, access, skill, and motivation in online and offline political discussion.

Findings support a cyberrealist perspective. A rather small percentage of all political discussion takes place on the Internet, which reduces the plausibility of the cyberoptimist perspective. Motivation matters almost as much as access, which also weakens optimism that eventual universal access will eliminate bars to online participation. Contrary to cyber-pessimists, demographics matter much less for online than offline discussion. A closer examination, however, reveals that much of the demographic difference is due to suppressed levels of participation by the educated and homeowners. Efforts to promote online discussion might introduce demographic disparities in online participation. These overall results are consistent with cyberskepticism—that on the whole IT makes little difference. They are also consistent with cyberrealism. The scales are tipped in favor of realism by evidence that there are important motivational differences between online and offline political discussants. Political interest proves crucial for offline but not for online discussion, which creates an opening for IT to mobilize people who are not normally active. Also, the patterns of motivation suggest online discussion may be more public and discomforting—attributes that raise the possibility of building a more vibrant public sphere online.

1. The Digital Divide: Access, Skill, and Motivation

Digital divide research usually focuses on three broad factors: access, skill, and motivation. Much research has focused on access to the Internet as an indicator of the digital divide (Katz, Rice, and Aspden 2001; McConnaughey et al. 2002; Rainie and Packel 2001; Victory and Cooper 2002). Some observers, however, believe access matters less over time because people are increasingly able to afford access (Eastin and LaRose 2000). A limited amount of research has been conducted on differences between people with skills necessary for using the Internet (Hargittai 2002), even though the notion of skills figures prominently in discussions of the influence of demographics on the digital divide (Norris 2001). Some research has examined the effect of motivation to use the Internet (Katz, Rice, and Aspden 2001; Lenhart et al. 2000). Again, motivation figures prominently in conceptualizations of the digital divide (Norris 2001). A limited amount of psychological work has examined Internet self-efficacy (Eastin and LaRose 2000; Torkzadeh and Van Dyke 2001), a construct related to motivation and skill. Access might be termed a "first-level" digital divide issue, while skill and motivation might be called "second-level" divide issues (Hargittai 2002)—that is, factors that matter after people acquire access.

2. Political Inequality and the Internet

The Internet may affect a particularly crucial type of inequality, political inequality. Verba, Schlozman, and Brady (1995) have shown that American politics involves high levels of demographic inequality in voting, donating money, and other types of political action. For example, people of modest means (family incomes of under $35,000) made up 55 percent of their nationally representative sample but only 46 percent of the vote in the 1988 presidential election—a difference that can matter. People of modest means also make up only 43 percent of campaign hours, 40 percent of contacts with the government, 42 percent of protests, and 16 percent of campaign dollars. Verba, Schlozman, and Brady also show that the policy concerns of lower-income Americans are systematically and substantially underrepresented in the political system.

The Internet may well matter for political inequality. Brady, Verba, and Schlozman (1995) lay much of the blame for inequalities in political participation on a lack of resources by members of various social groups. Resources include money, time, and civic skills such as speaking, writing, and organizing skills. The Internet may affect all of these resources. If people pay more attention to online political information from nonmainstream sources, the importance of money in politics would be reduced. Online civic participation could appreciably reduce time requirements for political activities. As for civic skills, the Internet might enhance the literacy and cognitive ability of its users, or it might serve as a bar to people with low skills.

In addition, the Internet could lower the barriers to entering the self-reinforcing "virtuous circle" between political interest, political knowledge, and participation (Neuman 1986; Norris 2001). In the virtuous circle, high levels of one of these factors tend to stimulate higher levels of the others, resulting in self-sustaining engagement. The Internet could lower barriers to entering the virtuous circle by providing low-cost political information and participation opportunities.

3. Hypotheses

I will test a number of hypotheses from the cyberrealist perspective. Cyberrealism holds that online political activity will be different only subtly from offline political activity in "normal political times"—which is certainly true of the year 2001, when this study was conducted. Cyberrealism concedes that the cyberskeptic view will hold for the most part. Nevertheless, there may be important yet subtle differences between online and offline participation that support cyberrealism. Because the costs of online engagement are lower, online participants might not be as interested in politics as offline participants. Also, given the public nature of much online discussion, they may need to be more inclined to discuss politics publicly. The following hypotheses should be supported:

> H1: There should not be an appreciable amount of online political discussion.

H2: The effect of demographics on amount of political discussion should matter as much online as offline.

H3: The second-level digital divides in motivation and Internet skill should matter as should the first-level divide in access. The second-level divides form a structural barrier to greater online participation, but one that can be affected by historical events.

4. Data and Methods

4.1. Participants

A sample of 1,200 Pittsburgh residents of voting age were selected from Cole Information Services' Marketshare directory of the Pittsburgh area. Because of its information sources, the directory likely overrepresents adults who have permanent residency and therefore underrepresents the economically disadvantaged, including ethnic minorities. Nevertheless, the Marketshare directory is superior to alternative directories. A sample was drawn that was stratified by gender, age, estimated household income, and geographical location. Mail survey data were obtained from 524 respondents, with a response rate of 65 percent. Nonrespondents and those who explicitly declined participation are counted toward the denominator of the response rate. Those not counted are the deceased, ineligible, and bad addresses.

Survey respondents were 54 percent male and 46 percent female, had a median age of forty-seven, and were 88 percent Caucasian, 8 percent African American, and 4 percent other. Median and mean education was "some college, no degree." Seventy-three percent of respondents owned their own home. Respondents represent a diverse cross section of people.

Pittsburgh is an ethnically varied and class-diverse community with a city population of 334,583; with the surrounding areas, the population is over 1 million, according to the 2000 census. Neighborhoods range from suburblike residential areas to areas of urban poverty. Although Pittsburgh is known to have a moderately high quality of life for a city its size, people intimately involved with public life in the city do not believe this leads to either an especially high level of political involvement or cordial public dialogue.

4.2. Materials and Procedures

Respondents were first sent a one-page prenotification letter indicating they had been selected for a Pittsburgh-wide mail survey being conducted by Community Connections, a nonprofit and nonpartisan community engagement project housed at Carnegie Mellon University. They were told the confidential questionnaire would arrive shortly with a small monetary gift and a coupon for a free Blockbuster video rental. They were also told that if they returned the questionnaire, they would be entered into three lotteries in which they could win up to $300. Three more waves of letters and a phone call awaited those who did not respond early.

4.3. Measures

4.3.1. Dependent Variables. The questions for overall discussion frequency and amount were: "Think back on the times you have discussed political issues. On average, about how many times a month do you discuss political issues? [__ times a month] On average, about how many minutes do these discussions last? (Your best estimate is fine.) [__ minutes]," The discussion frequency question was used as a dependent variable, and the product of frequency and amount was used to test an alternative hypothesis. These questions were preceded by a definition of *political* that included examples and the sentence "Political issues are issues that divide the public and which might need a government solution—at least according to some people." The dependent-variable questions were also preceded by a series of questions meant to help respondents remember where and when they discuss politics.

The other dependent variable, frequency of online political discussion, was measured by the question "How often do you go online to express an opinion about a political or social issue to a bulletin board, online newsgroup, or e-mail list [hardly ever, every couple of months, every couple of weeks, 1–2 days per week, 3–5 days per week, every day]?" This question was based on questions 63 and 66 of the Pew Research Center's Technology 1998 Survey. The online discussion question was converted to a more continuous scale. For comparability in ordered probit analysis, the continuous overall discussion frequency variable was converted to resemble the more categorical online discussion frequency variable by applying the same breakpoints and mean values as for the online question.

4.3.2. Independent Variables. The independent variables were as follows:

- *Political interest.* A weighted average of questions regarding how much the respondent follows politics and was interested in the presidential campaign. These are questions 310 and 313 from the 1952–92 cumulative code book of the American National Election Survey's (ANES) (1965–92 version with response categories presented as labels on a seven-point scale). Weights were assigned by principal components.
- *Talk motivation.* The question was "We are also hoping to develop a project in which we would bring small groups of Pittsburghers together for six hours on a weekend or evening to discuss matters of community concern. This would be a one-time commitment. If you

would like to learn more about this project, we could have someone phone you—assuming the project happens [yes, no]" (Muhlberger 2000, 2001; Muhlberger and Shane 2001).

- *Talk engagement.* A weighted average of the reversed responses to the questions "I'd rather not justify my political beliefs to someone who disagrees with me," "I would rather not reveal my political beliefs to someone who would disagree with me." All responses were on an eleven-point Likert scale. Responses were reversed by multiplying by -1. These questions were constructed and pretested for the purpose of this survey (Muhlberger 2000, 2001; Muhlberger and Shane 2001).
- *Talk with disagreement.* "I want to talk with people who disagree with me about political issues [Likert]."
- *Talk for job.* "Is discussing politics an important part of your employment [yes, no]?"
- *Internet skill.* "I am very skilled at using the World Wide Web (Internet) [Likert]," "I don't know much about using the World Wide Web (Internet)." Adapted from the computer skill scale in a HomeNet April 1998 survey.
- *Home Web access.* "Does your household have access to the Internet (World Wide Web) that lets you read whole Web pages? (Do not count mobile phones or other devices with limited access to Web pages.) [yes, no, don't know]." The answer "don't know" was coded as no. The question was adapted from the Commerce Department's 2000 digital divide survey.
- Web use. "On average, about how much time do you spend in the following activities on a typical day? (Just give your best estimate. Fill in the blank): using the Internet (World Wide Web) [__ hours, __ minutes]." Also included in analyses were similar questions for computer and e-mail use: "Using a computer at work, home, or school (include all activities)" and "Using electronic mail." These questions were derived from the HomeNet survey.
- *Demographics.* Standard demographic questions from the ANES and other sources.
- Additional independent variables. The following were also controlled for in analyses, although they are not depicted in tables because of space constraints, as they did not prove significant: internal and external political efficacy (standard ANES questions); perceived Internet information quality ("What do you think of the quality of online information?" [eleven-point scale, labels "very poor," "OK," "very good"]); Web information trust ("Information on the World Wide Web (Internet) can be trusted" [eleven-point scale, labels "not true," "moderately true," "very true"]); and Web privacy concerns ("I worry about my privacy on the World Wide Web (Internet) [same scale]").

- *Variables to test alternative explanations.* Party identification, ideology, and political values (humanitarianism, egalitarianism, individualism, traditionalism, and racism) were standard measures taken primarily from the ANES. Anti-instrumentalism was measured with such questions as "Sometimes people need to act politically even if the actions cannot succeed [Likert]." And free time was measured with such questions as "I have a lot of free time."

5. Results

5.1. The Prevalence of Online Political Discussion

The real significance of digital political speech should include its potential as much as the quantity of current levels of such speech. Nevertheless, an important datum in assessing current levels of digital political speech is its amount relative to political speech more generally. The data indicate that respondents on average discuss politics online eight times per year, compared with discussing politics both on and offline at a rate of eighty-four times per year. Thus, online discussion constitutes 9.8 percent of all discussion instances, with a confidence interval of 7.2 percent to 13.1 percent (bootstrapped bias-corrected 95 percent confidence interval, $N = 3,000$ for bootstraps, $N = 522$ for data). These levels of discussion may somewhat understate long-term rates of discussion because the study was conducted in 2001, a year largely without important elections.

5.2. Demographic Correlates of Online and Offline Discussion

Ordered probit analyses were conducted with two dependent variables (variables to be explained), online discussion and offline discussion. The explanatory variables were five demographic variables: education, gender, age, ethnicity, and home ownership. The analyses show that the proportion of variance of the dependent variable successfully predicted (R^2) is not particularly large for either online or all discussion. Nevertheless, the .07 R^2 of all discussion represents a quarter of all variance that appears explainable (the R^2 is .26 with all explanatory variables included). Interestingly, the proportion of variance explained by demographics ($R^2 = .02$) for online discussion is less than a third of that explained for all political discussion ($R^2 = .07$). This offers some cause for optimism that the Internet levels demographic differences. The digital divide in online discussion does not turn out to be a demographic divide. Though gender and education significantly and appreciably affect all political discussion, only age significantly affects online discussion. A further analysis of the data indicates that the negative relationship between age and online discussion is largely due to Internet access.

5.3. Total Possible Effects of Motivation, Access, and Demographics

Readers interested in the first- and second-level digital divide will want to know the overall impact of such groups of variables as political motivation, access and use, and demographics. They may also be interested in how much improvement is possible in discussion frequency. Table 16.1 shows what happens when groups of variables are "maximized"—that is, each variable is given its maximum observed value if its coefficient is positive or its minimum value if its coefficient is negative. Only variables within each group that prove significant in ordered probit analyses are maximized.

Table 16.1 shows an overall predicted mean for yearly online discussion frequency of 8.3, with no variables changed. When the significant access variables (home Web access and Web use) are maximized, the yearly frequency increases to 17.3, an increase of 109 percent from 8.3. Table 16.1 supports the notion of a second-level digital divide. Though access proves more important than political motivation for online discussion, motivation is not far behind. Thus, a second-level consideration—motivation—proves nearly as substantial as access. This result erases any doubt regarding the importance of the second-level digital divide for online discussion.

An important feature of Table 16.1 is the large possible improvement in online participation attributable to education and home ownership. Maximizing these variables involves setting all respondents to non-home-owners and to the lowest observed education, tenth grade (there is one observation at sixth grade, but setting the grade level to six would be extrapolating too much from the sample). Maximizing these variables increases discussion frequency 156 percent to 21.2, a substantial fraction of offline political discussion. Higher education and home ownership thus substantially suppress levels of online discussion, more than lack of access or low political motivation. Note that the effects reported here are total *direct* effects. The total direct and indirect effect of education and home-ownership is close to zero (analyses not shown). Table 16.1 shows that the educated and homeowners are participating much less than would be expected from their Internet access and use. The suppressive direct effects of demographics deserve discussion. Another noteworthy result of Table 16.1 is that it shows that very substantial improvements in online discussion would be possible by increasing more than one set of variables. Finally, offline discussion frequency reacts much as expected, with political motivation being the predominant factor.

6. Discussion

This essay tested five key cyberrealist hypotheses about online political discussion with generally supportive results. These hypotheses stipulate that online discussions do not have appreciable political effects currently but that online discussions will show motivational differences that could prove

TABLE 16.1 Possible Improvements in Yearly Political Discussion Frequency from Maximizing Significant Variables

	Variables improved (significant variables only)	Mean predicted yearly discussion frequency (% change from overall mean)
	Online Discussion	
Overall mean	None	8.3 (0%)
Maximized political motivation	Talk motivation, talk with disagreement	15.6 (88%)
Maximized access	Home Web access, Web use	17.3 (109%)
Maximized demographics	Education, owns home	21.2 (156%)
Maximized motivation and access	Talk motivation, talk with disagreement, home Web access, Web use	34.9 (321%)
Maximized motivation and demographics	Talk motivation, talk with disagreement, education, owns home	39.3 (374%)
Maximized access and demographics	Home Web access, web use, education, owns home	43.5 (425%)
Maximized all significant variables	All unique variables above	79.8 (863%)
	All Discussion	
Overall mean	None	69.2 (0%)
Maximized political motivation	Political interest, talk motivation, talk with disagreement	128.2 (85%)
Maximized demographics	Education	90.0 (30%)
Maximized all significant variables	All political motivations and education	160 (131%)

Note: Possible improvements calculated using ordered probit results. The overall mean is the overall yearly political discussion mean predicted given the explanatory variable values present in the data. Variables were "maximized" by setting them to their maximum value if their coefficient was positive or minimum if the coefficient was negative.

important under the right historical circumstances. These hypotheses are discussed below. Only hypothesis 2, that demographics should matter as much online as offline, is disconfirmed. Important caveats, however, apply to this result.

Contrary to the cyberoptimist viewpoint, but consistent with cyberrealism, findings indicate that online political discussion does not constitute an appreciable amount of all discussion. Online discussion makes up only

9.8 percent of all discussion, with a small confidence interval. Some will argue that even small amounts of discussion could play an important signaling role (Huckfeldt and Sprague 1991; Lupia and McCubbins 1998). Unless online discussion is far more politically potent than offline discussion (or there is a very low ceiling on effects), however, the more than 90 percent of discussion that takes place offline is bound to have a much greater political impact than online discussion.

Contrary to cyberrealism, but supportive of cyberoptimism, findings show that demographics matter more than a third less for online discussion than offline discussion. These results, however, must be interpreted in light of the low percentage of all discussion that takes place online, which greatly limits the potential benefits of online discussion in reducing demographic inequalities. This overall situation is consistent with the cyberrealist position that the Internet has untapped political potential. The demographic results must also be interpreted in light of the finding that education and homeownership matter considerably once Internet access and use are controlled (Table 16.1), even though neither matter when only demographic explanatory variables are regressed. These two findings indicate that the educated and homeowners discuss politics about as much as anyone else online, but much less than would be expected from their level of Internet access. A number of possible explanations suggest themselves. It may be that the educated and homeowners are too busy; that they believe online discussion will not affect political outcomes; that their ideology, political leanings, or political values differ from people online; that they have more discussions offline and so do not use online forums; and that they do not find Internet political discussion sufficiently high in quality or sufficiently pertinent to their concerns.

The low levels of participation by the educated and homeowners may best support a cyberpessimist view, with a caveat. The data show that getting these groups to participate more on the Internet would be by far the most effective means of improving the amount of online discussion. Their participation might be enhanced by forums that are more ideologically appealing, better connected to political outcomes, or focus on more communitycentric issues of interest to homeowners and on political issues of greater interest to more educated and politically mainstream people. Nevertheless, such attempts to boost online discussion would upset the current demographic balance of Internet discussion, confirming a cyberpessimist view. A caveat, however, is that in the longer term, the underlying reason for the greater potential participation of the educated and homeowners—namely, their greater access to and use of the Internet—may be mitigated by more universal access and use.

Consistent with cyberrealism (or cyberpessimism), political motivation matters. Motivational factors have almost as much effect as Internet access on the potential for improving discussion frequency. In addition, as just discussed, motivational considerations may be behind the sizable effect of demographics, which appear once Internet access is controlled. If so, the second-level divide of motivation would dwarf the effects of mere access. Findings on the role of education and homeownership, however, suggest the novel conclusion that some motivational considerations may actually narrow the gap between advantaged and disadvantaged population groups.

The findings of this essay gravitate toward cyberrealism. Online political discussion is too small a portion of overall political discussion to have appreciable political effects currently. Online discussion is more demographically balanced, which suggests some current-day positive implications of the Internet, but this finding must be interpreted in light of the low amount of online discussion and evidence that demographic equality results from suppressed levels of participation by the educated and homeowners. Online discussion is inhibited not only by Internet access but also by a second-level divide in political motivation. This second-level divide forms a structural barrier to greater online participation even if Internet access became widely available. It may, however, be a barrier that will vary with context—with current events and the specific format of discussion available. This offers some hope for the future potential of online discussion.

References

Aikens, G. S. 1996. "A History of Minnesota Electronic Democracy 1994." *First Monday* 1, 5. Available at http://www.firstmonday.dk/issues/issue5/aikens/#dep3.

Bimber, B. 1998. "The Internet and Political Mobilization: Research Note on the 1996 Election Season." *Social Science Computer Review* 16, 4: 391–401.

Bimber, B. 2000. "The Study of Information Technology and Civic Engagement." *Political Communication* 17: 329–33.

Brady, H. E., S. Verba, and K. L. Schlozman. 1995. "Beyond SES: A Resource Model of Political Participation." *American Political Science Review* 89, 2: 271–94.

Converse, P. E. 1964. "The Nature of Belief Systems in Mass Publics." In D. E. Apter, ed., *Ideology and Discontent*, 206–61. New York: Free Press.

Dahl, R. 1961. *Who Governs?: Democracy and Power in an American City.* New Haven: Yale University Press.

Eastin, M. S., and R. LaRose. 2000. "Internet Self-Efficacy and the Psychology of the Digital Divide." *Journal of Computer-Mediated Communication* 6, 1: n.p.

Gaventa, J. 1980. *Power and Powerlessness: Quiescence and Rebellion in an Appalachian Valley.* Urbana: University of Illinois Press.

Gilens, M. 2000. *Political Ignorance and American Democracy.* Paper presented at the annual meeting of the Midwest Political Science Association, Chicago.

Hargittai, E. 2002. "Second-Level Digital Divide in Internet Use: Mapping Differences in People's Online Skills." *First Monday* 7, 4.

Huckfeldt, Robert and John Sprague. 1991. "Discussant Effects on Vote Choice: Intimacy, Structure, and Interdependence." *Journal of Politics* 53, 1: 122–58.

Katz, J. E., R. E. Rice, and P. Aspden. 2001. "The Internet, 1995–2000: Access, Civic Involvement, and Social Interaction." *American Behavioral Scientist* 45, 3: 405–19.

Kiesler, S., J. Siegel, and T. W. McGuire. 1984. "Social Psychological Aspects of Computer-Mediated Communication." *American Psychologist* 39, 10: 1123–34.

Kiesler, S., and L. Sproull. 1992. "Group Decision Making and Communication Technology." *Organizational Behavior and Human Decision Processes* 52, 1: 96–123.

Kinder, D. R. 1983. "Diversity and Complexity in American Public Opinion." In A. Finifter, ed., *Political Science: The State of the Discipline,* 391–401. Washington, DC: American Political Science Association.

Kinder, D. R. 2003. "Pale Democracy: Opinion and Action in Post-War America." In E. D. Mansfield and R. Sisson, eds., *The Evolution of Political Knowledge.* Columbus: Ohio State University Press.

Kirschner, B. 1994. "PEN Lessons: An Interview with Ken Phillips." *Public Management* 12: 13.

Klofstad, C. A. 2001. "Social Networks and Political Behavior: The Impact of Political Talk on Civic Participation." Paper presented at the annual meeting of the American Political Science Association, San Francisco.

Lenhart, A., S. Fox, J. Horrigan, and T. Spooner. 2000. *Who's Not Online.* Washington, DC: Pew Internet and American Life Project.

Lupia, A., and M. D. McCubbins. 1998. *The Democratic Dilemma: Can Citizens Learn What They Need to Know?* Cambridge: Cambridge University Press.

Luskin, R. C. 1987. "Measuring Political Sophistication." *American Journal of Political Science* 31: 856–99.

Margolis, M., and D. Resnick. 2000. *Politics as Usual: The Cyberspace "Revolution."* Thousand Oaks, CA: Sage.

McChesney, R. W., E. M. Wood, and J. B. Foster. 1998. *Capitalism and the Information Age: The Political Economy of the Global Communication Revolution.* New York: Monthly Review Press.

McConnaughey, J. W., W. Lader, R. Chin, and D. Everette. 2002. *Falling Through the Net II: New Data on the Digital Divide.* Washington, DC: National Telecommunications and Information Administration.

Muhlberger, P. 2000. "Defining and Measuring Deliberative Participation and Potential: A Theoretical Analysis and Operationalization." Paper presented at the twenty-third annual scientific meeting of the International Society of Political Psychology, Seattle. Available at http://communityconnections.heinz.cmu.edu/papers..

Muhlberger, P. 2001. "Political Speech and Apathy in an American City: A Pilot Study." Paper presented at the annual meeting of the Midwest Political Science Association Annual Meeting, Chicago. Available at http://communityconnections.heinz.cmu.edu/papers.

Muhlberger, P., and P. Shane. 2001. "Prospects for Electronic Democracy: A Survey Analysis." Manuscript.

Neuman, W. R. 1986. *The Paradox of Mass Politics: Knowledge and Opinion in the American Electorate.* Cambridge, MA.: Harvard University Press.

Norris, P. 2001. *Digital Divide: Civic Engagement, Information Poverty, and the Internet Worldwide.* New York: Cambridge University Press.

Putnam, R. D. 2000. *Bowling Alone: The Collapse and Revival of American Community.* New York: Simon and Schuster.

Rainie, L., and D. Packel. 2001. *More Online, Doing More.* Washington, DC: Pew Internet and American Life Project.

Rheingold, H. 2000. *The Virtual Community: Homesteading on the Electronic Frontier.* Rev. ed. Cambridge, MA.: MIT Press.

Rothenberg, L. S. 1992. *Linking Citizens to Government: Interest Group Politics at Common Cause.* Cambridge: Cambridge University Press.

Schiller, H. I. 1989. *Culture, Inc.: The Corporate Takeover of Public Expression.* New York: Oxford University Press.

Schwartz, E. A. 1996. *Netactivism: How Citizens Use the Internet.* Sebastopol, CA: Songline Studios.

Torkzadeh, G., and T. P. Van Dyke. 2001. "Development and Validation of an Internet Self-Efficacy Scale." *Behaviour and Information Technology* 20, 4: 275–80.

Verba, S., K. L. Schlozman, and H. E. Brady. 1995. *Voice and Equality: Civic Voluntarism in American Politics.* Cambridge, MA: Harvard University Press.

Victory, N. J., and K. B. Cooper. 2002. *A Nation Online: How Americans Are Expanding Their Use of the Internet.* Washington, DC: U.S. Department of Commerce.

Watts, J. 2003. "Technology, Democracy a Potent Mix in South Korea." Christian Science Monitor Service, February 1.

Webster, F. 1995. "Information and the Idea of an Information Society." In *Theories of the Information Society.* New York: Routledge.

CHAPTER 17

Virtual Deliberation: Knowledge from Online Interaction Versus Ordinary Discussion

JASON BARABAS*

Most citizens know very little about the political world. In a wide variety of studies, scholars report that in many cases Americans cannot provide correct answers on a range of information questions and that their preferences differ typically from those of individuals who get these questions right (Althaus 1998; Bartels 1996; Delli Carpini and Keeter 1996; Gilens 2001). Worse yet, many times citizens are not only uninformed; they are misinformed, with a tendency to cling to inaccurate perceptions that shape their attitudes (Kuklinski et al. 2000; Hochschild 2001). Such findings have powerful implications for democratic theorists. To suggest that people may not know much or that their preferences would change were they more informed calls into question the very foundations of democracy.

In response to these bleak empirical findings concerning knowledge and the potential for unenlightened preferences, some theorists urge greater public deliberation. This process goes by many different names, such as "strong democracy" (Barber 1984), "unitary democracy" (Mansbridge 1980), "discursive democracy" (Dryzek 1990), or "deliberative democracy" (Gutmann and Thompson 1996), but one theme that unites them is that citizens are expected to learn. Deliberative activities ought to increase

*I thank Jennifer Jerit, Woody Stanley, Lori Weber, Tamara Witschge, and the participants at the Prospects for Electronic Democracy conference at Carnegie Mellon University for their helpful suggestions on an earlier version of this paper.

knowledge, according to Manin (1987), because no single individual can possess all the information deemed relevant to a decision, so deliberation can fill in the gaps (also see Benhabib 1996). Robert Dahl (1979) focuses on producing what he calls "enlightened understanding." Dahl writes, "In order to express his or her preferences accurately, each citizen ought to have adequate and equal opportunities for discovering and validating, in the time permitted by the need for a decision, what his or her preferences are on the matter to be decided" (1979: 104–5). Dahl proposes organizing statistically representative panels of citizens who would make recommendations on specific policy issues (also see Gastil 2000a).

Dahl's proposals may strike some as fanciful, but for James Fishkin something quite like it is already a reality. Fishkin (1991) argues that democracies need opportunities for deliberation. To promote participation, he proposes the "deliberative opinion poll," where representative samples of citizens gather in a single location to deliberate and to observe what an informed electorate would prefer. Enlightened consensus is a core goal for Fishkin (1991, 1995) who claims that a deliberative opinion poll models what the electorate *would* think if, hypothetically, it were immersed in intensive deliberative processes. Other formal deliberative processes have been proposed or implemented, such as citizen juries (Crosby 1995) and National Issues Forums (Gastil and Dillard 1999).

These deliberative venues can and do have a big impact on knowledge and preferences. Fishkin and Luskin (1999) report large information gains for citizens who attended the National Issues Convention in Austin, Texas, during the 1996 presidential race. Specifically, of eleven items in a questionnaire administered before and after the deliberation, six displayed significant increases in factual knowledge, including rather specific questions such as the percentage of children born out of wedlock, the percent of families on welfare, and the largest component of the U.S. budget. In a similar study with quasi-experimental survey data, Barabas (2002a) finds that knowledge increased significantly for several hundred citizens who attended a deliberative forum devoted to Social Security reform in the late 1990s.

Taken together, these and other studies (such as Gastil and Dillard 1999) provide at least tentative support for the idea that deliberation can lessen chronic lapses in public knowledge. The drawbacks with these deliberative forum solutions are that they are rare, expensive, and seriously limited in their scope. For instance, Benjamin I. Page (1996) estimates that citizens would have less than a second to speak their minds were citizens from a large country such as the United States brought together to deliberate about political matters. Page supports the idea of deliberation in a democracy, but he believes the mass media are much more likely to provide it and to provide it in sufficient depth.

Although some scholars pin their hopes on mass-mediated forms of mass deliberation, others suggest that political learning can take place electronically via the Internet. Depending upon the type of democracy one embraces, Internet-based communities can mimic many of the beneficial aspects of deliberative democracy (Dahlberg 2001; Barber, Matteson, and Peterson 1997). One of the earliest to recognize the potential for the Internet was Robert Dahl. In the late 1980s, Dahl (1989) proposed the idea of a "mini-populus," where a thousand citizens would deliberate on a single policy issue for more than a year. They would be connected electronically on an ongoing basis so that they could continue with the other important matters in their daily lives. Throughout Dahl's proposals, we see the importance of discussion and contemplation, even if carried out electronically.

While deliberative conferences similar to what Dahl proposes may increase *access* to information, we know very little about whether it improves actual knowledge. Furthermore, few studies compare in-person deliberation with computer-mediated forms to give us a sense of their comparative strengths (Gastil 2000b). The purpose of this study is to evaluate the effects of policy discussion and online activity on knowledge. Specifically, I attempt to determine whether activities such as policy discussion and Internet activity affect knowledge levels.

There are many reasons to expect that individuals who discuss politics or use the Internet often will have elevated levels of knowledge. The supply of facts may be more than what citizens typically encounter in the media, and citizens might replace incorrect assumptions with factual knowledge. The process of pooling partial understandings of the world could also bridge the gaps for many citizens (Stasser 1992). Providing motivation to learn (Lupia and McCubbins 1998) is yet another likely benefit of these activities, on the assumption that interacting with others provides additional incentives to be informed.

However, there is no guarantee that deliberative or interactive sources offer correct information. Using the Internet or talking with friends and colleagues may simply perpetuate errors unless there are penalties for lying and verification procedures (Lupia and McCubbins 1998). Moreover, having too much information available can lead to overload (Shenk 1998). Thus, while the balance of the literature discussed earlier as well as intuition suggests there may be an enlightening effect for both discussion and online activity, it remains an open question.

1. Data and Methods

One of the biggest analytical obstacles to discerning the effects of discussion and Internet activity is the lack of high-quality data with measures of both activities *and* political knowledge. The data used in this analysis are drawn from a series of questions tapping discussion habits, Internet usage, and political knowledge in two national surveys conducted by Princeton Survey Research Associates in March and July 1998 to measure awareness of Social Security reform issues.[1] The two cross-sectional surveys of approximately 1,200 respondents each have been pooled, so the total number of cases available for analysis is 2,402 across the two time periods.

The interviewers asked several generic policy discussion questions to discern general levels of discussion. Later in the survey, respondents were asked a more specific follow-up question: "Have you ever discussed your views about the way the Social Security program might be changed with a friend, neighbor, family member, or coworker?" The 58 percent who answered this filter question affirmatively were then asked, "Have you had a discussion like this in the past month or so, or not?" Thirty-eight percent claimed to have had a substantive Social Security policy discussion within a month prior to being interviewed. The analyses of this study concentrate on the most specific discussion question in the data set. A treatment dummy variable was constructed and coded as 1 if the respondent had discussed Social Security policy reforms within the last month and 0 otherwise.

The main Internet usage question was, "How often do you use a computer to go online to get information about current events, public issues, or politics? Would you say you do this regularly, sometimes, hardly ever, or never?" Most respondents (61 percent in March and 59 percent in July 1998) stated they never went online for this purpose. The percentage of respondents who claimed they hardly ever went online hovered just above 10 percent for both surveys, while 12 percent claimed they used a computer to get information "sometimes." The highest Internet usage category of "regularly" had 14 percent and 15 percent in the March and July surveys, respectively. While all of these response categories are somewhat subjective, we can plausibly assume that those who went online regularly had at least some significant exposure to the Internet. Thus, the main treatment variable for Internet activity is coded as 1 for regular users only and 0 otherwise.

It is important to note that ordinary discussion and online activity variables are related to deliberation but would probably not meet many of the stringent deliberative democracy requirements that some have proposed. Nevertheless, they are still quite useful. In the real world, meeting the various requirements is not easy, nor is finding high-quality data that permit an evaluation of their relative strengths. Part of the reason for this is that theorists do not agree on the precise requirements of the deliberative process. Habermas (1989) stresses three criteria.[2] Dahl (1989: 108–14) identifies four.[3] Bohman (1996: 16) highlights three.[4] Mendelberg and Oleske (2000) recognize eight criteria.[5] Instead of getting mired in the disagreements or different shades of meaning, the strategy adopted here is to focus on what they have in common.

While less controversial, the knowledge indices were somewhat more complex in the way they are constructed. Recent empirical evidence points to the need for a more nuanced understanding of knowledge. In their comprehensive study, Delli Carpini and Keeter (1996) argue that to be misinformed means something different than to be uninformed. More recently, Jeffery Mondak (2000) demonstrated that summing correct answers to political knowledge questions is of uncertain validity at best. The problem is that such a procedure treats "don't know" and incorrect answers equally. Mondak concludes that knowledge may not be discrete and that giving respondents a "don't know" option on surveys conflates personality traits and political knowledge. He argues that to be misinformed implies that exposure to information occurred and that the processing and storage of that information was somehow flawed. In contrast, to be uninformed implies that no information was received and stored (2000: 59). This study follows Mondak's suggestion that "[t]he common practice of grouping incorrect answers and [don't knows] must be discontinued" (2000, 80; Barabas 2002b) by separating out the various forms of knowledge into correct, incorrect, and "don't know" responses.

The analyses here concentrate upon sixteen factual questions. These questions were designed to measure awareness of Social Security reforms that became a part of the national agenda in America during the late 1990s.[6] The sixteen items were divided into three categories measuring programmatic, future funding, and personal financial knowledge as follows:

1. *Programmatic knowledge* (seven items). This index includes a question on the proportion of the federal budget spent on Social Security, five questions concerning Social Security eligibility, and a question about the pay-as-you-go nature of Social Security.
2. *Future funding knowledge* (seven items). This index includes a question on what happens to the system if no changes are made, five questions concerning various reasons for possible financial problems, and a follow-up question asking for the main reason for future funding problems.
3. *Personal financial knowledge* (two items). This index includes the amount financial experts recommend setting aside for retirement and the percentage of income experts think most people will need to maintain their standard of living.

Due to the nature of the questions, these last two questions in the personal financial battery were asked only of respondents who were not retired. The entire sample received the other questions. Table 17.1 displays basic descriptive statistics.

The first column lists the percentage of all respondents in each of the correct, incorrect, and "don't know" categories for the three varieties of knowledge. Most respondents performed quite well on the programmatic knowledge index. The average was 71 percent correct, while the percentages providing incorrect and "don't know" responses were much lower, at 18 and 12 percent, respectively. If we limit the sample to only those who

TABLE 17.1 Descriptive Statistics

	All	Discussion	Online	Neither
Programmatic Knowledge				
Correct	71%	74%	69%	69%
Incorrect	18%	16%	22%	17%
Don't know	12%	10%	9%	14%
N	2402	719	194	1329
Future Funding Knowledge				
Correct	43%	42%	45%	42%
Incorrect	49%	51%	49%	48%
Don't know	6%	5%	4%	8%
N	2402	719	194	1329
Financial Planning Knowledge				
Correct	43%	43%	51%	41%
Incorrect	46%	48%	44%	46%
Don't know	11%	10%	5%	14%
N	2402	533	181	943

engaged in policy discussion recently, then the average proportion correct rises to 74 percent. This is in contrast to the last two columns, which present the results for respondents who go online regularly but who do not discuss and respondents who neither go online nor discuss Social Security policy reforms. Those columns averaged only 69 percent correct, while the percentage incorrect is 22 percent for the online group.

The percentages correct for the future funding and personal financial knowledge indices were comparatively smaller. On average, fewer than half the respondents answered these questions correctly (43 percent). The online group did slightly better for both future funding and financial planning. The increases in correct responses seemed to be paired with corresponding decreases in the "don't know" categories, but verifying this will be the main objective of the empirical analyses in the next subsection. The main method of determining the effects of discussion and online activity on knowledge will be to examine differences in means for the proportions of correct, incorrect, and "don't know" answers. The analytical problem is that simple comparisons of the information levels between those who discuss politics and those who use the Internet are not possible.

Every day some individuals discuss politics or use the Internet, while others do not. This is, in essence, a natural experiment that researchers can use to gain analytical leverage on the question of whether these activities affect knowledge. We should be able to learn the effects of the discussion or online "treatments" by comparing the levels of political knowledge for those who engage in these activities to the levels of knowledge of those who do not. The problem is that these "field" or "quasi-" experiments typically do not use random assignment to assign subjects to the various treatment conditions (Cook and Campbell 1979). That is, individuals who discuss politics or use the Internet most certainly differ from those who do not because they self-select into these activities. A simple comparison, without adjusting for these important differences, would lead to incorrect inferences.

If assignment to the discussion and online conditions had been random, it would have been possible to compare the discussion or online respondents to the comparison group of those who did not engage in either of these activities.[7] However, in these quasi-experimental settings, simply analyzing differences between the treatment group and the nontreatment control group may lead to biased estimates of treatment effects to the extent that individuals self-select into the treatment and control groups. Propensity scores, defined as the conditional probability of assignment to treatment given a set of covariates, can be used to reduce bias by balancing the nonexperimental treatment and control groups (Rosenbaum and Rubin 1983).

The logic underlying propensity score analysis is that while comparisons between the treatment and comparison groups may not be valid if they differ in many important respects, it is possible to match respondents who have a high likelihood of engaging in the treatment activities *and* who actually reported doing them with those who have a similar likelihood but who did *not* do them. Such matching techniques reduce bias by adjusting estimates of the treatment effect as if the whole study were a randomized experiment (D'Agostino 1998; Dehejia and Wahba 1999). The variant of propensity score analysis employed here uses a simple probit technique to model the likelihood of discussion or online activity. The predictions from this probit model are used as propensity scores to help match up these respondents with others who did not receive the treatment.[8]

Unlike some statistical techniques, propensity score analyses yield readily interpretable results—in the form of means for the treated group and the matched control. Mean levels of knowledge can be subtracted to evaluate the effects of discussion and online activity compared with their control groups, who again are statistically as close as possible with the main exception that they did not receive the treatment. Just as we expect discussion and online activity to alter knowledge levels, we can test for these effects directly by examining differences in the knowledge proportions.

2. Findings

Whether discussion and going online simulate the effects of deliberation depends upon whether they increase correct knowledge above and beyond the factors that may drive participation in these activities. Viewed by these standards, the analyses here reveal that discussion consistently reduces proportions of "don't know" responses across all three forms of knowledge. The illustrations in panels A, B, and C of Figure 17.1 show significant decreases in "don't know" responses for those who discuss Social Security reforms compared with those who do not. Discussion reduces "don't know" responses on the programmatic knowledge index by three percentage points, by two percentage points on the future funding index, and by five percentage points on the personal financial knowledge batteries (all $p < 0.05$ for a two-tailed significance test).

Separating the responses gives us a considerable degree of analytical leverage. Only with programmatic knowledge do we see that the discussion-driven reductions in "don't know" responses lead to a corresponding four-percentage-point increase in the proportion correct. For the other two forms of knowledge, the reductions in "don't know" responses are offset by comparable three- and four-percentage-point *gains* in the average proportions of incorrect knowledge for future funding and financial planning.

The effects of online activity on knowledge are more in line with expectations. The right side of panel A shows a two-percentage-point movement from "don't know" to the correct category in the case of programmatic knowledge. These movements miss the conventional level of statistical significance but retain substantive meaning since they imply that going online improves knowledge, albeit slightly. In panel B, for knowledge of future funding, going online decreases correct responses and increases incorrect answers ($p < 0.10$). This is most unexpected and anomalous when we consider the final form of knowledge related to personal financial matters in the right side of panel C. There online activity has a large decrease (five percentage points) in "don't know" responses ($p < 0.05$) and a corresponding increase in correct knowledge.

Taken together, these findings suggest that discussion and online activity affect knowledge in a modest but similar fashion. The most consistent finding was the reduction in "don't know" responses. The analysis revealed that those who discuss Social Security and go online regularly offer fewer "don't know" responses for all three forms of knowledge. From a normative perspective this is a good thing. Discussion of Social Security reforms and going online lead to a reduction in "don't know" responses. However, the only time discussion had a statistically significant and positive effect on correct responses was with programmatic knowledge. For the kinds of knowledge that are most likely to affect preferences over reform packages or day-to-day individual saving habits, discussion actually made respondents more likely to offer incorrect responses. In two of the three online analyses, more respondents chose correct answers, but not enough to rule out chance variation.

3. Conclusion

Part of the allure behind using the Internet for everyday political discussions is that it has the potential to make democracy more deliberative. In a

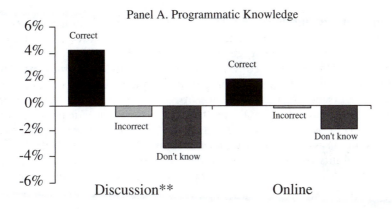

Panel A. Programmatic Knowledge

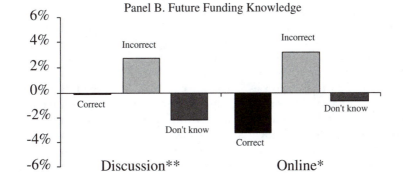

Panel B. Future Funding Knowledge

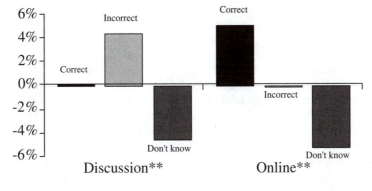

Panel C. Financial Planning Knowledge

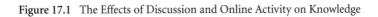

Note : ** *p* < .05; * *p* < .10

Figure 17.1 The Effects of Discussion and Online Activity on Knowledge

well-structured deliberative forum, information and discussion partners are plentiful. Conditions may not be quite as good in nondeliberative forum settings, but those who do not have access to a computer can presumably find a discussion partner. Similarly, isolated individuals or citizens who choose not to engage in ordinary verbal discussion can log onto the Internet to find both conversation partners and factual information. This study does not consider content or the quality of information provided via discussion and online activity. It is important to acknowledge that both activities could make matters worse if they provide poor-quality information. Nevertheless, a good first step is to explore their relative effects on the assumption that high-quality information is available. Given the availability of high-quality information, low transmission costs, and incentives to learn, one might expect policy discussion and going online to increase knowledge levels.

The consistent finding across the three analyses of knowledge was the reduction in "don't know" responses. Engaging in discussion of Social Security policy and going online made individuals less likely to opt out of political knowledge surveys by reporting "don't know." Sometimes, as in the case of the effect of discussion on programmatic knowledge or the effect that going online had on financial planning knowledge, the reduction in "don't know" responses was associated with an increase in the proportion of correct responses. These are clear and unambiguously positive results. But at other times, and especially when we consider the effect of discussion on knowledge of future funding or financial planning, the reductions in "don't know" responses were associated with increases in incorrect responses.

It is hard to claim that finding fewer "don't know" responses after citizens engage in discussion or go online is something to celebrate if the only offsetting change is to leave people with the wrong answer. Even theorists who encourage people to keep an open mind with respect to the various positions they bring into a deliberative dialogue concede that learning the correct answers to objective information questions is a good thing. Had we considered only knowledge of the Social Security program, then the overall conclusion would have been much more cheerful since both discussion and online activity have the net effect of increasing knowledge. Moving to the two other forms of knowledge—facts related to future funding for Social Security and financial planning—complicated the story because three out of the four analyses showed increases in incorrect knowledge.

Due to the propensity score method, which balances the comparison groups, we can be reasonably confident that these reductions in "don't know" responses are something more than mere differences in personality traits. Moreover, while crude in some respects (and dated, to be sure, at a time when Internet usage is expanding rapidly), these survey questions have the virtue of permitting simultaneous comparisons between these activities. Some, such as Michael Schudson (1997), argue that there is a distinction between conversation and deliberation. Others disagree (Wyatt, Kim, and Katz 2000a; 2000b) and argue that ordinary conversation can mimic some of the beneficial effects of deliberation. A fundamental premise underlying this investigation is that ordinary discussion and regular Internet usage are related to deliberation closely enough to consider whether they can deliver deliberation-like information improvements.

The lack of consistent findings across the various knowledge categories suggests that more research on other topics is needed, perhaps using different methods and better measures of discussion and online activity. If anything, the lack of uniformly positive effects implies that, at least according to these analyses, ordinary discussion and online activity do not completely mimic the beneficial effects of organized deliberative forums where others have shown unambiguous gains in political knowledge.

Notes

1. Both surveys used random-digit dialing and postsurvey weighting to ensure a nationally representative sample. The overall response rate was 50 percent (the product of a 69 percent contact rate, 75 percent cooperation rate, and 97 percent completion rate for the full interview among eligible respondents).
2. They are equal, open, and constraint-free discussion.
3. They are effective participation, equal voting opportunities, enlightened understanding, and agenda control.
4. They are inclusion, equality, and free and open exchange.
5. They are: (a) meetings are public; (b) citizens reflect and decide collectively rather than individually; (c) citizens have an equal opportunity to participate; (d) decisions turn on arguments, not on coercive power; (e) citizens are fully informed; (f) all alternatives are considered; (g) deliberation is an ongoing process supported by other institutions; and (h) arguments are based on general principles and appeal to the common good, not exclusively to self-interest.
6. Due to space limitations, detailed information regarding the survey questions and their wording could not be included but is available from the author upon request.
7. To gauge the relative effects of discussion, ideally we want a comparison group of respondents who do not discuss policy but who also do not go online regularly. Similarly, to judge the impact of online activity, we want to be sure to construct a comparison group with respondents who do not discuss policy regularly, or else we risk conflating the treatments.
8. The probit matching equation contains a variety of demographic characteristics such as gender, race, education, work status, marital status, age, and income as well as partisanship and a dummy variable to denote the second of two surveys. This process makes the treatment and control groups statistically indistinguishable on all factors except the key variables of interest: discussion and online activity.

References

Althaus, Scott L. 1998. "Information Effects in Collective Preferences." *American Political Science Review* 92: 545–58.

Barabas, Jason. 2002a. "How Deliberation Affects Public Opinion." Paper presented at the annual meeting of the Midwest Political Science Association, Chicago, April 25–28.

Barabas, Jason. 2002b. "Another Look at the Measurement of Political Knowledge." *Political Analysis* 10: 209.

Barber, Benjamin. 1984. *Strong Democracy: Participatory Politics for a New Age.* Berkeley: University of California Press.

Barber, Benjamin R., Kevin Matteson, and Michael Moody. 1997. "Creating Mall-Town Square: What Can be Done to Recreate Public Space in America's Suburbs?" New Brunswick, NJ: Walt Whitman Center.

Bartels, Larry M. 1996. "Uninformed Votes: Information Effects in Presidential Elections." *American Journal of Political Science* 40: 194–230.

Benhabib, Seyla. 1996. "Toward a Deliberative Model of Democratic Legitimacy." In S. Benhabib, ed., *Democracy and Difference*. Princeton, NJ: Princeton University Press.

Bohman, James. 1996. *Public Deliberation: Pluralism, Complexity, and Democracy*. Cambridge, MA: M.I.T. Press.

Cook, Thomas, and Donald Campbell. 1979. *Quasi-experimentation: Design and Analysis Issues for Field Settings*. Chicago: Rand McNally College.

Crosby, Ned. 1995. "Citizen Juries: One Solution for Difficult Environmental Questions." In O. Renn, T. Webler, and P. Wiedemann, eds. *Fairness and Competence in Citizen Participation: Evaluating Models for Environmental Discourse*, 157–74. Boston: Kluwer Academic.

D'Agostino, Ralph B., Jr. 1998. "Propensity Score Methods for Bias Reduction in the Comparison of a Treatment to a Non-Randomized Control Group." *Statistics in Medicine* 17: 2264–81.

Dahl, Robert A. 1979. "Procedural Democracy." In Peter Laslett and James Fishkin, eds., *Philosophy, Politics, and Society*, vol. 5. New Haven: Yale University Press.

Dahl, Robert A. 1989. *Democracy and Its Critics*. New Haven: Yale University Press.

Dahlberg, Lincoln. 2001. "The Internet and Democratic Discourse." *Information, Communication, and Society* 4: 615–33.

Dehejia, Rajeev H., and Sadek Wahba. 1999. "Causal Effects in Nonexperimental Studies: Reevaluating the Evaluation of Training Programs." *Journal of the American Statistical Association* 94: 1053–62.

Delli Carpini, Michael X., and Scott Keeter. 1996. *What Americans Know About Politics and Why It Matters*. New Haven: Yale University Press.

Dryzek, John S. 1990. *Discursive Democracy: Politics, Policy, and Political Science*. New York: Cambridge University Press.

Fishkin, James S. 1991. *Democracy and Deliberation: New Directions for Democratic Reform*. New Haven: Yale University Press.

Fishkin, James S. 1995. *The Voice of the People*. New Haven: Yale University.

Fishkin, James S., and Robert C. Luskin. 1999. "Bringing Deliberation to Democratic Dialogue." In M. E. McCombs and A. Reynolds, eds., *A Poll with a Human Face*. Mahwah, NJ: Lawrence Erlbaum.

Gastil, John. 2000a. *By Popular Demand: Revitalizing Representative Democracy Through Deliberative Elections*. Berkeley: University of California Press.

Gastil, John. 2000b. "Is Face-to-Face Citizen Deliberation a Luxury or a Necessity?" *Political Communication* 17: 357–61.

Gastil, John, and James P. Dillard. 1999. "Increasing Political Sophistication Through Public Deliberation." *Political Communication* 16: 3–23.

Gilens, Martin. 2001. "Political Ignorance and Collective Policy Preferences." *American Political Science Review* 95: 379–96.

Gutmann, Amy, and Dennis Thompson. 1996. *Democracy and Disagreement*. Cambridge, MA: Belknap Press.

Habermas, Jürgen. 1989. *The Structural Transformation of the Public Sphere: An Inquiry into a Category of Bourgeois Society*. Cambridge, M.A. M.I.T. Press.

Hochschild, Jennifer L. 2001. "Where You Stand Depends on What You See: Connections Among Values, Perceptions of Fact, and Political Prescriptions." In J. H. Kuklinski, ed., *Citizens and Politics: Perspectives from Political Psychology*. New York: Cambridge University Press.

Kuklinski, James H., Paul J. Quirk, Jennifer Jerit, David Schwieder, and Robert Rich. 2000. "Misinformation and the Currency of Citizenship." *Journal of Politics* 62: 790–816.

Lupia, Arthur, and Mathew D. McCubbins. 1998. *The Democratic Dilemma*. Cambridge: Cambridge University Press.

Manin, Bernard. 1987. "On Legitimacy and Political Deliberation." *Political Theory* 15: 338–68.

Mansbridge, Jane. 1980. *Beyond Adversary Democracy*. New York: Basic Books.

Mendelberg, Tali, and John Oleske. 2000. "Race and Public Deliberation." *Political Communication* 17: 169–191.

Mondak, Jeffery J. 2000. "Reconsidering the Measurement of Political Knowledge." *Political Analysis* 8: 57–82.

Page, Benjamin I. 1996. *Who Deliberates? Mass Media in Modern Democracy.* Chicago: University of Chicago Press.

Rosenbaum, Paul R., and Donald B. Rubin. 1983. "The Central Role of the Propensity Score in Observational Studies for Causal Effects." *Biometrika* 70: 41–55.

Schudson, Michael. 1997. "Why Conversation Is Not the Soul of Democracy." *Critical Studies in Mass Communication* 14: 297–309.

Shenk, David. 1998. *Data Smog: Surviving the Information Glut.* San Francisco: Harper.

Stasser, Garold. 1992. "Pooling of Unshared Information during Group Discussion." In S. Worchel, W. Wood, and J. Simpson, eds. *Group Process and Productivity.* Newbury Park: Sage.

Wyatt, Robert O., Elihu Katz, and Joohan Kim. 2000a. "Bridging the Spheres: Political and Personal Conversation in Public and Private Spaces." *Journal of Communication* 50: 71–92.

Wyatt, Robert O., Joohan Kim, and Elihu Katz. 2000b. "How Feeling Free to Talk Affects Ordinary Political Conversation, Purposeful Argumentation, and Civic Participation." *Journalism and Mass Communication Quartely* 77: 99–114.

CHAPTER 18

The Challenge of E-Democracy for Political Parties

GRANT KIPPEN AND GORDON JENKINS

> As the speed of information increases the tendency is for politics to move away from the representation and delegation of constituents toward immediate involvement of the entire community in the central acts of decision.
>
> —Marshall McLuhan

Over the past several years, governments worldwide have been attempting to transition their old command-and-control style operations to a new, more citizencentric approach. Although these important changes are still in their infancy, citizens are beginning to see meaningful improvements in the delivery of public sector services and in the information available to them from all levels of government. As consumers become more educated and demanding in this new globalized economic and social space, their desire increases for greater involvement and accountability among themselves, their governments, and their elected representatives.

Political parties are struggling with similar issues. But their struggles, as witnessed in both Canada and the United States, testify to an important truth. Although new information and communications technologies (ICTs) offer the potential to transform organizations in their own long-term interest, the logic of existing organizational processes, as well as the calculation of a political organization's short-term interests, may preclude adoption of ICT strategies that are most potentially helpful and transformative in the long run.

In this essay, we argue that political parties desperately need and could benefit enormously from e-democracy strategies that would deepen relationships between party organizations and their rank-and-file members. This is what we would call genuine e-democracy. At the same time, a variety of factors are impeding the adoption of such strategies. Based on our analysis of the hurdles to be overcome, we recommend public financing for new e-democracy approaches as a way to break the logjam and incentivize political party adoption of e-democracy strategies that would strengthen both the parties and government accountability more generally. Our approach is guided both by a review of books, studies, articles, and other related publications that explore the issue of e-democracy and the impact of the Internet on political parties as well as e-business and e-government, and by interviews we conducted with elected representatives, political party officials in Canada and the United States, the chief electoral officer of Canada, senior officials within the Parliamentary Centre and Congressional Management Foundation, and individuals involved in providing Internet campaign services to candidates in the United States.

1. Current Challenges to the Vitality of Political Parties

Over the past decade or so, signs have appeared that point to the erosion of political parties as dynamic and positive change agents. Some of these factors include:

- The rise in the number and the influence of single-issue interest groups, threatening the position of political parties as "integrators" of the diverse economic and social interests within society
- The increasing percentage of voters who do not participate in national, state/province, and local elections, a phenomenon that now exists in most Western democracies
- Eroding loyalty to traditional political parties
- A lack of transparency and accountability relative to the improvements that have been made with information and communications technologies, compared to what citizens expect

Political parties are likewise facing serious internal challenges. The desire of party members for greater involvement in internal party processes such as decision making and policy development is causing significant conflict. Carty, Cross and Young (2000) state that party activists in the old-line parties are showing a high degree of discontent over their limited roles in party decision making. The authors point out "that grass-roots involvement in party policy making is meaningful only if there is some connection between the policy positions of the party and the positions taken by its parliamentary caucus. This is a tension that is as old as organized political parties" (ibid.: 121).

It is clear that party members regard ongoing engagement within traditional party structures as having diminished in value. Compelling evidence of this appears in the low numbers of citizens who are active in political parties. In Canada, this problem is particularly acute, as a recent study examining political party membership points out. Cross and Young (2001) indicate that with just 2 percent of Canadian voters belonging to a political party, Canada ranks near the bottom among comparable countries in terms of political party membership. The time could hardly seem more ripe for political parties to adopt e-democracy strategies aimed first and foremost at deepening their relationship with rank-and-file voters.

2. Customer Relationship Management for Parties: Relationship Building in Business and Government

Fortunately for political parties, the pattern of recent ICT influence in the business and government sectors would seem to point precisely toward the potential for new ICT-enabled strategies to build relationships between organizations and their constituents. Not surprisingly, when the Internet went public, the business sector was quick to seize on its commercial potential. The declining costs of hardware and software relative to the performance of these components led to a burst of entrepreneurial creativity. Several aspects to the development of e-business have a direct bearing on the genesis of the e-democracy movement and potentially factor into the ways in which political parties can engage e-democracy strategies. These include the following:

- The rise in Internet usage in business and at home, as well as ICT knowledge and skills among the general populations within developed and developing countries
- The increasing importance of e-business, both business-to-business (B2B) and business-to-consumer (B2C), relative to the interconnected globalized economies of industrialized and developing countries
- The profound shifts from hierarchical command and control to flattened, horizontal organizational structures within most businesses
- The changing relationships that consumers have with companies in the e-business space

Although the research company IDC predicts that the e-commerce sector (B2B and B2C) will have grown from U.S. $131 billion in 1999 to over U.S. $5,300 billion by 2004, the real story of e-business is that as transaction costs fell, entire industry supply chains became disaggregated and reaggregated. The resulting supply chains began to take on forms ranging from hierarchical to self-organizing and in turn created new value propositions for the end customer. Investments not just in infrastructure but in applications such as supply chain management (SCM), enterprise resource planning (ERP), and customer relationship management (CRM) contributed to driving down costs, thus creating increased efficiencies and revenues for most companies.

The impact of new technologies and the Internet on e-business also contributed to fundamental restructuring of business organization and processes. Dell Computer is often singled out as one of the most successful examples of a company that completely redefined the role of a computer manufacturer by rewriting the book on supply chain management. With a flatter organizational structure, Dell was able to become more responsive to customer requirements, thereby enjoying a distinct competitive advantage over its competitors. The power behind this new model was that it allowed Dell to develop sophisticated databases populated with detailed consumer information from which it could anticipate future purchasing patterns. This "customercentric" approach has now permeated just about every aspect of the business and is evolving to a point where highly sophisticated customer relationship management (CRM) models are being used to strengthen the ongoing relationship between companies and their customers.

One of the profound changes precipitated by the Internet has been the shift in power between consumers and retailers. For businesses and consumers, value is not just about the product or just about service, but rather about the relationship that exists between buyer and seller. Frederick Newell (2000) states that the new basic principle is "to add value to the customer relationship in the customer's terms to maximize the value of the relationship to the customer for the customer's benefit and the company's profit."

The importance of the customer relationship is now viewed as an intrinsic business asset. Tapscott, Ticoll, and Lowy (2000) posit a new notion of relationship capital as follows: "The wealth embedded in customer relationships is now more important than the capital contained in land, factories, buildings and even big bank accounts. Relationships are now assets. A firm's ability to engage customers, suppliers and other partners in mutually beneficial value exchanges determines its relationship capital."

The same logic is appearing in the government sector. What initially caught the eye of government leaders with regard to new ICTs was the opportunity to improve services while actually reducing costs. Increasingly, however, governments have realized that the more profound opportunity for e-government is the potential to develop a stronger and more responsive relationship between the citizen and the state.

Over the past several years, e-government has become the focal point of public sector initiatives within most industrialized countries. While the roots for a more responsive client-centered government can be traced to the beginning of the previous decade, e-government is a more recent phenomenon and shadows the success of e-business within the corporate sector.

Well over a decade ago, the public sector began looking to and experimenting with new technologies with the objective of radically changing the paradigm of program delivery in terms of both cost and service. Spawned to a degree by the "reinventing government" approach as articulated by Osborne and Gaebler (1992) in the early 1990s, the Clinton-Gore administration championed this fresh new approach by introducing the National Performance Review (NPR) during its first term in office. Driven by the opportunity for greater cost efficiencies and the potential to meet (and perhaps exceed) changing customer/voter expectations of public service programs, the NPR signaled a major shift in public policy thinking. The driving concept was to match citizen expectations for service delivery by establishing performance standards across government departments and agencies in much the same way as consumers expect private sector companies to respond to their particular needs.

While government agencies, like businesses, were reliant on information technology from the start in order to drive many of their reengineering efforts brought about by the NPR, the advent of the World Wide Web in the early 1990s led both governments and businesses to examine the new ICT infrastructure as a channel for not only delivery but also communication. The first steps were to put government services online, a step that still remains a work in progress. To date, most technology-enabled government efforts have been less dramatic than private sector initiatives. Rather than disaggregate and rebuild entire supply chains (à la Dell), many governments have simply transferred their internal information and systems to the Web. To be sure, this has had a dramatic impact on service costs and efficiency. But replicating existing systems by transferring documents from a filing cabinet to a Web page has proven to be only an intermediary step.

Consistent with the trend in e-business, e-government initiatives are now beginning to focus on making the necessary changes that will allow for a strengthening of the relationship between state and citizen. According to an Accenture report, "Governments that adopt Customer Relationship Management or rather Citizen Relationship Management principles (client/citizen involvement) early in their eGovernment initiatives are improving at a much faster pace" (Accenture 2002). Another recent Accenture report (2001) makes the case that next generation advances in e-government will come about through the adoption of CRM. The fact that e-government initiatives are trending toward more direct and closer relationships between citizens and the state is a positive development from an e-democracy perspective and would seem to point to an obvious direction for the evolution in strategic thinking by political parties as well. The experience of e-business and e-government points to the possible adoption by political parties of a "life-cycle" approach to managing member and voter relationships that could provide political parties with a significant foundation for encouraging sustained citizen involvement, including voting. Because political parties vary in their structure and the constitutions that govern their activities as well as with regard to the environments within which they must operate, it won't be a case of one e-democracy model that works for all. The basic direction, however, is clear.

3. Impediments to the Transformation of Political Parties Through ICTs

The evolution of CRM in the business sector and "citizen relationship management" in the e-government sector would seem to signal to political parties a clear path for meeting their deepest long-term needs: the reengagement of rank-and-file voters in party affairs through ICTs. Yet while current trends within business and government point to greater transparency, openness, and accountability through appropriate governance structures, political parties continue to be characterized as closed organizations guided by back-room advisors. In speaking with elected representatives and party officials from federal political parties in Canada, we found only a small percentage of elected representatives and party officials even attuned to the issues and opportunities posed by e-democracy advances. None of the party officials interviewed felt that e-democracy was a priority issue facing their organizations. One Canadian Member of Parliament (MP) felt that out of a total of 301 elected representatives, only between ten and twenty of his colleagues from all parties were interested or somewhat knowledgeable about e-government and that an even smaller group was interested in the issue of e-democracy. Some MPs expressed frustration with the lack of support provided by their party on this issue and, in hopes of providing better representation to their constituents, have simply forged ahead on their own. But overall, very little attention is being paid to how ICTs could fundamentally alter the structure, organization, and functioning of parties in responding to changing voter expectations.

Our interviews, as well as a review of the literature, suggest at least five reasons for this state of affairs. In short, these are priorities, time scarcity, lack of leadership, the threat to established powers, and a paucity of financial resources. None may be surprising, but they cumulatively demonstrate the capacity of short-term difficulties to keep parties from acting in their own long-term best interests.

With regard to priorities, political parties are simply consumed with the immediate business of getting candidates elected in the next election cycle. As a result, longer-term issues, such as e-democracy, have difficulty capturing the attention of elected and senior officials responsible for setting the agenda of the parties. It may seem doubtful to party leaders that the parties should commit valuable time and resources responding to an approach that may or may not have an impact on the core business objective of getting elected. The question whether there is political value (votes and dollars) in building a sustainable e-democracy approach has yet to be answered.

For those dubious about e-democracy, it is even possible to characterize the debate over strategy as a debate over responsibility. While the percentage of the voting public continues to decline, it is unclear whether political parties should concern themselves chiefly with ensuring that the broadest possible group of citizens participate in the political process or whether they should focus their attentions on reaching those voters (even if a decreasing number) who will actually cast ballots.

This is not to say that winning elections is the parties' only function. Schmitter states that "electoral structuration is the primary function for parties, in the sense that it is this activity that constitutes their strongest claim to a distinctive political role" (quoted in Diamond and Gunther 2001: 74). But, while political parties do carry out other important functions, such as providing linkages between citizens and state, helping to set the policy agenda, participating in the formulation of policy, and recruiting elites, by and large their overriding focus is to ensure the success of the party, its leader, and its candidates during election campaigns (Meisel and Mendelsohn 1996: 179). Unless it is shown that e-democracy strategies akin to CRM, engaging greater numbers of voters in the political process, have the potential to translate into actual votes and increased financial support, parties may well remain unpersuaded of their importance.

Several other aspects of the current environment for political parties support their reluctance to change. One is simply the scarcity of time. With a twenty-four-hour-per-day news cycle, coupled with changing voter expectations, parties and politicians may simply be overwhelmed with the myriad demands placed on their time. There may be little time or appetite to examine new approaches toward political processes when current approaches are already so demanding.

Further, there is a relative absence of strong leadership on this issue. Tom Riley (2002: 6) suggests that "as with e-government, for e-democracy to grow it is going to need vision, strategy and political leadership." Vision, strategy and political leadership all have been present in successful e-business and e-government initiatives and will undoubtedly be required if e-democracy is to find a home within political parties. Although Prime Minister Tony Blair has been a champion on this issue with respect to the United Kingdom's e-government efforts, it has been hard to find an elected American or Canadian leader to articulate how e-democracy will be an important part of the future vision of any major political party.

It is likewise difficult to foresee how such leadership will emerge given the relative unfamiliarity of most politicians and party officials with new technologies. Jonah Seiger, cofounder and chief strategist for Mindshare Internet Campaigns, states that part of the current resistance toward the greater use of the Internet in campaigns is the fact that most professional campaign consultants, who are the decision makers in terms of campaign expenditures, are of the old school and therefore tend to favor the use of traditional approaches. To the extent this view is prevalent among senior party officials, it results in an inherent bias against greater reliance on ICTs, limiting the potential for e-democracy within political parties.

We have yet to see even universal adoption by elected officials of even the most rudimentary ICT tools. For example, a recent report by the Hansard Society in the United Kingdom indicated that one in four Westminster MPs had no functioning e-mail account in their parliamentary office and that 60 percent have no personal Web site. A similar survey conducted by the Centre for Collaborative Government examined Internet usage by Canadian parliamentarians and found that only 58 percent had official Web sites. Furthermore, only 27 percent of those with Web sites used any sort of interactive tools, such as feedback forms or online surveys.

These numbers may be unsurprising given that e-democracy is in the early stages of its diffusion cycle. However, if elected representatives are to become champions for e-democracy change, then greater emphasis on education, knowledge, and skills development will be required in order to make them more comfortable in this new medium. If e-democracy is to make a breakthrough within political parties, it will require a critical mass of elected representatives experimenting with this approach to move it forward.

In the United States and Canada elected representatives rely on two important nonpartisan, not-for-profit organizations to provide research, training, and tools to assist them in managing technological change. The Parliamentary Centre in Ottawa and the Congressional Management Foundation in Washington assist elected representatives in meeting the challenges brought about by the increasing reliance on technology within their office environments, but challenges do exist. Kathy Goldschmidt, director of technology at the Congressional Management Foundation, indicates that while Capitol Hill staffers need technology to do their jobs, most offices now are using technology as a business tool rather than as a constituency tool. The fact that a resource and skills gap exists in most offices means that elected representatives are not optimally positioned to adopt and use new technologies in more fundamental and transformative ways.

This view reflects the experience by the Liberal Party of Canada (LPC), which has developed, sold, and supported (through a partnership with a private sector company) a suite of software called ElecSys. The first product (AdminElect) assists members of Parliament to manage their constituency cases. The second product (ManagElect) is used by LPC candidates during election campaigns to track voter identification and GOTV (get out the vote) activities. Despite the investment made by the LPC in this software suite and the fact that it could assist MPs in managing their constituencies more effectively, it is used by less than 9 percent of the caucus. For the Liberal Party of Canada, this is clearly a disappointing return on investment.

There are those who would argue that parties will resist the transformative potential of e-democracy because it poses a serious threat to the order and structure that drives the present-day political system. Mark Walsh, chief technology advisor for the Democratic National Committee, believes that there is simply no natural migration path for e-democracy within political parties as there has been for e-business within the corporate sector. One of the main problems is that the demand for openness, accountability, and transparency that drives e-business works against the processes that run political parties. There are too many groups with short-term self-interests that dominate political parties who see no reason to change, if e-democracy might potentially benefit the party as well as society over the longer term.

The apprehensions of those already in power are fed, of course, by claims that the Internet will evolve to become the primary channel for citizen engagement. So dramatic a change in approach may well be too big a jump for many political players. Pippa Norris (2001: 167) argues that it is only reasonable to expect that digital technologies will supplement rather than replace the many functions and activities of political parties. To some extent, we can already see that evolution occurring. For example, the Canadian Alliance Party (CAP) has adopted an approach under which the Internet is used in a variety of ways to support, but not replace, internal party functions. Canadians can join the CAP or make a donation over the Internet, even though these same tasks can also be accomplished by walking into an Alliance office or over the telephone. The blending of traditional and modern approaches is extremely important to the CAP given the demographics of its membership. The party recognizes that a digital divide exists within its membership and, in order to keep members engaged, the party needs to offer multiple channels for interaction.

These initial efforts fall short, however, of realizing the potential of e-democracy to support a long-term sustainable citizen engagement model. Developments within the e-business and e-government sectors suggest that investment in citizencentric approaches would offer a substantial potential payoff for political parties and elected representatives should they decide to develop longer-term, more direct relationships with voters. So far, although both the Republican and Democratic parties in the United States are experimenting with CRM-type applications, the focus appears to be on fund-raising as opposed to citizen-engagement-type activities.

A final impediment to party adoption of citizencentric ICT approaches is cost. The poor rate of adoption reflects the lack of resources (financial and personnel) available either to the parties on an organizational basis or to MPs individually for citizen engagement activities. It is interesting to

262 • Grant Kippen and Gordon Jenkins

note that the average Canadian MP receives a support budget that works out to less than three dollars per year per constituent, an amount that should be reexamined in light of the need to be more responsive to the needs and expectations of today's citizens.

To implement the sorts of citizencentric relationship models that have transformed e-business and e-government initiatives requires significant direct investments in the technology infrastructures of both public and private organizations, as well as costs that result from secondary impacts of the new model on their organizational structures and processes. When compared to business and government citizencentric service initiatives, political parties and elected representatives appear to be at a distinct disadvantage simply by virtue of scale.

On an absolute basis, government departments enjoy considerably higher funding and resource levels than do political parties. While business and government funding models can support the investment required for citizencentric initiatives, one has to wonder whether political parties will ever be able to generate the levels of funding that will be required to implement similar large-scale, citizen-engagement initiatives.

While direct costs are one issue, there are other, intangible costs that would have to be borne by political parties in transitioning to an e-democracy approach. These costs would be reflected in the changes required to revamp existing political party structures and processes that have been institutionalized over time. Any such changes would need to be ratified by party members, which would likewise require a sustained long-term effort.

A crucial issue for political parties in considering e-democracy strategies will be financial sustainability. Parties cannot afford to ignore the long-term repercussions of declining voter participation. At present, political parties are becoming increasingly reliant on corporate donations, while the number of donations from individuals continues to decline. Calls to reform political party financing in Canada may, in the future, place restrictions on corporate fund-raising. Such a development would force parties to adopt more citizencentric engagement and fund-raising models while at the same time making the resource difficulties of moving to such approaches more onerous.

4. Overcoming Inertia: Public Financing for Political Parties

The spread of ambitious e-democracy efforts among political parties stands to benefit not only the parties themselves, but society more generally. Dr. Tom Flanagan, director of operations in the Office of the Official Opposition in Ottawa, states that in many respects, the debate around e-democracy shows the warts of our present-day democratic system. On one hand, the self-interest of the parties and candidates to be elected is paramount. Yet the egalitarian goal of attempting to raise the bar on democracy by encouraging greater voter participation ought be every bit as important. Carolyn Bennett, MP, sees e-democracy as a way to address the issues of transparency and accountability within political parties, which are critical public issues in the post-Enron era.

Robin Clarke makes the point that "public involvement should be about both achieving better quality decision and democratic renewal. Public involvement for better decision making offers instant returns, though a firm body of evidence is urgently needed to win over doubters. Public involvement as a means to democratic renewal is a trickier and, in reality, a long-term goal" (Clarke 2002: 53). Following Clarke's point, if e-democracy offers the potential to achieve better-quality decision making and democratic renewal, then it is important to consider both how success will be defined and whether the costs of achieving that success should be spread among the citizenry more generally.

One way to break the hold of short-term impediments to the adoption of potentially transformative e-democracy strategies would be to introduce financial incentives for political parties to move to citizencentric approaches. There is some precedent for this approach in Germany, where political parties have received government funding for undertaking education and citizen engagement activities. While the details would need to be worked out, the idea in the Canadian context would be that recognized political parties would receive a specific funding allotment from the government that would go to citizen engagement, e-democracy, education and outreach activities. These citizen engagement funds would provide parties with the flexibility and financial incentive to experiment with new approaches without forcing them to use funds that have been raised for electoral and ongoing party purposes. Such funding could be used to fund innovative online citizen engagement approaches through caucus members or using other party structures. Political parties could also choose to augment this funding with resources of their own, but all parties would be expected to account for this funding through appropriate disclosure mechanisms that address transparency and accountability issues.

The pervasiveness of e-business and e-government continues to drive fundamental economic and societal changes that are also having ramifications on the political landscape. Traditional political engagement models are no longer effective or sustainable, offering some hope that leaders will turn to more innovative e-democracy type approaches. E-democracy appears to pose compelling opportunities for political parties but, if history is any indication, change will occur at an evolutionary pace that may never enable e-democracy to reach its full transformative potential. In order to counteract the recent decline by citizens in the political process, political parties should seize upon the opportunity offered by the e-democracy movement and begin spending more time and effort experimenting, molding, and adapting this approach in order to reinvigorate the political process. It is unlikely they will do so, however, without a significant shift in incentives. That is where public funding can play its most useful role.

References

Accenture. 2001. *Customer Relationship Management: A Blueprint for Government*. Chicago: Accenture.

Accenture. 2002. *eGovernment Leadership: Realizing the Vision*. Chicago: Accenture.

Alexander, Cynthia J., and Leslie A. Pal, eds. 1998. *Digital Democracy: Policy and Politics in the Wired World*. Toronto: Oxford University Press.

Allison, Juliann Emmons, ed. 2002. *Technology, Development, and Democracy: International Conflict and Cooperation in the Information Age*. Albany: State University of New York Press.

Axworthy, Thomas, S. 1991. "Capital Intensive Politics: Money, Media and Mores in the United States and Canada." In F. Leslie Seidle, ed., *Issues in Party and Election Finance in Canada*. Toronto: Dundurn.

Barney, Darin. 2000. *Prometheus Wired: The Hope for Democracy in the Age of Network Technology*. Vancouver: University of British Columbia Press.

Blumler, Jay G., and Stephen Coleman. 2001. *Realising Democracy Online: A Civic Commons in Cyberspace*. London: Institute for Public Policy Research/Citizens Online.

Carty, R. Kenneth, William Cross, and Lisa Young. 2000. *Rebuilding Canadian Party Politics*. Vancouver: University of British Columbia Press.

Centre for Collaborative Government. 2002. *Canadian Federal Members of Parliament Online Website Prevalence*. Ottawa.

Clarke, Robin. 2002. *New Democratic Processes: Better Decisions, Stronger Democracy*. London: Institute for Public Policy Research.

Coleman, Stephen, ed. 2001. 2001: *Cyber Space Odyssey: The Internet in the UK Election*. London: Hansard Society.

Coleman, Stephen, ed. 2001. "*Elections in the Age of the Internet: Lessons from the United States*. London: Hansard Society.

Cross, William, and Lisa Young. 2001. "*Contours of Political Party Membership in Canada*." Manuscript.

Davis, Richard. 1999. *The Web of Politics: The Internet's Impact on the American Political System*. New York: Oxford University Press.

E-Voter Institute. 2001. *E-Voter 2001: Dawning of a New Era—Measuring the Initial Impact of the Internet on Political and Advocacy Communication*.

Friedman, Thomas L. 2000. *The Lexus and the Olive Tree*. New York: Anchor.

Gartner Dataquest Guide. 2002. *Infrastructure and Applications Worldwide Software Market Definitions*. Stamford, CT: Gartner.

Grossman, Lawrence K. 1995. *The Electronic Republic: Reshaping Democracy in the Information Age*. New York: Penguin.

Gunther, Richard, and Larry Diamond, eds. 2001. *Political Parties and Democracy*. Baltimore: Johns Hopkins University Press.

Hague, Barry N., and Brian D. Loader. 1999. *Digital Democracy: Discourse and Decision Making in the Information Age*. New York: Routledge.

Hanselmann, Calvin. 2001. *Electronically Enhanced Democracy in Canada*. Calgary: Canada West Foundation.

Hill, Kevin A., and John E. Hughes. 1998. *Cyberpolitics: Citizen Activism in the Age of the Internet*. Lanham, MD: Rowman and Littlefield.

Kamarck, Elaine Ciulla, and Joseph S. Nye Jr., eds. 2002. *Governance.com: Democracy in the Information Age*. Washington, DC: Brookings Institution.

Lenihan, Donald G. 2002a. *Realigning Governance: From E-Government to E-Democracy*. Ottawa: Centre for Collaborative Government.

Lenihan, Donald G. 2002b. *Survey on Canadian Federal MP Website Prevalence*. Ottawa: Centre for Collaborative Government.

Meisel, John, and Matthew Mendelsohn. 1996. "Meteor? Phoenix? Chameleon? The Decline and Transformation of Party in Canada." In Hugh G. Thorburn, ed., *Party Politics in Canada*. Scarborough, ON: Prentice Hall Canada.

Newell, Frederick. 2000. *Loyalty.com: Customer Relationship Management in the New Era of Internet Marketing*. New York: McGraw-Hill.

Norris, Pippa. 2001. *Digital Divide: Civic Engagement, Information Poverty, and the Internet Worldwide*. New York: Cambridge University Press.

Office of the e-Envoy. 2002. *In the Service of Democracy: A Consultation Paper on a Policy for Electronic Democracy.* London: Cabinet Office.

Osborne, David, and Ted Gaebler. 1992. *Reinventing Government.* Reading, MA: Addison-Wesley.

Pammett, Jon H., and Christopher Dornan. 2001. *The Canadian General Election of 2000.* Toronto: Dundurn.

Riley, Thomas B. 2002. *E-Democracy in the Future: Will We See Significant Change?* Ottawa: Riley Information Services.

Phillips, Susan D. 2002. *Mapping the Links: Citizen Involvement in Policy Processes.* Ottawa: Canadian Policy Research Networks.

Selnow, Gary W. 1998. *Electronic Whistle Stops: The Impact of the Internet on American Politics.* Westport, CT: Praeger.

Shine, Sean. 2002. *Building Customer Relationship Management in Government.* Dublin: Accenture.

Swerdlow, Joel L., ed. 1988. *Media Technology and the Vote.* Boulder, CO: Westview.

Tapscott, Don, Alex Ticoll, and Alex Lowy. 2000. *Digital Capital: Harnessing the Power of Business Webs.* Boston: Harvard Business School Press.

Thorburn, Hugh G., ed. 1996. *Party Politics in Canada.* Scarborough, Ontario: Prentice Hall Canada Inc.

The Government Executive Series. 2002. *eGovernment Leadership—Realizing the Vision.* Chicago: Accenture.

Wilhelm, Anthony G. 2000. *Democracy in the Digital Age: Challenges to Political Life in Cyberspace.* New York: Routledge.

Woodley, Bill. 2001. *The Impact of Transformative Technologies on Governance: Some Lessons from History.* Ottawa: Institute of Governance.

Contributors

Jason Barabas is Assistant Professor of Political Science at Southern Illinois University. His research in political behavior focuses on public opinion, political psychology, deliberation, and public policy. His work has been published in *Public Opinion Quarterly, International Studies Quarterly,* and *Political Analysis,* and by Oxford University Press. He was a postdoctoral fellow at the Center for the Study of Democratic Politics at Princeton University during 2000–01.

Thomas C. Beierle is a fellow in the Risk, Resource and Environmental Management Division at Resources for the Future, an environmental policy think tank in Washington, D.C. One of Beierle's primary areas of interest is the role of public participation in environmental policy, including the role of the Internet in fostering participation. He is the author of *Democracy in Practice* (RFF Press, 2002), an evaluative study of 239 cases of public involvement, and a number of articles and reports. Beierle received his Master of Public Affairs degree from Princeton University and a B.A. from Yale University.

James Bohman is Danforth Professor of Philosophy at St. Louis University. He is author of *Public Deliberation: Pluralism, Complexity and Democracy* (MIT Press, 1996) and *New Philosophy of Social Science: Problems of Indeterminacy* (MIT Press, 1991). He has also recently edited *Deliberative Democracy* (with William Rehg) and *Perpetual Peace: Essays on Kant's Cosmopolitan Ideal* (with Matthias Lutz-Bachmann), both with MIT Press. He is currently writing a book on cosmopolitan democracy. His other interests include philosophy of social science, critical social theory, and pragmatism.

A. Michael Froomkin is Professor at the University of Miami School of Law in Coral Gables, Florida, specializing in Internet law and administrative law. He is a member of the Royal Institute of International Affairs in

London and serves on the advisory boards of the BNA Electronic Information Policy and Law Report and on the editorial board of *Information,
Communication and Society* and is a founder editor of ICANNWatch.org.
Professor Froomkin writes primarily about the electronic commerce,
electronic cash, privacy, Internet governance, the regulation of
cryptography, and U.S. constitutional law. Before entering teaching, Professor Froomkin practiced international arbitration law in the London
office of Wilmer, Cutler and Pickering and clerked for Judge Stephen F.
Williams of the D.C. Circuit and Chief Judge John F. Grady of the North-
ern District of Illinois. He is a graduate of Yale Law School and has an
M.Phil. from Cambridge.

Paul G. Harwood is an Assistant Professor of Political Science at the
University of North Florida in Jacksonville. His dissertation, completed at
the University of Maryland, is entitled "Cyber-Interaction Matters: The
Net Impact on Civil Society." He came to the University of Maryland as a
scholar with support from the British Schools and Universities Founda-
tion. In 2002–03, Professor Harwood held a Maryland Executive-Legisla-
tive Public Service Fellowship. In 2001, he was awarded an International
Scholar Travel Grant from the American Political Science Association
(APSA), and a Carl and Lily Pforzheimer Fellowship from the National
Civic League. Professor Harwood has presented his work at numerous
conferences, including the annual meetings of the American Political
Science Association, the American Sociological Association, the Midwest
Political Science Association, and the American Politics Group, UK.

Dan Hunter (B.S., LL.B. (Hons.), LL.M., Ph.D.) is the Robert F. Irwin IV
Term Assistant Professor of Legal Studies at the Wharton School,
University of Pennsylvania, where he teaches electronic commerce law and
cyberlaw. He regularly publishes on issues dealing with the intersection
between computers and law, including papers dealing with the regulation
of the Internet, the use of artificial intelligence in law, and high technology
aspects of intellectual property. He is the coauthor of *Building Intelligent
Legal Information Systems,* published by Kluwer. He has been editor or
guest editor of a number of research journals, including *Journal of Law and
Information Science, Computers and Law,* and *International Journal of
Applied Expert Systems.*

Nicholas W. Jankowski is Associate Professor at the Department of
Communication, University of Nijmegen, The Netherlands. He has been
involved in the investigation of community media and other small-scale
communication facilities since the mid-1970s. His publications include: *A
Handbook of Qualitative Methodologies for Mass Communication Research*
(Routledge, 1991), *The People's Voice: Local Radio and Television in Europe*
(Libbey, 1992), *The Contours of Multimedia* (Luton, 1996), and *Commu-*

nity Media in the Information Age (Hampton, 2002). He is presently preparing a methodology textbook on new media research (Sage, 2003). One of his research interests involves the study of public discourse through Internet-based discussions. Jankowski is initiator and coeditor of the journal *New Media and Society* and editor of the Hampton Press book series *Communicative Innovations and Democracy.*

Gordon Jenkins is a Canadian consultant with Jenkins and Associates Inc., specializing in systems integration in the Internet with respect to both business and government. He has lived and worked in India, Singapore, Australia, Hong Kong and Sweden during the last eight of his eleven years with a private consulting company. He is at present working for the Canadian government in his home, Ottawa. His particular interest at the moment is Internet payments, as well as electronic government, electronic democracy, and electronic consultation. Mr. Jenkins is on the board of the U.S. International Institute of Business Technologies (www.iibt.org) in Washington, D.C., and is the editor of the *Journal of Internet Banking and Commerce* (www.arraydev.com/commerce/jibc/).

Grant Kippen is Country Director, Afghanistan, for the National Democratic Institute for International Affairs and is currently in Kabul, advising the newly constituted government of the Islamic Republic of Afghanistan on founding a new electoral system. He was formerly cofounder and principal of the Hillbrooke Group, an Ottawa-based consulting company that provides marketing, communications, and strategic management services to private and public sector organizations. Grant has worked for the Coopers and Lybrand Consulting Group within their Strategic Management practice and the Prime Minister's Office under the Right Honourable Pierre E. Trudeau, as well as having served as a Special Advisor to the Honourable Lloyd Axworthy. From the fall of 1990 until shortly after the 1993 federal election, Grant was the Director of Organization for the Liberal Party of Canada, where he was responsible for organization and training as well as the integration of information technology related to the Liberal Party's 1993 federal election campaign.

Nancy S. Marder, a graduate of Yale Law School, is a Professor of Law and Norman and Edna Freehling Scholar at Chicago-Kent College of Law. Before joining the faculty at Chicago-Kent, she taught at the University of Southern California Law School and clerked for Justice John Paul Stevens at the U.S. Supreme Court, for Judge William A. Norris on the Ninth Circuit, for Judge Leonard B. Sand in the Southern District of New York, and for Justice Edward C. King at the Supreme Court of the Federated States of Micronesia. She was also a litigator at Paul, Weiss, Rifkind, Wharton and Garrison in New York. Professor Marder has written extensively about the American jury system, including such articles as: "Juries, Justice and Multiculturalism," 75 *Southern California Law Review* 659 (2002); "Juries and Technology: Equipping Jurors for the Twenty-First Century," 66 *Brooklyn Law Review* 1257 (2001) (symposium issue); and "The Myth of the Nullifying Jury," 93 *Northwestern University Law Review* 877 (1999). Professor Marder is currently writing a book entitled *Jury Process,* to be published by Foundation Press, and teaches a law course entitled "Juries, Judges and Trials."

Wayne V. McIntosh is Associate Professor of Political Science, Associate Chair, and Director of Undergraduate Programs in the Department of Government and Politics at the University of Maryland, College Park. A specialist in law, judicial process, and information technology, Professor McIntosh has written or cowritten three books: *Law and the Web of Society* (2001) *Judicial Entrepreneurship* (1997), and *The Appeal of Civil Law* (1990), as well as numerous articles on litigation, the First Amendment, judicial politics, and information technology and society. He is currently working on several research projects, including a probe of corporations in the area of free speech in the United States and another assessing the role of information technologies in democratic society.

Jackie Mildener is director of elections at Capitol Advantage, which, in partnership with the League of Women Voters' DNet project in 2004, is devoted to supplying online solutions and publications that enable citizens to change the world through civic participation. She was formerly Director, E-Democracy, at the League of Women Voters Education Fund, where she functioned also as the Director of the DemocracyNet (DNet) program. Previously, Ms. Mildner served as Director of Programs at the International Women's Forum (IWF). She has worked at the Brookings Institution as an Executive Education Associate with the Center for Public Policy Education. While at Brookings, Ms. Mildner ran their Congressional Fellows Program. Ms. Mildner holds a bachelor's degree in International Relations from Bucknell University in Lewisburg, Pennsylvania, and a master's degree in International Relations from American University in Washington, DC.

Peter Muhlberger is E-Democracy Research Director at Carnegie Mellon University's Institute for the Study of Information Technology and Society (InSITeS) and Visiting Professor of Political Science at the H. John Heinz III School of Public Policy and Management. He was a founding member of Carnegie Mellon's Community Connections, an organization involved in the study of computer-mediated democratic deliberation. He conducts research on the social and psychological effects of political participation, with special interest in political agency, moral reasoning, and decision processes. Professor Muhlberger previously taught in the Information and Decision Systems program at Carnegie Mellon University.

Sean Murray is a master's student in political science at California State University, Chico. His primary areas of study are political parties and the media. He is currently working on a thesis that investigates the implications of Internet technology for third parties.

Juliet Musso is an Associate Professor of Public Policy at the School of Policy, Planning, and Development, University of Southern California. She holds a Ph.D. from the Goldman School of Public Policy, University of California at Berkeley. Professor Musso has expertise in urban policy, with specific research interests in community governance, local institutional reform, and federalism. She has researched government use of advanced telecommunications technologies to improve participation and service delivery, and currently is investigating the development of neighborhood councils in the City of Los Angeles.

Beth Simone Noveck is an Associate Professor of Law and Director of the Institute for Information Law and Policy at New York Law School, where she also directs the Democracy Design Workshop, an interdisciplinary project dedicated to deepening democratic practice in the digital age through technological and legal innovation. A founding fellow of the Yale Law School Information Society Project, Professor Noveck concentrates her research on information and technology law and policy with a focus on the intersection between technology and civil liberties. With the support of grants from the Rockefeller Brothers Fund, the Council of Europe, and AmericaSpeaks, Professor Noveck is currently at work on the Cairns Project, an online interactive inventory of collaborative practices. Professor Noveck is a founder of Bodies Electric LLC, designer of the Unchat software for real-time structured and democratic group deliberation in cyberspace. She is a member of the Legal Expert Network of the Institute for the Study of the Information Society and Technology (InSITeS) at the Carnegie Mellon Heinz School of Public Policy and Management, and a member of the advisory board of the Nanyang Technical University Centre on Asia Pacific Technology Law and Policy (CAPTEL) in Singapore, where she visited as a Fulbright Senior Specialist. Formerly a telecommunications and information technology lawyer practicing in New York City, Professor Noveck graduated from Harvard University with bachelor and master of arts degrees. She earned a J.D. from Yale Law School and a doctorate at the University of Innsbruck.

Oren Perez (LL.B., Tel Aviv University; LL.M., Ph.D., London School of Economics and Political Science) is currently an Assistant Professor on the Faculty of Law at Bar Ilan University, where he teaches courses in environmental law, international trade law, and torts. Dr. Perez has written on the implications of global legal pluralism for electronic democracy, and on transnational conflicts in environmental and public health policy. His recent publications include "Reflections on an Environmental Struggle: PandO, Dahanu and the Regulation of Multinational Enterprises." *George-town International Environmental Law Review* 15 (1): 1–27 (2002), "Normative Creativity and Global Legal Pluralism: Reflections on the Democratic Critique of Transnational Law," *Indiana Journal of Global Legal Studies,* 10 (2): 25–64 (2003), and *Ecological Sensitivity and Global Legal Pluralism: Rethinking the Trade and Environment Conflict,* forthcoming from Hart Publishing (spring 2004).

Alexandra Samuel is a Ph.D. candidate in political science at Harvard University. Her dissertation looks at the phenomenon of hacktivism, or politically motivated computer hacking. She also writes a weekly business column for the *Vancouver Sun.* In addition to her research and writing, Alexandra was the Research Director for Governance in the Digital Economy, an international research program. Alexandra's consulting work encompasses e-government and e-business strategy, as well as web design. She is the facilitator of DO-Consult, an e-mail list for experts and practitioners in the field of online consultation. She lives in Vancouver, Canada, where she recently finished teaching a course on the Internet and Politics at the University of British Columbia.

Peter M. Shane is the Joseph S. Platt–Porter, Wright, Morris and Arthur Professor of Law at the Ohio State University's Moritz College of Law, where he also directs the Center for Law, Policy, and Social Science. In addition, he serves as Distinguished Service Professor (Adjunct) of Law and Public Policy at Carnegie Mellon University's H. J. Heinz III School of Public Policy and Management, where he was the founding director of the Institute for the Study of Information Technology and Society (InSITeS). An internationally recognized authority on constitutional and administrative law, Peter was dean of the University of Pittsburgh School of Law from 1994 to 1998. Peter's increasing interest in the democratic and constitutional implications of information technology led him in 2000, along with Peter Muhlberger and other colleagues, to found Community Connections, a Carnegie Mellon–based research and outreach project on the uses of the Internet for civic engagement. Along with Peter Muhlberger and Robert Cavalier, he is principal investigator on a National Science Foundation Project to develop and test software to support online citizen public policy deliberation. Peter has also coauthored casebooks on administrative law and on separation of powers law and is working on a book on checks and balances in American government. With John Podesta and Richard Leone, he is co-editor of *A Little Knowledge: Privacy, Security, and Public Information After September 11* (New York: Century Foundation 2004).

J. Woody Stanley is Performance Planning Team Leader in the Federal Highway Administration. In his current position, he is primarily responsible for implementing strategic and performance management practices in the Agency. He has held similar positions in the National Highway Traffic Safety Administration and Federal Motor Carrier Safety Administration. Prior to joining the U.S. Department of Transportation in 1995, he was employed for sixteen years in management consulting and private industry. Woody received a Doctor of Public Administration (D.P.A.) from the University of Southern California in 2002. He also holds a M.B.A. from Duke University and a M.S. and B.A. from the University of North Carolina.

Nancy E. Tate is the Executive Director of the League of Women Voters of the United States and the League of Women Voters Education Fund. From 1994 until accepting the top staff position at the League in 2000, Ms. Tate was the Chief Operating Officer of the National Academy of Public Administration. Previously, Ms. Tate held a senior position in a management-consulting firm, where she managed a large multi-year contract focusing on the design and roll-out of a state-of-the-art computer system for all military hospitals. Before joining the private sector, Ms. Tate had a distinguished career in the federal government in the Department of Energy, the Department of Education, and the Office of Economic Opportunity. Ms. Tate has a B.A. in political science from Stanford University and a master's degree in public administration from George Washington University.

Renée van Os is currently a Ph.D. student at the Nijmegen Institute for Communications Research (NICoR), University of Nijmegen, The Netherlands. In her Ph.D. project, she focuses on how political actors involved in the campaign for the 2004 EU Parliament incorporate the Internet into strategies for dissemination of political information and organization of political debate. She is particularly interested in how this activity, together with its related citizen use, contributes to the development of a pan-European public sphere. She received her master's degree in communication science in September 2002. Her master's thesis was entitled "Digital Democracy: A Case Study Regarding the Role of Online Discussions Within the Local Political Process."

Christopher Weare is a research associate professor at the University of Southern California School of Policy, Planning, and Development. His research focuses on the effects of information and communication technologies on local governance and citizen political participation. Prior to his current position, he was a research fellow at the Public Policy Institute of California, an assistant professor at the Annenberg School for Communication at the University of Southern California, and a visiting assistant professor at the University of California, Berkeley. He also spent one year as a Congressional Fellow in the U.S. House of Representatives. He holds a

B.A. in government from Harvard College and a Ph.D. in public policy from the University of California, Berkeley.

Lori M. Weber received her Ph.D. in 2001 from the University of Colorado at Boulder. She received a National Science Foundation dissertation grant to complete her dissertation, "The Effect of Democratic Deliberation on Political Tolerance." Currently, she is collaborating on a project investigating the potential of new technology for democracy. This project, based at the Heinz School for Public Policy, Carnegie Mellon University, just received funding from the National Science Foundation Program on Social and Economic Implications of Technology. Professor Weber is an assistant professor in the Department of Political Science at California State University, Chico, and has published research on political parties, political participation, and deliberative democracy.

Tamara Witschge is a Ph.D. student at the Amsterdam School of Communications Research, University of Amsterdam. Her research focuses on the process and outcomes of online political discussions. With this study, she aims to gain better insights into the differences between online and offline deliberation. Tamara also teaches methods communication research at the International School of Humanities and Social Sciences. She received her MA degree in social cultural sciences in September 2001.

INDEX